Time Series Models

Time Series Models

Second Edition

ANDREW C. HARVEY

The MIT Press
Cambridge, Massachusetts

Second printing, 1994

First MIT Press edition, 1993

© 1981, 1993 Andrew C. Harvey

Printed and bound in Great Britain

ISBN 0-262-08224-1

Library of Congress Catalog Card Number 93-77076

To Catherine and Samuel

Contents

Figures

Preface to Second Edition

The revisions in this edition are substantial. There have been important developments in time series in the last ten years, and this has led to the addition of sections on topics such as non-linear models, fractional differencing, unit roots and co-integration. Furthermore, in the light of experience gained teaching from the book there has been some re-arrangement and change in emphasis. Thus the multivariate material is gathered together in a single chapter, and the miscellaneous regression topics of what was the last chapter have been dropped or worked into other sections. The chapter on modelling, formerly chapter 6, has been completely re-worked. This is partly because ARIMA methodology is now less dominant than it was when the first edition was written. In economic applications in particular, the use of unrestricted autoregressions, with associated tests for unit roots, has become popular, partly because of the way it leads into classes of multivariate models which are able to take account of long-run relationships between trending variables. In addition, structural time series models, which are models formulated directly in terms of components of interest, such as trends, seasonals and cycles, have advanced considerably. Some of the ideas of the structural approach were contained in the first edition, but they were not well developed. My recent monologue, *Forecasting, Structural Time Series Models and the Kalman Filter*, abbreviated as FSK in the text, attempts to provide a coherent approach to time series modelling via the structural approach, and argues, quite strongly, that it has considerable advantages over ARIMA modelling. In re-writing *Time Series Models*, I have tried to take a much more neutral line, concentrating primarily on laying out the basic techniques, rather than contrasting the various methodologies when they are used in practice.

I would like to thank all those who commented on the first edition. Special thanks must go to Naoto Kunitomo and Taku Yamamoto, who translated the book into Japanese. Siem Koopman and Esther Ruiz read several chapters of this new edition and made valuable suggestions. Of course, the responsibility for any errors rests solely with me.

London
July 1992

From the Preface to the First Edition

This book is concerned with the analysis and modelling of time series. It is designed primarily for use in courses given to final year undergraduates and postgraduates in statistics and econometrics. Although the emphasis is on economic time series, the material presented is also relevant in engineering and geography, and in other disciplines where time series observations are important.

Time Series Models can be regarded as a companion volume to *The Econometric Analysis of Time Series* the contents of which are listed on page xvi. The two books are essentially self-contained, although there is some cross-referencing. Here, reference to the earlier book will be indicated by the rather tasteless abbreviation 'EATS'.

As in EATS, the main concern in this book is to concentrate on models and techniques which are of practical value. There is more stress on creating an understanding of what the various models are capable of, and the ways in which they can be applied, than in proving theorems with the maximum of mathematical rigour. It is assumed that the reader is familiar with calculus and matrix algebra, although a good deal of the book can be read without any knowledge of matrices whatsoever. A basic knowledge of statistical inference is also assumed.

Equations are numbered according to the section. The chapter number is omitted except when referring to an equation in another chapter. Examples are numbered within each section and are referenced in the same way as equations. Tables and figures are numbered consecutively throughout each chapter and are independent of the section in which they appear. The term 'log' denotes a natural logarithm.

As in EATS, certain sections are starred (*). These sections contain material which is more difficult or more esoteric, or both. They can be omitted without any loss of continuity, although for a graduate course most of them would be included.

Parts of the book have been used as the basis for lectures at the LSE, and I'm grateful to all the students whose questions forced me to think more clearly about the exposition of certain topics. I'm also grateful to all the colleagues and friends who were kind enough to comment on various drafts of the book. Special thanks must go to Dick Baillie, Tom Cooley, James Davidson, Rob Engle, Katarina Juselius, Colin McKenzie and Bianca De Stavola. Of course, I am solely responsible for any errors which may remain. Finally, I'd like to thank Jill Duggan, Hazel Rice, Sue Kirkbride and Maggie Robertson for typing a difficult manuscript so efficiently.

London
February 1981

Note

The companion volume by A. C. Harvey, *The Econometric Analysis of Time Series* (The MIT Press, second edition 1990) has the following contents:

Chapter 1. Introduction

Chapter 2. Regression

Chapter 3. The Method of Maximum Likelihood

Chapter 4. Numerical Optimisation

Chapter 5. Test Procedures and Model Selection

Chapter 6. Regression Models with Serially Correlated Disturbances

Chapter 7. Dynamic Models I

Chapter 8. Dynamic Models II: Stochastic Difference Equations

Chapter 9. Simultaneous Equation Models

Abbreviations

Abbreviations used include:

ACF	– autocovariance, or autocorrelation, function
ACGF	– autocovariance generating function
AIC	– Akaike information criterion
ALS	– autoregressive least squares
AN	– asymptotically normal
AR	– autoregressive
ARCH	– autoregressive conditional heteroscedasticity
ARFIMA	– autoregressive-fractionally integrated-moving average
ARIMA	– autoregressive-integrated-moving average
ARMA	– autoregressive-moving average
BIC	– Bayes information criterion
BLUE	– best linear unbiased estimator
BLUP	– best linear unbiased predictor
BSM	– basic structural model
CSS	– conditional sum of squares
CUSUM	– cumulative sum
DW	– Durbin–Watson
ECM	– error correction model
EGARCH	– exponential generalised autoregressive conditional heteroscedasticity
EWMA	– exponentially weighted moving average
FD	– frequency domain
GARCH	– generalised autoregressive conditional heteroscedasticity
GLS	– generalised least squares
IID	– independently and identically distributed
KF	– Kalman filter
LM	– Lagrange multiplier
LR	– Likelihood ratio
MA	– moving average

MD   −martingale difference
ML   −maximum likelihood
MMSE   −minimum mean square estimator or estimate
MMSLE   −minimum mean square linear estimator
MSE   −mean square error
$NID(\mu, \sigma^2)$−normally and independently distributed with mean μ and variance σ^2
OLS   −ordinary least squares
PDF   −probability density function
P(S)D   −positive (semi-)definite
SGF   −spectral generating function
SSE   −sum of squared errors
SSF   −state space form
SURE   −seemingly unrelated regression equations
SUTSE   −seemingly unrelated time series equations
SV   −stochastic variance
TD   −time domain
UC   −unobserved components
VAR   −vector autoregression
VNR   −von Neumann ratio
WN   −white noise

In addition, FSK and EATS denote the books listed in the references as Harvey (1989, 1990).

1

Introduction

1.1 Analysing and Modelling Time Series

A time series typically consists of a set of observations on a variable, y, taken at equally spaced intervals over time. Economic variables are generally classified either as stocks or flows, the money supply being an example of a stock, and investment and gross national product being flows. The distinction between stocks and flows is important in dealing with aggregation or missing observations, but for most purposes it is irrelevant, and a series of T observations will be denoted by $y_1, \ldots, y_T$, irrespective of whether they refer to a stock or a flow variable.

There are two aspects to the study of time series – analysis and modelling. The aim of analysis is to summarise the properties of a series and to characterise its salient features. This may be done either in the time domain or in the frequency domain. In the time domain attention is focused on the relationship between observations at different points in time, while in the frequency domain it is cyclical movements which are studied. The two forms of analysis are complementary rather than competitive. The same information is processed in different ways, thereby giving different insights into the nature of the time series.

The main reason for modelling a time series is to enable forecasts of future values to be made. The distinguishing feature of a time series model, as opposed, say, to an econometric model, is that no attempt is made to formulate a behavioural relationship between y_t and other variables. The movements in y_t are 'explained' solely in terms of its own past, or by its position in relation to time. Forecasts are then made by extrapolation.

Stochastic Processes

Figure 1.1 shows a series of observations fluctuating around a fixed level, μ. If the observations were independent of each other, the best forecast of the

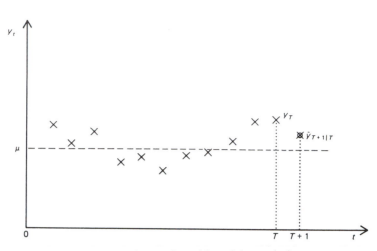

Figure 1.1 Time series with serial correlation.

next observation in the series, y_{T+1}, would simply be μ or, if this is unknown, a suitable estimate of μ such as the sample mean. However, the observations are clearly not independent. Each one tends to have a value which is closer to that of the observations immediately adjacent than to those which are further away. This type of structure is known as *serial correlation*. It is typical of time series observations and by taking account of the pattern of serial correlation better forecasts of future observations can be obtained. Thus, given the relationship between successive observations in figure 1.1, it would seem that a forecast lying somewhere between y_T and μ would be more appropriate than a forecast which is simply equal to μ.

The statistical approach to forecasting is based on the construction of a model. The model defines a mechanism which is regarded as being capable of having produced the observations in question. Such a model is almost invariably *stochastic*. If it were used to generate several sets of observations over the same time period, each set of observations would be different, but they would all obey the same probabilistic laws.

The first-order autoregressive model

$$y_t - \mu = \phi(y_{t-1} - \mu) + \varepsilon_t \tag{1.1}$$

is a simple example of a *stochastic process*. The uncertainty derives from the variable ε_t. This is a purely random disturbance term with a mean of zero and a variance of σ^2. The correlation between any two of its values at different points in time is zero, and if it is normally distributed such values are independent. The remaining features of the model are determined by the parameters μ and ϕ. If $|\phi| < 1$, the observations fluctuate around μ, which is then the mean of the process.

The parameters in (1.1) can be estimated by *ordinary least squares*

(OLS) regression. Given these estimates, $\tilde{\mu}$ and $\tilde{\phi}$, the next observation in the series can be forecast by

$$\tilde{y}_{T+1|T} = \tilde{\mu} + \tilde{\phi}(y_T - \tilde{\mu}) \qquad (1.2)$$

The closer $\tilde{\phi}$ is to one, the more weight is given to y_T. This is consistent with the intuitive argument given in connection with figure 1.1.

Constraining ϕ to lie between -1 and 1 in (1.1) means that the process is *stationary*. When a series of observations is generated by a stationary process, they fluctuate around a constant level and there is no tendency for their spread to increase or decrease over time. These are not the only properties of a stationary time series, but they are the most obvious ones and a casual inspection of the series in figure 1.1 indicates that it displays these characteristics.

Further lagged values, y_{t-2}, y_{t-3} and so on, could be added to (1.1), thereby enabling more complicated patterns of dependence to be modelled. Indeed, the properties of almost any stationary time series can be reproduced by introducing a sufficiently high number of lags. The disadvantage of modelling a series in this way is that when a large number of lagged values are needed, a large number of parameters must be estimated. One solution to this problem is to widen the class of models to allow for lagged values of the ε_t's. A model which contains lagged values of both the observed variable and the disturbance term is known as an *autoregressive-moving average* (ARMA) process. Such processes play an important role in dynamic modelling because they allow a *parsimonious* representation of a stationary time series. In other words, a model with relatively few parameters can be constructed. The simplest example is the ARMA(1, 1) model:

$$y_t - \mu = \phi(y_{t-1} - \mu) + \varepsilon_t + \theta\varepsilon_{t-1} \qquad (1.3)$$

where θ is a moving average parameter.

Local and Global Trends

The majority of time series do not fluctuate around a constant level, but instead show some kind of systematic upward or downward movement. Consider the observations in figure 1.2. They can be regarded as being scattered randomly around an upward sloping straight line. Thus a suitable model might be

$$y_t = \alpha + \beta t + \varepsilon_t, \qquad t = 1, \ldots, T \qquad (1.4)$$

where α and β are parameters and ε_t is a random process of the kind defined in (1.1).

Since (1.4) is a classical linear regression model, its parameters can be estimated by OLS. Forecasts of future values of y_t can be made by

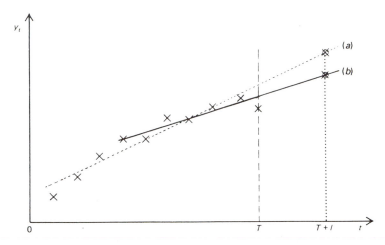

Figure 1.2 Local and global linear trends. Forecasting with (a) a global trend; (b) a local trend.

extrapolating the deterministic part of the fitted equation. Hence

$$\tilde{y}_{T+l|T} = a + b(T+l) = a + bT + bl, \qquad l = 1, 2, \dots \qquad (1.5)$$

where a and b denote the least squares estimators of α and β. A more general model could be formed by letting the disturbance term follow an ARMA(p, q) process. If such a model were constructed, the forecast in (1.5) would have to be modified to take account of the pattern of serial correlation.

The disadvantage of using (1.4) for forecasting purposes is that the trend is a *global* one. It is assumed to hold at all points in time with the parameters remaining constant throughout. However, a careful examination of the series seems to indicate that the slope is flattening out towards the end. This cannot be properly handled by (1.4). The question of whether the disturbance term is assumed to be random or a more general stationary ARMA process is irrelevant.

A more satisfactory forecasting procedure would allow the parameters to adapt to the change in the data. If relatively more weight is placed on the most recent observations, forecasts can be based on an estimate of the *local* trend. The lines drawn in figure 1.2 contrast the two approaches.

The Holt–Winters procedure is a popular method for making predictions of a local linear trend. It is a recursive procedure in which current estimates of the level and slope are revised as each new observation becomes available. In making predictions, the influence of past observations is discounted, but the way in which this is done is essentially *ad hoc*. A natural question to ask is whether there is a statistical model which can provide a rationale for such an approach.

The stochastic processes described in the previous sub-section were stationary. Although stationarity is a fundamental concept for the analysis of time series, stationary models are clearly not appropriate for modelling a series such as that shown in figure 1.2. The simplest non-stationary process is the *random walk*

$$y_t = y_{t-1} + \varepsilon_t$$

which can be obtained by setting $\phi = 1$ in (1.1). The first differences of this model, $y_t - y_{t-1}$, are, of course, stationary. This leads on to the idea of formulating a general class of models in which observations follow ARMA processes after they have been differenced, possibly more than once. Such models are called *autoregressive-integrated-moving average* (ARIMA) models. Forecasts of local trends can be produced by models from within this class. A rationale for Holt–Winters is provided by a model in which second differences follow a second-order moving average.

An approach to time series forecasting based on ARIMA models was developed by Box and Jenkins (1976), and their model fitting procedure is sometimes referred to as the *Box–Jenkins method*. The first step is to transform the series, by applying various operations such as logarithms and differences, until it is approximately stationary. The transformed series is then analysed and a tentative ARMA specification is chosen. The second step is to estimate the model and the third step is to subject the residuals to *diagnostic checking*. If the model appears to be satisfactory, it is used for forecasting. If it is not, the whole cycle is repeated.

A different way of providing a statistical rationale for local linear trend forecasting is to allow the parameters in the regression model (1.4) to evolve over time according to a stochastic process which is basically a multivariate version of the random walk. This approach can be generalised to any regression model which can be set up with explanatory variables which are functions of time. Thus not only deterministic trends, but also deterministic seasonals and cycles, can be made stochastic. Such models are called *structural time series models*. They have the additional attraction that unobserved components such as trends and cycles can be estimated, thereby providing a *description* of the series as well as a means of forecasting it.

Multivariate Models

In univariate analysis, attention is restricted to a single time series. When several variables are considered together, we have a multivariate time series. The observations then consist of a vector, $\mathbf{y}_t$, and a multivariate model will seek to capture the various inter-relationships between the different series. Generalising (1.1) leads to the first-order vector autoregressive process

$$\mathbf{y}_t = \mathbf{\Phi}\mathbf{y}_{t-1} + \boldsymbol{\varepsilon}_t, \qquad t = 1, \ldots, T \tag{1.6}$$

where $\mathbf{y}_t$ is an $N \times 1$ vector, the disturbance $\boldsymbol{\varepsilon}_t$ is also an $N \times 1$ vector, and $\boldsymbol{\Phi}$ is an $N \times N$ matrix of parameters. The disturbances are serially uncorrelated, but may be contemporaneously correlated. Thus $E(\boldsymbol{\varepsilon}_t\boldsymbol{\varepsilon}_t') = \boldsymbol{\Omega}$, where $\boldsymbol{\Omega}$ is an $N \times N$ matrix. A non-zero mean may be incorporated in the model as in (1.1). The essential point about the multivariate model is that each variable depends not only on its own past values, but on past values of the other variables as well. Thus if y_{it} denotes the ith element in $\mathbf{y}_t$, the ith row of (1.6) yields

$$y_{it} = \phi_{i1}y_{1,t-1} + \phi_{i2}y_{2,t-1} + \cdots + \phi_{iN}y_{N,t-1} + \varepsilon_{it}, \qquad i = 1, \ldots, N$$

The model in (1.6) may be extended in the same way as in the univariate case by bringing in more lags on $\mathbf{y}_t$ and introducing lags of $\boldsymbol{\varepsilon}_t$. This leads to the class of vector ARMA models, which when applied to differenced observations become vector ARIMA models. The relative difficulty of handling vector ARMA models has led to some emphasis on pure vector autoregressions. A model like (1.6) can be estimated by OLS, simply by regressing each variable on the lags of itself and the other variables. When the series are non-stationary, vector autoregressive models can be extended to incorporate constraints linking the various series together. This ties in with certain ideas in economics about steady-state relationships and a concept known as co-integration.

Structural time series models also extend to multivariate time series. Again various steady-state relationships between the series can be incorporated into the models, but this is done by means of common trend components.

The relationship between multivariate time series models and the systems of dynamic simultaneous equation models used in econometrics is explored in the last chapter of EATS (Harvey, 1990). Multivariate time series models do not attempt to model directly the behavioural relationships suggested by economic theory, although they may provide a useful first step towards the construction of such models.

1.2 Outline of the Book

Chapter 2 develops the basic concepts needed for the analysis of stochastic processes in the time domain. The rationale behind the ARMA class of models is explained and the properties of various members of the class are examined. The issues involved in treating series made up of several unobserved ARMA processes are then discussed. Finally various tests which can be applied to stationary time series are described.

Estimation and testing of ARMA models is the subject of chapter 3. The basic ideas of maximum likelihood are set out in the introduction, though for a fuller treatment the reader might refer to Silvey (1970) or EATS, chapters 3, 4 and 5. It is shown how maximum likelihood may be applied to ARMA models under certain simplifying assumptions; the question of algorithms for exact maximum likelihood is not taken up until chapter 4. The last section discusses the issue of model selection.

State space methods are fundamental to dynamic modelling. They were originally developed in control engineering for purposes such as tracking rockets, and it is only in recent years that their importance has come to be more widely recognised. Most time series models can be put in state space form and once this has been done, algorithms for prediction and signal extraction can be employed. The Kalman filter lies at the heart of these algorithms and also provides the basis for the construction of the likelihood function. The statistical treatment of structural time series models relies on state space methods, but as indicated in the previous paragraph, they are also useful for ARMA models. Indeed, once data irregularities, such as missing observations, need to be taken into account, the state space approach becomes even more important.

The material presented in chapters 2, 3 and 4 provides the basis for the development of univariate time series models which are actually used in practice. These models are described in chapter 5, after an opening section which sets the scene by treating data transformations and examining *ad hoc* forecasting procedures based on exponential smoothing. The three main approaches are classified as ARIMA models, structural time series models and autoregressions. Extensions to seasonal time series are also considered. Further material on the modelling of cycles, which is particularly important for the structural approach, is not considered until the frequency domain is covered in chapter 6.

The latter part of chapter 5 extends the models to include observable explanatory variables. The result is a combination of univariate time series models and regression, with the explanatory variables only accounting for part of the long term and seasonal movements in the variable of interest. Various approaches to modelling lags are considered, and the last section deals with intervention analysis, where the effect of an event or policy change on a series is modelled and assessed.

The first five chapters make up a self-contained course on basic time series. The inclusion of starred sections (*) is optional. The last three chapters take the subject further.

Chapter 6 introduces spectral analysis, starting from the idea of a fixed cycle and then moving on to show how cyclical behaviour can be accommodated within stochastic processes. The properties of ARMA models are analysed in the frequency domain, and it is shown how frequency domain analysis can provide insight into the effects of operations typically applied to time series. Seasonal adjustment is just one example. The way in which time series models can be estimated by maximum likelihood in the frequency domain is described. Such methods have little to do with the presence or otherwise of cycles in the data, the point being that a transformation to the frequency domain simply provides a convenient way of dealing with serial correlation. The approach is particularly attractive for dealing with unobserved components and fractional integration. Finally it is shown how certain features of regression models can be dealt with using frequency domain tools.

Methods for analysing and modelling multivariate time series are set out in chapter 7. As with chapter 5, the emphasis is on ARIMA, structural and autoregressive models. Some insight into the ideas underlying co-integrated time series is provided by looking at the issue in both the structural and autoregressive frameworks. Certain subjects, such as Granger causality and exogeneity, are not covered here, but can be found in EATS, chapter 8.

The final chapter looks at non-linear models. The basic ideas underlying such models are explored, and the notion of conditional Gaussianity introduced. Two approaches to modelling changes in variance are then described. The first is based on the idea of what is called autoregressive conditional heteroscedasticity (ARCH). The generalisation of this approach parallels ARMA modelling in some ways. Stochastic variance models, on the other hand, tie in more closely with the technique used to handle unobserved components. Both approaches have proved to be useful in practice. Markov chains are considered briefly in the penultimate section and linked in with autoregressive models. They are then used in the context of models for switching regimes.

2

Stationary Stochastic Processes and their Properties in the Time Domain

2.1 Basic Concepts

This book is primarily concerned with modelling time series as stochastic processes. Each observation in a stochastic process is a random variable, and the observations evolve in time according to certain probabilistic laws. Thus a stochastic process may be defined as a collection of random variables which are ordered in time.

The model defines the mechanism by which the observations are generated. A simple example is the first-order moving average process,

$$y_t = \varepsilon_t + \theta \varepsilon_{t-1}, \qquad t = 1, \ldots, T \qquad (1.1)$$

where ε_t is a sequence of independent random variables drawn from a distribution with mean zero and constant variance, and θ is a parameter. A particular set of values of $\varepsilon_0, \varepsilon_1, \ldots, \varepsilon_T$, results in a corresponding sequence of observations, $y_1, \ldots, y_T$. By drawing a different set of values of $\varepsilon_0, \varepsilon_1, \ldots, \varepsilon_T$, a different set of observations is obtained and model (1.1) can be regarded as being capable of generating an infinite set of such *realisations* over the period $t = 1, \ldots, T$. Thus, the model effectively defines a joint distribution for the random variables $y_1, \ldots, y_T$.

The moments of a stochastic process are defined with respect to the distribution of the random variables $y_1, \ldots, y_T$. The mean of the process at time t is

$$\mu_t = E(y_t), \qquad t = 1, \ldots, T \qquad (1.2)$$

and this can be interpreted as the average value of y_t taken over all possible realisations. Second moments have a similar interpretation. The variance at time t is defined by

$$\text{Var}(y_t) = E[(y_t - \mu_t)^2], \qquad t = 1, \ldots, T \tag{1.3}$$

while the covariance between y_t and $y_{t-\tau}$ is given by

$$\text{Cov}(y_t, y_{t-\tau}) = E[(y_t - \mu_t)(y_{t-\tau} - \mu_{t-\tau})], \qquad t = \tau + 1, \ldots, T \tag{1.4}$$

If several realisations are available, the above quantities can be sensibly estimated by 'ensemble' averages. For example,

$$\hat{\mu}_t = m^{-1} \sum_{j=1}^{m} y_t^{(j)}, \qquad t = 1, \ldots, T \tag{1.5}$$

where $y_t^{(j)}$ denotes the jth observation on y_t and m is the number of realisations. However, in most time series problems, only a single series of observations is available. In these circumstances, no meaningful inferences can be made about the quantities defined in (1.2) to (1.4), unless some restrictions are placed on the process which is assumed to be generating the observations. This leads to the concept of stationarity.

Stationarity

When only a single realisation of observations is available, attention must shift from the aggregation of observations at particular points *in* time, to the averaging of observations *over* time. This is only possible if the data generating process is such that the quantities (1.2), (1.3) and (1.4) are independent of time. Thus, for example, if $\mu_t = \mu$ for $t = 1, \ldots, T$, it can be estimated by taking the average of the observations $y_1, \ldots, y_T$.

For a stochastic process to be *stationary*, the following conditions must be satisfied for all values of t:

$$E(y_t) = \mu \tag{1.6}$$

$$E[(y_t - \mu)^2] = \sigma_y^2 = \gamma(0) \tag{1.7}$$

and

$$E[(y_t - \mu)(y_{t-\tau} - \mu)] = \gamma(\tau), \qquad \tau = 1, 2, \ldots \tag{1.8}$$

Expressions (1.6) and (1.7) define the mean and variance of the data generating process, while (1.8) gives the autocovariance at lag τ. The implications of (1.6) and (1.7) were noted in the discussion surrounding figure 1.1.

The quantities (1.6) to (1.8) can be estimated from a single series of observations as follows:

$$\hat{\mu} = \bar{y} = T^{-1} \sum_{t=1}^{T} y_t \tag{1.9}$$

$$\hat{\gamma}(0) = c(0) = T^{-1} \sum_{t=1}^{T} (y_t - \bar{y})^2 \tag{1.10}$$

and

$$\hat{\gamma}(\tau) = c(\tau) = T^{-1} \sum_{t=\tau+1}^{T} (y_t - \bar{y})(y_{t-\tau} - \bar{y}), \qquad \tau = 1, 2, 3, \ldots \tag{1.11}$$

If the process is *ergodic*, these statistics give consistent estimates of the mean, variance and autocovariances. Ergodicity will not be defined formally here, but what it basically requires is that observations sufficiently far apart should be almost uncorrelated. For all the models considered in this chapter, stationarity implies ergodicity. The cyclical process in (6.3.1) is an example of non-ergodicity.

The conditions (1.6) to (1.8) provide a definition of *weak* or *covariance* stationarity. Occasionally the condition of *strict* stationarity is imposed. This is a stronger condition whereby the joint probability distribution of a set of r observations at times $t_1, t_2, \ldots, t_r$ is the same as the joint probability of the observations at times $t_1 + \tau, t_2 + \tau, \ldots, t_r + \tau$. Strict stationarity implies weak stationarity provided that the first two moments of the joint distribution exist. In this chapter, the term stationarity will always refer to weak stationarity, though it should be noted that if a series is weakly stationary and normally distributed, then it is also stationary in the strict sense.

The simplest example of a covariance stationary stochastic process is a sequence of uncorrelated random variables with constant mean and variance. A process of this kind is known as *white noise* (WN), a terminology borrowed from the engineering literature. Throughout this book the symbol ε_t will always denote a white noise variable, and unless explicitly stated otherwise, such a variable will have a mean of zero and a variance of σ^2. Because the variables in a white noise sequence are uncorrelated, the autocovariances at non-zero lags are all zero. Thus

$$E(\varepsilon_t \varepsilon_{t-\tau}) = \begin{cases} \sigma^2, & \tau = 0 \\ 0, & \tau \neq 0 \end{cases} \tag{1.12}$$

Autocovariance and Autocorrelation Functions

When a stochastic process is stationary, its time domain properties can be summarised by plotting $\gamma(\tau)$ against τ. This is known as the *autocovariance function*. Since $\gamma(\tau) = \gamma(-\tau)$, it is unnecessary to extend the plot over negative values of τ.

The autocovariances may be standardised by dividing through by the variance of the process. This yields the autocorrelations,

$$\rho(\tau) = \gamma(\tau)/\gamma(0), \qquad \tau = 0, \pm 1, \pm 2, \ldots \tag{1.13}$$

A plot of $\rho(\tau)$ against non-negative values of τ gives the *autocorrelation function*. Note that $\rho(0) = 1$ by definition.

The time domain properties of the moving average model (1.1) are relatively easy to derive. Since ε_t is a white noise variable with mean 0 and variance σ^2, it follows that

$$\mu = E(\varepsilon_t) + \theta E(\varepsilon_{t-1}) = 0 \tag{1.14a}$$

while

$$
\begin{aligned}
\gamma(0) &= E[(\varepsilon_t + \theta\varepsilon_{t-1})(\varepsilon_t + \theta\varepsilon_{t-1})] \\
&= E(\varepsilon_t^2) + \theta^2 E(\varepsilon_{t-1}^2) + 2\theta E(\varepsilon_t\varepsilon_{t-1}) \\
&= (1 + \theta^2)\sigma^2
\end{aligned}
\tag{1.14b}
$$

Similarly,

$$
\begin{aligned}
\gamma(1) &= E[(\varepsilon_t + \theta\varepsilon_{t-1})(\varepsilon_{t-1} + \theta\varepsilon_{t-2})] \\
&= E(\varepsilon_t\varepsilon_{t-1}) + \theta E(\varepsilon_{t-1}^2) + \theta E(\varepsilon_t\varepsilon_{t-2}) + \theta^2 E(\varepsilon_{t-1}\varepsilon_{t-2}) \\
&= \theta E(\varepsilon_{t-1}^2) \\
&= \theta\sigma^2
\end{aligned}
\tag{1.14c}
$$

and

$$\gamma(\tau) = 0, \qquad \tau = 2, 3, 4, \ldots \tag{1.14d}$$

The mean, variance and covariances are therefore independent of t and the process is stationary. Note that it is not necessary to specify the full distribution of ε_t for (1.14) to hold.

The autocovariance and autocorrelation functions have exactly the same shape and provide the same information on the nature of the process. It is more usual to plot the autocorrelation function since it is dimensionless. Standardising (1.14c) gives

$$\rho(1) = \theta/(1 + \theta^2) \tag{1.15}$$

and the autocorrelation function for $\theta = 0.5$ is shown in figure 2.1.

When θ is positive, successive values of y_t are positively correlated and so the process will tend to be smoother than the random series, ε_t. On the other hand, a negative value of θ will yield a series which is more irregular than a random series, in the sense that positive values of y_t tend to be followed

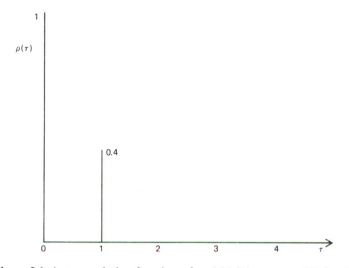

Figure 2.1 Autocorrelation function of an MA(1) process with $\theta = 0.5$.

by negative values and *vice versa*. This is reflected in the autocorrelation function, as $\rho(1)$ is negative for $\theta < 0$.

The Correlogram

The quantities defined in (1.9), (1.10) and (1.11) are the *sample mean, sample variance* and *sample autocovariances* respectively. The sample autocovariances may be standardised in the same way as theoretical autocovariances. This yields the *sample autocorrelations,*

$$r(\tau) = c(\tau)/c(0), \qquad \tau = 1, 2, \ldots \tag{1.16}$$

and a plot of $r(\tau)$ against non-negative values of τ is known as the sample autocorrelation function or *correlogram.*

The sample autocorrelations are estimates of the corresponding theoretical autocorrelations for the stochastic process which is assumed to be generating the data. They will therefore be subject to sampling variability, and so although the correlogram will tend to mirror the properties of the theoretical autocorrelation function, it will not reproduce them exactly. The sample autocorrelations from a white noise process, for example, will typically be close to zero but will not, in general, be identically equal to zero.

The correlogram is the main tool for analysing the properties of a series of observations in the time domain. However, in order to interpret the correlogram it is necessary to know something, firstly about the sampling variability of the estimated autocorrelations, and secondly about the

autocovariance functions of different stochastic processes. The sections which
follow examine the nature of the autocorrelation function for various special
cases within the class of autoregressive-moving average models. This provides
the basis for the model building strategy developed in chapter 3. The question
of sampling variability, together with the related question of test procedures
associated with the correlogram, is taken up at the end of this chapter.

The Lag Operator

The *lag operator*, L, plays an extremely useful role in carrying out algebraic
manipulations in time series analysis. It is defined by the transformation

$$Ly_t = y_{t-1} \qquad (1.17)$$

Applying L to y_{t-1} yields $Ly_{t-1} = y_{t-2}$. Substituting from (1.17) gives
$L(Ly_t) = L^2 y_t = y_{t-2}$ and so, in general,

$$L^\tau y_t = y_{t-\tau}, \qquad \tau = 1, 2, 3, \ldots \qquad (1.18)$$

It is logical to complete the definition by letting L^0 have the property
$L^0 y_t = y_t$ so that (1.18) holds for all non-negative integers. Allowing τ to be
negative defines a lead operation, which can be conveniently expressed in
terms of a forward or *lead operator*, $F = L^{-1}$.

The lag operator can be manipulated in a similar way to any algebraic
quantity. Consider an infinite moving average process in which the coefficient
of ε_{t-j} is ϕ^j for $j = 0, 1, 2, \ldots$, and $|\phi| < 1$. The model may be written as

$$y_t = \sum_{j=0}^{\infty} (\phi L)^j \varepsilon_t \qquad (1.19)$$

and if L is regarded as having the property $|L| \leqslant 1$, it follows that $|\phi L| < 1$
and so the series $1, \phi L, (\phi L)^2, \ldots$ may be summed as an infinite geometric
progression. Thus (1.19) becomes

$$y_t = \varepsilon_t / (1 - \phi L) \qquad (1.20)$$

and this may be re-arranged to give the first-order autoregressive process

$$y_t = \phi y_{t-1} + \varepsilon_t \qquad (1.21)$$

The *first difference operator*, Δ, can be manipulated in a similar way to
the lag operator, since $\Delta = 1 - L$. The relationship between the two operators
can often be usefully exploited. For example,

$$\Delta^2 y_t = (1 - L)^2 y_t = (1 - 2L + L^2) y_t = y_t - 2y_{t-1} + y_{t-2} \qquad (1.22)$$

Autoregressive-moving Average Processes

A general class of stochastic processes can be formed by introducing an infinite number of lags into a moving average. This yields the representation

$$y_t = \sum_{j=0}^{\infty} \psi_j \varepsilon_{t-j} \qquad (1.23)$$

where $\psi_0, \psi_1, \psi_2, \ldots$ are parameters. The condition

$$\sum_{j=0}^{\infty} \psi_j^2 < \infty \qquad (1.24a)$$

must be imposed in order to ensure that the process has finite variance. For some purposes, the slightly stronger condition

$$\sum_{j=0}^{\infty} |\psi_j| < \infty \qquad (1.24b)$$

is needed; see Fuller (1976, ch. 2).

Any model which can be written in the form (1.23) is said to be an *indeterministic* or *linear process*. However, the model itself will only be described as being linear if the ε_t's are independent, rather than merely uncorrelated; see chapter 8.

A linear process is stationary and its properties may be expressed in terms of the autocovariance function. These properties can be approximated, to any desired level of accuracy, by a model drawn from the class of autoregressive-moving average processes. An autoregressive-moving average process of order (p, q), which is normally abbreviated as ARMA(p, q), is written as

$$y_t = \phi_1 y_{t-1} + \cdots + \phi_p y_{t-p} + \varepsilon_t + \theta_1 \varepsilon_{t-1} + \cdots + \theta_q \varepsilon_{t-q} \qquad (1.25)$$

As will be shown in the next section, certain restrictions must be placed on the autoregressive parameters, $\phi_1, \ldots, \phi_p$, if the model is to be stationary.

An ARMA process can be written more concisely by defining *associated polynomials* in the lag operator. If

$$\phi(L) = 1 - \phi_1 L - \cdots - \phi_p L^p \qquad (1.26a)$$

and

$$\theta(L) = 1 + \theta_1 L + \cdots + \theta_q L^q \qquad (1.26b)$$

model (1.25) becomes

$$\phi(L) y_t = \theta(L) \varepsilon_t \qquad (1.27)$$

This representation has certain technical, as well as notational, advantages. For example, if a non-zero mean, μ, is introduced into a stationary model it becomes

$$y_t = \mu + \phi^{-1}(L)\theta(L)\varepsilon_t \tag{1.28}$$

On multiplying through by $\phi(L)$, it is apparent that the same effect could be achieved by adding a parameter

$$\theta_0 = \phi(L)\mu = \phi(1)\mu = (1 - \phi_1 - \cdots - \phi_p)\mu$$

to the right hand side of (1.27).

The next three sections explore the properties of pure autoregressive, pure moving average and mixed (ARMA) processes. It is assumed throughout that the processes have zero mean, i.e. $\mu = 0$. This is purely for convenience and implies no loss in generality.

2.2 Autoregressive Processes

An autoregressive process of order p is written as

$$y_t = \phi_1 y_{t-1} + \cdots + \phi_p y_{t-p} + \varepsilon_t, \qquad t = 1, \ldots, T \tag{2.1}$$

This will be denoted by writing $y_t \sim \text{AR}(p)$. Autoregressive processes have always been popular, partly because they have a natural interpretation, and partly because they are easier to estimate than MA or mixed processes.

The first point to establish about an AR model is the conditions under which it is stationary. This amounts to determining whether it can be written in the form (1.23) with condition (1.24a) holding. Once this has been done, the autocorrelation function can be derived.

Stationarity for the First-Order Model

The AR(1) process is

$$y_t = \phi y_{t-1} + \varepsilon_t, \qquad t = 1, \ldots, T \tag{2.2}$$

Although the series is first observed at time $t = 1$, the process is regarded as having started at some time in the remote past. Substituting repeatedly for lagged values of y_t gives

$$y_t = \sum_{j=0}^{J-1} \phi^j \varepsilon_{t-j} + \phi^J y_{t-J} \tag{2.3}$$

The right hand side of (2.3) consists of two parts, the first of which is a moving average of lagged values of the white noise variable driving the process. The second part depends on the value of y_t at time $t - J$. Taking expectations and treating y_{t-J} as a fixed number yields

$$E(y_t) = E\left(\sum_{j=0}^{J-1} \phi^j \varepsilon_{t-j}\right) + E(\phi^J y_{t-J}) = \phi^J y_{t-J} \qquad (2.4)$$

If $|\phi| \geqslant 1$, the mean value of the process depends on the starting value, y_{t-J}. Expression (2.3) therefore contains a deterministic component and a knowledge of y_{t-J} enables non-trivial prediction to be made for future values of the series, no matter how far ahead. If, on the other hand, ϕ is less than one in absolute value, this deterministic component is negligible if J is large. As $J \to \infty$, it effectively disappears and so if the process is regarded as having started at some point in the remote past, it is quite legitimate to write (2.2) in the form

$$y_t = \sum_{j=0}^{\infty} \phi^j \varepsilon_{t-j}, \qquad t = 1, \ldots, T \qquad (2.5)$$

On comparing (2.5) with (1.23), it can be seen that an $AR(1)$ process with $|\phi| < 1$ is indeterministic, since summing the squared coefficients as a geometric progression yields

$$\sum_{j=0}^{\infty} \phi^{2j} = 1/(1 - \phi^2) \qquad (2.6)$$

The expectation of y_t is zero for all t, while

$$\gamma(0) = E(y_t^2) = E\left(\sum_{j=0}^{\infty} \phi^j \varepsilon_{t-j}\right)^2 = \sum_{j=0}^{\infty} \phi^{2j} E(\varepsilon_{t-j}^2)$$

$$= \sigma^2 \sum_{j=0}^{\infty} \phi^{2j} = \sigma^2/(1 - \phi^2) \qquad (2.7)$$

Stationarity for the Second-Order Model

The second-order autoregressive process is defined by

$$y_t = \phi_1 y_{t-1} + \phi_2 y_{t-2} + \varepsilon_t, \qquad t = 1, \ldots, T \qquad (2.8)$$

As with the first-order model, it is possible to decompose (2.8) into two parts, one stochastic and the other deterministic. The deterministic part depends on a pair of starting values, but if the process is stationary, their influence is negligible for a starting point some time in the remote past.

In order to study the nature of the deterministic component, we suppress the disturbance term in (2.8). This yields the homogeneous difference equation,

$$\bar{y}_t - \phi_1 \bar{y}_{t-1} - \phi_2 \bar{y}_{t-2} = 0 \qquad (2.9)$$

where the bar over y_t indicates that we are now dealing with the mean of the process. The solution to (2.9) depends on the roots of the characteristic equation,

$$x^2 - \phi_1 x - \phi_2 = 0 \qquad (2.10)$$

Since (2.10) is a quadratic equation, these roots, m_1 and m_2, satisfy

$$(x - m_1)(x - m_2) = 0 \qquad (2.11)$$

and they may be found in the usual way from the formula

$$m_1, m_2 = (\phi_1 \pm \sqrt{\phi_1^2 + 4\phi_2})/2 \qquad (2.12)$$

Three possible cases arise with regard to the solution of (2.12) depending on whether the term under the square root is positive, zero or negative. In the first case, the roots are both real and the solution to (2.9) is given by

$$\bar{y}_t = k_1 m_1^J + k_2 m_2^J \qquad (2.13)$$

where k_1 and k_2 are constants which depend on the starting values, $\bar{y}_{t-J}$ and $\bar{y}_{t-J+1}$. If both m_1 and m_2 are less than unity in absolute value, $\bar{y}_t$ will be close to zero if J is large.

When $\phi_1^2 + 4\phi_2 < 0$, the roots are a pair of complex conjugates. The solution is again of the form (2.13), but it may be rewritten as

$$\bar{y}_t = k_3 r^J \cos(\lambda J + k_4) \qquad (2.14)$$

where k_3 and k_4 are constants which depend on the starting values of the series, r is the modulus of the roots and λ is defined by

$$\lambda = \tan^{-1}[\text{Im}(m_1)/\text{Re}(m_1)] = \tan^{-1}[(-\phi_1^2 - 4\phi_2)^{1/2}/\phi_1]$$

$$= \cos^{-1}[\phi_1/(2\sqrt{-\phi_2})] \qquad (2.15)$$

and measured in radians. The time path followed by $\bar{y}_t$ is cyclical, but if the modulus of the roots is less than unity it is damped and $\bar{y}_t$ is negligible if J is large.

When the roots are real and equal, the solution to (2.9) takes a slightly different form from (2.13), but the condition that this root be less than unity is necessary for $\bar{y}_t$ to be negligible.

If J is allowed to tend to infinity and the roots of (2.10) are less than one in absolute value, the deterministic component in (2.8) disappears completely. This leaves a linear process, (1.23). The coefficients in this process can be derived most easily by defining the polynomials

$$\phi(L) = 1 - \phi_1 L - \phi_2 L^2 \qquad (2.16)$$

and

$$\psi(L) = \psi_0 + \psi_1 L + \psi_2 L^2 + \cdots + \psi_\tau L^\tau + \cdots \qquad (2.17)$$

and noting that (2.8) and (1.23) can be written as

$$y_t = \phi^{-1}(L)\varepsilon_t \tag{2.18}$$

and

$$y_t = \psi(L)\varepsilon_t \tag{2.19}$$

respectively. On comparing (2.18) and (2.19) it will be seen that

$$\phi(L)\psi(L) = 1 \tag{2.20}$$

This can be expanded to yield

$$(1 - \phi_1 L - \phi_2 L^2)(\psi_0 + \psi_1 L + \psi_2 L^2 + \cdots) = 1$$

which on re-arrangement becomes:

$$\psi_0 + (\psi_1 - \phi_1\psi_0)\,L + (\psi_2 - \phi_1\psi_1 - \phi_2\psi_0)\,L^2$$
$$+ (\psi_3 - \phi_1\psi_2 - \phi_2\psi_1)\,L^3 + \cdots = 1 \tag{2.21}$$

The coefficients of L, L^2, L^3 ... on the right hand side of (2.21) are all zero and so

$$\psi_1 - \phi_1 = 0$$
$$\psi_j - \phi_1\psi_{j-1} - \phi_2\psi_{j-2} = 0, \qquad j \geqslant 2 \tag{2.22}$$

For $j \geqslant 2$, ψ_j is determined by the second-order difference equation, (2.22), with starting values $\psi_0 = 1$ and $\psi_1 = \phi_1$. This difference equation has exactly the same form as (2.9). Its roots are given by (2.12) and if they are both less than one in absolute value, ψ_j will tend towards zero as $j \to \infty$. It can be shown that this movement towards zero takes place quickly enough for (1.24a) to be satisfied and the condition that the roots of (2.10) have modulus less than unity is sufficient to ensure stationarity.

The conditions for stationarity may be defined in terms of the parameters ϕ_1 and ϕ_2 as follows:

$$\phi_1 + \phi_2 < 1 \tag{2.23a}$$

$$-\phi_1 + \phi_2 < 1 \tag{2.23b}$$

$$\phi_2 > -1 \tag{2.23c}$$

see, for example, Goldberg (1958, pp. 171–2). The roots of the homogeneous equation will be complex if

$$\phi_1^2 + 4\phi_2 < 0 \tag{2.24}$$

although a necessary condition for complex roots is simply that $\phi_2 < 0$. These conditions are conveniently summarised in figure 2.2, where all the points which actually lie *within* the triangle (but not *on* the boundary) correspond to values of ϕ_1 and ϕ_2 in a stationary process. The shaded area indicates complex roots.

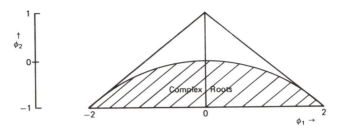

Figure 2.2 Admissible region for ϕ_1 and ϕ_2 in a stationary AR(2) process.

Stationarity for the pth-Order Model

The AR(p) model, (2.1), will be stationary if the roots of the characteristic equation

$$x^p - \phi_1 x^{p-1} - \cdots - \phi_p = 0 \qquad (2.25)$$

are less than one in absolute value, i.e. if they lie within the unit circle. An alternative way of expressing this condition is in terms of the associated polynomial, (1.26a). The polynomial equation,

$$1 - \phi_1 L - \cdots - \phi_p L^p = 0 \qquad (2.26)$$

is similar in form to (2.25) except that x is replaced by $1/L$ and the whole equation is multiplied through by L^p. The stationarity condition is that the roots of (2.26) should be *outside* the unit circle.

Autocovariance and Autocorrelation Functions

When $|\phi| < 1$, the AR(1) model, (2.2), has a mean of zero and a variance given by (2.7). The autocovariance at lag τ can be derived by expressing y_t as a linear combination of $y_{t-\tau}$ and $\varepsilon_t, \varepsilon_{t-1}, \ldots, \varepsilon_{t-\tau+1}$. This is achieved by setting $J = \tau$ in (2.3) and so

$$\gamma(\tau) = E(y_t y_{t-\tau}) = E\left[\left(\phi^\tau y_{t-\tau} + \sum_{j=0}^{\tau-1} \phi^j \varepsilon_{t-j} \right) y_{t-\tau} \right]$$

Since $\varepsilon_t, \ldots, \varepsilon_{t-\tau+1}$ are all uncorrelated with $y_{t-\tau}$, this expression reduces to

$$\gamma(\tau) = \phi^\tau E(y_{t-\tau}^2) = \phi^\tau \gamma(0), \qquad \tau = 1, 2, \ldots \qquad (2.27)$$

The autocovariances depend only on τ, confirming that the process is stationary.

The autocovariances may be derived by a more direct method if stationarity is assumed from the outset. Multiplying both sides of (2.2) by

$y_{t-\tau}$ and taking expectations gives

$$E(y_t y_{t-\tau}) = \phi E(y_{t-1} y_{t-\tau}) + E(\varepsilon_t y_{t-\tau}), \qquad \tau = 0, 1, 2, \ldots \quad (2.28)$$

For a stationary process, $E(y_{t-1} y_{t-\tau}) = E(y_t y_{t-\tau+1}) = \gamma(\tau - 1)$ and, if $\tau > 0$, the last term is zero, as ε_t is uncorrelated with past values of y_t. Therefore

$$\gamma(\tau) = \phi \gamma(\tau - 1), \qquad \tau = 1, 2, \ldots \quad (2.29)$$

This is a first-order difference equation with a solution given by (2.27). The expression for the variance of the process may be derived by a similar method by noting that $E(\varepsilon_t y_t) = \sigma^2$.

The autocorrelation takes the form

$$\rho(\tau) = \phi^\tau, \qquad \tau = 0, 1, 2, \ldots \quad (2.30)$$

and for positive values of ϕ this exhibits a smooth exponential decay as shown in figure 2.3(a). When ϕ is negative, the autocorrelation function again decays exponentially, but it oscillates between negative and positive values as shown in figure 2.3(b). When ϕ is positive, the series is 'slowly changing' in that the differences between successive observations tend to be relatively small. A negative ϕ leads to a very irregular pattern, since adjacent observations are negatively correlated.

The variance and autocovariance of the AR(2) process may be obtained by generalising (2.28). Multiplying (2.8) by $y_{t-\tau}$ and taking expectations yields

$$E(y_t y_{t-\tau}) = \phi_1 E(y_{t-1} y_{t-\tau}) + \phi_2 E(y_{t-2} y_{t-\tau}) + E(\varepsilon_t y_{t-\tau}) \quad (2.31)$$

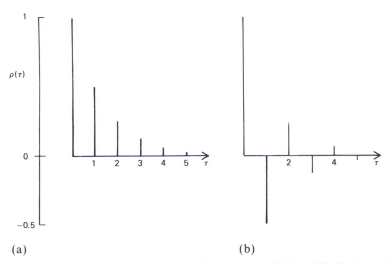

(a)   (b)

Figure 2.3 Autocorrelation functions for AR(1) processes: (a) $\phi = 0.5$; (b) $\phi = -0.5$.

The last term is zero for $\tau > 0$ and so

$$\gamma(\tau) = \phi_1\gamma(\tau - 1) + \phi_2\gamma(\tau - 2), \qquad \tau = 1, 2, \ldots \qquad (2.32)$$

Dividing through by $\gamma(0)$ gives a second-order difference equation for the autocorrelation function, i.e.

$$\rho(\tau) = \phi_1\rho(\tau - 1) + \phi_2\rho(\tau - 2), \qquad \tau = 1, 2, \ldots \qquad (2.33)$$

Since $\rho(-1) = \rho(1)$, setting $\tau = 1$ yields

$$\rho(1) = \phi_1 + \phi_2\rho(1)$$

and so starting values for the autocorrelation function are given by

$$\rho(0) = 1$$

and

$$\rho(1) = \phi_1/(1 - \phi_2)$$

Equation (2.33) is of exactly the same form as the homogeneous equation (2.9). Its solution will therefore exhibit the same characteristics as the deterministic component of the AR(2) process. In particular, for complex roots it may show damped cyclical behaviour as illustrated in figure 2.4.

The variance of the AR(2) process may be obtained from (2.31) with $\tau = 0$. The last term is no longer zero as

$$E(\varepsilon_t y_t) = E[\varepsilon_t(\phi_1 y_{t-1} + \phi_2 y_{t-2} + \varepsilon_t)]$$

$$= \phi_1 E(\varepsilon_t y_{t-1}) + \phi_2 E(\varepsilon_t y_{t-2}) + E(\varepsilon_t^2)$$

$$= 0 + 0 + \sigma^2 = \sigma^2$$

and so

$$\gamma(0) = \phi_1\gamma(1) + \phi_2\gamma(2) + \sigma^2 \qquad (2.34)$$

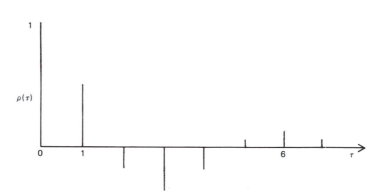

Figure 2.4 Autocorrelation function for an AR(2) process with $\phi_1 = 0.7$ and $\phi_2 = -0.5$.

Dividing through by $\gamma(0)$ and rearranging gives

$$\gamma(0) = \frac{\sigma^2}{1 - \rho(1)\phi_1 - \rho(2)\phi_2} \tag{2.35}$$

but since $\rho(1) = \phi_1/(1 - \phi_2)$ and $\rho(2) = \phi_1\rho(1) + \phi_2$, $\gamma(0)$ may be expressed in terms of ϕ_1 and ϕ_2 as

$$\gamma(0) = \left(\frac{1 - \phi_2}{1 + \phi_2}\right)\frac{\sigma^2}{[(1 - \phi_2)^2 - \phi_1^2]} \tag{2.36}$$

The same techniques may be used to derive the time domain properties of any AR process. Multiplying (2.1) by $y_{t-\tau}$, taking expectations and dividing by $\gamma(0)$ gives the pth-order difference equation

$$\rho(\tau) = \phi_1\rho(\tau - 1) + \cdots + \phi_p\rho(\tau - p), \qquad \tau = 1, 2, \ldots \tag{2.37}$$

When $\tau = 0$, the following expression for the variance is obtained after some rearrangement:

$$\gamma(0) = \sigma^2/[1 - \rho(1)\phi_1 - \cdots - \rho(p)\phi_p] \tag{2.38}$$

For all stationary $AR(p)$ processes the autocorrelation function 'damps down', in the sense that $\rho(\tau)$ tends to zero as $\tau \to \infty$. The actual behaviour it exhibits, for example with regard to cyclical movements, depends on the roots of the characteristic equation, (2.25).

2.3 Moving Average Processes

A moving average process of order q is written as

$$y_t = \varepsilon_t + \theta_1\varepsilon_{t-1} + \cdots + \theta_q\varepsilon_{t-q}, \qquad t = 1, \ldots, T \tag{3.1}$$

and denoted by $y_t \sim MA(q)$. A finite moving average process is always stationary. Condition (1.24) is satisfied automatically and the covariances can be derived without placing any restrictions on the parameters $\theta_1, \ldots, \theta_q$. However, it is sometimes necessary to express an MA process in autoregressive form. If this is to be done, the MA parameters must satisfy conditions similar to those which have to be imposed on AR parameters in order to ensure stationarity. If these conditions are satisfied, the MA process is said to be invertible.

Autocovariance and Autocorrelation Functions

Taking expectations in (3.1) immediately shows that y_t has zero mean, while

$$\gamma(0) = E(y_t^2) = (1 + \theta_1^2 + \cdots + \theta_q^2)\sigma^2 \tag{3.2}$$

The autocovariances are given by

$$\gamma(\tau) = \begin{cases} (\theta_\tau + \theta_1\theta_{\tau+1} + \cdots + \theta_{q-\tau}\theta_q)\sigma^2, & \tau = 1, \ldots, q \\ 0, & \tau > q \end{cases} \tag{3.3}$$

compare (1.14c) and (1.14d). Since the autocovariances at lags greater than q are zero, the autocovariance function, and therefore the autocorrelation function, has a distinct 'cut-off' at $\tau = q$. This contrasts with the autocovariance function for an AR process which gradually decays towards zero. If q is small, the maximum value of $|\rho(1)|$ is well below unity. It can be shown that

$$|\rho(1)| \leqslant \cos[\pi/(q+2)] \tag{3.4}$$

For $q = 1$, this means that the maximum value of $|\rho(1)|$ is 0.5, a point which can be verified directly from (1.15).

Invertibility

The MA(1) process, (1.1), can be expressed in terms of lagged values of y_t by substituting repeatedly for lagged values of ε_t. This yields

$$y_t = \theta y_{t-1} - \theta^2 y_{t-2} + \cdots - (-\theta)^J y_{t-J} + \varepsilon_t - (-\theta)^{J+1}\varepsilon_{t-J-1} \tag{3.5}$$

compare (2.3). If y_t is not to depend on a shock to the system arising at some point in the remote past, θ must be less than one in absolute value. If J is allowed to go to infinity, the last term in (3.5) disappears and y_t may be written as an infinite autoregressive process with declining weights, i.e.

$$y_t = -\sum_{j=1}^{\infty} (-\theta)^j y_{t-j} + \varepsilon_t \tag{3.6}$$

An MA(1) model with $|\theta| > 1$ is not invertible, but it is still stationary. However, its autocorrelation function can be reproduced exactly by an invertible process with parameter $1/\theta$. This can be seen by substituting in (1.15) to give

$$\rho(1) = \frac{1/\theta}{1 + (1/\theta)^2} = \frac{\theta}{1 + \theta^2} \tag{3.7}$$

Except for the case of $|\theta| = 1$, therefore, a particular autocorrelation function will be compatible with two processes, only one of which is invertible. Restricting attention to invertible processes resolves the problem of identifiability.

An MA(1) process with $|\theta| = 1$ is something of an anomaly, since it may be uniquely identified from the autocorrelation function. Although such processes are not *strictly* invertible, they can arise in certain circumstances, and perfectly sensible predictions can be based on them.

The concept of invertibility extends to higher order MA processes. The conditions necessary for invertibility may be expressed in terms of the associated MA polynomial, (1.26b), by requiring that the roots of

$$\theta(L) = 0 \tag{3.8}$$

lie outside the unit circle.

2.4 Mixed Processes

The general autoregressive-moving average process was defined in (1.25) and such a process is indicated by the notation $y_t \sim \text{ARMA}(p, q)$. The $\text{AR}(p)$ and $\text{MA}(q)$ models are special cases and it is quite legitimate to denote them by $\text{ARMA}(p, 0)$ and $\text{ARMA}(0, q)$ respectively. However, a mixed process will always be taken to mean one in which both p and q are greater than zero.

Stationarity and Invertibility

Whether or not a mixed process is stationary depends solely on its autoregressive part. The conditions may be expressed in terms of the autoregressive polynomial associated with (1.27) by requiring that the roots of $\phi(L) = 0$ lie outside the unit circle. In a similar way, the invertibility condition is exactly the same as for an $\text{MA}(q)$ process, namely that the roots of (3.8) should lie outside the unit circle.

The reason why stationarity depends on the AR part of the model becomes apparent as soon as an attempt is made to express a mixed process as an infinite moving average. The $\text{ARMA}(1, 1)$ process

$$y_t = \phi y_{t-1} + \varepsilon_t + \theta \varepsilon_{t-1}, \qquad t = 1, \ldots, T \tag{4.1}$$

is the simplest mixed process and it would be possible to substitute repeatedly for lagged values of y_t as in (2.3). An alternative way of going about this is to write (4.1) in the form

$$(1 - \phi L)y_t = (1 + \theta L)\varepsilon_t \tag{4.2}$$

and to divide both sides by $(1 - \phi L)$. This yields

$$y_t = \frac{\varepsilon_t}{1 - \phi L} + \frac{\theta \varepsilon_{t-1}}{1 - \phi L} \tag{4.3}$$

If L is deemed to satisfy the condition $|L| \leqslant 1$, the term $1/(1 - \phi L)$ can be regarded as the sum of the infinite geometric progression $1, \phi L, (\phi L)^2, \ldots$

when $|\phi| < 1$, and so (4.3) can be re-written as

$$y_t = \sum_{j=0}^{\infty} (\phi L)^j \varepsilon_t + \theta \sum_{j=0}^{\infty} (\phi L)^j \varepsilon_{t-1}$$

$$= \sum_{j=0}^{\infty} \phi^j \varepsilon_{t-j} + \theta \sum_{j=0}^{\infty} \phi^j \varepsilon_{t-j-1}$$

$$= \varepsilon_t + \sum_{j=1}^{\infty} (\theta \phi^{j-1} + \phi^j) \varepsilon_{t-j} \tag{4.4}$$

When $\theta = 0$, this expression reduces to (2.5). Given that $|\phi| < 1$, the weights in (4.4) decline sufficiently rapidly for the process to have finite variance and for the autocovariances to exist.

For $p > 1$, the infinite MA representation may be obtained by a similar device which entails factorising $\phi(L)$ and expanding $\phi^{-1}(L)\theta(L)$ in partial fractions. A more convenient way of proceeding is to equate coefficients of powers of L in the expression

$$\theta(L) = \phi(L)\psi(L) \tag{4.5}$$

where $\theta(L)$ and $\phi(L)$ are the polynomials defined in (1.26). The infinite MA polynomial, $\psi(L)$, was defined in (2.17) and expression (4.5) is simply a generalisation of the equation (2.20) used to obtain MA coefficients in the AR(2) case. After some re-arrangement (4.5) yields

$$\psi_0 = 1$$

$$\psi_j = \theta_j + \sum_{i=1}^{\min(j,p)} \phi_i \psi_{j-i}, \qquad j = 1, \ldots, q$$

$$\psi_j = \sum_{i=1}^{\min(j,p)} \phi_i \psi_{j-i}, \qquad j > q \tag{4.6}$$

For $j \geqslant \max(p, q+1)$, the ψ_j's are determined by the difference equation (4.6) with starting values given by the previous p values of ψ_j.

Example 1   In the AR(2) model it was shown earlier that the MA coefficients depend on the difference equation (2.22) for $j \geqslant 2$, with starting values $\psi_0 = 1$ and $\psi_1 = \phi_1$.

Example 2   For the ARMA(1, 1) model, (4.1), the ψ_j's are computed from the difference equation

$$\psi_j = \phi \psi_{j-1}, \qquad j \geqslant 2 \tag{4.7}$$

with starting value

$$\psi_1 = \theta + \phi \psi_0 = \theta + \phi \tag{4.8}$$

Similar techniques may be used to obtain the infinite autoregressive representation of an invertible ARMA process.

Autocovariance and Autocorrelation Functions

The time domain properties of mixed models incorporate features of both AR and MA processes. This is illustrated clearly by the ARMA$(1, 1)$ model. Multiplying (4.1) through by $y_{t-\tau}$ and taking expectations gives

$$\gamma(\tau) = \phi\gamma(\tau - 1) + E(\varepsilon_t y_{t-\tau}) + \theta E(\varepsilon_{t-1} y_{t-\tau}), \qquad \tau = 0, 1. 2, \ldots \qquad (4.9)$$

The last two expectations are zero for $\tau > 1$. For $\tau = 1$, the second of the expectations becomes

$$E(\varepsilon_{t-1} y_{t-1}) = E[\varepsilon_{t-1}(\phi y_{t-2} + \varepsilon_{t-1} + \theta\varepsilon_{t-2})] = \sigma^2$$

although the first remains zero. When $\tau = 0$, both expectations are non-zero, being given by

$$E(\varepsilon_t y_t) = \sigma^2$$

and

$$E(\varepsilon_{t-1} y_t) = E[\varepsilon_{t-1}(\phi y_{t-1} + \varepsilon_t + \theta\varepsilon_{t-1})]$$
$$= \phi E(\varepsilon_{t-1} y_{t-1}) + \theta\sigma^2$$
$$= \phi\sigma^2 + \theta\sigma^2$$

The autocovariance function is therefore

$$\gamma(0) = \phi\gamma(1) + \sigma^2 + \theta\phi\sigma^2 + \theta^2\sigma^2 \qquad (4.10a)$$

$$\gamma(1) = \phi\gamma(0) + \theta\sigma^2 \qquad (4.10b)$$

$$\gamma(\tau) = \phi\gamma(\tau - 1), \qquad \tau = 2, 3, \ldots \qquad (4.10c)$$

Substituting for $\gamma(1)$ from the second of these equations into the first yields

$$\gamma(0) = \frac{1 + \theta^2 + 2\phi\theta}{1 - \phi^2} \sigma^2 \qquad (4.11)$$

and so

$$\gamma(1) = \frac{(1 + \phi\theta)(\phi + \theta)}{1 - \phi^2} \sigma^2 \qquad (4.12)$$

Dividing (4.12) and (4.10c) by (4.11) gives the autocorrelation function

$$\rho(1) = \frac{(1 + \phi\theta)(\phi + \theta)}{1 + \theta^2 + 2\phi\theta} \qquad (4.13a)$$

$$\rho(\tau) = \phi\rho(\tau - 1), \qquad \tau = 2, 3, \ldots \qquad (4.13b)$$

On inspecting the autocorrelation function, it will be seen that, for $\tau > 1$, its behaviour is governed by the first-order difference equation (4.13b). Thus the autocorrelations exhibit exponential decay, with oscillations when ϕ is negative. This is exactly as in the AR(1) case. However, while the starting value for the difference equation in the AR(1) model is simply $\rho(0) = 1$, in the ARMA(1, 1) model the starting value is given by $\rho(1)$. As expression (4.13a) makes clear, $\rho(1)$ depends on both ϕ and θ, and the sign of $\rho(1)$ will depend on the sign of $(\phi + \theta)$.

As an illustration of the kind of pattern exhibited by the autocorrelation function, suppose $\phi = 0.3$ and $\theta = 0.9$. In this case $\rho(1) = 0.649$, and the autocorrelations follow the scheme in figure 2.5(a). Changing the moving average parameter to $\theta = -0.9$ gives $\rho(1) = -0.345$. The autocorrelations once again decay exponentially, but from a negative rather than a positive starting value. This is shown in figure 2.5(b). All in all there are six distinct patterns for the autocorrelation function from an ARMA(1, 1) model, depending on the different values taken by ϕ and θ.

The properties of higher order ARMA models may be derived in a similar fashion. The general pattern which emerges for the autocorrelation function is that the first q autocorrelations depend on both the moving average and the autoregressive parameters. Higher order autocorrelations are given by a pth-order difference equation of the form (2.37), with $\rho(q)$, $\rho(q - 1), \ldots, \rho(q - p + 1)$ as starting values.

Autocovariance Generating Function

For some purposes it is convenient to work with the *autocovariance generating function* (ACGF) of a stationary process. This is defined as a polynomial in

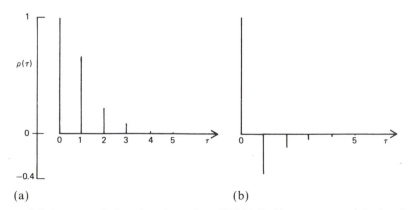

Figure 2.5 Autocorrelation functions for ARMA(1, 1) processes: (a) $\phi = 0.3$, $\theta = 0.9$; (b) $\phi = 0.3$, $\theta = -0.9$.

the lag operator, $g(L)$, such that

$$g(L) = \sum_{\tau = -\infty}^{\infty} \gamma(\tau)L^\tau \qquad (4.14)$$

The coefficient of L^j gives the autocovariance at lag τ. For an infinite MA process, (1.23), written in terms of a polynomial in the lag operator, $\psi(L)$,

$$g(L) = |\psi(L)|^2 = \psi(L)\psi(L^{-1})\sigma^2 \qquad (4.15)$$

This result can be shown as follows. Firstly, letting q go to infinity in (3.3) and changing the notation, it can be seen that

$$\gamma(\tau) = \sum_{j=0}^{\infty} \psi_j \psi_{j+\tau}$$

Substituting in (4.14) gives

$$g(L) = \sigma^2 \sum_{\tau = -\infty}^{\infty} \sum_{j=0}^{\infty} \psi_j \psi_{j+\tau} L^\tau = \sigma^2 \sum_{j=0}^{\infty} \sum_{\tau = -j}^{\infty} \psi_j \psi_{j+\tau} L^\tau$$

since $\psi_j = 0$ for $j < 0$. Writing $j + \tau = h$, so that $\tau = h - j$,

$$g(L) = \sigma^2 \sum_{j=-\infty}^{\infty} \sum_{h=0}^{\infty} \psi_j \psi_h L^{h-j} = \sigma^2 \sum_{h=0}^{\infty} \psi_h L^h \sum_{j=0}^{\infty} \psi_j L^{-j}$$

which is (4.15).

It follows from (4.5) that for an ARMA process

$$g(L) = \frac{|\theta(L)|^2}{|\phi(L)|^2}\sigma^2 = \frac{\theta(L)\theta(L^{-1})}{\phi(L)\phi(L^{-1})}\sigma^2 \qquad (4.16)$$

Example 3   In the MA(1) model, (1.1),

$$g(L) = (1 + \theta L)(1 + \theta L^{-1})\sigma^2$$
$$= (1 + \theta^2)\sigma^2 + \sigma^2\theta L + \sigma^2\theta L^{-1}$$
$$= \gamma(0) + \gamma(1)L + \gamma(-1)L^{-1}$$

The resulting autocovariances are as given in (1.14).

Common Factors

If the AR and MA polynomials in (1.27) have a root which is the same, they are said to have a *common factor*. In this case the model is over-parameterised, since a model with identical properties can be constructed by reducing both p and q by one. It is important to recognise common factors, since if they exist the model will not be identifiable and computational problems may arise; see EATS, section 3.6.

Example 4   In the ARMA $(2, 1)$ model

$$y_t = 0.2y_{t-1} + 0.15y_{t-2} + \varepsilon_t + 0.3\varepsilon_{t-1} \tag{4.17}$$

the AR polynomial may be factorised as

$$(1 - 0.2L - 0.15L^2) = (1 - 0.5L)(1 + 0.3L)$$

On re-writing the model in the form

$$y_t = \phi^{-1}(L)\theta(L)\varepsilon_t = \frac{(1 + 0.3L)}{(1 - 0.5L)(1 + 0.3L)}\varepsilon_t$$

it is immediately apparent that (4.14) has exactly the same MA representation as the AR (1) model

$$y_t = 0.5y_{t-1} + \varepsilon_t \tag{4.18}$$

Hence (4.17) and (4.18) have identical autocovariance functions and so (4.17) is over-parameterised.

2.5 Unobserved Components

A time series model may sometimes be formulated in terms of components. These components are not observed directly, but are assumed to have ARMA representations. In non-stationary time series, an unobserved components (UC) representation is often a natural way in which to proceed because the components can be identified with features such as trends, seasonals and cycles. This issue is taken up in the discussion of structural time series models in chapter 5. For the moment we restrict ourselves to stationary time series and establish some basic results.

It will be assumed that the observed series, y_t, is made up of two stationary and invertible ARMA processes, μ_t and ξ_t, driven by mutually uncorrelated white noise disturbances, η_t and ε_t, with variances σ_η^2 and σ_ε^2 respectively. Thus, writing the ARMA models in terms of polynomials as in (1.27), and assuming them to have zero means, we have

$$y_t = \mu_t + \xi_t = \frac{\theta_\mu(L)}{\phi_\mu(L)}\eta_t + \frac{\theta_\xi(L)}{\phi_\xi(L)}\varepsilon_t \tag{5.1}$$

The generalisation of results to series with more than two components is straightforward.

Autocorrelations

The autocorrelations of a UC model are obtained in the usual way by first computing the autocovariances.

Example 1 A stationary AR(1) process is observed with a white noise error so that

$$y_t = \mu_t + \varepsilon_t \qquad (5.2a)$$

$$\mu_t = \phi\mu_{t-1} + \eta_t, \qquad |\phi| < 1 \qquad (5.2b)$$

where $|\phi| < 1$ and η_t and ε_t are mutually uncorrelated white noise disturbances with variances σ_η^2 and σ_ε^2 respectively. The observed series, y_t, has zero mean as each of the components has zero mean. Since the two components are uncorrelated with each other, the autocovariance of the observed series is equal to the sum of the autocovariances of the individual series. Thus

$$\gamma(\tau) = \gamma_\mu(\tau) + \gamma_\varepsilon(\tau), \qquad \tau = 0, 1, 2, \ldots$$

where $\gamma_\mu(\tau)$ is the τth autocovariance of μ_t. From (2.27)

$$\gamma_\mu(\tau) = \phi^\tau\gamma_\mu(0) = \phi^\tau\sigma_\eta^2/(1 - \phi^2)$$

and so the autocorrelation function of the observations is:

$$\rho(\tau) = \frac{\phi^\tau\sigma_\eta^2/(1 - \phi^2)}{\sigma_\eta^2/(1 - \phi^2) + \sigma_\varepsilon^2}, \qquad \tau = 0, 1, 2, 3, \ldots \qquad (5.3)$$

A useful result in the context of UC representations is that the ACGF of the series is the sum of the individual ACGFs. Thus in (5.1) we have, using obvious notation,

$$g(L) = g_\mu(L) + g_\xi(L) = \frac{|\theta_\mu(L)|^2}{|\phi_\mu(L)|^2}\sigma_\eta^2 + \frac{|\theta_\xi(L)|^2}{|\phi_\xi(L)|^2}\sigma_\varepsilon^2 \qquad (5.4)$$

Reduced Form

The sum of two uncorrelated ARMA processes is itself an ARMA process. This process is known as the *reduced form*.

Example 2 If in (5.1) μ_t is an MA(1) process with parameter θ and the other component is white noise, the result is

$$y_t = \eta_t + \theta\eta_{t-1} + \varepsilon_t \qquad (5.5)$$

The autocorrelation function of this process is

$$\rho(\tau) = \begin{cases} \sigma_\eta^2\theta/[\sigma_\eta^2(1 + \theta^2) + \sigma_\varepsilon^2], & \tau = 1 \\ 0, & \tau \geqslant 2 \end{cases} \qquad (5.6)$$

This has exactly the same form as the autocorrelation function of an MA(1) process. Thus y_t is an MA(1) process. Its moving average parameter can be expressed in terms of the UC parameters by equating the formulae for $\rho(1)$.

Example 3 In the AR(1) plus noise model of (5.2) multiplying throughout by the AR polynomial, $\phi_\mu(L) = 1 - \phi L$, gives

$$y_t - \phi y_{t-1} = \eta_t + \varepsilon_t - \phi \varepsilon_{t-1} \qquad (5.7)$$

From the argument in the previous example, the right hand side is equivalent to an MA(1) process, and the net result is that y_t is ARMA(1,1) with AR parameter ϕ.

The general result, which was proved by Granger and Morris (1976), is as follows. *If, in (5.1), μ_t is ARMA(p_1, q_1) and ξ_t is ARMA(p_2, q_2), then y_t is ARMA(p, q), where $p \leqslant p_1 + p_2$ and $q \leqslant max(p_1 + q_2, p_2 + q_1)$.*
The basic rationale underlying the result can be seen by multiplying (5.1) through by the AR polynomials to give

$$\phi_\mu(L)\phi_\xi(L)y_t = \theta_\mu(L)\phi_\xi(L)\eta_t + \theta_\xi(L)\phi_\mu(L)\varepsilon_t \qquad (5.8)$$

The inequalities in the expressions for p and q are necessary because some cancellation may occur, as illustrated in the following example.

Example 4 If the components are AR(1) processes with a common parameter, ϕ, that is

$$\mu_t = \phi\mu_{t-1} + \eta_t \qquad (5.9a)$$

$$\xi_t = \phi\xi_{t-1} + \varepsilon_t \qquad (5.9b)$$

then

$$\mu_t + \xi_t = \phi(\mu_{t-1} + \xi_{t-1}) + \eta_t + \varepsilon_t$$

and so

$$y_t = \phi y_{t-1} + \omega_t \qquad (5.10)$$

where ω_t is white noise. Hence y_t is AR(1) rather than ARMA(2, 1).

Although the reduced form parameters are easily obtained in the above examples, deriving general expressions is not straightforward. An algorithm is given in Maravall and Mathis (1993).

2.6 Prediction and Signal Extraction

We show below how optimal predictions of future observations in ARMA models can be made by a straightforward recursive procedure. A method for obtaining predictions for unobserved components models *via* the state space form is discussed later in chapter 4. The state space approach also allows exact finite sample predictions to be made for ARMA models under fairly general assumptions concerning initial conditions. Similarly it provides the general solution to the optimal estimation of unobserved components in finite examples. This is known as *signal extraction*. The classical results on signal extraction presented here apply to large samples, but their appeal lies in the insight they give into the form of the estimators.

Minimum Mean Square Error Estimation

Given the availability of a set of observations up to, and including, y_T, the *optimal predictor* l steps ahead is the expected value of y_{T+l} conditional on the information at time $t = T$. This may be written as

$$\tilde{y}_{T+l|T} = E(y_{T+l}|Y_T) = \underset{T}{E}(y_{T+l}) \qquad (6.1)$$

where Y_T denotes the information set $\{y_T, y_{T-1}, \ldots\}$ and the T below the expectation conveys the same message as explicitly conditioning on Y_T. The predictor is optimal in the sense that it has minimum mean square error. This is easily seen by observing that for any predictor, $\hat{y}_{T+l|T}$, constructed on the basis of the information available at time T, the estimation error can be split into two parts:

$$y_{T+l} - \hat{y}_{T+l|T} = [y_{T+l} - E(y_{T+l}|Y_T)] + [E(y_{T+l}|Y_T) - \hat{y}_{T+l|T}]$$

Since the second term on the right hand side is fixed at time T, it follows that, on squaring the whole expression and taking expectations at time T, the cross-product term disappears leaving

$$\text{MSE}(\hat{y}_{T+l|T}) = \text{Var}(y_{T+l}|Y_T) + [\hat{y}_{T+l|T} - E(y_{T+l}|Y_T)]^2 \qquad (6.2)$$

The first term on the right hand side of (6.2), the conditional variance of y_{T+l}, does not depend on $\hat{y}_{T+l|T}$. Hence the *minimum mean square estimate* (MMSE) of y_{T+l} is given by the conditional mean (6.1) and it is unique. When (6.1) is viewed as a rule rather than a number, it is an estima*tor* rather than an estima*te* of y_{T+l}. It can be shown that it is the *minimum mean square estimator* (also abbreviated as MMSE) since it minimises the MSE when the expectation is taken over all the observations in the information set. (This follows from the law of iterated expectations given in chapter 8.) When the observations are normally distributed, the expression corresponding to $\text{Var}(y_{T+l}|Y_T)$ in (6.2) does not depend on the observations and so can be interpreted as the MSE of the estimator. However, as we shall see shortly, normality of the observations is not always needed for the MSE to have this property.

More generally, the MMSE of any random variable is its expectation conditional on the relevant information set. Thus the MMSE of the unobserved component μ_t in (5.1) is $E(\mu_t | Y_T)$ for t either within or outside the sample.

Conditional expectations may not be linear combinations of the observations. If attention is restricted to the class of linear estimators, the best such estimator is the *minimum mean square linear estimator* (MMSLE) or *best linear unbiased predictor* (BLUP). Further discussion on such estimators may be found in chapter 4.

Optimal Predictions for ARMA Models

We now consider the question of how to construct an MMSE of a future observation from an ARMA process, given observations up to and including time T. The ARMA process is assumed to be stationary and invertible, with known parameters and *independent* disturbances with mean zero and constant variance, σ^2. It is further assumed that, for MA and mixed processes, all present and past disturbances, $\varepsilon_T, \varepsilon_{T-1}, \varepsilon_{T-2}, \ldots$, are known. This is effectively the same as assuming an infinite realisation of observations going back in time. Such an assumption is obviously unrealistic, though as we shall see it may be easily modified so as to yield a predictor which can be computed from a finite sample.

The equation of an ARMA(p, q) model at time $T + l$ is

$$y_{T+l} = \phi_1 y_{T+l-1} + \cdots + \phi_p y_{T+l-p} + \varepsilon_{T+l} + \cdots + \theta_q \varepsilon_{T+l-q} \qquad (6.3)$$

The MMSE of a future observation is its expectation conditional on the information at time T, (6.1). On taking conditional expectations in (6.3), future values of ε_t are set to zero since, being independent, they cannot be predicted. This yields

$$\tilde{y}_{T+l|T} = \phi_1 \tilde{y}_{T+l-1|T} + \cdots + \phi_p \tilde{y}_{T+l-p|T}$$

$$+ \tilde{\varepsilon}_{T+l|T} + \cdots + \theta_q \tilde{\varepsilon}_{T+l-q|T}, \qquad l = 1, 2, \ldots \qquad (6.4)$$

where $\tilde{y}_{T+j|T} = y_{T+j}$ for $j \leq 0$, and

$$\tilde{\varepsilon}_{T+j|T} = \begin{cases} 0 & \text{for } j > 0 \\ \varepsilon_{T+j} & \text{for } j \leq 0 \end{cases}$$

Expression (6.4) provides a recursion for computing optimal predictions of future observations.

Example 1   For the AR(1) process, expression (6.4) leads directly to the difference equation

$$\tilde{y}_{T+l|T} = \phi \tilde{y}_{T+l-1|T}, \qquad l = 1, 2, \ldots \qquad (6.5)$$

The starting value is given by $\tilde{y}_{T|T} = y_T$, and so (6.5) may be solved to yield

$$\tilde{y}_{T+l|T} = \phi^l y_T \tag{6.6}$$

Thus the predicted values decline exponentially towards zero, and the forecast function has exactly the same form as the autocovariance function.

Example 2   At time $T + 1$, the equation for an MA(1) process is of the form

$$y_{T+1} = \varepsilon_{T+1} + \theta\varepsilon_T \tag{6.7}$$

Since ε_{T+1} is unknown, it is set equal to zero in the corresponding prediction equation which is

$$\tilde{y}_{T+1|T} = \theta\varepsilon_T \tag{6.8}$$

For $l > 1$, $\tilde{y}_{T+l|T} = 0$, and so knowledge of the data generating process is of no help in predicting more than one period ahead.

Example 3   Consider the ARMA(2, 2) process

$$y_t = 0.6y_{t-1} + 0.2y_{t-2} + \varepsilon_t + 0.3\varepsilon_{t-1} - 0.4\varepsilon_{t-2}$$

and suppose that $y_T = 4.0$, $y_{T-1} = 5.0$, $\varepsilon_T = 1.0$ and $\varepsilon_{T-1} = 0.5$. Then

$$\tilde{y}_{T+1|T} = 0.6y_T + 0.2y_{T-1} + 0.3\varepsilon_T - 0.4\varepsilon_{T-1} = 3.5$$

and

$$\tilde{y}_{T+2|T} = 0.6\tilde{y}_{T+1|T} + 0.2y_T - 0.4\varepsilon_T = 2.5$$

Thereafter forecasts are generated by the difference equation

$$\tilde{y}_{T+l|T} = 0.6\tilde{y}_{T+l-1|T} + 0.2\tilde{y}_{T+l-2|T}, \qquad l = 3, 4, \ldots$$

To find the forecast MSE, note that since y_t has the infinite MA representation, (1.23), we can write

$$y_{T+l} = \sum_{j=1}^{l} \psi_{l-j}\varepsilon_{T+j} + \sum_{j=0}^{\infty} \psi_{l+j}\varepsilon_{T-j} \tag{6.9}$$

Taking conditional expectations shows that the second term on the right hand side of (6.9) gives the expression for the MMSE of y_{T+l} in terms of past ε_t's, namely

$$\tilde{y}_{T+l|T} = \sum_{j=0}^{\infty} \psi_{l+j}\varepsilon_{T-j} \tag{6.10}$$

Thus the first term on the right hand side of (6.9) is the error in predicting l steps ahead, and its variance is the prediction MSE, that is

$$\mathrm{MSE}(\tilde{y}_{T+l|T}) = (1 + \psi_1^2 + \cdots + \psi_{l-1}^2)\sigma^2 \tag{6.11}$$

The expression for the MSE is independent of the observations, and so if (6.10) is regarded as an estima*tor*, (6.11) gives its unconditional MSE, that is, the MSE averaged over all possible realisations of observations.

Example 4   For the AR(1) model $\psi_{l+j} = \phi^{l+j}$, and so

$$\tilde{y}_{T+l|T} = \sum_{j=0}^{\infty} \phi^{l+j} \varepsilon_{T-j} = \phi^l \sum_{j=0}^{\infty} \phi^j \varepsilon_{T-j} = \phi^l y_T$$

as in (6.6). The MSE of $y_{T+l|T}$ is given by

$$\text{MSE}(\tilde{y}_{T+l|T}) = [1 + \phi^2 + \cdots + \phi^{2(l-1)}]\sigma^2$$
$$= \frac{1 - \phi^{2l}}{1 - \phi^2} \sigma^2 \qquad (6.12)$$

As $l \to \infty$, this expression tends towards $\sigma^2/(1 - \phi^2)$ which is simply the variance of y_t.

Making the additional assumption that the ε_t's are normally distributed means that the conditional distribution of y_{T+l} is also normal. A 95% prediction interval is given by

$$y_{T+l} = \tilde{y}_{T+l|T} \pm 1.96 \left(1 + \sum_{j=1}^{l-1} \psi_j^2 \right)^{1/2} \sigma \qquad (6.13)$$

This can be interpreted as saying that, given a particular sample, there is a 95% chance that y_{T+l} will lie within the designated range.

Returning to the issue concerning knowledge of the ε_t's into the infinite past, an alternative approach is to make assumptions about initial conditions which permit the recursive computation of the values of the required disturbances; see section 3.3. The theory above still applies, though, of course, the predictions will not be optimal if the assumptions about initial conditions are violated. A method of computing exact optimal finite sample predictions without making such assumptions is described in section 4.4.

Example 5*   The assumption that ε_0 is zero in the MA(1) model allows the disturbances to be calculated from the recursion

$$\varepsilon_t = y_t - \theta\varepsilon_{t-1}, \qquad t = 1, \ldots, T \qquad (6.14)$$

The consequences of this assumption can be seen by writing down (6.14) for $t = T$ and repeatedly substituting for lagged values of ε_t. This yields

$$\varepsilon_T = y_T + (-\theta)y_{T-1} + \theta^2 y_{T-2} + \cdots + (-\theta)^{T-1}y_1 + (-\theta)^T\varepsilon_0 \qquad (6.15)$$

Incorrectly assuming that ε_0 is zero induces an error in the predictor, (6.8), which is equal to $\theta(-\theta)^T\varepsilon_0$. This error may not be negligible if T is small and $|\theta|$ is close to one. If $\varepsilon_0 \sim N(0, \sigma^2)$, the MSE taken over all possible realisations is increased by $\theta^{2(T+1)}\sigma^2$.

Best Linear Unbiased Predictor

The assumption that the disturbances in an ARMA model are independent is needed for deriving the MMSE of a future observation. If the assumption of independence is relaxed to one of uncorrelatedness, the result does not go through because the conditional expectation of a future disturbance is not necessarily zero; see the examples in chapter 8, section 8.1. However, if we restrict ourselves to linear predictors, the predictor given by the right hand side of (6.10) is still the best in the sense that it minimises the unconditional prediction MSE. In other words, it is the MMSLE or BLUP.

A linear predictor is a linear function of the observations, and is therefore a linear function of current and past disturbances. Any such predictor may be written as

$$\hat{y}_{T+l|T} = \sum_{j=0}^{\infty} \psi_{l+j}^* \varepsilon_{T-j} \tag{6.16}$$

where the ψ_{l+j}^*'s are pre-specified weights. The predictor is unbiased in the sense that the unconditional expectation of the prediction error

$$y_{T+l} - \hat{y}_{T+l|T} = \varepsilon_{T+l} + \psi_1 \varepsilon_{T+l-1} + \cdots + \psi_{l-1} \varepsilon_{T+1}$$
$$+ (\psi_l - \psi_l^*)\varepsilon_T + (\psi_{l+1} - \psi_{l+1}^*)\varepsilon_{T-1} + \cdots$$

is zero. Its MSE is given by

$$\mathrm{MSE}(\hat{y}_{T+l|T}) = \sigma^2(1 + \psi_1^2 + \cdots + \psi_{l-1}^2) + \sigma^2 \sum_{j=0}^{\infty} (\psi_{l+j} - \psi_{l+j}^*)^2$$

This is minimised by setting $\psi_{l+j}^* = \psi_{l+j}$. The MMSLE of y_{T+l} is therefore given by (6.10) with MSE as in (6.11).

*Signal Extraction**

Signal extraction is concerned with finding the optimal estimate or estimator of an unobserved component at some point in the sample. In what follows, the problem of estimating μ_t in the model (5.1) will be considered. The extension to models with more than two components is straightforward.

The MMSE of the component of interest, μ_t, is its expectation conditional on the full set of observations, $y = (y_1, y_2, \ldots, y_T)'$, that is

$$\tilde{\mu}_{t|T} = E(\mu_t | y) \tag{6.17}$$

compare (6.1). The classical Wiener–Kolmogorov approach to signal extraction assumes an infinite sample; thus we write (6.17) as $\tilde{\mu}_{t|\infty}$. More precisely, the sample is said to be doubly infinite, meaning that there are an infinite number of observations on either side of the time period, t. In practice this means that the formulae obtained tend not to be particularly useful guides to the weighting which should be adopted near the beginning or end of a finite sample.

As in the sub-sections on prediction, the parameters are taken to be known. The disturbances η_t and ε_t are assumed to be normally distributed and mutually independent. This leads to MMSEs of the unobserved components. If the disturbances are only assumed to be mutually uncorrelated white noise processes, the resulting formulae yield MMSLEs.

The expression for the MMSE of μ_t, which is derived shortly, is

$$\tilde{\mu}_{t|\infty} = \sum_{j=-\infty}^{\infty} w_j y_{t+j} = w(L)y_t \tag{6.18a}$$

where the weight, w_j, is the coefficients of L^j in the polynomial

$$w(L) = \frac{|\theta_\mu(L)/\phi_\mu(L)|^2 \sigma_\eta^2}{|\theta_\mu(L)/\phi_\mu(L)|^2 \sigma_\eta^2 + |\theta_\xi(L)/\phi_\xi(L)|^2 \sigma_\varepsilon^2} \tag{6.18b}$$

In view of (5.4), the denominator can be set equal to $g(L)$, the autocovariance generating function of y_t itself. If desired, $g(L)$ can be expressed in terms of the coefficients of the reduced form ARMA model, as in (4.16).

Example 6 In the AR(1) plus noise model (5.2)

$$w(L) = \frac{\sigma_\eta^2/|1 - \phi L|^2}{\sigma_\eta^2/|1 - \phi L|^2 + \sigma_\varepsilon^2} \tag{6.19}$$

As shown in (5.7), the reduced form is an ARMA(1, 1) process, and so

$$g(L) = \sigma^2 |1 + \theta L|^2 / |1 - \phi L|^2$$

Substituting in the denominator gives

$$w(L) = \frac{\sigma_\eta^2/|1 - \phi L|^2}{\sigma^2 |1 + \theta L|^2 / |1 - \phi L|^2} = \frac{\sigma_\eta^2}{\sigma^2} \frac{1}{|1 + \theta L|^2} \tag{6.20}$$

Now $|1 + \theta L|^2 = (1 + \theta L)(1 + \theta L^{-1})$. Expanding $1/(1 + \theta L)$ as $1 + (-\theta)L + (-\theta)^2 L^2 + \ldots$, and similarly for $1/(1 + \theta L^{-1})$, and collecting terms, shows that w_j is

$$w_j = [\sigma_\eta^2/\{\sigma^2(1 - \theta^2)\}](-\theta)^{|j|}, \qquad j = \ldots -2, -1, 0, 1, 2, \ldots \tag{6.21}$$

The weights assigned to observations therefore decline exponentially on either side of the time period of interest.

Formula (6.18) can be derived from the joint density function of the observations and the component of interest, μ_t. Since this is a multivariate normal distribution, a conditional mean (6.17) is the same as a conditional mode and so can be found by partial differentiation. The details are as follows.

Conditional on the μ_t's, the joint density of the observations y_t, $t = 1, \ldots, T$, is the same as the joint density of the component $\xi_t = y_t - \mu_t$, $t = 1, \ldots, T$. This is generated by an ARMA process, and in the next chapter it is shown that if the pre-sample values of ξ_t, and its associated disturbance term ε_t, are set to zero, the logarithm of the joint density function of $\boldsymbol{\xi} = (\xi_1, \ldots, \xi_T)'$ is

$$\log p(\boldsymbol{\xi}) = -\tfrac{1}{2}T \log 2\pi - \tfrac{1}{2}T \log \sigma_\varepsilon^2 - \sum_{t=1}^{T} (\varepsilon_t^2/\sigma_\varepsilon^2)$$

with the summation going from 1 to T. The joint density of the μ_t's themselves, denoted $p(\boldsymbol{\mu})$, is given by a similar expression with ε_t replaced by η_t. Thus the logarithm of the joint density of $\mathbf{y}$ and $\boldsymbol{\mu}$ is

$$\log p(\mathbf{y}, \boldsymbol{\mu}) = \log[p(\mathbf{y}|\boldsymbol{\mu})p(\boldsymbol{\mu})] = \log p(\boldsymbol{\xi}) + \log p(\boldsymbol{\mu})$$
$$= -T \log 2\pi - \tfrac{1}{2}T \log \sigma_\varepsilon^2 - \tfrac{1}{2}T \log \sigma_\eta^2 - \tfrac{1}{2}\sum (\varepsilon_t^2/\sigma_\varepsilon^2)$$
$$- \tfrac{1}{2}\sum (\eta_t^2/\sigma_\eta^2) \tag{6.22}$$

Since $\mu_t = \{\theta_\mu(L)/\phi_\mu(L)\}\eta_t$ and $y_t - \mu_t = \xi_t = \{\theta_\xi(L)/\phi_\xi(L)\}\varepsilon_t$, substituting for ε_t and η_t gives

$$\log p(\mathbf{y}, \boldsymbol{\mu}) = -T \log 2\pi - \tfrac{1}{2}T \log \sigma_\varepsilon^2 - \tfrac{1}{2}T \log \sigma_\eta^2$$
$$- \tfrac{1}{2}\sum [\{\phi_\xi(L)/\theta_\xi(L)\}(y_t - \mu_t)]^2/\sigma_\varepsilon^2$$
$$- \tfrac{1}{2}\sum [\{\phi_\mu(L)/\theta_\mu(L)\}\mu_t]^2/\sigma_\eta^2 \tag{6.23}$$

If the sample is taken to be (doubly) infinite, differentiating with respect to μ_t yields $\mu_t/g_\mu(L) - (y_t - \mu_t)/g_\xi(L)$ where $g_\mu(L)$ and $g_\xi(L)$ are the ACGFs of μ_t and ξ_t respectively. Equating this expression to zero and re-arranging gives the classical signal extraction formula

$$\mu_{t|\infty} = \frac{g_\mu(L)}{g_\mu(L) + g_\xi(L)} y_t \tag{6.24}$$

which is the same as (6.18).

2.7 Properties of the Correlogram and Other Sample Statistics

The correlogram is the basic tool of analysis in the time domain. An inspection of the correlogram may lead to the conclusion that the series is random, or that it exhibits a pattern of serial correlation which can perhaps be modelled by a particular stochastic process. In order to make judgements of this kind, it is necessary to know something about the sampling properties of the correlogram and related statistics such as the sample mean and auto-covariances. These issues are examined in this section while section 2.8 looks at various test statistics.

*Sample Mean**

The sample mean, $\bar{y}$, given in (1.9), is an unbiased estimator of the mean of a stationary process, μ. This follows immediately on taking expectations. The variance is

$$\text{Var}(\bar{y}) = \frac{1}{T^2} \sum_{s=1}^{T} \sum_{t=1}^{T} \text{cov}(y_s, y_t) = \frac{\gamma(0)}{T^2} \sum_{s=1}^{T} \sum_{t=1}^{T} \rho(t-s) \qquad (7.1)$$

If we make a change of variable from s and t to s and $\tau = t - s$ we can sum over the diagonals of the correlation matrix of $y_1, \ldots, y_T$, rather than over the rows. The summation over τ goes from $-(T-1)$ to $T-1$; for $\tau > 0$, s goes from 1 to $T - \tau$, while for $\tau < 0$, s goes from $-\tau$ to T. The summation in (7.1) is a function of τ only, and hence summation over s gives the expression $T - |\tau|$ for both positive and negative τ. Therefore

$$\text{Var}(\bar{y}) = \frac{\gamma(0)}{T^2} \sum_{\tau=-(T-1)}^{T-1} (T - |\tau|)\rho(\tau) = \frac{\gamma(0)}{T} \sum_{-(T-1)}^{T-1} \left(1 - \frac{|\tau|}{T}\right)\rho(\tau) \qquad (7.2)$$

This expression is exact. However, as the sample size goes to infinity, the weights attached to the low order autocorrelations tend to one, while if the series is ergodic, $\rho(\tau) \to 0$ as $T \to \infty$. Thus

$$\lim_{T \to \infty} \gamma(0) \sum_{\tau=-(T-1)}^{T-1} \left(1 - \frac{|\tau|}{T}\right)\rho(\tau) = \gamma(0) \sum_{\tau=-\infty}^{\infty} \rho(\tau) \qquad (7.3)$$

see Priestley (1981, p. 320) for a formal discussion. It follows that dividing the right hand side of (7.3) by T gives the asymptotic variance of the sample mean, that is

$$\text{Avar}(\bar{y}) = \frac{\gamma(0)}{T} \sum_{\tau=-\infty}^{\infty} \rho(\tau) \qquad (7.4)$$

Given the convergence of the expression in (7.3) to a fixed number, it follows that the variance of $\bar{y}$ tends to zero as $T \to \infty$, so since $\bar{y}$ is unbiased, it is also consistent.

Example 1 For an AR(1) process, $\rho(\tau) = \phi^\tau$, and so

$$\text{Avar}(\bar{y}) = \frac{\gamma(0)}{T} \left(2 \sum_{t=0}^{\infty} \rho(\tau) - 1\right) = \frac{\gamma(0)}{T} \left(\frac{2}{1-\phi} - 1\right)$$

$$= \frac{\gamma(0)}{T} \frac{(1+\phi)}{(1-\phi)} = \frac{\sigma^2}{T} \frac{1}{(1-\phi)^2} \qquad (7.5)$$

For any linear process of the form (1.23) with a non-zero mean, that is

$$y_t = \mu + \sum_{j=0}^{\infty} \psi_j \varepsilon_{t-j} \qquad (7.6)$$

with the ε_t's independently and identically distributed, and condition (1.24b) satisfied, it is possible to go further and show that the limiting distribution of $T^{\frac{1}{2}}(\bar{y} - \mu)$ is normal; see Anderson (1971, p. 478). In other words, $\bar{y}$ is asymptotically normal with mean μ and variance (7.4).

*Sample Autocovariances**

If the mean, μ, is known

$$\gamma^*(\tau) = \frac{1}{T - \tau} \sum_{\tau=0}^{T-\tau} (y_t - \mu)(y_{t-\tau} - \mu), \qquad \tau = 0, 1, 2, \ldots \qquad (7.7)$$

is an unbiased estimator of $\gamma(\tau)$. The effect of replacing μ by the sample mean is to introduce a small bias into the estimator, but this bias disappears as $T \to \infty$, so the estimator is asymptotically unbiased. The sample autocovariance, $c(\tau)$, introduced earlier in (1.11), has a divisor of T, and so is biased even when μ is known. When μ is estimated, its bias is greater than that of the estimator based on a divisor of $T - \tau$. Nevertheless, $c(\tau)$ tends to be the preferred estimator, one reason being that for large τ its MSE is smaller than that of the estimator based on a divisor of $T - \tau$, and so the somewhat erratic behaviour of the latter at higher order lags is mitigated to a certain extent. At smaller lags the difference between the two estimators is negligible, with the bias disappearing as $T \to \infty$. In what follows, therefore, attention will be restricted to $c(\tau)$.

For a process of the form (7.6), Bartlett (1946) derived the following large sample approximations to the variance of $c(\tau)$ and the covariance between estimators at different lags:

$$\text{Avar}\{c(\tau)\} = \frac{1}{T} \sum_{j=-\infty}^{\infty} [\gamma(j)^2 + \gamma(j + \tau)\gamma(j - \tau)] \qquad (7.8)$$

and

$$\text{Acov}\{c(\tau), c(\tau + v)\}$$
$$= \frac{1}{T} \sum_{j=-\infty}^{\infty} [\gamma(j)\gamma(j + v) + \gamma(j + \tau + v)\gamma(j - \tau)] \qquad (7.9)$$

In the special case when $\tau = 0$, expression (7.8) gives the variance of the sample variance, namely

$$\text{Avar}\{c(0)\} = \frac{2\gamma^2(0)}{T} \sum_{\tau=-\infty}^{\infty} \rho^2(\tau) \qquad (7.10)$$

Example 2   For an AR(1) process

$$\text{Avar}\{c(0)\} = \frac{2\gamma^2(0)}{T} \frac{(1 + \phi^2)}{(1 - \phi^2)} \tag{7.11}$$

*Sample Autocorrelations**

The sample autocorrelation, $r(\tau)$, was defined in (1.16) as the ratio of $c(\tau)$ to $c(0)$. Unlike an estimator based on autocovariances with a divisor of $T - \tau$, it is the case that

$$|r(\tau)|^2 \leqslant 1, \qquad \text{for all } \tau$$

For a linear process, (7.6), with the condition $\sum j\psi_j < \infty$, it can be shown that, for a fixed number of lags, n, the estimators $r(1), \ldots, r(n)$ are asymptotically normal with mean zero and covariances

$$\text{Acov}\{r(\tau), r(\tau + v)\} = T^{-1} \sum_{j=-\infty}^{\infty} [\rho(j)\rho(j + v) + \rho(j + \tau + v)\rho(j - \tau)$$

$$+ 2\rho(\tau)\rho(\tau + v)\rho^2(j) - 2\rho(\tau)\rho(j)\rho(j - \tau - v)$$

$$- 2\rho(\tau + v)\rho(j)\rho(j - \tau)] \tag{7.12}$$

for $\tau, \tau + v > 0$. The expression for the asymptotic variance of $r(\tau)$ is obtained by setting $v = 0$. Again, see Bartlett (1946) and Anderson (1971, p. 478).

For independent observations, it follows immediately on setting $\rho(\tau)$ to zero for $\tau \neq 0$, that for all τ

$$\text{Avar}\{r(\tau)\} = 1/T \tag{7.13}$$

while estimators at different lags are asymptotically independent. On the other hand, (7.12) implies that serial correlation in the observations will tend to be reflected in the correlogram. Thus sample autocorrelations which are quite close together may be quite highly correlated, and when combined with the sampling error, this has the effect that the correlogram may provide a distorted picture of the underlying autocorrelation function.

Example 3   For an AR(1) process

$$\text{Avar}\{r(\tau)\} = \frac{1}{T} \frac{(1 + \phi^2)}{(1 - \phi^2)}, \qquad \tau = 1, 2, \ldots \tag{7.14}$$

while

$$\text{Acov}\{r(\tau), r(\tau + v)\} = \frac{\phi^v}{T} \left[\frac{(1 + \phi^2)}{(1 - \phi^2)} + v \right], \qquad \tau, v = 1, 2, \ldots \tag{7.15}$$

Thus with ϕ taking the moderate value of 0.5, the correlation between successive values of $r(\tau)$ is approximately 0.80.

2.8 Tests for Randomness and Normality

Testing for randomness is a fundamental aspect of time series analysis. A random series is one which is white noise, that is the observations are serially uncorrelated. Randomness could also be defined in terms of the observations being independent. The distinction between uncorrelatedness and independence will become clear when non-linear models are discussed in chapter 8. For the moment we concentrate on how to test for uncorrelatedness, bearing in mind that if we conclude that the series has this property, there is no point in attempting to fit a linear model to the data.

Another important question is whether or not the observations are Gaussian. This is examined in the last sub-section.

Tests on Sample Autocorrelations

Tests of randomness are usually based on the sample autocorrelations. As we indicated by (7.13), the sample autocorrelations are asymptotically normal with mean zero and variance $1/T$ when the observations are independent. Although, following the discussion opening this section, what is actually required is the distribution under the weaker assumption of uncorrelatedness, this turns out to be rather complicated. Hence tests are based on the distributional theory implied by an assumption of independence, even though a failure to reject the null is interpreted only as a failure to reject uncorrelatedness. Proceeding on this basis, a test may be carried out on the sample autocorrelation at a particular lag, τ, by treating $T^{1/2} r(\tau)$ as a standardised normal variate. At the 5% level of significance, the null hypothesis is rejected if $|T^{1/2}r(\tau)| > 1.96 \simeq 2$.

A test on a particular sample autocorrelation is only valid if the lag is specified in advance. This implies some *a priori* knowledge of the nature of the series. For example, with quarterly data a test of the significance of $r(4)$ would clearly be relevant. Except for the case of a seasonal effect, however, such *a priori* knowledge is likely to be the exception rather than the rule, and formal test procedures are generally restricted to the first-order autocorrelation, $r(1)$. For this reason some effort has been devoted to developing exact test procedures for hypotheses concerning $\rho(1)$. These are discussed in the next sub-section.

Notwithstanding the above remarks, it is nevertheless very useful to plot two lines on the correlogram, one at a height of $2/\sqrt{T}$ above the horizontal axis and the other at the same distance below. These may be used as a yardstick for assessing departures from randomness. If the underlying series is white noise, most of the sample autocorrelations will lie within these limits. Values outside are an indication of non-randomness, although for a white noise process, about one in twenty of the autocorrelations will be significant.

The von Neumann Ratio

The von Neumann ratio is defined by

$$\text{VNR} = \frac{T}{T-1}\left[\sum_{t=2}^{T}(y_t - y_{t-1})^2 \Big/ \sum_{t=1}^{T}(y_t - \bar{y})^2\right] \tag{8.1}$$

where $\bar{y}$ is the sample mean. This statistic is closely related to $r(1)$. Writing $y_t - y_{t-1} = y_t - \bar{y} - (y_{t-1} - \bar{y})$, substituting in the numerator of (8.1), and expanding shows that

$$\text{VNR} \simeq 2[1 - r(1)] \tag{8.2}$$

The approximation arises simply because of the treatment of the end point. Its effect is negligible in moderate or large samples.

If the observations are normally distributed white noise, i.e. if $y_t \sim \text{NID}(0, \sigma^2)$, the small sample distribution of (8.1) is known. An exact test may therefore be carried out using the significance values tabulated by Hart (1942). From (8.2) it can be seen that when $r(1) = 0$, the von Neumann ratio is approximately equal to two, but as $r(1)$ tends towards one, VNR tends towards zero. A one-sided test against positive serial correlation is therefore carried out by looking up the appropriate significance point and rejecting the null hypothesis if VNR falls below it. Conversely, a test against negative serial correlation is based on the upper tail of the distribution. Anderson (1971, chapter 6) shows that against a one-sided alternative, the von Neumann ratio test is uniformly most powerfully unbiased.

If T is large, the distribution of VNR may be approximated by a normal distribution with a mean of $2T/(T-1)$ and a variance $4/T$. This may be used as the basis for a test procedure, although what amounts to the same test may be carried out directly on $r(1)$.

The Portmanteau Test Statistic

The result on the asymptotic distribution of the sample autocorrelations suggests that a general test of randomness might be based on the first P autocorrelations, through the statistic

$$Q = T \sum_{\tau=1}^{P} r^2(\tau) \tag{8.3}$$

Since the $r(\tau)$s are independently distributed in large samples, Q will be asymptotically χ_P^2 for data from a white noise process. If a number of the sample autocorrelations are not close to zero, Q will be inflated.

The choice of P is somewhat arbitrary. Setting P high means that we capture what might be highly significant $r(\tau)$'s at relatively high lags. On the other hand, by making P high, a good deal of power may be lost. As an example, suppose that the true model is an MA(1) process. While a test based on $r(1)$ or the von Neumann ratio may have a relatively high power against such an alternative, the portmanteau test may be ineffective. Although $r(1)$ may be some way from zero, its influence in the Q-statistic will be diluted by the remaining $P - 1$ autocorrelations. The portmanteau test should not therefore be regarded as a substitute for examining the correlogram, since an insignificant result may easily mask some distinctive feature.

The justification for the portmanteau test is an asymptotic one. In small samples it has been found that χ_P^2 does not provide a particularly good approximation to the distribution of Q under the null hypothesis. A modification, which is rather more satisfactory in this respect, is

$$Q^* = T(T+2) \sum_{\tau=1}^{P} (T-\tau)^{-1} r^2(\tau) \tag{8.4}$$

see Ljung and Box (1978).

Tests for Normality

Many estimation and testing procedures are based on the assumption of normally distributed observations. One way of assessing whether a series of independent observations is normal is by a normal probability plot. Alternatively tests may be carried out on the sample measures of skewness and kurtosis. These are the standardised third and fourth moments of the observations about the mean, namely

$$\sqrt{b_1} = \hat\sigma_y^{-3} \sum (y_t - \bar y)^3 / T \tag{8.5}$$

and

$$b_2 = \hat\sigma_y^{-4} \sum (y_t - \bar y)^4 / T \tag{8.6}$$

where $\hat\sigma_y^2$ is $c(0)$. When the observations are normally and independently distributed with constant mean and variance, these statistics are asymptotically normally distributed such that

$$\sqrt{b_1} \sim AN(0, 6/T)$$

and

$$b_2 \sim AN(3, 24/T)$$

see Bowman and Shenton (1975). They are also independent of each other in large samples and so a test for normality may be based on

$$N = (T/6)b_1 + (T/24)(b_2 - 3)^2 \tag{8.7}$$

Under the null hypothesis, this statistic has a χ_2^2 distribution in large samples. Of course, separate tests on skewness and kurtosis may sometimes be desirable. A test for excess kurtosis may be particularly useful as an indicator of outliers.

A drawback to basing tests on the measures of skewness and kurtosis is that their behaviour may be rather erratic in small samples. Other tests of non-normality, such as the Shapiro–Wilk test, may therefore be considered.

Tests based on $\sqrt{b_1}$ and b_2 can still be carried out when the observations are serially correlated. However, allowance must be made for the fact that their variances will be affected. As a generalisation of the earlier result, it can be shown that for a linear process

$$\mathrm{Avar}(\sqrt{b_1}) = (6/T) \sum_{\tau = -\infty}^{\infty} \rho^3(\tau)$$

and

$$\mathrm{Avar}(b_2) = (24/T) \sum_{\tau = -\infty}^{\infty} \rho^4(\tau)$$

The correction terms implied by these expressions may be estimated by taking finite sums of powers of sample autocorrelations. Granger and Newbold (1977, p. 315) cite evidence which suggests that the resulting test statistics will be reasonably well behaved in moderate sized samples, but may be less satisfactory when the sample is small.

Exercises

1. Are the following stochastic processes stationary?
   (a) $y_t = \varepsilon_t + \varepsilon_{t-1}$, $\varepsilon_t \sim \mathrm{NID}(0, \sigma^2)$;
   (b) $y_t = \alpha \cos \lambda t + \beta \sin \lambda t$, where $\alpha \sim N(0, \sigma^2)$, $\beta \sim N(0, \sigma^2)$ and α and β are independent;
   (c) $y_t = y_{t-1} + \varepsilon_t$, $\varepsilon_t \sim \mathrm{NID}(0, \sigma^2)$ and y_0 fixed;
   (d) $y_t = \varepsilon_{1t} + t\varepsilon_{2t}$, $\varepsilon_{it} \sim \mathrm{NID}(0, \sigma_i^2)$, $i = 1, 2$, and $E(\varepsilon_{1t}\varepsilon_{2s}) = 0$, all t, s;
   (e) $y_t - y_{t-1} + 0.5y_{t-2} = \varepsilon_t$;
   (f) $y_t \sim \mathrm{NID}(1, 1)$ for t odd, y_t exponentially and independently distributed with mean 1 for t even;
   (g) y_t is a series of independent and identically distributed Cauchy variables.
2. Determine the autocorrelation function of the following stochastic process:

$$y_t = 14 + \varepsilon_t + 0.4\varepsilon_{t-1} - 0.2\varepsilon_{t-2}$$

3. Calculate the first five autocorrelations for an AR(2) process with
    (a) $\phi_1 = 0.6$, $\phi_2 = -0.2$;
    (b) $\phi_1 = -0.6$, $\phi_2 = 0.2$.
    Sketch the autocorrelation functions.
4. (a) Sketch the autocorrelation function of the process

    $$y_t = -0.5y_{t-1} + \varepsilon_t - 0.8\varepsilon_{t-1}$$

    (b) Find the coefficients, ψ_j, in the infinite MA representation.
5. Is the model

    $$y_t = -0.2y_{t-1} + 0.48y_{t-2} + \varepsilon_t + 0.6\varepsilon_{t-1} - 0.16\varepsilon_{t-2}$$

    over-parameterised?
6. If $y_T = 2.6$ and $\varepsilon_T = 1.2$ make predictions one and two steps ahead from an MA(1) model with $\theta = 0.5$.
7. Given that $y_T = 2.0$, $y_{T-1} = 1.0$ and $\varepsilon_T = 0.5$, make predictions one, two and three steps ahead from the model

    $$y_t = 0.6y_{t-1} + 0.2y_{t-2} + \varepsilon_t + 0.6\varepsilon_{t-1}, \qquad t = 1, \ldots, T$$

    Compute the corresponding MSEs.
8. Compute predictions and their MSEs from an AR(2) model with $\phi_1 = 0.5$ and $\phi_2 = -0.2$ for $l = 1, 2$ and 3, if $y_{T-1} = 1$, $y_T = 2$ and $\sigma^2 = 3$.
9. Write down an expression for the asymptotic variance of the sample mean of an ARMA(1, 1) process in terms of its parameters.
10. Show that the sum of two independent AR(2) processes is an ARMA(p, q) process. What are the maximum values of p and q? Are there any circumstances when (a) $p = 3$, $q = 1$, (b) $p = 2$, $q = 0$?
11. If an AR(1) process is observed every other time period, show that the observed process is still AR(1). Express the parameters of the new process in terms of those of the original.

    If the sum of two consecutive values of an AR(1) process is observed every other time period, show that the observed series is ARMA(1, 1).

3

Estimation and Testing of Autoregressive-Moving Average Models

3.1 Introduction

This chapter deals with the estimation of $ARMA(p, q)$ models. The models are assumed to be stationary and invertible. Issues concerned with non-stationarity are addressed in chapter 5.

Under the assumption that the observations are normally distributed, it is shown how maximum likelihood estimators can be constructed. By making suitable assumptions about initial conditions, these estimators can be obtained by minimising a residual sum of squares function. This must be done iteratively for MA and mixed models, but the procedure is relatively straightforward. The question of exact maximum likelihood estimation is taken up in chapter 4, within a state space framework.

The introduction of a non-zero mean, μ, into an ARMA model has no important implications for the estimation of the AR and MA parameters. As illustrated for an AR model in section 3.2, the sample mean, $\bar{y}$, is an asymptotically efficient estimator of μ, and so the AR parameters can be estimated by putting the observations in deviation from the mean form.

The likelihood approach provides the basis for the development of formal hypothesis tests. The likelihood ratio, Wald and Lagrange multiplier tests are all discussed. The Lagrange multiplier test is particularly interesting insofar as it is able to provide a rationale for various diagnostics used in model selection.

We begin by reviewing some basic results on ML estimation and then show how the approach extends to time series models. Further details can be found in EATS, chapters 3 and 4.

48

Maximum Likelihood Estimation

The classical theory of maximum likelihood (ML) concerns estimation related to a sample of independent and identically distributed observations. The joint probability density function (PDF) of the full set of observations is then just the product of the individual probability density functions. Once the observations are known, the joint density function is re-interpreted as a likelihood function. This is denoted $L(\psi)$, indicating that it is to be regarded as a function of the unknown parameters in the $n \times 1$ vector ψ. Maximising the likelihood function with respect to ψ yields the ML estimator $\tilde{\psi}$.

It is usual to work with the logarithm of the likelihood function, so the ML estimator satisfies the *likelihood equations*, which are obtained by differentiating $\log L$ with respect to each of the unknown parameters and setting the result to zero. Thus, writing the derivatives as a vector, we have

$$\frac{\partial \log L}{\partial \psi} = 0 \tag{1.1}$$

As a rule, the likelihood equations are non-linear and so the ML estimates must be found by some kind of iterative procedure.

Under fairly general regularity conditions, the ML estimator is consistent and asymptotically efficient. It can be shown that $\sqrt{T}(\tilde{\psi} - \psi)$ converges in distribution to a multivariate normal, with mean vector zero and covariance matrix equal to the inverse of the asymptotic information matrix. This matrix is defined by

$$\mathbf{IA}(\psi) = p \lim T^{-1} \left(-\frac{\partial^2 \log L}{\partial \psi \, \partial \psi'} \right) \tag{1.2}$$

The matrix of second derivatives in (1.2), which has $\partial^2 \log L / \partial \psi_i \, \partial \psi_j$ as its ijth element, is known as the *Hessian*. Taking the expectation of the negative Hessian gives the information matrix, $\mathbf{I}(\psi)$, and of course the probability limit of $T^{-1}\mathbf{I}(\psi)$ is also $\mathbf{IA}(\psi)$.

Since the asymptotic distribution is used in practice to give an approximation to the distribution of the estimator in finite samples, we say that $\tilde{\psi}$ is *asymptotically normal* (AN) with mean ψ and covariance matrix

$$\text{Avar}(\tilde{\psi}) = T^{-1}\mathbf{IA}^{-1}(\psi) \tag{1.3}$$

and express this concisely by writing

$$\tilde{\psi} \sim \text{AN}\{\psi, T^{-1}\mathbf{IA}^{-1}(\psi)\} \tag{1.4}$$

In practice the asymptotic covariance matrix, $\text{Avar}(\tilde{\psi})$, must be estimated from the sample. In order to construct asymptotically valid test statistics, it is necessary for an estimator, $\text{avar}(\tilde{\psi})$, to satisfy the condition that

$$p \lim\{T. \, \text{avar}(\tilde{\psi})\} = \mathbf{IA}^{-1}(\psi) \tag{1.5}$$

If this condition is satisfied, the square roots of the diagonal elements of avar($\tilde{\psi}$) are *asymptotic standard errors*.

In many applications each observation depends on some function of the parameters ψ and a random variable, ε_t, which is normally distributed with mean zero and variance σ^2. The parameter σ^2 is an additional parameter, not included in ψ, and the log–likelihood function is of the form

$$\log L = -\tfrac{1}{2}T \log 2\pi - \tfrac{1}{2}T \log \sigma^2 - \tfrac{1}{2}\sigma^{-2}S(\psi) \tag{1.6}$$

where $S(\psi)$ is the sum of squares function

$$S(\psi) = \sum_{t=1}^{T} \varepsilon_t^2(\psi) \tag{1.7}$$

The notation $\varepsilon_t(\psi)$ stresses the point that ε_t is no longer a disturbance, but a residual which depends on the value taken by the variables in ψ. However, in what follows ε_t, rather than $\varepsilon_t(\psi)$, will be used provided the meaning is clear. The likelihood equations obtained by differentiating $\log L$ with respect to ψ are

$$\frac{\partial \log L}{\partial \psi} = -\frac{1}{\sigma^2}\sum_{t=1}^{T}\frac{\partial \varepsilon_t}{\partial \psi}\varepsilon_t = \frac{1}{\sigma^2}\sum_{t=1}^{T} \mathbf{z}_t\varepsilon_t = 0 \tag{1.8}$$

where

$$\mathbf{z}_t = -\partial \varepsilon_t/\partial \psi$$

but the solution does not depend on σ^2 and exactly the same result is obtained by differentiating $S(\psi)$ with respect to ψ. Thus the ML estimator of ψ is obtained by minimising $S(\psi)$ and the minimised value of $S(\psi)$ provides the ML estimator of σ^2 since, after differentiating $\log L$ with respect to σ^2, we find

$$\tilde{\sigma}^2 = T^{-1}S(\tilde{\psi}) = T^{-1}\sum_{t=1}^{T} \varepsilon_t^2(\tilde{\psi}) \tag{1.9}$$

In the Hessian, the elements which involve second derivatives are all small and disappear when expectations are taken so that the information matrix is just σ^{-2} multiplied by the cross-product matrix of the first derivatives. The asymptotic information matrix is

$$\mathbf{IA}(\psi) = \sigma^{-2}p \lim T^{-1}\sum_{t=1}^{T} \mathbf{z}_t\mathbf{z}_t' \tag{1.10}$$

Example 1   Consider the non-linear regression model

$$y_t = f(\mathbf{x}_t; \psi) + \varepsilon_t, \qquad \varepsilon_t \sim \text{NID}(0, \sigma^2), \qquad t = 1, \ldots, T \tag{1.11}$$

where $f(\mathbf{x}_t; \psi)$ depends on a set of explanatory variables, $\mathbf{x}_t$. In this case

$$S(\psi) = \sum_{t=1}^{T} \{y_t - f(\mathbf{x}_t; \psi)\}^2 = \sum_{t=1}^{T} \varepsilon_t^2(\psi)$$

The asymptotic variance is estimated by

$$\text{avar}(\tilde{\psi}) = \tilde{\sigma}^2 \left[\sum_{t=1}^{T} \mathbf{z}_t \mathbf{z}_t' \right]^{-1} \tag{1.12}$$

In a linear regression model, $f(\mathbf{x}_t; \psi) = \mathbf{x}_t' \psi$. Thus $\mathbf{z}_t = \mathbf{x}_t$, and solving the likelihood equations gives the OLS estimator of ψ.

Maximisation of a Likelihood Function

There are a number of different approaches to numerical optimisation. However, when the problem is to maximise a likelihood function, an important class of algorithms is defined by iterations of the form

$$\psi^* = \hat{\psi} + [\mathbf{I}^*(\hat{\psi})]^{-1} \{\partial \log L / \partial \psi\} \tag{1.13}$$

$\mathbf{I}^*(\psi)$ denotes the information matrix, or an approximation to it, and in (1.13) this is evaluated at the current estimate, $\hat{\psi}$. The vector of derivatives, $\partial \log L / \partial \psi$, is also evaluated at $\hat{\psi}$ and application of (1.13) yields an updated estimate ψ^*. This process is repeated until convergence. In practice, some modification of the scheme will usually be made, for example by the introduction of a variable step length; see EATS, section 4.3.

When $\mathbf{I}^*(\psi)$ is defined as the Hessian of $-\log L$, the iterative procedure in (1.13) is known as *Newton–Raphson*. Taking the expectation of the Hessian yields the information matrix itself and the scheme is then known as the *method of scoring*. In the special case when maximising the likelihood function is equivalent to minimising a sum of squares function, defining $\mathbf{I}^*(\psi)$ as

$$\mathbf{I}^*(\psi) = \sigma^{-2} \sum \mathbf{z}_t \mathbf{z}_t'$$

and using (1.8), leads to the iterative scheme

$$\psi^* = \hat{\psi} + \left(\sum \mathbf{z}_t \mathbf{z}_t' \right)^{-1} \sum \mathbf{z}_t \varepsilon_t \tag{1.14}$$

This is known as *Gauss–Newton*. At each step, ε_t and its vector of derivatives, $\mathbf{z}_t$, are evaluated at the current estimate, $\hat{\psi}$. This estimate is then 'corrected' by regressing ε_t on $\mathbf{z}_t$. The iterative scheme is completely independent of the parameter σ^2. Once the procedure has converged, this can be estimated from the residual using (1.9).

Equation (1.13) can be used as the basis for deriving asymptotically efficient *two-step* estimators. If $\hat{\psi}$ is a *consistent* estimator of ψ and certain regularity conditions are satisfied, ψ^* will have the same asymptotic distribution as the ML estimator. However, its small sample properties may be very different.

Dependent Observations

When the observations are dependent, their joint density function is constructed in terms of a series of conditional probability density functions. Suppose that there are only two observations. Their joint density function can be factorised as

$$p(y_2, y_1) = p(y_2|y_1)p(y_1) \qquad (1.15)$$

where $p(y_2|y_1)$ denotes the PDF of y_2, conditional on the value of the previous observation, y_1. In a similar way, the joint PDF for three observations can be written as

$$p(y_3, y_2, y_1) = p(y_3|y_2, y_1)p(y_2, y_1)$$

and, on substituting from (1.1),

$$p(y_3, y_2, y_1) = p(y_3|y_2, y_1)p(y_2|y_1)p(y_1)$$

It should now be clear that the likelihood function for T observations can be obtained from the conditional PDFs by writing the joint PDF as

$$L(\mathbf{y}; \psi) = \prod_{t=1}^{T} p(y_t|Y_{t-1}) \qquad (1.16)$$

where Y_{t-1} denotes the set of observations up to, and including, y_{t-1}, and $p(y_1|Y_0)$ is to be interpreted as $p(y_1)$, the unconditional PDF of y_1.

Many time series models are effectively specified in terms of a conditional distribution for each observation. Thus the first-order autoregressive model

$$y_t = \phi y_{t-1} + \varepsilon_t, \qquad \varepsilon_t \sim \text{NID}(0, \sigma^2) \qquad (1.17)$$

can also be specified by stating that the distribution of y_t, conditional on y_{t-1}, is normal with mean ϕy_{t-1} and variance, σ^2. In other words $p(y_t|Y_{t-1})$ is $N(\phi y_{t-1}, \sigma^2)$. Given this interpretation, the log–likelihood function can be written down directly:

$$\log L(\phi, \sigma^2) = \frac{-(T-1)}{2} \log 2\pi - \frac{(T-1)}{2} \log \sigma^2$$

$$- \frac{1}{2\sigma^2} \sum_{t=2}^{T} (y_t - \phi y_{t-1})^2 + \log p(y_1) \qquad (1.18)$$

If y_1 is regarded as being fixed in repeated realisations, then $p(y_1)$ does not enter into the likelihood function and the last term in (1.18) can be dropped. The ML estimator of ϕ is then linear, being given by a regression of y_t on y_{t-1}. On the other hand, if it can be assumed that $|\phi| < 1$, so that the process is stationary, the unconditional distribution of y_1 is known to be normal with mean zero and variance $\sigma^2/(1 - \phi^2)$. The likelihood function is therefore

$$
\log L(\phi, \sigma^2) = -\frac{T}{2} \log 2\pi - \frac{T}{2} \log \sigma^2 + \frac{1}{2} \log(1 - \phi^2)
$$

$$
-\frac{1}{2} \sigma^{-2}(1 - \phi^2) y_1^2 - \frac{1}{2} \sigma^{-2} \sum_{t=2}^{T} (y_t - \phi y_{t-1})^2 \quad (1.19)
$$

In this case, the ML estimator is no longer linear as the likelihood equation (1.1) is a cubic in ϕ. A method of calculating the unique real root in the range $[-1, 1]$ is given in Beach and MacKinnon (1978). On the other hand, if the third and fourth terms are dropped from (1.19), the corresponding approximate ML estimator of ϕ is the same as the estimator obtained under the assumption that y_1 is fixed. The large sample properties are not affected.

Prediction Error Decomposition

It was shown in chapter 2 that the mean of the conditional distribution of y_t, $E(y_t|Y_{t-1})$, is the optimal predictor of y_t in the sense that it minimises the prediction mean square error; see (2.6.1). The variance of the corresponding prediction error

$$
v_t = y_t - E(y_t|Y_{t-1}) \tag{1.20}
$$

is the same as the conditional variance of y_t, that is

$$
\mathrm{Var}(v_t) = \mathrm{Var}(y_t|Y_{t-1}) \tag{1.21}
$$

When the observations are normally distributed, the likelihood function can be expressed in terms of the prediction errors. This is known as the *prediction error decomposition*. It is often convenient to write

$$
\mathrm{Var}(v_t) = \sigma^2 f_t, \qquad t = 1, \ldots, T \tag{1.22}
$$

where σ^2 is a scale parameter, in which case the prediction error decomposition form of the logarithm of the joint density function is

$$
\log L(\mathbf{y}; \boldsymbol{\psi}) = -\frac{T}{2} \log 2\pi - \frac{T}{2} \log \sigma^2 - \frac{1}{2} \sum_{t=1}^{T} \log f_t
$$

$$
-\frac{1}{2} \sigma^{-2} \sum_{t=1}^{T} v_t^2 / f_t \tag{1.23}
$$

Thus for the AR(1) model, $f_t = 1$ for $t = 2, \ldots, T$ while $f_1 = 1/(1 - \phi^2)$; compare with (1.19).

Further insight into the prediction error decomposition is obtained by noting that the joint density function of a linear Gaussian model can be expressed in terms of a multivariate normal distribution. Thus $\mathbf{y} \sim N(\boldsymbol{\mu}, \sigma^2 \mathbf{V})$, where $\boldsymbol{\mu}$ is a $T \times 1$ mean vector, $\mathbf{V}$ is a $T \times T$ positive definite matrix and the scalar parameter σ^2 appears explicitly as a matter of convenience. In a stationary model the elements of $\boldsymbol{\mu}$ are the same while the ijth element of $\mathbf{V}$ is the autocovariance at lag $i - j$. For the AR(1) model in (1.17), $\boldsymbol{\mu} = 0$ and

$$
\mathbf{V} = \frac{1}{1 - \phi^2}
\begin{bmatrix}
1 & \phi & \phi^2 & \cdots & \phi^{T-1} \\
\phi & 1 & \phi & \cdots & \phi^{T-2} \\
\phi^2 & \phi & 1 & \cdots & \phi^{T-3} \\
\vdots & \vdots & \vdots & \vdots & \vdots \\
\phi^{T-1} & \phi^{T-2} & \phi^{T-3} & \cdots & 1
\end{bmatrix}
\tag{1.24}
$$

In general $\boldsymbol{\mu}$ and $\mathbf{V}$ will depend on the parameters in $\boldsymbol{\psi}$ and the joint density function is

$$
\log \mathbf{L}(\mathbf{y}; \boldsymbol{\psi}) = -\frac{T}{2} \log 2\pi - \frac{T}{2} \log \sigma^2 - \frac{1}{2} \log |\mathbf{V}|
$$

$$
- \frac{1}{2} \sigma^{-2} (\mathbf{y} - \boldsymbol{\mu})' \mathbf{V}^{-1} (\mathbf{y} - \boldsymbol{\mu})
\tag{1.25}
$$

The construction and inversion of the $T \times T$ matrix V may be time consuming and so evaluating the likelihood function directly from (1.25) may not be an attractive proposition, particularly if this has to be carried out repeatedly within a numerical optimisation procedure. The usual approach is to carry out a Cholesky decomposition of $\mathbf{V}^{-1}$. If $\bar{\mathbf{L}}$ is a lower triangular matrix with ones on the leading diagonal, $\mathbf{V}^{-1}$ may be factorised as

$$
\mathbf{V}^{-1} = \bar{\mathbf{L}}' \mathbf{D} \bar{\mathbf{L}}
\tag{1.26}
$$

where $\mathbf{D} = \text{diag}(f_1^{-1}, \ldots, f_T^{-1})$. This factorisation is unique and the $T \times 1$ vector of prediction errors $v = (v_1, \ldots, v_T)'$ is given by the transformation $v = \bar{\mathbf{L}} \mathbf{y}$. Thus substituting for $\mathbf{V}^{-1}$ in (1.25) and noting that

$$
|\mathbf{V}^{-1}| = |\bar{\mathbf{L}}| \cdot |\mathbf{D}| \cdot |\bar{\mathbf{L}}| = |\mathbf{D}| = \prod_{t=1}^{T} f_t
$$

leads directly to the prediction error decomposition form of the likelihood function (1.23).

The exact likelihood function of any ARMA model may be obtained by casting it in state space form, and computing the prediction error decomposition form of the likelihood function using the Kalman filter or some modification of it. This is described in the next chapter. However, as in the pure autoregressive case, ML estimation may be simplified considerably by making appropriate assumptions about the initial observations and/or disturbances. Maximising the resulting likelihood function is then equivalent to minimising a sum of squares function, but this has to be done iteratively.

3.2 Autoregressive Models

The likelihood function for an $AR(1)$ model was derived in (1.19). The same approach may be adopted for an $AR(p)$ model. Corresponding to (1.18) we obtain

$$\log L(\mathbf{y}) = \sum_{t=p+1}^{T} \log p(y_t | y_{t-1}, \ldots, y_1) + \log p(\mathbf{y}_p) \qquad (2.1)$$

where $p(\mathbf{y}_p)$ is the joint distribution of the first p observations, $\mathbf{y}_p = (y_1, \ldots, y_p)'$. If the covariance matrix of $\mathbf{y}_p$ is denoted by $\sigma^2 \mathbf{V}_p$, the full log–likelihood function may be written as

$$\log L(\boldsymbol{\phi}, \sigma^2) = -(1/2) T \log 2\pi - (1/2) T \log \sigma^2 - (1/2) \log |\mathbf{V}_p|$$
$$- (1/2) \sigma^{-2} \left[\mathbf{y}_p' \mathbf{V}_p^{-1} \mathbf{y}_p + \sum_{t=p+1}^{T} (y_t - \phi_1 y_{t-1} - \cdots \right.$$
$$\left. - \phi_p y_{t-p})^2 \right] \qquad (2.2)$$

where $\boldsymbol{\phi}$ denotes the parameter vector $(\phi_1, \ldots, \phi_p)'$. The parameter σ^2 may be concentrated out of the likelihood function. However, the resulting function is still non-linear in $\boldsymbol{\phi}$, and ML estimation must be carried out by numerical optimisation. The matrix $\mathbf{V}_p^{-1}$ may be obtained directly, a number of methods being available; see Box and Jenkins (1976) or Galbraith and Galbraith (1974).

Least Squares

The estimation of AR models may be simplified considerably by regarding the first p observations, $y_1, \ldots, y_p$, as fixed. This provides a theoretical justification for dropping the last term in (2.1), with the result that maximising the likelihood function becomes equivalent to minimising the conditional sum of squares function

$$S(\boldsymbol{\phi}) = \sum_{t=p+1}^{T} (y_t - \phi_1 y_{t-1} - \cdots - \phi_p y_{t-p})^2 \qquad (2.3)$$

The ML estimator of $\boldsymbol{\phi}$ is therefore obtained by an OLS regression of y_t on its lagged values, $y_{t-1}, \ldots, y_{t-p}$.

In large samples it makes very little difference whether estimation is carried out by exact ML or by regression. In the $AR(1)$ model, for example, it can be seen from (1.19) that the only distinguishing feature of the exact likelihood function is the inclusion of the terms involving y_1^2 and $\log(1 - \phi^2)$. These terms are swamped by the remainder of the likelihood function if T is at all large, and the asymptotic distribution of the estimators of ϕ and σ^2 is unaffected if they are omitted.

Estimation from the Correlogram: the Yule–Walker Equations

Estimates of the parameters in ϕ may also be obtained from the correlogram. For a pure $AR(p)$ model, the autocorrelations are given by the pth-order difference equation (2.2.37). Writing out this equation for $\tau = 1, \ldots, p$ gives

$$
\begin{pmatrix}
1 & \rho(1) & \cdots & \rho(p-1) \\
\rho(1) & 1 & \cdots & \rho(p-2) \\
\vdots & \vdots & \vdots & \vdots \\
\rho(p-1) & \rho(p-2) & \cdots & 1
\end{pmatrix}
\begin{pmatrix}
\phi_1 \\
\phi_2 \\
\vdots \\
\phi_p
\end{pmatrix}
=
\begin{pmatrix}
\rho(1) \\
\rho(2) \\
\vdots \\
\rho(p)
\end{pmatrix}
\tag{2.4}
$$

These are known as the *Yule–Walker equations*. Replacing $\rho(\tau)$ by $r(\tau)$ yields a set of linear equations which may be solved directly to yield estimates of $\phi_1, \ldots, \phi_p$.

Example 1   For the $AR(2)$ model

$$
\hat{\phi}_1 = \frac{r(1)[1 - r(2)]}{1 - r^2(1)}, \qquad \hat{\phi}_2 = \frac{r(2) - r^2(1)}{1 - r^2(1)}
\tag{2.5}
$$

Apart from the 'end effects', the estimators obtained in this way are the same as those obtained by regressing y_t on p lagged values of itself. The estimators obtained from the Yule–Walker equations therefore have the same asymptotic distribution as the ML estimators.

Asymptotic Properties

The information matrix obtained from the likelihood function in (2.2) is

$$
I(\phi, \sigma^2) = -E
\begin{bmatrix}
\dfrac{\partial^2 \log L}{\partial \phi\, \partial \phi'} & \dfrac{\partial^2 \log L}{\partial \phi\, \partial \sigma^2} \\[2ex]
\dfrac{\partial^2 \log L}{\partial \phi\, \partial \sigma^2} & \dfrac{\partial^2 \log L}{\partial \sigma^4}
\end{bmatrix}
$$

$$
= E
\begin{bmatrix}
\sigma^{-2} \sum y_{t-1} y'_{t-1} & \sigma^{-4} \sum y_{t-1}\varepsilon_t \\[1ex]
\sigma^{-4} \sum \varepsilon_t y'_{t-1} & \sigma^{-6} \sum \varepsilon_t^2
\end{bmatrix}
= T
\begin{bmatrix}
V_p & 0 \\
0 & \tfrac{1}{2}\sigma^{-4}
\end{bmatrix}
\tag{2.6}
$$

where, it will be recalled, $\sigma^2 V_p$ is the covariance matrix of the $p \times 1$ vector of lagged observations, $y_{t-1} = (y_{t-1}, \ldots, y_{t-p})'$. The ML estimator of ϕ is asymptotically normally distributed with mean ϕ and covariance matrix given by the inverse of the expression above, that is

$$\text{Avar}(\tilde{\phi}) = T^{-1}\mathbf{V}_p^{-1} \tag{2.7}$$

In the special case of an AR(1) model

$$\text{Avar}(\tilde{\phi}) = (1 - \phi^2)/T \tag{2.8}$$

As regards σ^2, this is asymptotically normal with

$$\text{Avar}(\tilde{\sigma}^2) = 2\sigma^4/T \tag{2.9}$$

Expression (2.7) can also be obtained by evaluating (1.10) with $\mathbf{z}_t = \mathbf{y}_{t-1}$. It can be estimated by replacing ϕ by $\tilde{\phi}$ or by using (1.12). The latter estimator is produced directly when ϕ is estimated by a least squares regression.

It can be shown that the asymptotic distribution of the least squares estimator of ϕ is unchanged even if the disturbances are not Gaussian. This is the Mann and Wald (1943) result. Some restrictions are needed on the distribution of the disturbance, in particular the fourth moment is assumed to be finite. Of course, it must be remembered that the estimator will not be efficient as compared with an ML estimator based on the true distribution.

Estimation of the Mean

If an AR(1) model has a non-zero mean, μ, the conditional sum of squares function becomes

$$S(\phi, \mu) = \sum_{t=2}^{T} [y_t - \mu - \phi(y_{t-1} - \mu)]^2 \tag{2.10}$$

Differentiating with respect to μ yields

$$\tilde{\mu} = \frac{\sum_{t=2}^{T} y_t - \tilde{\phi} \sum_{t=1}^{T-1} y_t}{(T-1)(1-\tilde{\phi})} \simeq \bar{y} \tag{2.11}$$

Thus the ML estimator of μ is approximately equal to the sample mean, and so can be computed independently of ϕ. By evaluating the information matrix, it is not difficult to show that the asymptotic variance of $\bar{y}$ is as given in (2.7.5).

The same argument can be applied to show that the sample mean is approximately the ML estimator of μ for any AR(p) model. Furthermore, from the information matrix,

$$\text{Avar}(\bar{y}) = T^{-1}\sigma^2/(1 - \phi_1 - \phi_2 - \ldots - \phi_p)^2 \tag{2.12}$$

The efficiency of the sample mean can also be demonstrated in the frequency domain; see section 6.8.

*Prediction with Estimated Parameters**

In practice, predictions are almost invariably made with estimated parameters. This creates an additional source of variability, which should ideally be incorporated in the expression for the prediction MSE.

Consider the AR(1) process. When ϕ is known, the MMSE for l periods ahead is given by (2.6.6). When ϕ is unknown it will be replaced by its ML estimator, $\tilde{\phi}$, or by an estimator which is asymptotically equivalent. The actual predictor is therefore

$$\tilde{y}^*_{T+l|T} = \tilde{\phi}^l y_T \qquad (2.13)$$

In more general cases, $\bar{y}^*_{T+l|T}$ can be computed by a difference equation having exactly the same form as (2.6.4).

The prediction error for (2.13) may be decomposed into two parts by writing

$$y_{T+l} - \tilde{y}^*_{T+l|T} = (y_{T+l} - \tilde{y}_{T+l|T}) + (\tilde{y}_{T+l|T} - \tilde{y}^*_{T+l|T}) \qquad (2.14)$$

The first term on the right hand side of (2.14) is the prediction error when ϕ is known, while the second term represents the error arising from the estimation of ϕ. This decomposition is appropriate for all ARMA models. In the present case it specialises to

$$y_{T+l} - \tilde{y}^*_{T+l|T} = (y_{T+l} - \tilde{y}_{T+l|T}) + (\phi^l - \tilde{\phi}^l)y_T \qquad (2.15)$$

Now consider the one-step ahead predictor. The MSE may be written as

$$\text{MSE}(\tilde{y}^*_{T+l|T}) = \text{MSE}(\tilde{y}_{T+l|T}) + y_T^2 E[(\tilde{\phi} - \phi)^2] \qquad (2.16)$$

In formulating the contribution of the estimation error to (2.16), y_T is taken as fixed, whereas $\tilde{\phi}$ is a random variable. This may appear to be contradictory, as y_T is actually used to construct $\tilde{\phi}$. However, (2.16) provides a sensible definition of MSE in this context, since any prediction is always made conditional on the sample observations being known. Replacing $E[(\tilde{\phi} - \phi)^2]$ by its asymptotic variance gives an approximation to the mean square error, that is

$$\text{MSE}(\tilde{y}^*_{T+l|T}) \simeq \sigma^2 + y_T^2(1 - \phi^2)/T \qquad (2.17)$$

The AR(1) model is often estimated by OLS. Applying the usual regression formula for estimating the MSE of $\tilde{y}^*_{T+l|T}$ gives

$$\text{mse}(\tilde{y}^*_{T+1|T}) = s^2 \left(1 + y_T^2 \bigg/ \sum_{t=2}^{T} y_{t-1}^2 \right) \qquad (2.18)$$

This is closely related to (2.19) since

$$\sum_{t=2}^{T} y_{t-1}^2 \simeq T\sigma^2/(1 - \phi^2)$$

in large samples. Fuller and Hasza (1981) provide evidence indicating that the usual regression formula is, in fact, an excellent estimator of the prediction MSE for multi-step prediction in more general AR models.

When $l > 1$, the last term in (2.16) is $y_T^2 E[(\hat{\phi}^l - \phi^l)^2]$. Writing

$$\phi^l - \tilde{\phi}^l = \phi^l - \phi^l \left[1 - \frac{(\phi - \tilde{\phi})}{\phi} \right]^l$$

and expanding the term in square brackets yields

$$\phi^l - \tilde{\phi}^l \simeq l\phi^{l-1}(\phi - \tilde{\phi})$$

when higher order terms are ignored. Therefore

$$E[(\tilde{\phi}^l - \phi^l)^2] \simeq l^2 \phi^{2(l-1)} E[(\tilde{\phi} - \phi)^2]$$

Together with the result in (2.6.12) this gives

$$\text{MSE}(y_{T+l|T}^*) \simeq \sigma^2 \frac{1 - \phi^{2l}}{1 - \phi^2} + y_T^2 \frac{(1 - \phi^2)l^2\phi^{2(l-1)}}{T} \qquad (2.19)$$

Expression (2.19) is an approximation to the MSE of the multi-step predictor for a particular sample. In order to get some idea of the MSE of such a predictor *on average*, y_T^2 is replaced by its expected value $\sigma^2/(1 - \phi^2)$. The resulting expression is known as the *asymptotic mean square error* (AMSE). Thus

$$\text{AMSE}(\tilde{y}_{T+l|T}^*) \simeq \sigma^2 \left[\frac{1 - \phi^{2l}}{1 - \phi^2} + \frac{l^2\phi^{2(l-1)}}{T} \right], \qquad l = 1, 2, \ldots \qquad (2.20)$$

For the special case of $l = 1$,

$$\text{AMSE}(\tilde{y}_{T+1|T}^*) = \sigma^2(1 + T^{-1}) \qquad (2.21)$$

In both (2.20) and (2.21), the contribution arising from the error in estimating ϕ is a term of $0(T^{-1})$. This will be dominated by the expression for the MSE of the optimal predictor when ϕ is known. Although ignoring the effect of estimating ϕ will lead to an underestimate of the variability of the prediction error, the bias is unlikely to be severe unless T is very small. These findings carry over to more general models. Further discussion will be found in Box and Jenkins (1976, pp. 267–9) and Yamamoto (1976).

3.3 Moving Average and Mixed Processes

The likelihood function for any $\text{ARMA}(p, q)$ process may be constructed from the prediction error decomposition. If the model is cast in state space form, the prediction errors may be calculated by the Kalman filter, and the exact likelihood function constructed; see section 4.4. However, finding a way of computing the likelihood function is only the first step in an algorithm, for the function must then be maximised with respect to the elements in ϕ and θ. This may be very time consuming, particularly if $p + q$ is large.

If certain assumptions are made about initial values of the disturbances and/or the observations, a *conditional* likelihood function is obtained. In the pure AR case this led to a linear ML estimator of ϕ. For MA and mixed processes the ML estimator is still non-linear, but the calculation of the likelihood function is simplified considerably. Furthermore, analytic derivatives are readily available and these can be important in improving the efficiency of the optimisation procedure.

The Conditional Sum of Squares Estimator for the MA(1) Model

The MA(1) model

$$y_t = \varepsilon_t + \theta\varepsilon_{t-1}, \qquad \varepsilon_t \sim \text{NID}(0, \sigma^2), \qquad t = 1, \ldots, T \qquad (3.1)$$

provides the simplest illustration of the techniques used to estimate models which are not purely autoregressive. The distribution of y_t conditional on the disturbance in the previous time period is normal with mean $\theta\varepsilon_{t-1}$ and variance σ^2. The problem is that ε_{t-1} is not directly observable. However, conditional on ε_0 being taken to be fixed and equal to zero, the full set disturbances can be computed recursively by re-arranging (3.1) to give

$$\varepsilon_t = y_t - \theta\varepsilon_{t-1}, \qquad t = 1, \ldots, T \qquad (3.2)$$

The likelihood function is therefore

$$\log L(\theta, \sigma^2) = -\frac{T}{2}\log 2\pi - \frac{T}{2}\log \sigma^2 - \frac{1}{2\sigma^2}\sum_{t=1}^{T}(y_t - \theta\varepsilon_{t-1})^2$$

Maximising this likelihood with respect to θ is equivalent to minimising the conditional sum of squares function

$$S(\theta) = \sum_{t=1}^{T}(y_t - \theta\varepsilon_{t-1})^2 = \sum_{t=1}^{T}\varepsilon_t^2 \qquad (3.3)$$

The resulting estimator is known as the *conditional sum of squares* (CSS) estimator. Using the notation $\varepsilon_t(\theta)$ in (3.3) would stress the point that ε_t is no longer a disturbance, but a residual which depends on the value taken by the variable θ; compare with (1.7).

The likelihood equations are non-linear since the derivative of ε_t must involve θ. This is in contrast to the AR(1) model where the derivative of the residual with respect to the unknown AR parameter is minus y_{t-1}. A suitable method for minimising $S(\theta)$ with respect to θ is therefore needed. Since only one parameter is involved, a grid search over the range $[-1, 1]$ could be carried out. For more general models this approach may not be viable and the obvious algorithm to adopt is Gauss–Newton, or a suitable modification of it. For the MA(1) model, differentiating (3.3) yields

$$\frac{\partial \varepsilon_t}{\partial \theta} = -\theta \frac{\partial \varepsilon_{t-1}}{\partial \theta} - \varepsilon_{t-1}, \qquad t = 1, \ldots, T \tag{3.4}$$

Since ε_0 is fixed, it follows that $\partial \varepsilon_0 / \partial \theta = 0$. Thus the derivatives are produced by a recursion running parallel to (3.3), with the initialisation handled in similar fashion. Given an estimate of θ, the algorithm proceeds by computing ε_t and $\partial \varepsilon_t / \partial \theta$, and then updating the estimate from a regression of ε_t on $\partial \varepsilon_t / \partial \theta$, as in (1.14).

Exact ML estimation requires the initial disturbance to have the same property as the other disturbances, namely to be normal with mean zero and variance σ^2. This being the case, the ε_t's can no longer be constructed by a simple recursion, as in (3.2). (A modified recursion is given in chapter 4.) For most practical purposes, setting ε_0 equal to zero makes very little difference and it can be shown that the CSS estimator has the same asymptotic distribution as exact ML provided that $|\theta| < 1$.

The Conditional Sum of Squares in the General Case

For higher order MA models, the conditional likelihood function is given by taking $\varepsilon_{1-q}, \ldots, \varepsilon_0$ to be equal to zero in all realisations. The residuals used to compute the CSS function are then obtained from the recursion

$$\varepsilon_t = y_t - \theta_1 \varepsilon_{t-1} - \cdots - \theta_q \varepsilon_{t-q}, \qquad t = 1, \ldots, T \tag{3.5}$$

with $\varepsilon_{1-q} = \varepsilon_{2-q} = \cdots = \varepsilon_0 = 0$.

Similar procedures may be adopted for mixed models, although in such cases there is the additional problem of handling the initial observations. Consider the ARMA(1, 1) model, (2.4.1). If y_1 is taken to be fixed, the prediction error may be computed from the recursion

$$\varepsilon_t = y_t - \phi y_{t-1} - \theta \varepsilon_{t-1}, \qquad t = 2, \ldots, T \tag{3.6}$$

with $\varepsilon_1 = 0$. An alternative approach would be to start the recursion at $t = 1$, with y_0 and ε_0 set equal to zero. However, although this yields T, rather than $T - 1$, residuals, it is not to be recommended, since arbitrarily setting $y_0 = 0$ introduces a distortion into the calculations. In general, the appropriate procedure for an ARMA(p, q) model is to compute $T - p$ prediction errors from a recursion of the form

$$\varepsilon_t = y_t - \phi_1 y_{t-1} - \cdots - \phi_p y_{t-p} - \theta_1 \varepsilon_{t-1} - \cdots - \theta_q \varepsilon_{t-q},$$

$$t = p + 1, \ldots, T \quad (3.7)$$

with $\varepsilon_p = \varepsilon_{p-1} = \cdots = \varepsilon_{p-q+1} = 0$.

The derivatives needed to implement the Gauss–Newton algorithm can again be computed by recursions. For the ARMA$(1, 1)$ model,

$$\frac{\partial \varepsilon_t}{\partial \phi} = -y_{t-1} - \theta \frac{\partial \varepsilon_{t-1}}{\partial \phi}, \qquad t = 2, \ldots, T \quad (3.8a)$$

$$\frac{\partial \varepsilon_t}{\partial \theta} = -\theta \frac{\partial \varepsilon_{t-1}}{\partial \theta} - \varepsilon_{t-1}, \qquad t = 2, \ldots, T \quad (3.8b)$$

with $\partial \varepsilon_1 / \partial \phi = \partial \varepsilon_1 / \partial \theta = 0$. In general, $p + q$ derivatives will be needed. However, these may be obtained on the basis of only two recursions, one for the AR and the other for the MA components; see Box and Jenkins (1976, p. 237).

Asymptotic Properties

Provided the model is both stationary and invertible, the exact ML and CSS estimators have the same asymptotic distribution. As in pure AR models, the ML estimator of σ^2 is distributed independently of the other estimators in large samples with a variance $2\sigma^4 / T$. Since the conditional likelihood function is of the form (1.6), an expression for the asymptotic covariance matrix of the ML estimator of the ARMA parameters, $\psi = (\phi', \theta')'$, may be obtained by evaluating the inverse of

$$\mathbf{IA}(\psi) = \sigma^{-2} p \lim T^{-1} \sum \mathbf{z}_t \mathbf{z}_t' \quad (3.9)$$

where $\mathbf{z}_t = -\partial \varepsilon_t / \partial \psi$, and dividing by T; see (1.10). In fact the estimator obtained by minimising the CSS function has the same distribution even if the disturbances are not Gaussian. All that is required is that they be independent with finite fourth moments; see Fuller (1976).

For the MA(1) model, $\partial \varepsilon_t / \partial \theta$ obeys the recursion (3.4) and so z_t follows an AR(1) process,

$$z_t = (-\theta) z_{t-1} + \varepsilon_{t-1}, \qquad t = 1, \ldots, T \quad (3.10)$$

Hence

$$p \lim T^{-1} \sum_{t=1}^{T} z_t^2 = \text{Var}(z_t) = \sigma^2 / (1 - \theta^2) \quad (3.11)$$

and so $\tilde\theta$ is asymptotically normally distributed with mean θ and variance

$$\text{Avar}(\tilde\theta) = (1 - \theta^2)/T \tag{3.12}$$

Mixed models may be handled in the same way. In the ARMA$(1, 1)$ case, it follows from (3.8b) that $z_{2t} = -\partial\varepsilon_t/\partial\theta$ is generated by an AR(1) process similar in form to (3.10). On the other hand, setting $z_{1t} = -\partial\varepsilon_t/\partial\phi$ yields

$$z_{1t} = -\theta z_{1,t-1} + y_{t-1}$$

This may be re-written as

$$z_{1t} = \frac{y_{t-1}}{1 + \theta L} = \frac{1}{1 + \theta L}\frac{1 + \theta L}{1 - \phi L}\varepsilon_{t-1} = \frac{\varepsilon_{t-1}}{1 - \phi L}$$

and so z_{1t} also obeys an AR(1) process,

$$z_{1t} = \phi z_{1,t-1} + \varepsilon_{t-1}$$

with the same disturbance term as z_{2t}.

Expression (3.9) may be evaluated by taking note of (3.11), and writing

$$E(z_{1t}z_{2t}) = E\left[\left(\frac{\varepsilon_{t-1}}{1 - \phi L}\right)\left(\frac{\varepsilon_{t-1}}{1 + \theta L}\right)\right]$$

$$= E\{[\varepsilon_{t-1} + \phi\varepsilon_{t-2} + \phi^2\varepsilon_{t-3} + \cdots]$$

$$\times [\varepsilon_{t-1} + (-\theta)\varepsilon_{t-2} + (-\theta)^2\varepsilon_{t-3} + \cdots]\}$$

$$= \sigma^2[1 + (-\phi\theta) + (-\phi\theta)^2 + \cdots] = \sigma^2/(1 + \phi\theta)$$

The asymptotic covariance matrix of the ML estimator of ϕ and θ is therefore

$$\text{Avar}(\tilde\phi, \tilde\theta) = \frac{1}{T}\frac{1 + \phi\theta}{(\phi + \theta)^2}\begin{pmatrix} (1 - \phi^2)(1 + \phi\theta) & -(1 - \phi^2)(1 - \theta^2) \\ -(1 - \phi^2)(1 - \theta^2) & (1 - \theta^2)(1 + \phi\theta) \end{pmatrix}$$

$$\tag{3.13}$$

Estimators from the Correlogram

Starting values are needed for the Gauss–Newton iterations. For an MA(1) model it would be possible to begin by setting $\hat\theta = 0$, but a similar strategy could not be adopted for a mixed model. Setting $\hat\phi = \hat\theta = 0$ in the ARMA$(1, 1)$ model would result in the two derivatives being identical. Hence the algorithm would immediately break down due to perfect multicollinearity in the regression of ε_t on $\partial\varepsilon_t/\partial\phi$ and $\partial\varepsilon_t/\partial\theta$.

A better way of starting the iterations is to begin from consistent estimates of the parameters. One possibility is to obtain estimates from the correlogram.

Consider the MA(1) model. If $\rho(1)$ is replaced by $r(1)$ in (2.1.15), an estimator of θ is obtained by solving the quadratic equation,

$$\hat{\theta}^2 r(1) - \hat{\theta} + r(1) = 0 \qquad (3.14)$$

This has two solutions, but since

$$r^{-1}(1) = \hat{\theta} + \hat{\theta}^{-1}$$

one root is clearly the reciprocal of the other. The problem of deciding which root to select is resolved by the invertibility condition. The estimator is therefore

$$\hat{\theta}_c = \{1 - [1 - 4r^2(1)]^{1/2}\}/2r(1) \qquad (3.15)$$

The other solution, $\hat{\theta}_c^{-1}$, is ruled out, since it will have an absolute value greater than one.

The only case when (3.14) does not have two different solutions is when $r(1) = \pm 0.5$. The estimator is then $\hat{\theta}_c = \pm 1$. If $|r(1)| > 0.5$, there is no real solution to (3.15), since the theoretical first-order autocorrelation cannot exceed 0.5 for an MA(1) model. An $r(1)$ of this magnitude would probably suggest that an MA(1) model should not be entertained, although in small samples such a value could arise from an MA(1) process due to sampling fluctuations.

A similar technique may be employed for estimating the parameters in an ARMA(1, 1) model. The autocorrelation function is given by (2.4.13), which suggests estimating ϕ by

$$\hat{\phi}_c = r(2)/r(1) \qquad (3.16)$$

If $\rho(1)$ and ϕ are replaced by $r(1)$ and $\hat{\phi}_c$ in (2.4.13a), an estimator is again given by the solution to a quadratic equation. This approach may be generalised to higher order models, although it does begin to get complicated; see Godolphin (1976). An alternative method for obtaining starting values is described in Box and Jenkins (1976, pp. 201–5).

Although consistent estimators may be obtained from the correlogram, they will not be asymptotically efficient if the model contains an MA component. In the MA(1) case, for example, $\text{Eff}(\hat{\theta}_c) = 0.49$ when $\theta = \pm 0.5$, and as $|\theta| \to 1$, $\text{Eff}(\hat{\theta}_c) \to 0$. This implies that the higher order autocorrelations contain information which is not in $r(1)$.

3.4 Hypothesis Tests and Confidence Intervals

Methods of testing hypotheses can be derived systematically using a maximum likelihood approach. The basic procedure is the likelihood ratio test, but two other tests, the Wald test and the Lagrange multiplier test, share some of the properties of the likelihood ratio test and are sometimes easier to compute. All three tests are reviewed briefly in the first sub-section. A more detailed description can be found in chapter 5 of EATS.

The classical framework within which the likelihood ratio, Wald and Lagrange multiplier tests operate assumes that the null hypothesis is nested within a more general model, in other words it is a special case. Thus a test of an AR(1) model against an MA(1) cannot be carried out although a test of AR(1) against an ARMA(1, 1) alternative is quite legitimate. Nevertheless, discrimination between non-nested models does play an important role in model selection, and the issue is discussed to some extent in section 3.6.

Note that it is not possible to test restrictions imposed simultaneously on the autoregressive and moving average parts of a model. This is because if the null hypothesis is true, the unrestricted model will contain common factors and so will not be identifiable. Thus, the null hypothesis of an ARMA(1, 1) model cannot be tested against the alternative of ARMA(2, 2).

Classical Test Procedures

The likelihood ratio (LR) test is primarily concerned with testing the validity of a set of restrictions on the parameter vector, ψ. When these restrictions are linear, they may be expressed in the form

$$\mathbf{R}\psi = \mathbf{r} \tag{4.1}$$

where $\mathbf{R}$ is an $m \times n$ matrix of fixed values, $\mathbf{r}$ is an $m \times 1$ vector of fixed values and m, the number of restrictions, is less than n.

Under the null hypothesis, H_0, ψ satisfies the restrictions in (4.1). When the restrictions are imposed, the ML estimator of $\tilde{\psi}$ is denoted by $\tilde{\psi}_0$ and this may be contrasted with the unrestricted estimator, $\tilde{\psi}$. If the maximised likelihood function under H_0, $L(\tilde{\psi}_0)$, is much smaller than the unrestricted maximised likelihood, $L(\tilde{\psi})$, there is evidence against the null hypothesis. This result is formalised in the Neyman–Pearson lemma which shows that a test based on the likelihood ratio,

$$\lambda = L(\tilde{\psi}_0)/L(\tilde{\psi}) \tag{4.2}$$

has certain desirable statistical properties.

It is sometimes possible to transform the likelihood ratio into a statistic, the exact distribution of which is known under H_0. When this cannot be done, a large sample test is carried out. This is based on the result that the statistic

$$\text{LR} = -2 \log \lambda \tag{4.3}$$

is asymptotically distributed as χ^2_m under H_0.

The disadvantage of the LR test is that the model must be estimated under both the null and alternative hypotheses. A different procedure, the

Wald test, only requires an estimate of ψ from the unrestricted model. The usual form of the test statistic is

$$W = (\mathbf{R}\tilde{\psi} - \mathbf{r})'[\mathbf{R}\mathbf{I}^{-1}(\tilde{\psi})\mathbf{R}']^{-1}(\mathbf{R}\tilde{\psi} - \mathbf{r}) \tag{4.4}$$

where $\mathbf{I}(\tilde{\psi})$ is the information matrix evaluated at the unrestricted estimate $\tilde{\psi}$. Under H_0, W is asymptotically χ_m^2 and its large sample properties can be shown to be similar to those of the LR test.

If the model is easier to estimate under the null hypothesis, a *Lagrange multiplier* test may be appropriate. The test statistic, which again is asymptotically χ_m^2 under H_0, takes the form

$$\text{LM} = \left(\frac{\partial \log L}{\partial \psi}\right)' \mathbf{I}^{-1}(\tilde{\psi}_0) \left(\frac{\partial \log L}{\partial \psi}\right) \tag{4.5}$$

where $\partial \log L / \partial \psi$ is evaluated at the restricted estimate, $\tilde{\psi}_0$. As with the Wald test, the large sample properties of the LM test are similar to those of the LR test, but estimation of the more general, unrestricted model is avoided.

When maximising the likelihood function of the unrestricted model is equivalent to minimising a sum of squares function, a minor modification of (4.5) leads to a particularly convenient form of the test statistic. If the residual, ε_t, and its $m \times 1$ vector of derivatives, $\partial \varepsilon_t / \partial \psi$, are evaluated at $\psi = \tilde{\psi}_0$, ε_t may be regressed on $\partial \varepsilon_t / \partial \psi$ to yield a coefficient of multiple correlation, R^2. The statistic

$$\text{LM}^* = TR^2 \tag{4.6}$$

is then asymptotically equivalent to the LM statistic, (4.5), and it can be tested as a χ_m^2 variate in the usual way. On occasion it is convenient to adopt a 'modified LM test' based on the F-distribution. The general principle underlying this approach should be clear from the examples given.

Wald and Likelihood Ratio Tests for ARMA Models

If an ARMA model is estimated by Gauss–Newton, the natural large sample estimator of $\mathbf{I}^{-1}(\tilde{\psi})$ in the Wald statistic (4.4) is

$$\text{avar}(\tilde{\psi}) = \tilde{\sigma}^2 \left(\sum \mathbf{z}_t \mathbf{z}_t'\right)^{-1} \tag{4.7}$$

where $\mathbf{z}_t = -\partial \varepsilon_t / \partial \psi$ is evaluated at $\psi = \tilde{\psi}$. The regression methodology of Gauss–Newton suggests a modification of the above procedure, in which a test is based on the classical F-statistic in the regression of $\varepsilon_t(\tilde{\psi})$ on $\mathbf{z}_t(\tilde{\psi})$. The estimator of σ^2 has a divisor of $T - p - q$, thereby corresponding to the estimator s^2 in classical linear regression, while dividing W by m, the number of restrictions under H_0, converts the χ^2-statistic into an F. The use of the

F-distribution should not be taken to imply that the test is exact. The F-test is mainly used as a matter of convenience, although the analogy with classical regression does suggest that it might be more accurate. A test on a single parameter in the model can be based on the classical t-statistic. Again the test will not be exact. The terms 'asymptotic t-ratio' and 'asymptotic F-ratio' are often employed in this context.

Example 1 In an AR(1) model the CSS estimator of ϕ is obtained directly by regressing y_t on y_{t-1}. The asymptotic t-ratio is

$$\tilde{\phi}/(s/\sqrt{\sum y_{t-1}^2}) \tag{4.8}$$

where s^2 corresponds to the unbiased estimator of σ^2 in classical linear regression. A test based on (4.8) is asymptotically equivalent to a test which uses the square root of $(1 - \tilde{\phi}^2)/T$ as an estimate of the standard error. This is because

$$p \lim (s^{-2} \sum y_{t-1}^2/T) = 1/(1 - \phi^2) \tag{4.9}$$

Example 2 If an MA(1) model is estimated by Gauss–Newton, a test on θ can be carried out on convergence. This is based on the asymptotic t-ratio associated with $\partial \varepsilon_t/\partial \theta$.

The LR test statistic is

$$\text{LR} = T \log(\tilde{\sigma}_0^2/\tilde{\sigma}^2) = T \log(\text{SSE}_0/\text{SSE}) \tag{4.10}$$

where SSE_0 and SSE are the residual sums of squares, $\sum \varepsilon_t^2$, for the restricted and unrestricted models respectively. The analogy with classical linear regression again suggests a modified test in which

$$\text{LR*} = \frac{(\text{SSE}_0 - \text{SSE})/m}{\text{SSE}/(T - p - q)} \tag{4.11}$$

is taken to have an F-distribution with $(m, T - p - q)$ degrees of freedom under H_0.

Lagrange Multiplier Tests

Suppose the restricted form of the model has been estimated. An LM test of H_0 can then be based on a single iteration of Gauss–Newton. This leads to the TR^2-statistic, (4.6), which can be tested as a χ_m^2 variate.

Example 3 Suppose that an AR(1) model has been fitted, and that we wish to test for the addition of an MA component. In other words, the unrestricted model is ARMA(1, 1), while $H_0: \psi = \psi_0$ has $\psi_0 = (\phi, 0)'$.

The residual function of an $ARMA(1, 1)$ process is

$$\varepsilon_t = y_t - \phi y_{t-1} - \theta \varepsilon_{t-1} \tag{4.12}$$

and the derivatives of ε_t with respect to ϕ and θ are given by the recursive expressions (3.8a) and (3.8b). The LM procedure is based on a regression of $\varepsilon_t(\tilde{\psi}_0)$ on its derivatives evaluated at $\tilde{\psi}_0$. Since $\theta = 0$ under H_0, this reduces to a regression of ε_t on y_{t-1} and ε_{t-1}. The test is carried out by treating TR^2 as a χ_1^2 variate. The 'modified LM test' takes the form of a t-test on the coefficient of ε_{t-1}.

Example 4 If the null hypothesis in the previous example had been $H_0: \phi = \theta = 0$, the test would have broken down. Since $\partial \varepsilon_t / \partial \theta = -\varepsilon_{t-1} = -y_{t-1}$ when $\phi = \theta = 0$ and since $\partial \varepsilon_t / \partial \phi = -y_{t-1}$, the two explanatory variables in the regression of ε_t on its derivatives are perfectly collinear. The fact that the LM statistic cannot be computed in this case is a reflection of the point on common factor restrictions made at the beginning of this section.

Confidence Intervals

The most straightforward way of constructing a confidence interval for a single parameter is based on standard regression methodology. An estimate of the asymptotic standard error of a parameter will appear as part of a Gauss–Newton optimisation algorithm, and an approximate confidence interval may then be based on the t-distribution.

An alternative approach is based on finding a contour for the sum of squares surface. For a single parameter this will not necessarily give the same answer as the method described above, although any discrepancy is likely to be small. The advantage of the sum of squares approach is that it can be used to construct a confidence region for several parameters. Suppose that m parameters are being considered and that $\chi_m^2(\alpha)$ is the χ^2 significance value for a test of size α. An approximate $1 - \alpha$ confidence region is then bounded by the contour on the sum of squares surface for which

$$SSE(\psi) = SSE(\tilde{\psi})[1 + \chi_m^2(\alpha)/T] \tag{4.13}$$

Further details will be found in Box and Jenkins (1976, pp. 228–31).

3.5 Small Sample Properties

Although some work has been done in the pure AR case, few analytic results are available for the distribution of estimators of ARMA models. It is therefore necessary to rely on Monte Carlo studies to provide evidence on small sample properties. In this section an attempt is made to bring together some of the results reported in the literature, the survey being based primarily on the work of Ansley and Newbold (1980), Davidson (1981), Dent and Min (1978), Harvey and Phillips (1977), Kang (1975), Nelson (1974, 1976) and Nelson and O'Shea (1979).

Autoregressive Processes

For the AR(1) process it is clear from (1.19) that the likelihood function is not defined for $|\phi| \geqslant 1$. As a result, the exact ML estimator will always lie within the unit circle. This is not necessarily the case when other methods, such as least squares, are used. Nevertheless the evidence suggests that unless T is very small, and $|\phi|$ is close to 1, the difference between the full ML and the least squares estimator is likely to be negligible. In both cases there is a downward bias, which is approximately equal to $2\phi/T$; see Shenton and Johnson (1965).

While there is little to choose between the various asymptotically equivalent estimators in the AR(1) case, it appears that this is no longer true for higher order models. For $T = 100$ and $p = 2$ and 3, Dent and Min (1978) report sample MSEs for the ML estimates which, in some cases, are appreciably smaller than the MSEs obtained by other methods. As might be expected, the differences between the various procedures become more marked when the true parameters are close to the boundary of the stationarity region.

Confidence intervals and 't-statistics' can be constructed very easily when AR models are estimated by regression; compare with example 4.1. Unless the true parameters are near to the stationarity boundary, these statistics appear to be quite reliable; see Ansley and Newbold (1980).

Moving Average and Mixed Models

As usual, the simple MA(1) model provides important insights into the behaviour of models other than pure autoregressions. The question of estimates on or outside the invertibility region is now of some importance. A model with $|\theta| > |$ is still a stationary process with a properly defined likelihood function. Carrying out unconstrained optimisation of this exact likelihood function, thereby allowing non-invertible estimates, means that the likelihood equation has more than one solution, and so an identification problem arises. For every value of θ outside the unit circle, there is a value of θ inside the unit circle with the same autocorrelation function. This follows because (2.1.15) takes the same value when θ is replaced by its reciprocal $1/\theta$. The implication is that the (exact) likelihood function will have two maxima, one at $\tilde{\theta}$ and one at $1/\tilde{\theta}$. The only exception to this rule is when the maximum is actually on the unit circle, i.e. $\tilde{\theta} = \pm 1$. Insisting that estimates of θ satisfy the invertibility conditions removes the ambiguity arising from multiple solutions.

Unconstrained exact ML estimation is feasible because an estimate of θ outside the unit circle can be converted to an invertible estimate by simply taking its reciprocal. The CSS function, on the other hand, has no meaning for values of θ outside the unit circle. However, in small samples it may sometimes be the case that the CSS function has no minimum within the invertibility region, with the result that an unconstrained optimisation procedure may not converge or, if it does converge, will produce meaningless estimates. While such behaviour is only likely with $|\theta|$ close to 1 and T small, it nevertheless points to the importance of taking account of the invertibility constraints in an estimation procedure.

Allowing the full likelihood function to be maximised without imposing restrictions reveals a rather interesting result. For small samples, and a true value of θ close to the unit circle, a relatively high number of global maxima are located at a value of θ *exactly* equal to plus or minus one. The effect of this is shown in figure 3.1, which is constructed from a simple Monte Carlo experiment reported in Harvey and Phillips (1977). For $T = 25$ and $\theta = 0.9$, approximately half of the estimates computed in each of 200 replications form a typical 'bell-shaped' distribution centred on $\theta \simeq 0.85$. The remaining 103 estimates are exactly equal to unity; compare with figure 1 in Ansley and Newbold (1980). The notion that an estimator can take a particular value with a non-zero probability might appear rather implausible. However, Sargan and Bhargava (1983) have provided analytic evidence on this point. They set out a method for evaluating the probability that $\tilde{\theta} = \pm 1$ for given values of θ and T.

In the same set of replications used to construct figure 3.1 CSS estimates were also computed. In 32 cases the minimum was at $\theta = 1$, but only because estimates outside the unit circle were deemed to be inadmissible. Thus, unlike the ML case, they did not represent global solutions to the optimisation problem. Given these results on the distribution of the ML estimator, care must be exercised in comparisons between estimators based on sample MSEs, since this does not capture the rather unusual bimodality of θ in the distribution of the ML estimator. However, most of the results quoted below are based on $T = 100$, and for a sample size of that order the effect is relatively unimportant unless θ is close to the unit circle. Nevertheless, the fact that a true value of θ equal to minus one can arise when over-differencing takes place should be borne in mind when evaluating different estimators.

Nelson (1974), Davidson (1981) and Dent and Min (1978) compare a variety of estimation procedures over a range of values of θ. Nelson, unfortunately, does not include the ML estimator in his experiments, preferring to regard the 'unconditional sum of squares' as a reasonable

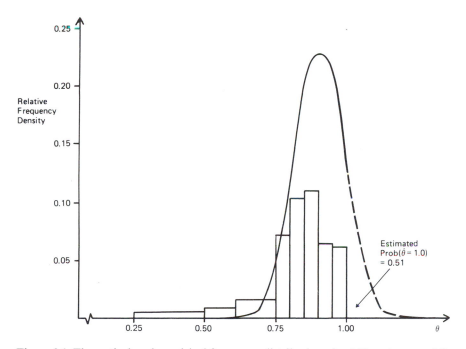

Figure 3.1 Theoretical and empirical frequency distributions for ML estimator of θ in an MA(1) process with $\theta = 0.9$ ($T = 25$).

approximation. The unconditional sum of squares estimator is obtained by maximising the exact likelihood function, but without the determinantal term, $\log |V|$. For a large value of T this estimator is similar to exact ML. However, if T is small and θ is close to the unit circle, it can be very different, and the evidence presented by Kang (1975) and Davidson (1981) suggests that there is little to recommend it. The main conclusions of the three studies are as follows. Firstly, for $T = 30$, the CSS estimator is clearly biased towards zero when $\theta = \pm 0.9$, but the extent of this bias is considerably reduced when $T = 100$. Secondly, the ML estimator is to be preferred to the CSS estimator on an MSE criterion when the true value of θ is close to the unit circle. However, when $T = 100$, the results of Dent and Min suggest that there is very little to choose between the two estimators for $|\theta|$ less than about 0.8. In fact, if anything, the CSS estimator has a smaller MSE. Supporting evidence is provided by Davidson.

Nelson also examines another aspect of inference, namely the estimator of standard errors. These may be computed from the cross-product matrix which emerges in the Gauss–Newton method, or by numerically evaluating the Hessian. For the CSS estimator, the estimated standard errors tend to be a good deal smaller than the corresponding MSEs given over all replications. The result is that the dispersion of 't-ratios' is too wide, and so a null hypothesis will tend to be rejected much too often. For $T = 30$, Nelson's results indicate that a nominal test size of 0.05 is likely to produce an actual test size of around 0.10 for most values of θ. Some improvement is observed as the sample size increases, but, as might be expected, values of θ close to the unit circle continue to give rise to problems in this respect. For example, with $T = 100$, a nominal test size of 0.05 implies an actual size of around 0.12 when $\theta = 0.9$. Nelson sums up these findings by observing that the t-ratios in MA models are likely to be 'treacherous' in small samples. Supporting evidence is provided in Nelson and O'Shea (1979) and Ansley and Newbold (1980).

The performance of estimators other than ML and CSS is also reported in some papers. Of principal interest is the correlogram estimator, $\hat{\theta}_c$, defined in (3.15). When θ is close to zero, $\hat{\theta}_c$ has an MSE close to that of the CSS estimator, but its relative efficiency declines fairly rapidly as $|\theta|$ tends towards one. Although its MSE diminishes as T increases, its relative performance with respect to CSS actually gets worse. In Nelson's study, the sample MSE of $\hat{\theta}_c$ is about twice that of the corresponding MSE for the CSS estimator when $\theta = 0.5$ and $T = 30$, but around three times the size for $T = 100$. The asymptotic efficiency of $\hat{\theta}_c$ is 0.49 for $\theta = 0.5$. The results given by Dent and Min for $T = 100$ are very similar. The overall conclusion is that although $\hat{\theta}_c$ might not be entertained as a final estimator, it is nevertheless a satisfactory way of generating starting values for iterative schemes. To quote Nelson (1974, p. 127) '... the GN method led to the global minimum (for CSS) reliably and quickly when $\hat{\theta}_c$ was used as an initial guess value'.

For the MA(2) process, the results in Dent and Min again indicate that there is little to choose between the ML and CSS estimators, except when the parameters are close to the boundary of the invertibility region. In such cases there appears to be a gain in using the ML estimator. The conclusion reached by Dent and Min (1978, p. 38) that '... for pure moving average models the conditional least squares (CSS) estimator may be marginally superior to the maximum likelihood estimator' is not particularly well supported by their results for the MA(2) process. The MSEs quoted for the CSS estimator fall below the corresponding MSEs in less than half of the models studied, and the differences are so small that it is difficult to draw firm conclusions on the basis of only one hundred replications.

For the ARMA(1, 1) model, the results in Dent and Min show the ML and CSS estimators to be performing equally well; no clear pattern of superiority of one over the other emerges. The results in Ansley and Newbold (1980), on the other hand, indicate a clear gain from using full ML for both ϕ and θ. As in the MA(1) case, the 'pile up' effect of estimates of θ when the true value is close to the unit circle should be borne in mind in any comparison of MSEs. For $\theta = 0.9$ and $\phi = 0.9$, Harvey and Phillips (1977) found that, for $T = 25$, between 40% and 50% of the ML estimates of θ

were exactly equal to unity. A similar proportion was observed when ϕ was set equal to 0.5.

Ansley and Newbold (1980) also studied the reliability of confidence intervals for mixed models. They found particularly severe problems when there was 'anything approaching parameter redundancy'. In such cases the computed confidence intervals can be far too narrow.

3.6 Model Selection

The earlier part of this chapter discussed the estimation of parameters in an $\text{ARMA}(p, q)$ model for *given* values of p and q. In modelling a particular stationary time series, however, p and q will not, in general, be known. Prior to estimation, therefore, a suitable model must be selected. This involves choosing p and q in such a way that a good fit is obtained with a minimum number of parameters. This is known as the principle of *parsimony*.

From the statistical point of view, the best approach to model selection is to start from the most general model and to test successively more and more stringent restrictions. This approach would be feasible in the present context if it were reasonable to regard a pure AR (or pure MA) process as the most general formulation. Thus, given an $\text{AR}(p)$ model, the first hypothesis to be tested is that the process is of order p. The next hypothesis in the nest is that the process is of order $p - 1$ and so on. The order of the model is then fixed when a particular hypothesis is rejected. Full details of such an approach will be found in Anderson (1971, pp. 270–6). Unfortunately the procedure is open to two objections, one minor and the other major. The minor objection is that the set of ordered hypotheses which have been defined may not always be appropriate. The best model may have an order greater than the number of non-zero parameters; for example, an $\text{AR}(2)$ model may have $\phi_1 = 0$. However, except in seasonal cases, such formulations are relatively uncommon, and once p has been determined it would not be difficult to detect zero coefficients in any case. The more basic objection is that it may take a relatively large number of AR parameters to approximate a particular linear process at all well. This has two implications. Firstly, the initial general model should be chosen with a sufficiently high order. Secondly, once a model has been selected by the sequential testing procedure it may well contain a very large number of parameters, thereby violating the principle of parsimony.

A mixed ARMA model has the advantage that it can usually approximate a linear process with relatively few parameters. The problem with a mixed model is that there is no longer any natural ordering of hypotheses. Furthermore, a technical difficulty arises when such a model is over-parameterised. As a simple example suppose that an $\text{ARMA}(1, 1)$ model

$$y_t = \phi y_{t-1} + \varepsilon_t + \theta \varepsilon_{t-1} \qquad (6.1)$$

is fitted to a set of observations from a white noise process. Model (6.1) reduces to white noise when $\phi = -\theta$, but when this constraint is imposed the asymptotic information matrix (3.13) is singular. This is likely to cause computational problems, since most ML estimation procedures rely on a matrix which is asymptotically equivalent to the information matrix. If the routine does not actually fail, but converges to estimates for which $\tilde{\phi} \neq -\tilde{\theta}$, an important clue to the over-parameterisation will lie in the estimated standard errors, which because of the near singularity of the estimated information matrix will tend to be high.

The above considerations led Box and Jenkins (1976) to advocate a strategy for model selection based on a three-stage iterative procedure. In the first stage, *identification*, a tentative model is selected on the basis of the appearance of the correlogram and other related statistics. Given p and q, the parameters are then estimated by one of the methods described earlier. As a by-product of this *estimation* stage, residuals are computed and these may be used as the basis for *diagnostic checking*. A significant departure from randomness indicates that the model is, in some sense, inadequate. A return to the identification stage is then called for, and the complete cycle is repeated until a suitable formulation is found.

Identification

The correlogram provides the most important means by which a suitable ARMA(p, q) process may be identified. Provided the sample is reasonably large, the correlogram should mirror the theoretical autocorrelation function of the underlying process. In chapter 2 the behaviour of the autocorrelation function was examined and certain salient characteristics were noted for particular processes. Thus, a pure MA(q) process exhibits a cut-off in its autocorrelation function for lags greater than q. On the other hand, the autocorrelations of an AR or mixed process gradually tail off to zero. A correlogram of the type shown in figure 3.2 would therefore probably lead to an MA(2) model being initially entertained. While the autocorrelations beyond $\tau = 2$ are not identically equal to zero, they are small enough in comparison with $r(1)$ and $r(2)$ to suggest that their size is primarily due to sampling error.

If the theoretical autocorrelations beyond a certain point, q, are zero, it follows from (2.7.12) that the sample autocorrelations are approximately normally distributed in large samples with mean zero and variance

$$\text{Avar}[r(\tau)] = \left[1 + 2 \sum_{j=1}^{q} \rho^2(j) \right] \bigg/ T, \qquad \tau > q \qquad (6.2)$$

An estimate of $\text{Avar}[r(\tau)]$ can be obtained by replacing the theoretical autocorrelations in (6.2) by the corresponding sample autocorrelations. The

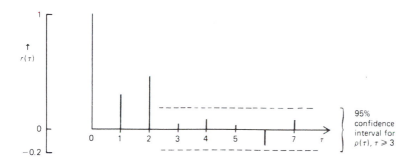

Figure 3.2 Sample autocorrelations for 200 observations from an MA(2) process.

broken lines in figure 3.2 indicate approximate 95% confidence intervals for each $r(\tau)$, $\tau > 2$, under the assumption that the process is indeed MA(2).

The order of a pure AR process is rather more difficult to determine from the correlogram, except perhaps when $p = 1$. A complementary procedure is therefore often used. This is based on the sample *partial autocorrelation function*. Let $\tilde{\phi}(\tau)$ denote the estimated coefficient of $y_{t-\tau}$ in an AR(τ) model. The sample partial autocorrelation function is then defined by a plot of $\tilde{\phi}(\tau)$ against τ. The important point to note about this function is that its behaviour is the opposite of that exhibited by the autocorrelation function. For a pure AR(p) process, the theoretical partial autocorrelations are zero at lags beyond p, while for an MA process they die away gradually. If the observations are generated by an AR(p) process, the sample partial autocorrelations beyond lag p are normally distributed with mean zero and variance,

$$\text{Avar}[\tilde{\phi}(\tau)] = 1/T \qquad (6.3)$$

If the data can be reasonably well approximated by a pure AR or MA model, it should not prove too difficult to select a suitable value of p or q by examining the estimated autocorrelation, or partial autocorrelation, function. The identification of both p and q in a mixed model is somewhat more problematic. Neither the autocorrelation function nor the partial autocorrelation function has a definite cut-off point, and considerable skill may be needed to interpret the patterns obtained. In these circumstances the complete cycle of identification, estimation and diagnostic checking may have to be repeated several times before a suitable model is found.

The above difficulties may be seriously compounded by sampling error. For example, for an AR(1) process it follows from (2.7.14) that with $\phi = 0.9$ and $T = 100$, the asymptotic standard error of $r(1)$ is 0.3. Furthermore, the strong correlation between successive sample autocorrelations, noted below (2.7.15), may lead to a very distorted picture of the underlying ACF.

Diagnostic Checking

Diagnostic checking of the model may be carried out by examining the residuals for departures from randomness. Formal tests can be based on the correlogram, although this should not be seen as a substitute for a direct plot of the residuals. To quote Box and Jenkins (1976, p. 289): 'It cannot be too strongly emphasized that visual inspection of a plot of the residuals themselves is an indispensable first step in the checking process.'

Although plotting and examining functions of the residuals is an extremely valuable exercise, some care should be taken in interpreting the results. Tests associated with these procedures are often constructed on the assumption that the residuals have the same properties as the disturbances when the model is correctly specified. Unfortunately this assumption is invalid for residuals from ARMA models, even when the sample size is large. For example, if an AR(1) model is fitted to the data, it can be shown that the first-order autocorrelation in the residuals has an asymptotic variance of ϕ^2/T. This can be substantially less than $1/T$, which is the variance of $r(1)$ for a white noise process. However, for higher order lags the bias in variance is considerably less serious. This is indicative of the behaviour of the residual autocorrelations for any fitted ARMA(p, q) process. In all cases, a reduction in variance tends to occur at low lags. Furthermore, the $r(\tau)$'s at these lags can be highly correlated. Although such effects usually disappear at higher lags, they are often sufficiently important to impart a severe bias to the portmanteau statistic. The net result is that this test procedure tends to underestimate the significance of apparent discrepancies.

Although the tests associated with the graphical procedures are not generally valid in this situation, they can nevertheless provide useful guidelines. However, a valid test statistic is clearly desirable. Box and Pierce (1970) have shown that, provided P is reasonably large, the portmanteau statistic constructed from ARMA residuals is appropriate if it is taken to have a χ^2_{P-p-q} distribution under the null hypothesis. The reduction in degrees of freedom is to allow for the fitted parameters, and the net result is that the probability of rejecting the null hypothesis is increased as compared with a portmanteau test based on a χ^2-distribution with the full P degrees of freedom. Unfortunately the statistic still suffers from the small sample defects described in section 2.8, and the preferred approach is now to calculate the modified portmanteau statistic (2.8.4). This is then tested against an appropriate significance value from the χ^2_{P-p-q} distribution. When (2.8.3) and (2.8.4) are used in this way, the resulting procedures are often referred to as the *Box–Pierce test* and the *modified Box–Pierce* (or *Box–Ljung*) *test* respectively. Note that in both cases P should be chosen so as to be reasonably large compared with $p + q$. A useful rule of thumb is to set P equal to $\sqrt{T}$, although formally P should increase at the same rate as T for the asymptotic theory to go through.

Other diagnostic tests may be carried out. In particular we may wish to construct tests for heteroscedasticity or non-normality.

Lagrange Multiplier Tests as Diagnostics

The portmanteau test, and indeed the Box–Pierce test, were set up as what are sometimes called *pure significance tests*. There is no specific alternative hypothesis in mind. The idea is simply that any departures from randomness will be reflected in the sample autocorrelations, leading to a significant value of the test statistic.

A more formal approach is to construct a Lagrange multiplier test of the null hypothesis that a series is Gaussian white noise against the alternative that it follows a Gaussian AR(P) or MA(P) process. Such a test turns out to be identical to the portmanteau test based on (2.8.3). Thus, to the extent that a high order AR or MA process may be regarded as an approximation to any linear process, the portmanteau test is a general test against non-randomness.

Consider the alternative of an AR(P) model and assume, for simplicity, that the process is known to have zero mean. Since the asymptotic information matrix for an AR(P) process is block diagonal with respect to ϕ and σ^2, the LM statistic is given directly by (4.5) with $\psi = \phi$. From (2.6),

$$\mathbf{IA}(\phi) = \mathbf{V}_P \tag{6.4}$$

where $\sigma^2 \mathbf{V}_P$ is the covariance matrix of the observation over P successive time periods. Under the null hypothesis, $H_0 : \phi_1 = \phi_2 = \cdots = \phi_P = 0$, $\mathbf{V}_P$ reduces to the identity matrix, and so the LM statistic is

$$\mathrm{LM} = T^{-1} \left(\frac{\partial \log L}{\partial \phi} \right)' \left(\frac{\partial \log L}{\partial \phi} \right) = T^{-1} \sum_{i=1}^{P} \left(\frac{\partial \log L}{\partial \phi_i} \right)^2 \tag{6.5}$$

evaluated at $\phi = 0$. The conditional log–likelihood function is

$$\log L = -(1/2) T \log 2\pi - (1/2) T \log \sigma^2 - (1/2) \sigma^{-2} S(\phi)$$

where $S(\phi)$ is defined in (2.3). Differentiating with respect to the elements of ϕ gives

$$\frac{\partial \log L}{\partial \phi_i} = \sigma^{-2} \sum_{t=P+1}^{T} y_{t-i} (y_t - \phi_1 y_{t-1} - \cdots - \phi_P y_{t-P}),$$
$$i = 1, \ldots, P \tag{6.6}$$

Under H_0, $\tilde{\sigma}_0^2 = T^{-1} \sum y_t^2$, and (6.6) becomes

$$\left. \frac{\partial \log L}{\partial \phi_i} \right|_{\phi=0} = \tilde{\sigma}_0^{-2} \sum_{t=P+1}^{T} y_{t-i} y_t = Tr(i), \qquad i = 1, \ldots, P \tag{6.7}$$

On substituting in (6.5) it follows immediately that

$$LM = T \sum_{\tau=1}^{P} r^2(\tau) \qquad (6.8)$$

This is identical to the portmanteau test statistic, (2.8.3), except that $r(\tau)$ is defined without $\bar{y}$ appearing in the autocovariances. This is simply a consequence of the assumption that the process has zero mean.

The portmanteau test may also be derived as a test against an $MA(P)$ alternative. As with the $AR(P)$ process, the information matrix under H_0 is equal to T multiplied by a $P \times P$ identity matrix. The LM statistic is similar in form to (6.5), but with $\partial \log L / \partial \phi_i$ replaced by

$$\frac{\partial \log L}{\partial \theta_j} = \sigma^{-2} \sum_{t=1}^{T} \left(\varepsilon_{t-j} + \sum_{i=1}^{q} \theta_i \frac{\partial \varepsilon_{t-i}}{\partial \theta_j} \right) \varepsilon_t, \qquad j = 1, \ldots, P$$

However, under the null hypothesis $\theta_i = 0$ for $i = 1$ to q and $\varepsilon_t = y_t$, so

$$\left. \frac{\partial \log L}{\partial \theta_j} \right|_{\theta=0} = Tr(j), \qquad j = 1, \ldots, P \qquad (6.9)$$

and the argument goes through as before.

An alternative approach in both the AR and MA cases is to equate maximising the likelihood function with minimising the conditional sum of squares. A test may then be based on the TR^2-statistic, where R^2 is the coefficient of multiple correlation obtained by regressing ε_t on z_t, its vector of partial derivatives. In both cases, this amounts simply to regressing y_t on $y_{t-1}, y_{t-2}, \ldots, y_{t-P}$. The TR^2-statistic is then tested as a χ^2 variate with P degrees of freedom. This form of the LM test may be generalised so as to construct a diagnostic check when an $ARMA(p, q)$ model has been fitted. The model is nested within an $ARMA(p + P, q)$ process and a Lagrange multiplier test of the hypothesis $H_0: \phi_{p+1} = \phi_{p+2} = \cdots = \phi_{p+P} = 0$ is carried out. The residual ε_t is regressed on the full set of $p + P + q$ derivatives evaluated under H_0 and the resulting TR^2-statistic is treated as a χ_P^2 variate. The 'modified' LM procedure consists of carrying out an asymptotic F-test on the joint significance of the derivatives with respect to ϕ_{p+1} to ϕ_{p+P}.

Example 1 Suppose that an $ARMA(1, 1)$ model has been estimated. A test against an $ARMA(1 + P, 1)$ specification involves the evaluation of the derivatives of the residual function,

$$\varepsilon_t = y_t - \phi_1 y_{t-1} - \cdots - \phi_{1+P} y_{t-1-P} - \theta \varepsilon_{t-1},$$

$$t = 2 + P, \ldots, T \qquad (6.10)$$

with $\varepsilon_{1+P} = 0$. These derivatives are

$$\frac{\partial \varepsilon_t}{\partial \phi_i} = -y_{t-i} - \theta \frac{\partial \varepsilon_{t-1}}{\partial \phi_i} = -\sum_{j=0}^{t-P-2} (-\theta)^j y_{t-i-j},$$

$$t = 2 + P, \ldots, T \qquad (6.11)$$

for $i = 1, \ldots, 1 + P$, and

$$\frac{\partial \varepsilon_t}{\partial \theta} = -\varepsilon_{t-1} - \theta \frac{\partial \varepsilon_{t-1}}{\partial \theta} = -\sum_{j=0}^{t-P-2} (-\theta)^j \varepsilon_{t-1-j},$$

$$t = 2 + P, \ldots, T \qquad (6.12)$$

Note that since ε_{1+P} is assumed to be fixed, all the derivatives at $t = 1 + P$ are equal to zero.

Evaluating these expressions under the null hypothesis leads to a regression of $y_t - \phi_1 y_{t-1} - \theta \varepsilon_{t-1}$ on (6.11) with ϕ_1, θ and the ε_t's replaced by their estimated values. The resulting TR^2-statistic is tested against a χ_P^2-distribution.

An LM test could also be set up by augmenting the MA component to yield an $ARMA(p, q + P)$ process. (Example 3 in section 3.4 is a special case.) At first sight this would seem to yield a different test to the one described above, but in fact it turns out that the two TR^2-statistics are identical; see Poskitt and Tremayne (1980).

A final point to note about these LM tests is that they are valid for any value of P. This is an advantage over the Box–Pierce test, where, as noted earlier, a reasonably large value of P is needed for the asymptotic theory to go through.

Goodness of Fit

In a given application, the Box–Jenkins model selection procedure may suggest several specifications, each of which satisfies the diagnostic checks. Some kind of measure of goodness of fit is therefore needed to distinguish between different models in these circumstances. One possibility is the *Akaike information criterion* (AIC), where the decision rule is to select the model which minimises

$$\text{AIC} = -2 \log L(\tilde{\psi}) + 2n \qquad (6.13)$$

where $L(\tilde{\psi})$ is the maximised value of the likelihood function and n is the number of parameters; see Akaike (1974). For an $ARMA(p, q)$ model this can be conveniently expressed in the form

$$\text{AIC}^\dagger = \tilde{\sigma}^2 \exp[\log |\mathbf{V}| + 2(p + q)/T] \qquad (6.14)$$

where $\sigma^2 \mathbf{V}$ is the covariance matrix of the observations. The term $\log |\mathbf{V}|$ goes to zero as the sample size increases and disappears completely under the assumptions of the CSS estimator. The preferred model is the one for which $\text{AIC}^\dagger$ is a minimum. The term $2(p + q)/T$ assigns a penalty to models which are not suitably parsimonious.

There are a number of other model selection criteria which are distinguished from the AIC by the penalty which they give to the number of parameters in the model. For example in the *Bayes information criterion* (BIC), the $2n$ in (6.13) and (6.14) is replaced by $n \log T$. There is evidence to suggest that the BIC is more satisfactory than the AIC as an ARMA model selection criterion since the AIC has a tendency to pick models which are over-parameterised; see Sneek (1984) and Hannan (1980).

One of the disadvantages of the Box–Jenkins strategy is that it requires a good deal of time and skill, particularly at the identification stage. An alternative approach is to use the AIC or the BIC more comprehensively. The range of possible models is defined on the basis of *a priori* information, or by a rather crude identification procedure, and the one for which (6.14) is a minimum is selected. This implies a shift in emphasis towards the computer. However, although the procedure may be applied in a semi-automatic fashion, it would be unwise not to submit a model chosen in this way to diagnostic checking.

Exercises

1. If the sample autocorrelations at lags 1 and 2 are 0.8 and 0.5 respectively, find asymptotically efficient estimators of the parameters in an $\text{AR}(2)$ model.
2. If a stationary $\text{AR}(1)$ model with zero mean is estimated by regression, show that $R^2 \simeq \hat{\phi}^2$.
3. Show that the Yule–Walker equations for an $\text{AR}(2)$ model give approximately the same estimators of ϕ_1 and ϕ_2 as a regression of y_t on y_{t-1} and y_{t-2}. Find an expression for the asymptotic covariance matrix of these estimators in terms of ϕ_1 and ϕ_2.
4. Obtain an expression for the exact likelihood function of a stationary $\text{AR}(2)$ model in terms of the parameters in the model. How can this expression be modified so as to give a linear estimator of the autoregressive parameters?
5. For the set of observations 6, -4, -2, 0, 2 calculate the conditional sum of squares for an MA process with $\theta = -0.5$. Make predictions one, two and three steps ahead and calculate their MSEs.
6. How would you estimate ϕ and θ in an $\text{ARMA}(1, 1)$ model from the first two sample autocorrelations?
7. In question 5, how would you test the null hypothesis that $\theta = -0.5$ using a Wald test? How would you test the null hypothesis that (a) $\theta = -0.5$; (b) $\theta = 0$, using an LM test?
8. If an $\text{AR}(2)$ model is fitted, construct an LM test against an $\text{ARMA}(2, Q)$ alternative and compare the form of this test to the Box–Pierce test applied to the residuals.

9. Derive an LM test for testing the hypothesis that a model is $ARMA(1, 1)$ against the alternative that it is $ARMA(1, 3)$. How would you carry out a modified LM test based on the F-distribution?

10. Show that the LM test of $\theta = 0$ in the $ARMA(1, 1)$ model is equivalent to a test based on the first autocorrelation, $r(1)$, computed from the residuals from an $AR(1)$ model, with $r(1)$ regarded as being asymptotically normal with mean zero and variance ϕ^2/T.

11. Suppose that an $MA(2)$ model is estimated when the second moving average parameter, θ_2, is actually equal to zero. Find an expression for the relative efficiency of the resulting estimator of θ_1 as compared with the estimator obtained from an $MA(1)$ model.

    How would you construct a Lagrange multiplier test of the hypothesis that $\theta_2 = 0$?

12. If $r(1) = 0.7$ and $r(2) = 0.5$ calculate the first two sample partial auto-correlations. Comment on the implications for model identification.

13. (a) A time series analyst fitted an $AR(6)$ model and obtained the following estimates of the parameters:

$$\hat{\pi}_1 = 0.40, \qquad \hat{\pi}_2 = -0.36, \qquad \hat{\pi}_3 = 0.32, \qquad \hat{\pi}_4 = -0.29$$

$$\hat{\pi}_5 = 0.26, \qquad \hat{\pi}_6 = -0.23$$

Show how these estimates could be accounted for by the values implied by the two parameters of an $ARMA(1, 1)$ process.

(b) Derive the autocorrelation function for an $ARMA(1, 1)$ process, and compute the first four autocorrelations using the estimates computed in (a). Sketch this autocorrelation function and explain why an $AR(1)$ specification would have been rejected if the correlogram had had this shape.

4

State Space Models and the
Kalman Filter

4.1 State Space Form

The state space form is a powerful tool which opens the way to handling a wide range of time series models. Once a model has been put in state space form, the Kalman filter may be applied and this in turn leads to algorithms for prediction and smoothing. In a Gaussian model, the Kalman filter provides the means of constructing the likelihood function by the prediction error decomposition. The application of this technique to the exact ML estimation of ARMA and time-varying parameter regression models is described in the last two sections. Further examples of the use of state space methods will be found later in the book particularly in the context of structural time series models.

Although we are only interested in univariate time series at present, the general state space form (SSF) applies to multivariate time series. It is no more difficult to develop algorithms for this set-up than it is to develop the corresponding algorithms for a univariate series. Results are therefore presented for the general case, although some attention is paid to the special features of univariate models.

The $N \times 1$ vector of observed variables at time t, $\mathbf{y}_t$, is related to an $m \times 1$ vector, $\boldsymbol{\alpha}_t$, known as the *state vector*, via a *measurement equation*

$$\mathbf{y}_t = \mathbf{Z}_t \boldsymbol{\alpha}_t + \mathbf{d}_t + \boldsymbol{\varepsilon}_t, \qquad t = 1, \ldots, T \tag{1.1a}$$

where $\mathbf{Z}_t$ is an $N \times m$ matrix, $\mathbf{d}_t$ is an $N \times 1$ vector and $\boldsymbol{\varepsilon}_t$ is an $N \times 1$ vector of serially uncorrelated disturbances with mean zero and covariance matrix $\mathbf{H}_t$, that is

$$E(\boldsymbol{\varepsilon}_t) = \mathbf{0} \qquad \text{and} \qquad \text{Var}(\boldsymbol{\varepsilon}_t) = \mathbf{H}_t \tag{1.1b}$$

In general the elements of $\boldsymbol{\alpha}_t$ are not observable. However, they are known to be generated by a first-order Markov process,

$$\boldsymbol{\alpha}_t = \mathbf{T}_t \boldsymbol{\alpha}_{t-1} + \mathbf{c}_t + \mathbf{R}_t \boldsymbol{\eta}_t, \qquad t = 1, \ldots, T \qquad (1.2a)$$

where $\mathbf{T}_t$ is an $m \times m$ matrix, $\mathbf{c}_t$ is an $m \times 1$ vector, $\mathbf{R}_t$ is an $m \times g$ matrix and $\boldsymbol{\eta}_t$ is a $g \times 1$ vector of serially uncorrelated disturbances with mean zero and covariance matrix, $\mathbf{Q}_t$, that is

$$E(\boldsymbol{\eta}_t) = \mathbf{0} \quad \text{and} \quad \text{Var}(\boldsymbol{\eta}_t) = \mathbf{Q}_t \qquad (1.2b)$$

Equation (1.2a) is the *transition equation*. The inclusion of the matrix $\mathbf{R}_t$ in front of the disturbance term is, to some extent, arbitrary. The disturbance term could always be redefined so as to have a covariance matrix $\mathbf{R}_t \mathbf{Q}_t \mathbf{R}_t'$. Nevertheless the representation in (1.2a) is often more natural when $\boldsymbol{\eta}_t$ is identified with a particular set of disturbances in the model.

The specification of the state space system is completed by two further assumptions:

(a) The initial state vector, $\boldsymbol{\alpha}_0$, has a mean of $\mathbf{a}_0$ and a covariance matrix $\mathbf{P}_0$, that is

$$E(\boldsymbol{\alpha}_0) = \mathbf{a}_0 \quad \text{and} \quad \text{Var}(\boldsymbol{\alpha}_0) = \mathbf{P}_0 \qquad (1.3)$$

(b) The disturbances $\boldsymbol{\varepsilon}_t$ and $\boldsymbol{\eta}_t$ are uncorrelated with each other in all time periods, and uncorrelated with the initial state, that is

$$E(\boldsymbol{\varepsilon}_t \boldsymbol{\eta}_s') = \mathbf{0} \quad \text{for all } s, t = 1, \ldots, T \qquad (1.4a)$$

and

$$E(\boldsymbol{\varepsilon}_t \boldsymbol{\alpha}_0') = \mathbf{0}, \qquad E(\boldsymbol{\eta}_t \boldsymbol{\alpha}_0') = \mathbf{0} \quad \text{for } t = 1, \ldots, T \qquad (1.4b)$$

Relaxing the assumption in (1.4a) leads to modifications in the various algorithms; see FSK, sub-section 3.2.5.

The matrices $\mathbf{Z}_t$, $\mathbf{d}_t$ and $\mathbf{H}_t$ in the measurement equation and the matrices $\mathbf{T}_t$, $\mathbf{c}_t$, $\mathbf{R}_t$ and $\mathbf{Q}_t$ in the transition equation will be referred to as the *system matrices*. Unless otherwise stated, it will be assumed that they are non-stochastic. Thus, although they may change with time, they do so in a way which is pre-determined. As a result the system is *linear* and for any value of t, $\mathbf{y}_t$ can be expressed as a linear combination of present and past $\boldsymbol{\varepsilon}_t$'s and $\boldsymbol{\eta}_t$'s and the initial state vector, $\boldsymbol{\alpha}_0$. The consequences of allowing the system matrices to depend on past observations are explored in chapter 8.

If the system matrices $\mathbf{Z}_t$, $\mathbf{d}_t$, $\mathbf{H}_t$, $\mathbf{T}_t$, $\mathbf{c}_t$, $\mathbf{R}_t$ and $\mathbf{Q}_t$ do not change over time, the model is said to be *time invariant* or *time homogeneous*. Stationary models are a special case. The transition equation in a time invariant model is a first-order vector autoregressive process.

Example 1   The AR(1) plus noise model

$$y_t = \mu_t + \varepsilon_t, \qquad\qquad \mathrm{Var}(\varepsilon_t) = \sigma_\varepsilon^2 \qquad\qquad (1.5a)$$

$$\mu_t = \phi\mu_{t-1} + \eta_t, \qquad \mathrm{Var}(\eta_t) = \sigma_\eta^2 \qquad\qquad (1.5b)$$

is a time invariant state space model with μ_t being the state.

The definition of α_t for any particular statistical model is determined by construction. Its elements may or may not be identifiable with components which have a substantive interpretation. From the technical point of view, the aim of the state space formulation is to set up α_t in such a way that it contains all the relevant information on the system at time t and that it does so by having as small a number of elements as possible. The fact that the transition equation is a first-order process is not restrictive, since higher order processes can easily be cast in the Markov form.

Example 2   Two possible state space representations for the second-order autoregressive process (2.2.8) are

$$y_t = (1 \quad 0)\alpha_t \qquad\qquad (1.6a)$$

$$\alpha_t = \begin{bmatrix} y_t \\ \phi_2 y_{t-1} \end{bmatrix} = \begin{bmatrix} \phi_1 & 1 \\ \phi_2 & 0 \end{bmatrix} \alpha_{t-1} + \begin{bmatrix} 1 \\ 0 \end{bmatrix} \varepsilon_t \qquad\qquad (1.6b)$$

and

$$y_t = (1 \quad 0)\alpha_t^* \qquad\qquad (1.7a)$$

$$\alpha_t^* = \begin{bmatrix} y_t \\ y_{t-1} \end{bmatrix} = \begin{bmatrix} \phi_1 & \phi_2 \\ 1 & 0 \end{bmatrix} \alpha_{t-1}^* + \begin{bmatrix} 1 \\ 0 \end{bmatrix} \varepsilon_t \qquad\qquad (1.7b)$$

A model does not have to be autoregressive to be put in SSF. It will be shown how any ARMA model can be put in SSF in section 4.4. For the moment we just consider the MA(1).

Example 3   The MA(1) model

$$y_t = \varepsilon_t + \theta\varepsilon_{t-1}, \qquad t = 1, \ldots, T \qquad\qquad (1.8)$$

can be put in state space form by defining the state vector $\alpha_t = (y_t, \theta\varepsilon_t)'$ and writing

$$y_t = (1 \quad 0)\alpha_t, \qquad t = 1, \ldots, T \qquad\qquad (1.9a)$$

$$\alpha_t = \begin{bmatrix} 0 & 1 \\ 0 & 0 \end{bmatrix} \alpha_{t-1} + \begin{bmatrix} 1 \\ \theta \end{bmatrix} \varepsilon_t \qquad\qquad (1.9b)$$

If $\alpha_t = (\alpha_{1t}, \alpha_{2t})'$, then $\alpha_{2t} = \theta\varepsilon_t$ and $\alpha_{1t} = \alpha_{2,t-1} + \varepsilon_t = \varepsilon_t + \theta\varepsilon_{t-1}$. Thus the first element in the state is y_t, and this is extracted by the measurement equation. A feature of this representation is that there is no measurement equation noise. There are alternative state space representations which keep the dimension of the state vector to one in this case, but at the cost of introducing correlation between the measurement and transition equation disturbances.

4.2 Filtering, Smoothing and Prediction

Once a model is in state space form, the way is open for the application of various algorithms. At the centre of these is the Kalman filter, which is a recursive procedure for calculating the optimal estimator of the state vector given all the information which is currently available; see Kalman (1960) and Kalman and Bucy (1961). Once the end of the series is reached, optimal predictions of future observations can be made. A backward recursion, known as smoothing, enables optimal estimators of the state vector to be calculated at all points in time using the full sample.

Kalman Filter

Let $\mathbf{a}_t$ denote the optimal estimator of the state vector, $\boldsymbol{\alpha}_t$, based on all the observations up to, and including, $\mathbf{y}_t$. Let $\mathbf{P}_t$ denote the $m \times m$ covariance matrix of the associated estimation error, that is

$$\mathbf{P}_t = E[(\boldsymbol{\alpha}_t - \mathbf{a}_t)(\boldsymbol{\alpha}_t - \mathbf{a}_t)'] \tag{2.1}$$

This may also be referred to as the mean square error (MSE) matrix of $\mathbf{a}_t$; it cannot properly be called the covariance matrix of $\mathbf{a}_t$ since the vector to be estimated, $\boldsymbol{\alpha}_t$, consists of random variables rather than fixed parameters.

Suppose that we are at time $t - 1$, and that $\mathbf{a}_{t-1}$ and $\mathbf{P}_{t-1}$ are given. The optimal estimator of $\boldsymbol{\alpha}_t$ is then given by the *prediction equations*

$$\mathbf{a}_{t|t-1} = \mathbf{T}_t \mathbf{a}_{t-1} + \mathbf{c}_t \tag{2.2a}$$

and

$$\mathbf{P}_{t|t-1} = \mathbf{T}_t \mathbf{P}_{t-1} \mathbf{T}_t' + \mathbf{R}_t \mathbf{Q}_t \mathbf{R}_t', \qquad t = 1, \ldots, T \tag{2.2b}$$

while the corresponding estimator of y_t is

$$\tilde{\mathbf{y}}_{t|t-1} = \mathbf{Z}_t \mathbf{a}_{t|t-1} + \mathbf{d}_t, \qquad t = 1, \ldots, T \tag{2.3a}$$

The MSE of the prediction error, or *innovation*, vector

$$v_t = \mathbf{y}_t - \tilde{\mathbf{y}}_{t|t-1} = \mathbf{Z}_t(\boldsymbol{\alpha}_t - \mathbf{a}_{t|t-1}) + \varepsilon_t, \qquad t = 1, \ldots, T \tag{2.3b}$$

is

$$\mathbf{F}_t = \mathbf{Z}_t \mathbf{P}_{t|t-1} \mathbf{Z}_t' + \mathbf{H}_t \tag{2.3c}$$

Once the new observation becomes available, the estimator of the state can be updated. The *updating equations* are

$$\mathbf{a}_t = \mathbf{a}_{t|t-1} + \mathbf{P}_{t|t-1}\mathbf{Z}_t'\mathbf{F}_t^{-1}(\mathbf{y}_t - \mathbf{Z}_t\mathbf{a}_{t|t-1} - \mathbf{d}_t) \tag{2.4a}$$

and

$$\mathbf{P}_t = \mathbf{P}_{t|t-1} - \mathbf{P}_{t|t-1}\mathbf{Z}_t'\mathbf{F}_t^{-1}\mathbf{Z}_t\mathbf{P}_{t|t-1}, \qquad t = 1, \dots, T \tag{2.4b}$$

It will be observed that the prediction error vector, $\mathbf{v}_t$, plays a key role in the updating. The more the predictor of observation deviates from its realised value, the bigger the change made to the estimator of the state.

Taken together, equations (2.2) and (2.4) make up the *Kalman filter* (KF). Given initial conditions, $\mathbf{a}_0$ and $\mathbf{P}_0$, the Kalman filter delivers the optimal estimator of the state as each new observation becomes available. When all T observations have been processed, the estimator $\mathbf{a}_T$ contains all the information needed to make predictions of future observations.

Prediction

The formulae for predicting more than one step ahead are given by simply by-passing the updating equations. Thus the optimal estimator of the state vector at times $T + l$, based on information at time T is given by

$$\mathbf{a}_{T+l|T} = \mathbf{T}_{T+l}\mathbf{a}_{T+l-1} + \mathbf{c}_{T+l}, \qquad l = 1, 2, \dots \tag{2.5a}$$

with $\mathbf{a}_{T|T} = \mathbf{a}_T$, while the associated MSE matrix is obtained from

$$\mathbf{P}_{T+l|T} = \mathbf{T}_{T+l}\mathbf{P}_{T+l-1|T}\mathbf{T}_{T+l}' + \mathbf{R}_{T+l}\mathbf{Q}_{T+l}\mathbf{R}_{T+l}', \qquad l = 1, 2, \dots \tag{2.5b}$$

with $\mathbf{P}_{T|T} = \mathbf{P}_T$. The predictor of $\mathbf{y}_{T+l}$ is

$$\tilde{\mathbf{y}}_{T+l|T} = \mathbf{Z}_{T+l}\mathbf{a}_{T+l|T} + \mathbf{d}_{T+l}, \qquad l = 1, 2, \dots \tag{2.6a}$$

with prediction MSE

$$\mathrm{MSE}(\tilde{\mathbf{y}}_{T+l|T}) = \mathbf{Z}_{T+l}\mathbf{P}_{T+l|T}\mathbf{Z}_{T+l}' + \mathbf{H}_{T+l} \tag{2.6b}$$

When the model is Gaussian, (2.6b) can be used to construct prediction intervals.

Example 1 In the AR(1) plus noise model of (1.5),

$$\tilde{y}_{T+l|T} = \phi^l a_T, \qquad l = 1, 2, \dots \tag{2.7}$$

Thus the forecast function damps down exponentially to zero as in a standard AR(1) model, but it starts from an estimator of the unobserved component, μ_T, rather than from the last observation itself. Solving (2.5b) and substituting in (2.6b) gives the forecast MSE

$$\mathrm{MSE}(\tilde{y}_{T+l|T}) = \phi^{2l}P_T + (1 + \phi^2 + \cdots + \phi^{2(l-1)})\sigma_\eta^2 + \sigma_\varepsilon^2 \tag{2.8}$$

compare with (2.6.12).

Smoothing

The aim of filtering is to estimate the state vector, $\boldsymbol{\alpha}_t$, conditional on the information available at time t. The aim of smoothing is to take account of the information made available after time t. The smoothed estimator, known simply as the *smoother* and denoted $\mathbf{a}_{t|T}$, is based on more information than the filtered estimator, and so it will have an MSE matrix, $\mathbf{P}_{t|T}$, which, in general, is smaller than that of the filtered estimator.

There are basically three smoothing algorithms in a linear model. *Fixed-point* smoothing is concerned with computing smoothed estimators of the state vector at some fixed point in time. Thus it gives $\mathbf{a}_{\tau|t}$ for particular values of τ at all time periods $t > \tau$. *Fixed-lag* smoothing computes smoothed estimators for a fixed delay, that is $\mathbf{a}_{t-j|t}$ for $j = 1, \ldots, M$, where M is some maximum lag. Both of these algorithms can be applied in an *on-line* situation. *Fixed-interval* smoothing, on the other hand, is concerned with computing the full set of smoothed estimators for a fixed span of data. Hence it is an *off-line* technique which yields $\mathbf{a}_{t|T}$, $t = 1, \ldots, T$. It therefore tends to be the most widely used algorithm for economic and social data. The basic algorithm is set out below, although it should be noted that there are many ways in which its computational efficiency can be improved; see Koopman (1993).

The fixed-interval smoothing algorithm consists of a set of recursions which start with the final quantities, $\mathbf{a}_T$ and $\mathbf{P}_T$, given by the Kalman filter and work backwards. The equations are

$$\mathbf{a}_{t|T} = \mathbf{a}_t + \mathbf{P}_t^*(\mathbf{a}_{t+1|T} - \mathbf{T}_{t+1}\mathbf{a}_t - \mathbf{c}_{t+1}) \qquad (2.9a)$$

and

$$\mathbf{P}_{t|T} = \mathbf{P}_t + \mathbf{P}_t^*(\mathbf{P}_{t+1|T} - \mathbf{P}_{t+1|t})\mathbf{P}_t^{*\prime} \qquad (2.9b)$$

where

$$\mathbf{P}_t^* = \mathbf{P}_t\mathbf{T}_{t+1}'\mathbf{P}_{t+1|t}^{-1}, \qquad t = T-1, \ldots, 1 \qquad (2.9c)$$

with $\mathbf{a}_{T|T} = \mathbf{a}_T$ and $\mathbf{P}_{T|T} = \mathbf{P}_T$. As it stands, the algorithm therefore requires that $\mathbf{a}_t$ and $\mathbf{P}_t$ be stored for all t so that they can be combined with $\mathbf{a}_{t+1|T}$ and $\mathbf{P}_{t+1|T}$.

State space smoothing algorithms are more general than the classical signal extraction algorithms of section 2.6 since they apply to finite samples and to systems which need not be time invariant. The attraction of the classical formulae is that they are easy to interpret.

Initialisation of the Kalman Filter

If the state is generated by a stationary process, the initial conditions for the Kalman filter are given by its unconditional mean and variance.

Example 1 (contd)   In the AR(1) plus noise model the unconditional mean and variance are zero and

$$P_0 = \sigma_\eta^2/(1 - \phi^2) \tag{2.10}$$

respectively; see (2.2.7).

More generally, for a stationary, time invariant transition equation of the form (1.2) the mean is

$$\mathbf{a}_0 = (\mathbf{I} - \mathbf{T})^{-1}\mathbf{c} \tag{2.11a}$$

while the unconditional covariance matrix is given by

$$\text{vec}(\mathbf{P}_0) = [\mathbf{I} - \mathbf{T} \otimes \mathbf{T}]^{-1}\text{vec}(\mathbf{RQR}') \tag{2.11b}$$

see (7.3.12). This is valid even if the matrices $\mathbf{Z}_t$, $\mathbf{H}_t$ and $\mathbf{d}_t$ in the measurement equation are not time invariant.

If the transition equation is not stationary, and the initial conditions are not given as part of the model specification, they must be estimated from the observations themselves. There are two approaches. The first assumes that the initial state, $\boldsymbol{\alpha}_0$, is fixed. Its distribution is then degenerate as $\mathbf{P}_0 = \mathbf{0}$. However, since $\boldsymbol{\alpha}_0$ is unknown, its elements must be estimated by treating them as unknown parameters in the model. The second approach assumes that $\boldsymbol{\alpha}_0$ is random and has a *diffuse* distribution, that is its covariance matrix is $\mathbf{P}_0 = \kappa\mathbf{I}$, with $\kappa \to \infty$. This says that nothing is known about the initial state. The result is that starting values are effectively constructed from the initial observations.

Example 2   If in (1.5) ϕ is 1, so that μ_t is a random walk, the Kalman filter equations yield the following estimator of μ_1:

$$a_1 = a_0 + \frac{P_0 + \sigma_\eta^2}{P_0 + \sigma_\eta^2 + \sigma_\varepsilon^2}(y_1 - a_0) \tag{2.12a}$$

The corresponding MSE is

$$P_1 = P_0 + \sigma_\eta^2 - \frac{(P_0 + \sigma_\eta^2)^2}{P_0 + \sigma_\eta^2 + \sigma_\varepsilon^2} \tag{2.12b}$$

In the limit as $P_0 \to \infty$,

$$a_1 = y_1 \quad \text{and} \quad P_1 = \sigma_\varepsilon^2$$

irrespective of the value given to a_0. Thus a diffuse prior for μ_0 gives the same result as explicitly using y_1 as an estimator of μ_1 and noting that the associated estimation error is

$$E[(y_1 - \mu_1)^2] = E(\varepsilon_t^2) = \sigma_\varepsilon^2$$

Starting the Kalman filter off with κ equal to a large but finite number can give an approximation to the filter which would be obtained with diffuse initial conditions. However, this is not entirely satisfactory, particularly as the presence of large numbers in the filter can lead to numerical instability. Algorithms which overcome these problems have been designed by Ansley and Kohn (1985) and de Jong (1991).

4.3 Gaussian Models and the Likelihood Function

In a Gaussian state space model, the disturbances ε_t and η_t, and the initial state vector, α_0, are normally distributed. Under these assumptions it is relatively straightforward to derive the Kalman filter. The way in which the likelihood function can be constructed from the prediction errors then follows almost immediately.

Derivation of the Kalman Filter

The initial state is normally distributed with mean $\mathbf{a}_0$ and covariance matrix $\mathbf{P}_0$. The state vector at time $t = 1$ is given by

$$\alpha_1 = \mathbf{T}_1\alpha_0 + \mathbf{c}_1 + \mathbf{R}_1\eta_1 \tag{3.1}$$

Thus α_1 is a linear combination of two vectors of random variables, both of which have multivariate normal distributions, and a vector of constants. Hence it is also normal, with mean

$$\mathbf{a}_{1|0} = \mathbf{T}_1\mathbf{a}_0 + \mathbf{c}_1 \tag{3.2a}$$

and covariance matrix

$$\mathbf{P}_{1|0} = \mathbf{T}_1\mathbf{P}_0\mathbf{T}_1' + \mathbf{R}_1\mathbf{Q}_1\mathbf{R}_1' \tag{3.2b}$$

The notation $a_{1|0}$ serves to indicate the mean of the distribution of α_1 conditional on the information at time $t = 0$.

In order to obtain the distribution of α_1 conditional on y_1, we write

$$\alpha_1 = \mathbf{a}_{1|0} + (\alpha_1 - \mathbf{a}_{1|0}) \tag{3.3a}$$

$$\mathbf{y}_1 = \mathbf{Z}_1\mathbf{a}_{1|0} + \mathbf{d}_1 + \mathbf{Z}_1(\alpha_1 - \mathbf{a}_{1|0}) + \varepsilon_t \tag{3.3b}$$

The second of these equations is simply a re-arrangement of the measurement equation. It can be seen directly from (3.3) that the normally distributed vector $(\alpha_1'\ \mathbf{y}_1')'$ has a mean and covariance matrix given by

$$\begin{bmatrix} \mathbf{a}_{1|0} \\ \mathbf{Z}_1\mathbf{a}_{1|0} + \mathbf{d}_1 \end{bmatrix} \quad \text{and} \quad \begin{bmatrix} \mathbf{P}_{1|0} & \mathbf{P}_{1|0}\mathbf{Z}_1' \\ \mathbf{Z}_1\mathbf{P}_{1|0} & \mathbf{Z}_1\mathbf{P}_{1|0}\mathbf{Z}_1' + \mathbf{H}_1 \end{bmatrix}$$

respectively. It now follows from the properties of the multivariate distribution, as given in appendix A, that the distribution of $\boldsymbol{\alpha}_1$, conditional on a particular realised value of $\mathbf{y}_1$, is multivariate normal with mean

$$\mathbf{a}_1 = \mathbf{a}_{1|0} + \mathbf{P}_{1|0}\mathbf{Z}_1'\mathbf{F}_1^{-1}(\mathbf{y}_1 - \mathbf{Z}_1\mathbf{a}_{1|0} - \mathbf{d}_1) \qquad (3.4a)$$

and covariance matrix

$$\mathbf{P}_1 = \mathbf{P}_{1|0} - \mathbf{P}_{1|0}\mathbf{Z}_1'\mathbf{F}_1^{-1}\mathbf{Z}_1\mathbf{P}_{1|0} \qquad (3.4b)$$

where

$$\mathbf{F}_1 = \mathbf{Z}_1\mathbf{P}_{1|0}\mathbf{Z}_1' + \mathbf{H}_1 \qquad (3.4c)$$

Repeating the above steps for $t = 2, \ldots, T$ gives the Kalman filter. This derivation enables us to interpret $\mathbf{a}_t$ and $\mathbf{P}_t$ as the mean and covariance matrix of the conditional distribution of $\boldsymbol{\alpha}_t$. However, the argument in section 2.6 tells us that this conditional mean is the *minimum mean square estimate* of $\boldsymbol{\alpha}_t$. Furthermore, if $\mathbf{a}_t$ is regarded as an estima*tor* rather than an estima*te*, it can be shown to minimise the MSE when the expectation is taken over all the observations in the information set rather than being conditional on a particular set of values; see Anderson and Moore (1979, pp. 29–32) for a detailed discussion. Thus the conditional mean estimator is the *minimum mean square estimator* (MMSE) of $\boldsymbol{\alpha}_t$.

The estimator $\mathbf{a}_t$ is unbiased in the sense that the expectation of the estimation error is zero. Since this expectation can be taken over all observations in the information set, this property is sometimes referred to as unconditional unbiasedness. Furthermore, since the $\mathbf{P}_t$ matrix is independent of the observations, it is also the *unconditional* error covariance matrix associated with $\mathbf{a}_t$. In other words the expectation in (2.1) need not be conditional on the realised observation up to and including time t.

When the disturbances in the state space model are not normally distributed, it is no longer true, in general, that the Kalman filter yields the conditional mean of the state vector. However, if attention is restricted to estimators which are *linear* combinations of the observations, then $\mathbf{a}_t$ is the one which minimises the MSE. Thus $\mathbf{a}_t$ is the *minimum mean square linear estimator* (MMSLE) of $\boldsymbol{\alpha}_t$ based on observations up to and including time t. This estimator is unconditionally unbiased and the unconditional covariance matrix of the estimation error is again the $\mathbf{P}_t$ matrix given by the Kalman filter; see Duncan and Horn (1972).

The above points apply in exactly the same way to $\mathbf{a}_{t|t-1}$ and $\mathbf{P}_{t|t-1}$. Furthermore, the conditional mean of $\mathbf{y}_t$ at time $t-1$, namely $\tilde{\mathbf{y}}_{t|t-1}$ of (2.3a), can be interpreted as the MMSE of $\mathbf{y}_t$ in a Gaussian model, and as the MMSLE otherwise.

Maximum Likelihood

In a state space model the system matrices will usually depend on a set of unknown parameters. These will be denoted by the $n \times 1$ vector ψ and referred to as *hyperparameters*. For example, in the AR(1) plus noise model of (1.5), the hyperparameters are σ_η^2, ϕ and σ_ε^2. ML estimation of the hyper-parameters can be carried out by using the Kalman filter to construct the likelihood function and then maximising it using a suitable numerical optimisation procedure.

As was shown in section 3.1, the joint density function of a set of T observations can be expressed in terms of conditional distributions. For a multivariate model

$$L(\mathbf{y};\psi) = \prod_{t=1}^{T} p(\mathbf{y}_t | Y_{t-1}) \qquad (3.5)$$

where $p(\mathbf{y}_t | Y_{t-1})$ denotes the distribution of y_t conditional on the information set at time $t-1$, that is $Y_{t-1} = \{\mathbf{y}_{t-1}, \mathbf{y}_{t-2}, \ldots, \mathbf{y}_1\}$. From the derivation of the Kalman filter in the previous sub-section, it will be recalled that, conditional on Y_{t-1}, α_t is normally distributed with a mean of $\mathbf{a}_{t|t-1}$ and a covariance matrix of $\mathbf{P}_{t|t-1}$. If the measurement equation is written as

$$\mathbf{y}_t = \mathbf{Z}_t \mathbf{a}_{t|t-1} + \mathbf{Z}_t(\alpha_t - \mathbf{a}_{t|t-1}) + \mathbf{d}_t + \varepsilon_t \qquad (3.6)$$

it can be seen immediately that the conditional distribution of y_t is normal with mean

$$\tilde{\mathbf{y}}_{t|t-1} = \mathbf{Z}_t \mathbf{a}_{t|t-1} + \mathbf{d}_t \qquad (3.7)$$

and a covariance matrix, $\mathbf{F}_t$, given by (2.3c). For a Gaussian model, therefore, the likelihood function (3.5) can be written down immediately as

$$\log L(\psi) = -\frac{NT}{2} \log 2\pi - \frac{1}{2} \sum_{t=1}^{T} \log |\mathbf{F}_t| - \frac{1}{2} \sum_{t=1}^{T} \mathbf{v}_t' \mathbf{F}_t^{-1} \mathbf{v}_t \qquad (3.8)$$

where v_t is the vector of prediction errors, (2.3b). Expression (3.8) is known as the *prediction error decomposition* form of the likelihood, and it generalises (3.1.23).

A univariate model can usually be re-parameterised so that $\psi = (\psi_*', \sigma_*^2)'$ where ψ_* is a vector containing $n-1$ parameters and σ_*^2 is a scale factor, usually corresponding to the variance of one of the disturbances in the model. The measurement equation may be written as

$$y_t = \mathbf{z}_t' \alpha_t + d_t + \varepsilon_t, \qquad \text{Var}(\varepsilon_t) = \sigma_*^2 h_t, \qquad t = 1, \ldots, T \qquad (3.9)$$

where z_t is an $m \times 1$ vector and h_t is a scalar, while the transition equation is unchanged except that the covariance matrix of the disturbance η_t is redefined as $\sigma_*^2 \mathbf{Q}_t$. If the initial covariance matrix, $\mathbf{P}_0$, is also specified up to the factor of proportionality, σ_*^2, that is $\mathrm{Var}(\boldsymbol{\alpha}_0) = \sigma_*^2 \mathbf{P}_0$, the Kalman filter can be run independently of σ_*^2. The main reason for proceeding in this way is that if σ_*^2 is an unknown parameter, it can be concentrated out of the likelihood function. The prediction errors are unaffected by the omission of σ_*^2 from the Kalman filter, but their variances can now be expressed as

$$\mathrm{Var}(v_t) = \sigma_*^2 f_t \tag{3.10}$$

In terms of (3.8), $\mathbf{F}_t = \sigma_*^2 f_t$, and so the log–likelihood function is

$$\log L(\boldsymbol{\psi}_*, \sigma_*^2) = -\frac{T}{2} \log 2\pi - \frac{T}{2} \log \sigma_*^2$$

$$-\frac{1}{2} \sum_{t=1}^{T} \log f_t - \frac{1}{2\sigma_*^2} \sum_{t=1}^{T} v_t^2 / f_t \tag{3.11}$$

This is basically the same as (3.2.21) where σ_*^2 is defined unambiguously as the variance of the single disturbance term.

Since v_t and f_t do not depend on σ_*^2, differentiating (3.11) with respect to σ_*^2 and equating to zero gives

$$\tilde{\sigma}_*^2(\boldsymbol{\psi}_*) = \frac{1}{T} \sum_{t=1}^{T} \frac{v_t^2}{f_t} \tag{3.12}$$

The notation $\tilde{\sigma}_*^2(\boldsymbol{\psi}_*)$ indicates that (3.12) is the ML estimator of σ_*^2 conditional on a given value of $\boldsymbol{\psi}_*$. Substituting in (3.11) gives the concentrated log–likelihood function

$$\log L_c(\boldsymbol{\psi}_*) = -\frac{T}{2}(\log 2\pi + 1) - \frac{1}{2} \sum_{t=1}^{T} \log f_t - \frac{T}{2} \log \tilde{\sigma}_*^2(\boldsymbol{\psi}_*) \tag{3.13a}$$

which must be maximised with respect to the elements of $\boldsymbol{\psi}_*$. Alternatively the modified sum of squares function

$$S(\boldsymbol{\psi}_*) = \left(\prod_{t=1}^{T} f_t \right) \sum_{t=1}^{T} (v_t^2 / f_t) \tag{3.13b}$$

may be minimised.

Example 1 The AR(1) plus noise model (1.5) may be re-parameterised by letting σ_ε^2 play the role of σ_*^2. Thus

$$\mathrm{Var}(\varepsilon_t) = \sigma_\varepsilon^2 \qquad \text{and} \qquad \mathrm{Var}(\eta_t) = \sigma_\varepsilon^2 q$$

so that $\boldsymbol{\psi}_*$ only contains q, the signal–noise ratio. The Kalman filter depends only on q, with the initial conditions such that, instead of (2.10),

$$P_0 = q / (1 - \phi^2) \tag{3.14}$$

As illustrated by the above example, the Kalman filter can be initialised with the mean and covariance matrix of the unconditional distribution of α_t when α_t is stationary. For non-stationary state vectors, a likelihood function can be formed from all T prediction errors as in (3.8), only if prior information is available such that α_0 has a proper distribution with known mean, $\mathbf{a}_0$, and bounded covariance matrix, $\mathbf{P}_0$. However, outside a Bayesian framework, a proper prior distribution for the initial state is rarely part of the model specification. In such cases, the initial state effectively has a *diffuse prior*. As was noted in section 4.2, diffuse initial conditions lead to starting values being formed from the observations. If the state vector in a univariate model contains d non-stationary elements, it is normally the case that a proper distribution for the state can be constructed at time $t = d$, using the first d observations. The joint density function of $y_{d+1}, \ldots, y_T$, conditional on $y_1, \ldots, y_d$ is then given by the prediction error decomposition (3.11), with the summations running from $t = d + 1$ instead of $t = 1$. A more formal justification for this argument can be found in de Jong (1988). An algorithm for carrying out the computations in the general case is given in de Jong (1991).

Example 1 (contd)   Suppose that the parameter ϕ in (1.5) is not assumed to be less than one in absolute value and that σ_ε^2 is zero, so there is no measurement error. A Gaussian likelihood function can be constructed conditional on the first observation, as noted below (3.1.18). The ML estimator is then given by regressing y_t on y_{t-1} for $t = 2, \ldots, T$.

When σ_ε^2 is not zero, the use of a diffuse prior for μ_0 leads to μ_1 having the proper distribution

$$\mu_1 \sim N(y_1, \sigma_\varepsilon^2)$$

see the result below (2.12). The likelihood function is then constructed from the prediction error decomposition with the summation from 2 to T.

If the initialisation problem is handled by treating α_0 as a vector of fixed parameters which have to be estimated, these parameters can be concentrated out of the likelihood function; see Rosenberg (1973) and de Jong (1988). However, the properties of estimators obtained in this way appear to be less satisfactory than estimators based on the diffuse prior approach. This argument is strengthened by the observation that the diffuse prior likelihood is, in fact, the *marginal likelihood* for the model with α_0 fixed. The use of a marginal likelihood is generally regarded as being preferable when a model contains nuisance parameters, in this case the elements of α_0; see Shephard (1993).

Example 1 (contd)   As previously, suppose that the autoregressive parameter ϕ is not assumed to be less than one in absolute value and that σ_ε^2 is zero. If y_0 is treated as an unknown parameter, the likelihood function is

$$\log L(\phi, \sigma_\eta^2) = -\frac{T}{2} \log 2\pi - \frac{T}{2} \log \sigma_\eta^2 - \frac{1}{2\sigma_\eta^2} \sum_{t=1}^{T} (y_t - \phi y_{t-1})^2$$

The ML estimator of y_0 is y_1/ϕ, but the ML estimator of ϕ is exactly as before. The only difference is that the estimator of σ_η^2 has a divisor of T rather than $T - 1$; although it is nominally based on T prediction errors, the first is identically zero.

If σ_ε^2 is not assumed to be zero, but ϕ is assumed to be one, the estimator of the signal–noise ratio, q, has some unsatisfactory features when μ_0 is treated as an unknown parameter; see Shephard and Harvey (1990).

Residuals and Diagnostic Checking

In a Gaussian model, the joint density function of the observations is given by the right hand side of (3.8). This is also the joint density function of the innovations which are consequently independently and normally distributed, that is

$$\mathbf{v}_t \sim \text{NID}(\mathbf{0}, \mathbf{F}_t), \qquad t = 1, \ldots, T \qquad (3.15)$$

The standardised residuals, $\mathbf{F}_t^{-1/2}\mathbf{v}_t$, are therefore useful for diagnostic checking, although if the system matrices contain unknown hyperparameters which are replaced by estimators, (3.15) does not usually hold exactly. For a univariate model, formulated as in (3.9), with the state containing d non-stationary elements, it follows from (3.10) that we can write

$$\tilde{v}_t = v_t/\sqrt{f_t} \sim \text{NID}(0, \sigma_*^2), \qquad t = d + 1, \ldots, T \qquad (3.16)$$

In the absence of the normality assumption the mean of the innovation vector is still a zero vector, while its covariance matrix at time t is $\mathbf{F}_t$. In addition the innovations in different time periods can be shown to be uncorrelated.

Other residuals can also be constructed, although they will not have the independence property of the innovations. Nevertheless, they may play a useful role as diagnostics. In particular, the estimators of the measurement equation noise, $\boldsymbol{\varepsilon}_t$, and the transition equation noise, $\boldsymbol{\eta}_t$, calculated from the smoother as

$$\tilde{\boldsymbol{\varepsilon}}_{t|T} = \mathbf{y}_t - \mathbf{Z}_t \mathbf{a}_{t|T} - \mathbf{d}_t \qquad (3.17\text{a})$$

and

$$\tilde{\boldsymbol{\eta}}_{t|T} = \mathbf{a}_{t|T} - \mathbf{T}_t \mathbf{a}_{t-1|T} - \mathbf{c}_t, \qquad t = 1, \ldots, T \qquad (3.17\text{b})$$

can help to detect outliers and structural breaks; see Koopman (1993).

Missing Observations and Other Data Irregularities

Missing observations pose no problems when handled in the state space framework. If an observation is missing at a particular point in time, $t = \tau$, the Kalman filter updating equations are redundant. Thus

$$\mathbf{a}_\tau = \mathbf{a}_{\tau|\tau-1} \quad \text{and} \quad \mathbf{P}_\tau = \mathbf{P}_{\tau|\tau-1}$$

The prediction equations then yield what is actually a two-step ahead predictor and the updating equations are applied in the usual way when the observation $\mathbf{y}_{\tau+1}$ becomes available. The smoothing equations give an estimator of the state at time τ. Hence the estimator of the missing observation, together with its MSE, can be computed.

The likelihood function is computed in the usual way using the innovations from the Kalman filter, except, of course, that there is no innovation corresponding to the missing observation. Thus there are no terms at time τ, and the innovation at time $\tau + 1$ is a two-step ahead prediction error. In terms of (3.5), there is no conditional distribution at time τ, and the distribution at time $\tau + 1$ is conditional on the information at time $\tau - 1$.

Example 2 In the AR(1) plus noise model it follows from (2.7) and (2.8) that the distribution of $y_{\tau+1}|Y_{\tau-1}$ is normal with mean $\phi^2 a_{\tau-1}$ and variance $\phi^4 P_{\tau-1} + (1 + \phi^2)\sigma_\eta^2 + \sigma_\varepsilon^2$.

The above results generalise straightforwardly to any linear Gaussian state space model irrespective of how many missing observations there are, and where they are located. Thus, for example, if m consecutive observations are missing, the mean and variance of an $m + 1$-step ahead predictive distribution will enter into the likelihood.

The Kalman filter can also handle situations where observations are aggregated over time, and only the aggregate is observed. This happens if a series on a flow variable, such as national income, consists of some annual observations, followed by quarterly observations. The solution is to extend the state vector to include a variable which is able to cumulate the series at the points where it is not observed.

Other types of data irregularity can be treated by the state space approach. For example, a model can be built to account for the data revisions which are often made to time series by government agencies. Further details can be found in FSK, section 6.4.

4.4 Autoregressive-Moving Average Models

The Kalman filter can be used to construct the exact likelihood function of an ARMA model. If we define $m = \max(p, q + 1)$, the general ARMA(p, q)

model, (2.1.27), can be written in the form

$$y_t = \phi_1 y_{t-1} + \cdots + \phi_m y_{t-m} + \varepsilon_t + \theta_1 \varepsilon_{t-1} + \cdots + \theta_{m-1} \varepsilon_{t-m+1} \qquad (4.1)$$

where some of the AR or MA coefficients will be zero unless $p = q + 1$. A Markovian representation of (4.1) is then obtained by defining an $m \times 1$ vector, $\boldsymbol{\alpha}_t$, which obeys the multivariate AR(1) model

$$\boldsymbol{\alpha}_t = \begin{bmatrix} \phi_1 & \\ \phi_2 & \\ \vdots & \mathbf{I}_{m-1} \\ \phi_m & \mathbf{0}' \end{bmatrix} \boldsymbol{\alpha}_{t-1} + \begin{bmatrix} 1 \\ \theta_1 \\ \vdots \\ \theta_{m-1} \end{bmatrix} \varepsilon_t \qquad (4.2a)$$

This may be regarded as a transition equation (1.2) in which $\mathbf{T}_t$ and $\mathbf{R}_t$ are constant and $\mathbf{Q}_t = \sigma^2$. The original ARMA model may easily be recovered by noting that the first element of $\boldsymbol{\alpha}_t$ is identically equal to y_t. This can be seen by repeated substitution, starting at the bottom row of the system. The role of the measurement equation is simply to extract the first element of the state vector. Thus

$$y_t = \mathbf{z}_t' \boldsymbol{\alpha}_t, \qquad t = 1, \ldots, T \qquad (4.2b)$$

where $\mathbf{z}_t' = (1 \ \mathbf{0}_{m-1}')'$. The disturbance term is identically zero, unless the model is subject to measurement error as, for example, in (1.5).

The AR(2) model as formulated in (1.6) is a special case of the above state space representation, as is the MA(1) model of (1.9). As indicated in the previous sub-section, missing observations are easily handled in this framework; see Jones (1980).

Provided the model is stationary, the initial conditions for the state are given by (2.11a). The Kalman filter then gives the likelihood function in the form (3.11). In order to illustrate this and clarify the difference with the CSS algorithm we focus attention on the MA(1) model.

The transition equation for an MA(1) model was given in (1.9b). The initial state vector is $\mathbf{a}_0 = \mathbf{a}_{1|0} = \mathbf{0}$. Since $\boldsymbol{\alpha}_t = (y_t, \theta \varepsilon_t)'$, the initial matrix $\mathbf{P}_0 = \mathbf{P}_{1|0}$ may be obtained directly as

$$\mathbf{P}_{1|0} = \mathbf{P}_0 = \sigma^{-2} E(\boldsymbol{\alpha}_t \boldsymbol{\alpha}_t') = \begin{bmatrix} 1 + \theta^2 & \theta \\ \theta & \theta^2 \end{bmatrix} \qquad (4.3)$$

The first prediction error is $v_1 = y_1$, while $f_1 = 1 + \theta^2$. Application of the updating formulae gives

$$\mathbf{a}_1 = \begin{pmatrix} y_1 \\ \theta y_1/(1 + \theta^2) \end{pmatrix} \quad \text{and} \quad \mathbf{P}_1 = \begin{pmatrix} 0 & 0 \\ 0 & \theta^4/(1 + \theta^2) \end{pmatrix} \qquad (4.4)$$

The prediction equations for α_2 are

$$\mathbf{a}_{2|1} = \begin{pmatrix} y_1\theta/(1+\theta^2) \\ 0 \end{pmatrix} \tag{4.5}$$

and

$$\mathbf{P}_{2|1} = \begin{pmatrix} \theta^4/(1+\theta^2) & 0 \\ 0 & 0 \end{pmatrix} + \begin{pmatrix} 1 & \theta \\ \theta & \theta^2 \end{pmatrix}$$

$$= \begin{pmatrix} (1+\theta^2+\theta^4)/(1+\theta^2) & \theta \\ \theta & \theta^2 \end{pmatrix} \tag{4.6}$$

and so

$$v_2 = y_2 - \theta y_1/(1+\theta^2) \text{ and } f_2 = (1+\theta^2+\theta^4)/(1+\theta^2) \tag{4.7}$$

On repeating this process further, it will be seen that the Kalman filter is effectively computing the prediction errors from the recursion

$$v_t = y_t - \theta v_{t-1}/f_{t-1}, \qquad t = 1, \ldots, T \tag{4.8}$$

where $v_0 = 0$, and

$$f_t = 1 + \theta^{2t}/[1 + \theta^2 + \cdots + \theta^{2(t-1)}] \tag{4.9}$$

An examination of the equations (4.4) to (4.9) is instructive, in that it provides a useful insight into the relationship between the conditional and exact likelihood functions. In both procedures the first prediction error is y_1, but in CSS the assumption that $\varepsilon_0 = 0$ means that $\mathrm{Var}(y_1) = \mathrm{Var}(\varepsilon_1) = \sigma^2$. On the other hand, if ε_0 is taken to be random, $\mathrm{Var}(y_1) = \sigma^2(1+\theta^2)$. This is reflected in f_1. Allowing for the distribution of ε_0 is also apparent in the second prediction error, (4.7), and its associated variance. In terms of the recursion in (4.8), the simplifying assumption in CSS means that f_{t-1} is effectively set equal to unity for all t.

When $|\theta| < 1$, f_t tends towards unity as t increases. Thus for a sufficiently large value of t, the prediction error recursion, (4.8), may be approximated by the CSS recursion (3.3.2). This feature is exploited in the algorithm by Gardner *et al.* (1980), where f_t is monitored. Once it becomes 'reasonably close' to unity, the program switches to evaluating the prediction errors from a CSS recursion. A small number, δ, defines what is meant by 'reasonably close' in this context, the switch being made when $f_t < 1 + \delta$. Making δ smaller has the effect of diminishing the error in the approximation, but at the cost of increasing t^*, the value of t at which the switch takes place. A guide to the choice of δ is given in Gardner *et al.* (1980) where table I shows the trade-off between t^* and the error of approximation. Setting $\delta = 0.01$ appears to be a reasonable compromise.

When $|\theta| > 1$

$$\lim_{t \to \infty} f_t = \theta^2 > 1, \qquad |\theta| > 1 \tag{4.10}$$

Non-invertible solutions will therefore be detected by monitoring f_t. However, a non-invertible θ will give exactly the same prediction errors, and exactly the same likelihood function, as the corresponding invertible parameter, $1/\theta$. Note that when $|\theta| = 1$, f_t converges to unity, but does so more slowly than when $|\theta| < 1$, since it is equal to $(1 + t)/t$ for $t = 1, 2, \ldots, T$.

Efficient filtering algorithms for ARMA models have been developed by Mélard (1984) and Mittnik (1991). However, computing the exact likelihood will always be more time consuming than computing the conditional sum of squares. Furthermore, the fact that analytic derivatives are readily available in the CSS case means that numerical optimisation can, as a rule, be carried out more efficiently. Nevertheless, exact ML estimation may have some statistical advantages, particularly if the MA parameters lie close to, or on, the boundary of the invertibility region. The evidence for this assertion was presented in section 3.6.

4.5 Regression and Time-Varying Parameters

Consider a classical linear regression model,

$$y_t = \mathbf{x}_t' \boldsymbol{\beta} + \varepsilon_t, \qquad t = 1, \ldots, T \tag{5.1}$$

where $\mathbf{x}_t$ is a $k \times 1$ vector of exogenous explanatory variables and $\boldsymbol{\beta}$ is the corresponding $k \times 1$ vector of unknown parameters. The first sub-section below shows how the OLS estimator may be computed recursively, and how this may be regarded as an application of the Kalman filter. The model is then extended so that $\boldsymbol{\beta}$ is allowed to evolve over time according to various stochastic processes. The statistical treatment of such models via state space methods is described.

Recursive Least Squares

Suppose that an estimator of $\boldsymbol{\beta}$ in (5.1) has been calculated using the first $t - 1$ observations. The tth observation may be used to construct a new estimator without inverting a cross-product matrix as implied by a direct use of the OLS formula

$$\mathbf{b}_t = \left(\sum_{j=1}^{t} \mathbf{x}_j \mathbf{x}_j' \right)^{-1} \sum_{j=1}^{t} \mathbf{x}_j y_j \tag{5.2}$$

This is done by means of recursive updating formulae. If $\mathbf{X}_t = (\mathbf{x}_1, \ldots, \mathbf{x}_t)'$, then

$$\mathbf{b}_t = \mathbf{b}_{t-1} + (\mathbf{X}'_{t-1}\mathbf{X}_{t-1})^{-1}\mathbf{x}_t(y_t - \mathbf{x}'_t\mathbf{b}_{t-1})/f_t \tag{5.3a}$$

and

$$(\mathbf{X}'_t\mathbf{X}_t)^{-1} = (\mathbf{X}'_{t-1}\mathbf{X}_{t-1})^{-1}$$
$$- (\mathbf{X}'_{t-1}\mathbf{X}_{t-1})^{-1}\mathbf{x}_t\mathbf{x}'_t(\mathbf{X}'_{t-1}\mathbf{X}_{t-1})^{-1}/f_t \tag{5.3b}$$

where

$$f_t = 1 + \mathbf{x}'_t(\mathbf{X}'_{t-1}\mathbf{X}_{t-1})^{-1}\mathbf{x}_t, \qquad t = k+1, \ldots, T \tag{5.3c}$$

A minimum of k observations are needed to compute an OLS estimator of β. If $\mathbf{X}_k$ is of full rank, the estimator based on the first k observations is

$$\mathbf{b}_k = (\mathbf{X}'_k\mathbf{X}_k)^{-1}\mathbf{X}'_k\mathbf{y}_k = \mathbf{X}_k^{-1}\mathbf{y}_k \tag{5.4}$$

where $\mathbf{y}_k = (y_1, \ldots, y_k)'$. This provides a starting value and the estimators $\mathbf{b}_{k+1}, \ldots, \mathbf{b}_T$ can be computed with no further matrix inversions. The final estimator, $\mathbf{b}_T$, is identical to the standard OLS estimator based on all T observations.

The *recursive least squares* updating formulae can be derived using the matrix inversion lemma given in appendix B. However, they are a special case of the Kalman filter. The regression model in (5.1) may be identified directly with a measurement equation of the form (3.9) by setting $\mathbf{z}_t = \mathbf{x}_t$, $h_t = 1$ and $\boldsymbol{\alpha}_t = \boldsymbol{\beta}$. The transition equation is simply $\boldsymbol{\alpha}_t = \boldsymbol{\alpha}_{t-1}$ and so $\mathbf{T} = \mathbf{I}$ while $\mathbf{Q} = \mathbf{0}$. The prediction equations are therefore trivial as they reduce to the identities $\mathbf{a}_{t|t-1} = \mathbf{a}_{t-1}$ and $\mathbf{P}_{t|t-1} = \mathbf{P}_{t-1}$, while the OLS updating formulae are obtained directly from the updating equations (2.4) with

$$\mathbf{P}_t = (\mathbf{X}'_t\mathbf{X}_t)^{-1}, \qquad t = k, \ldots, T$$

The initialisation in (5.4) is implied by the use of a diffuse prior to initialise the Kalman filter.

When the OLS estimator is computed recursively, a set of $T - k$ prediction errors

$$v_t = y_t - \mathbf{x}'_t\mathbf{b}_{t-1}, \qquad t = k+1, \ldots, T \tag{5.5}$$

are obtained. These have zero mean, variance $\sigma^2 f_t$ and are uncorrelated; see (3.16) and EATS, section 2.6. The standardised prediction errors

$$\tilde{v}_t = v_t/\sqrt{f_t}, \qquad t = k+1, \ldots, T \tag{5.6}$$

are known as *recursive residuals* and they figure prominently in procedures for checking the specification and stability of regression models. A full description of these methods will be found in EATS, section 5.2. Remember that if the disturbances in (5.1) are normally distributed, the recursive residuals are also normal; that is $\varepsilon_t \sim \text{NID}(0, \sigma^2)$ implies $\tilde{v}_t \sim \text{NID}(0, \sigma^2)$.

The recursive residuals feature in the updating formula for the residual sum of squares, or sum of squared errors (SSE). This recursion is

$$\text{SSE}_t = \text{SSE}_{t-1} + v_t^2, \qquad t = k+1, \ldots, T \qquad (5.7)$$

where

$$\text{SSE}_t = (y_t - \mathbf{X}_t \mathbf{b}_t)'(y_t - \mathbf{X}_t \mathbf{b}_t), \qquad t = k, \ldots, T \qquad (5.8)$$

Since $\text{SSE}_k = 0$ it follows that the residual sum of squares from all T observations is equal to the sum of the squares of the recursive residuals, that is

$$\text{SSE}_T = \sum_{t=k+1}^{T} v_t^2 \qquad (5.9)$$

The use of (5.7) in conjunction with (5.3) allows the covariance matrix of $\mathbf{b}_t$ to be estimated as the recursion proceeds.

Random Walk Parameters

The random walk time-varying parameter model is

$$y_t = \mathbf{x}_t' \boldsymbol{\beta}_t + \varepsilon_t, \qquad t = 1, \ldots, T \qquad (5.10a)$$

where $\varepsilon_t \sim \text{NID}(0, \sigma^2)$ and the vector $\boldsymbol{\beta}_t$ is generated by the process

$$\boldsymbol{\beta}_t = \boldsymbol{\beta}_{t-1} + \boldsymbol{\eta}_t \qquad (5.10b)$$

where $\boldsymbol{\eta}_t \sim \text{NID}(0, \sigma^2 \mathbf{Q})$. Because $\boldsymbol{\beta}_t$ is non-stationary, it is able to evolve in such a way that the model can accommodate fundamental changes in structure. The $k \times k$ PSD matrix $\mathbf{Q}$ determines the extent to which it can vary. If $\mathbf{Q} = \mathbf{0}$, the model collapses to a regression model, as in (5.1), since $\boldsymbol{\beta}_t = \boldsymbol{\beta}_{t-1}$. On the other hand, if $\mathbf{Q}$ is PD, all k parameters will be time varying.

The model is already in state space form, with $\boldsymbol{\beta}_t$ being the state. As in recursive least squares, the use of a diffuse prior leads to the first k observations being used to construct starting values. This may be done explicitly by expressing the first $k - 1$ coefficient vectors in terms of the kth. Thus, for example,

$$\boldsymbol{\beta}_k = \boldsymbol{\beta}_{k-1} + \boldsymbol{\eta}_t = \boldsymbol{\beta}_{k-2} + \boldsymbol{\eta}_{t-1} + \boldsymbol{\eta}_t \qquad (5.11)$$

leading to

$$\boldsymbol{\beta}_{k-2} = \boldsymbol{\beta}_k - \boldsymbol{\eta}_{t-1} - \boldsymbol{\eta}_t$$

and similarly for the other coefficient vectors. The first k equations in (5.10a) CE1may therefore be written as

$$y_t = \mathbf{x}_t' \boldsymbol{\beta}_k + \zeta_t, \qquad t = 1, \ldots, k \qquad (5.12a)$$

where $\zeta_k = \varepsilon_k$ and

$$\zeta_t = \varepsilon_t - \mathbf{x}_t'(\boldsymbol{\eta}_{t+1} + \cdots + \boldsymbol{\eta}_k), \qquad t = 1, \ldots, k-1 \qquad (5.12\text{b})$$

The covariance matrix of the disturbance vector, $\boldsymbol{\zeta}_k = (\zeta_1, \ldots, \zeta_k)'$, is $\sigma^2 \mathbf{V}$, where the ijth element of $\mathbf{V}$ is

$$v_{ij} = \delta_{ij} + [\min(k-i, k-j)] \mathbf{x}_i' \mathbf{Q} \mathbf{x}_j, \qquad i, j = 1, \ldots, k$$

where δ_{ij} is one for $i = j$ and zero otherwise; see Cooley and Prescott (1978). Writing the equations in (5.12a) in matrix form, and re-arranging, gives

$$\boldsymbol{\beta}_k = \mathbf{X}_k^{-1} \mathbf{y}_k - \boldsymbol{\zeta}_k \qquad (5.13)$$

from which it can be seen that, conditional on the first k observations, $\mathbf{y}_k$, the coefficient vector $\boldsymbol{\beta}_k$ is normally distributed with mean

$$\mathbf{b}_k = \mathbf{X}_k^{-1} \mathbf{y}_k \qquad (5.14\text{a})$$

and covariance matrix $\sigma^2 \mathbf{P}_k$, where

$$\mathbf{P}_k = (\mathbf{X}_k \mathbf{V}_k^{-1} \mathbf{X}_k')^{-1} \qquad (5.14\text{b})$$

The Kalman filter can be run using (5.14) as initial values, and the log–likelihood function constructed as in (3.11) with the summations running from $t = k + 1$, $\boldsymbol{\psi}_*$ denoting the distinct elements of $\mathbf{Q}$, and σ_*^2 being σ^2.

Example 2 Using annual observations for the period 1916–1966, Garbade (1977) estimated the following demand for money equation by OLS:

$$\Delta \widehat{\log} M1_t = 0.002 - 0.083 \, \Delta \log Rcp_t + 0.495 \, \Delta \log y_t$$

$$R^2 = 0.36, \qquad s = 0.051 \qquad \text{and} \qquad DW = 1.43$$

The variables are the narrow money supply per capita (M1), the commercial paper yield (Rcp), which is taken to represent the rate of interest, and real income per capita (y). Garbade proceeded to estimate the model under the assumption that the parameters had been generated by a random walk process, (5.10b). The matrix $\mathbf{Q}$ was taken to be diagonal and ML estimates of the three elements, q_1, q_2 and q_3, were computed by exploiting the Kalman filter in essentially the way as described above. This gave the following results:

$$\tilde{q}_1 = 0.198, \qquad \tilde{q}_2 = 2.679, \qquad \tilde{q}_3 = 5.457 \qquad \text{and} \qquad \tilde{\sigma} = 0.034$$

Having estimated $\mathbf{Q}$, Garbade smoothed estimates of the β_t's. The graphs in his paper show substantial and well-defined fluctuations in the estimates of β_{1t} and β_{2t}, but the estimated income elasticity, β_{3t}, appears to stabilise in the mid 1930s at around 0.5. However, it may be that these parameter variations are symptomatic of a mis-specified dynamic model rather than an indication of a fundamental change in the process generating the data. Indeed, it has been argued that tracking the parameters in this way is a very useful diagnostic checking procedure.

Return to Normality Model*

In the *return to normality* model the time-varying parameters in (5.10a) are generated by a stationary vector AR(1) process

$$\boldsymbol{\beta}_t = \bar{\boldsymbol{\beta}} + \boldsymbol{\Phi}(\boldsymbol{\beta}_{t-1} - \bar{\boldsymbol{\beta}}) + \boldsymbol{\eta}_t \tag{5.15}$$

where $\boldsymbol{\eta}_t \sim \text{NID}(\mathbf{0}, \sigma^2 \mathbf{Q})$. Since the matrix $\boldsymbol{\Phi}$ contains k^2 parameters, it will often be taken to be diagonal, in which case the stationarity condition is simply that its diagonal elements should be less than one in absolute value. In contrast to the model in the previous sub-section, the parameters generated in this way move around a fixed mean. Schaefer *et al.* (1975) found evidence for this kind of parameter variation in modelling a share's market risk; see also Rosenberg (1973). Note that if $\mathbf{x}_t$ contains a constant term, the disturbance term ε_t can be included in $\boldsymbol{\beta}_t$ and allowed to follow an AR(1) process.

Substituting (5.15) into (5.10a) gives the regression model

$$y_t = \mathbf{x}'_t \bar{\boldsymbol{\beta}} + u_t, \qquad t = 1, \ldots, T \tag{5.16a}$$

with a disturbance term

$$u_t = \mathbf{x}'_t (\boldsymbol{\beta}_t - \bar{\boldsymbol{\beta}}) + \varepsilon_t \tag{5.16b}$$

which is easily seen to have an expected value of zero. The *random coefficient* model is a special case in which $\boldsymbol{\Phi} = \mathbf{0}$. This is relatively straightforward to estimate as all that needs to be handled is the heteroscedasticity in the disturbances. In the more general model, the disturbances are serially correlated as well as heteroscedastic.

A regression model of the form (5.16) can be handled by treating $\bar{\boldsymbol{\beta}}$ as part of a state vector. If we let $\boldsymbol{\beta}_t^* = \boldsymbol{\beta}_t - \bar{\boldsymbol{\beta}}$, then

$$y_t = (\mathbf{x}'_t \, \mathbf{x}'_t)\boldsymbol{\alpha}_t + \varepsilon_t, \qquad t = 1, \ldots, T \tag{5.17a}$$

and

$$\boldsymbol{\alpha}_t = \begin{bmatrix} \bar{\boldsymbol{\beta}}_t \\ \boldsymbol{\beta}_t^* \end{bmatrix} = \begin{bmatrix} \mathbf{I} & \mathbf{0} \\ \mathbf{0} & \boldsymbol{\Phi} \end{bmatrix} \begin{bmatrix} \bar{\boldsymbol{\beta}}_{t-1} \\ \boldsymbol{\beta}_{t-1}^* \end{bmatrix} + \begin{bmatrix} \mathbf{0} \\ \boldsymbol{\eta}_t \end{bmatrix} \tag{5.17b}$$

A diffuse prior is used for $\bar{\boldsymbol{\beta}}_t$, which effectively means that the starting values are constructed from the first k observations. The initialisation of $\boldsymbol{\beta}_t^*$ poses no problem since it is a stationary vector AR(1) process with mean zero and covariance matrix given by (2.11b).

An alternative approach is to write the state space model as

$$y_t - \mathbf{x}_t'\boldsymbol{\beta} = \mathbf{x}_t'\boldsymbol{\beta}_t^* + \varepsilon_t, \qquad t = 1, \ldots, T \qquad (5.18a)$$

$$\boldsymbol{\beta}_t^* = \boldsymbol{\Phi}\boldsymbol{\beta}_{t-1}^* + \boldsymbol{\eta}_t \qquad (5.18b)$$

and to recognise that the Kalman filter which is appropriate for $y_t - \mathbf{x}_t'\bar{\boldsymbol{\beta}}$ can be applied separately to y_t and the elements of $\mathbf{x}_t$. The GLS estimator of $\bar{\boldsymbol{\beta}}$ is then obtained by regressing the standardised innovations from y_t on the standardised innovations from $\mathbf{x}_t$; see Kohn and Ansley (1985). Given $\mathbf{Q}$, both approaches deliver the same estimator of $\bar{\boldsymbol{\beta}}$. In both cases, full ML estimation may be carried out by maximising the concentrated likelihood function with respect to $\mathbf{Q}$. The algorithm of de Jong (1991) actually contains elements of the second approach, although it is primarily based on the first.

When $\mathbf{Q}$ and $\boldsymbol{\Phi}$ are diagonal, initial estimators of their elements q_i and $\phi_i, i = 1, \ldots, k$, may be obtained from the OLS residuals, $\hat{u}_t$. The covariances of the disturbances in (5.16) are

$$E(u_t u_s) = \sum_{i=1}^{k} x_{it} x_{is} q_i \phi_i^{\tau} / (1 - \phi_i^2), \qquad t, s = 1, \ldots, T \qquad (5.19)$$

and replacing $E(u_t u_s)$ by $\hat{u}_t \hat{u}_s$ for $s = t$ and $s = t - 1$ suggests two regressions, one of $\hat{u}_t^2$ on $x_{2t}^2, \ldots, x_{kt}^2$ and the other of $\hat{u}_t \hat{u}_{t-1}$ on $x_{2t} x_{2,t-1}, \ldots, x_{kt} x_{k,t-1}$. This yields $2k$ estimated coefficients from which it is possible to solve for the $2k$ unknown parameters in $\boldsymbol{\Phi}$ and $\mathbf{Q}$. Thus if $\hat{\gamma}_{i,0}$ denotes the ith regression coefficient in the equation for $\tau = 0$, and $\hat{\gamma}_{i,1}$ denotes the corresponding coefficient for $\tau = 1$, ϕ_i may be estimated by $\hat{\phi}_i = \hat{\gamma}_{i,1}/\hat{\gamma}_{i,0}$. Once estimates of the ϕ_i's have been obtained, estimating the q_i's is straightforward. Note that the initial covariance matrix of $\boldsymbol{\beta}^*$ in this case is diagonal with ith diagonal element given by $q_i/(1 - \phi_i^2)$. The estimators computed in this way may be used to start off a numerical optimisation procedure for calculating ML estimates. Alternatively they may be used to compute a two-step feasible GLS estimator of $\bar{\boldsymbol{\beta}}$ as described above; see the Monte Carlo results in Harvey and Phillips (1982).

Appendix A Properties of the Multivariate Normal Distribution

Let the pair of vectors $\mathbf{x}$ and $\mathbf{y}$ be jointly multivariate normal such that $(\mathbf{x}', \mathbf{y}')'$ has mean and covariance matrix given by

$$\boldsymbol{\mu} = \begin{bmatrix} \boldsymbol{\mu}_x \\ \boldsymbol{\mu}_y \end{bmatrix} \quad \text{and} \quad \boldsymbol{\Sigma} = \begin{bmatrix} \boldsymbol{\Sigma}_{xx} & \boldsymbol{\Sigma}_{xy} \\ \boldsymbol{\Sigma}_{yx} & \boldsymbol{\Sigma}_{yy} \end{bmatrix}$$

respectively. Then the distribution of $\mathbf{x}$ conditional on $\mathbf{y}$ is also multivariate normal with mean

$$\boldsymbol{\mu}_{x|y} = \boldsymbol{\mu}_x + \boldsymbol{\Sigma}_{xy}\boldsymbol{\Sigma}_{yy}^{-1}(\mathbf{y} - \boldsymbol{\mu}_y) \qquad (A.1)$$

and covariance matrix

$$\Sigma_{xx|y} = \Sigma_{xx} - \Sigma_{xy}\Sigma_{yy}^{-1}\Sigma_{yx} \tag{A.2}$$

Note that (A.2) does not depend on $\mathbf{y}$. Note also that Σ and Σ_{yy} are assumed to be non-singular, although in fact Σ_{yy}^{-1} can be replaced by a pseudo inverse.

A proof of the above lemma can be found in FSK, pp. 165–6, or Anderson and Moore (1979), although the result is a standard one.

Appendix B Matrix Inversion Lemma

Let $\mathbf{D}$ be an $n \times n$ matrix defined by

$$\mathbf{D} = [\mathbf{A} + \mathbf{BCB'}]^{-1} \tag{B.1}$$

where $\mathbf{A}$ and $\mathbf{C}$ are non-singular matrices of order n and m respectively, and $\mathbf{B}$ is $n \times m$. Then

$$\mathbf{D} = \mathbf{A}^{-1} - \mathbf{A}^{-1}\mathbf{B}[\mathbf{C}^{-1} + \mathbf{B'A}^{-1}\mathbf{B}]^{-1}\mathbf{B'A}^{-1} \tag{B.2}$$

The result may be verified directly by showing that $\mathbf{DD}^{-1} = \mathbf{I}$. Let $\mathbf{E} = \mathbf{C}^{-1} + \mathbf{B'A}^{-1}\mathbf{B}$. Then

$$\mathbf{D}^{-1}\mathbf{D} = \mathbf{I} - \mathbf{BE}^{-1}\mathbf{B'A}^{-1} + \mathbf{BCB'A}^{-1} + \mathbf{BCB'A}^{-1}\mathbf{BE}^{-1}\mathbf{B'A}^{-1}$$

$$= \mathbf{I} + [-\mathbf{BE}^{-1} + \mathbf{BC} - \mathbf{BCB'A}^{-1}\mathbf{BE}^{-1}]\mathbf{B'A}^{-1}$$

$$= \mathbf{I} + \mathbf{BC}[-\mathbf{C}^{-1}\mathbf{E}^{-1} + \mathbf{I} - \mathbf{B'A}^{-1}\mathbf{BE}^{-1}]\mathbf{B'A}^{-1}$$

$$= \mathbf{I} + \mathbf{BC}[\mathbf{I} - \mathbf{EE}^{-1}]\mathbf{B'A}^{-1} = \mathbf{I}$$

An important special case arises when $\mathbf{B}$ is an $n \times 1$ vector, $\mathbf{b}$, and $\mathbf{C} = 1$. Then

$$(\mathbf{A} + \mathbf{bb'})^{-1} = \mathbf{A}^{-1} - \frac{\mathbf{A}^{-1}\mathbf{bb'A}^{-1}}{1 + \mathbf{b'A}^{-1}\mathbf{b}} \tag{B.3}$$

A number of other useful results on matrix inversion will be found in Jazwinski (1970, pp. 261–2).

Exercises

1. Consider an AR(1) model in which the first observation is fixed. Write down the likelihood function if the observation at time τ is missing.

   Given a value of the AR parameter, ϕ, show that the estimator of the missing observation obtained by smoothing is

$$\tilde{y}_{\tau|T} = \varphi(y_{\tau-1} + y_{\tau+1})/(1 + \phi^2)$$

2. Show that for an MA(1) model with $|\theta| > 1$, the prediction errors are the same as for a model with parameter $1/\theta$ when the Kalman filter is initialised with (4.3). Show also that f_t in the filter is θ^2 times the f_t obtained with $1/\theta$, and hence show that the likelihood functions are the same. What happens to the CSS recursion when $|\theta| > 1$?

3. Consider a random walk plus noise model, that is (1.5) with $\phi = 1$. If σ_η^2 is zero, show that running the Kalman filter initialised with a diffuse prior yields an estimator of μ_t equal to the mean of the first t observations. Show that the variance of this estimator is calculated by the Kalman filter to be σ_ε^2/t.

4. How would you estimate the parameters ϕ, θ and σ^2 in an ARMA(1, 1) model by exact ML?

5
Time Series Models

5.1 Introduction

Most time series encountered in practice are non-stationary. The methods described in chapters 2 and 3 are for stationary time series, but the ideas may be adapted for use with non-stationary series. As indicated in the opening chapter, there is more than one way to proceed. The ARIMA methodology, developed by Box and Jenkins, is based on the idea that series can be made stationary by operations such as differencing. Once this has been done, the model-fitting techniques described in chapter 3 can be applied directly. All that remains is to reverse the differencing operations so as to make forecasts in levels.

In the structural approach, models are set up explicitly in terms of components of interest such as trends, seasonals and cycles. The statistical treatment is based on the state space form. Non-stationarity is handled directly, without the need for explicit differencing operations. Nevertheless, the basic models can be reduced to a stationary form by such operations, and when this is done the formal links with ARIMA models become apparent.

A third approach is to estimate autoregressive models in levels without imposing any stationarity restrictions. This is rather limited as a means of modelling univariate time series since it lacks the generality needed to model adequately many of the features typically present. Its appeal lies in the fact that it provides a framework within which to test for non-stationarity and the way in which this can be generalised to testing for long-run relationships between non-stationary variables in multivariate models.

Before embarking on a detailed treatment of the various modelling methodologies, some relevant preliminary ideas will be discussed.

Plots and Transformations

The first step in model building is to plot the data. Many of the salient features, such as trends and cycles can be seen directly, and it might

106

even be possible to spot unusual observations which may be tentatively identified as outliers. If the data are monthly or quarterly, seasonal fluctuations can be expected, while with daily observations a seven-day pattern is likely to arise. A plot of the data re-confirms the existence of such patterns, gives an idea of their importance and perhaps even indicates whether there is any change over time.

A plot may also indicate the need for certain instantaneous transformations. The main question is whether to take logarithms. For most economic time series the answer is usually in the affirmative, since if, as in the structural approach, a series is viewed as consisting of components, such as trend and seasonal, these components tend to combine multiplicatively. Taking logarithms leads to the additive formulation upon which the statistical treatment is based. A plot is often helpful in this respect since one can examine whether, for example, a seasonal pattern appears more stable after logarithms have been taken.

More generally, the *Box–Cox transform* may be applied. This is defined by

$$y_t^{(\lambda)} = \begin{cases} (y_t^\lambda - 1)/\lambda, & 0 < \lambda \leqslant 1 \\ \log y_t, & \lambda = 0 \end{cases} \tag{1.1}$$

Thus levels, $\lambda = 1$, and logarithms appear at the extremes as special cases. There may sometimes be reasons for imposing intermediate values of λ. For example, with count data a more stable variance can often be obtained by setting λ equal to a half or two-thirds. Alternatively λ can be treated as a free parameter and estimated along with the other parameters in the model.

For data lying within a specific range a *logistic transformation* may be appropriate. Thus for a proportion, lying between zero and one, we construct a new variable,

$$y_t^* = \log\{y_t/(1 - y_t)\} \tag{1.2}$$

which can be anywhere in the range minus infinity to plus infinity.

Differencing is a fundamental operation in time series modelling. Many non-stationary series appear to be more or less stationary after applying the first difference operator, $\Delta = 1 - L$. If the original series is in logarithms, the first differences will be a series of growth rates, $g_t = \Delta y_t/y_{t-1}$, as

$$\Delta \log y_t = \log(y_t/y_{t-1}) = \log(1 + g_t) \simeq g_t \qquad \text{for } g_t \text{ small}$$

For example, taking differences of the logarithm of the price level gives the rate of inflation. Third differences are rarely used in practice since, as will be seen in the next section, this would imply a model with a quadratic forecast function.

Summation operators may be used to remove periodic movements, such as seasonals. The basic operation is

$$S_\tau(L) = 1 + L + L^2 + \cdots + L^{\tau-1}, \qquad \tau = 1, 2, \ldots \tag{1.3}$$

where τ is the length of the period in question. Thus for monthly data $\tau = 12$. When used in connection with seasonality, (1.3) will be called the *seasonal summation operator*, and the τ subscript will be droppped. Periodic effects may also be removed by τth differencing.

$$\Delta_\tau = 1 - L^\tau, \qquad \tau = 1, 2, \ldots \tag{1.4}$$

When used to remove seasonal effects, (1.4) will be called the *seasonal difference operator*, and denoted Δ_s where s is the number of seasons in the year. There is an important relationship between the summation and difference operators, namely

$$\Delta_\tau = \Delta \cdot S_\tau(L) \tag{1.5}$$

This may be verified directly by multiplying the two right hand side operators and simplifying the resulting expression. In the light of this result it can be seen that seasonal differencing is doing two things; firstly it is smoothing out the seasonal and secondly it is differencing to remove the trend.

The differencing and summation operations are special cases of *linear filters*. The summation operation is essentially a moving average filter, the distinction being that such filters usually sum over later as well as previous observations and divide the result by the number of observations in the sum. More general moving average filters have different weights and are used for such purposes as removing cycles and detrending. However, considerable care must be taken if filtering operations are applied prior to any analysis, and the filtered series is then treated as though it were the raw data. The danger is that the filtering operations can induce spurious movements in the series, with the result that incorrect conclusions are drawn. This issue is best examined in the frequency domain; see section 6.6. The overall conclusion is that filtering operations should be used as an integral part of a process which combines analysis and model building.

A final point to stress is that although much analysis and model building is based on the assumption that a series can be made stationary, such an assumption is quite an heroic one. There is no theorem which says that a series can be made stationary by the kind of operations discussed above, and it is important to recognise that the stationarity assumption may be violated in many different ways; for example, the structure of the series may change.

Deterministic Trends

A deterministic trend model is of the form

$$y_t = f(t) + u_t, \qquad t = 1, \ldots, T \tag{1.6}$$

where u_t is a stationary ARMA(p, q) process and $f(t)$ is a deterministic function of time. In the absence of any prior knowledge on the form of the deterministic trend, the obvious thing to do is to model it as a polynomial. Thus

$$f(t) = \alpha + \beta_0 t + \beta_1 t^2 + \cdots + \beta_h t^h \tag{1.7}$$

where h is the order of the polynomial. Even though the disturbance may be serially correlated, it can be shown that the unknown parameters in $f(t)$, that is $\alpha, \beta_1, \ldots, \beta_h$, may be estimated efficiently by OLS. An ARMA model may then be fitted in the usual way from the residuals.

A model with a linear trend and a white noise disturbance may be written as

$$y_t = \alpha + \beta t + \varepsilon_t \tag{1.8}$$

The l-step ahead prediction is given by

$$\tilde{y}_{T+l|T} = a + b(T + l) \tag{1.9}$$

where a and b are the OLS estimators of α and β. The prediction mean square error is:

$$\text{MSE}(\tilde{y}_{T+l|T}) = \sigma^2 \left\{ 1 + \frac{2[(2T-1)(T-1) + 6l(T+l-1)]}{T(T^2-1)} \right\} \tag{1.10}$$

and this may be estimated by replacing σ^2 by its unbiased estimator, i.e. the residual sum of squares divided by $T - 2$. Lower case letters will be used to denote the estimated mean square error and the corresponding root mean square error. The $100(1 - \alpha)\%$ prediction interval for y_{T+l} is therefore

$$\tilde{y}_{T+l|T} \pm t_{T-2}^{(\alpha/2)} \cdot \text{rmse}(\tilde{y}_{T+l|T})$$

where $t_{T-2}^{(\alpha/2)}$ is the point on the t-distribution with $(T - 2)$ degrees of freedom such that the probability to the right of it is $\alpha/2$.

The drawback with models like (1.6) is that they are rarely appropriate. The trend is a deterministic function of time and so all observations receive the same weight when predictions are made. This is unreasonable, and so it is necessary to formulate models which lead to the discounting of past observations. *Ad hoc* methods of discounting are described in the next sub-section. Structural time series models, in which the discounting is achieved by setting up a model in which the trend parameters are allowed to evolve over time as stochastic processes, are described in section 5.4.

Local Trends and Ad Hoc Forecasting

The notion of discounting past observations embodies the idea of a *local*, as opposed to a *global*, trend. A global trend may be represented by a deterministic function of time as in (1.6). A local trend may change direction during the sample and it is the most recent direction which we want to extrapolate into the future.

The construction of forecast functions based on discounted past observations is most commonly carried out by exponential smoothing procedures. These procedures have the attraction that they allow the forecast function to be updated very easily each time a new observation becomes available. Storage requirements are kept to a minimum. Exponential smoothing procedures have become justifiably popular, particularly in operational research, since they are easy to implement and can be quite effective. However, they are *ad hoc* in that they are implemented without respect to a properly defined statistical model.

The simplest *ad hoc* forecasting procedure is the *exponentially weighted moving average* (EWMA). Rather than estimate the level of a series of observations by the sample mean and use this as the basis for forecasting observations, it is more appealing to put more weight on the most recent observations. Thus the estimate of the current level of the series is taken to be

$$m_T = \sum_{j=0}^{T-1} w_j y_{T-j} \tag{1.11}$$

where the w_js are a set of weights which sum to unity. This estimate is then taken to be the forecast of future observations, so that

$$\hat{y}_{T+l|T} = m_T, \qquad l = 1, 2, \ldots \tag{1.12}$$

and the forecast function is a horizontal straight line. If the weights decline exponentially

$$m_T = \lambda \sum_{j=0}^{T-1} (1 - \lambda)^j y_{T-j} \tag{1.13}$$

where λ is a *smoothing constant* in the range $0 < \lambda \leqslant 1$. If T is large, the condition that the weights sum to unity is approximately satisfied since

$$\lim_{T \to \infty} \sum_{j=0}^{T-1} w_j = \lambda \lim_{T \to \infty} \sum_{j=0}^{T-1} (1 - \lambda)^j = 1$$

If expression (1.13) is defined for any value of t from $t = 1$ to T, it can be split into two parts to give the recursion

$$m_t = (1 - \lambda)m_{t-1} + \lambda y_t, \qquad t = 1, \ldots, T \tag{1.14}$$

with $m_0 = 0$. The current value, m_T, can then be computed recursively. A modification, which is slightly more satisfactory, is to set m_1 equal to y_1 and to start the recursion at $t = 2$. This gives a slightly different result from (1.13), since y_1 receives a weight of $(1 - \lambda)^T$ rather than $\lambda(1 - \lambda)^T$. However, the weights in (1.11) do sum to unity, even in small samples.

Since m_T is the appropriate forecast of y_{t+1}, the recursion in (1.14) is often written as

$$\hat{y}_{t+1|t} = (1 - \lambda)\hat{y}_{t|t-1} + \lambda y_t \tag{1.15}$$

Thus next period's forecast is a weighted average of the current observation and the forecast of the current observation made in the previous time period. Alternatively

$$\hat{y}_{t+1|t} = \hat{y}_{t|t-1} + \lambda(y_t - \hat{y}_{t|t-1}) \tag{1.16}$$

so that forecasts are modified according to the size of the forecast error in the current period. If a value of λ equal to zero were admissible, it would mean that no updating would take place. A value of unity for λ means that all the information needed for forecasting is contained in the current observation. The value of λ is often set on *a priori* grounds, in which case it is usually somewhere between 0.05 and 0.30. However, if a reasonable number of observations are available, λ can be chosen as that value which minimises the sum of squares of the one-step ahead forecast errors, that is

$$S(\lambda) = \sum \hat{v}_t^2 \tag{1.17}$$

where

$$\hat{v}_t = y_t - \hat{y}_{t|t-1} \tag{1.18}$$

If the recursion in (1.15) is started off with $\hat{y}_{2|1}$ equal to y_1, which is equivalent to setting m_1 equal to y_1 in (1.14), the forecast errors are defined for $t = 2, \ldots, T$.

The *Holt–Winters* forecasting procedure extends the EWMA to a local linear trend. Bringing a slope, b_T, into the forecast function gives

$$\hat{y}_{T+l|T} = m_T + b_T l, \qquad l = 1, 2, \ldots \tag{1.19}$$

The updating scheme of Holt (1957) and Winters (1960) calculates m_T and b_T by a scheme in which past observations are discounted by two smoothing constants, λ_0 and λ_1, in the range $0 < \lambda_0, \lambda_1 < 1$. Let m_{t-1} and b_{t-1} denote the estimates of the level and slope at time $t - 1$. The one-step ahead forecast is then

$$\hat{y}_{t|t-1} = m_{t-1} + b_{t-1} \tag{1.20}$$

As in the EWMA, the updated estimate of the level, m_t, is a linear combination of $\hat{y}_{t|t-1}$ and y_t. Thus

$$m_t = \lambda_0 y_t + (1 - \lambda_0)(m_{t-1} + b_{t-1}) \tag{1.21a}$$

From this new estimate of m_t, an estimate of the slope b_t can be constructed as $m_t - m_{t-1}$. This suggests that an updated estimate, b_t, be formed by a linear combination of $m_t - m_{t-1}$ and the previous estimate, and so

$$b_t = \lambda_1(m_t - m_{t-1}) + (1 - \lambda_1)b_{t-1} \tag{1.21b}$$

Following the argument given for the EWMA, starting values may be constructed from the initial observations as $m_2 = y_2$ and $b_2 = y_2 - y_1$.

The recursions in (1.21) can be re-arranged so as to be in terms of the one-step ahead forecast error, $\hat{v}_t$, defined in (1.18). Thus

$$m_t = m_{t-1} + b_{t-1} + \lambda_0 \hat{v}_t \tag{1.22a}$$

$$b_t = \qquad b_{t-1} + \lambda_0 \lambda_1 \hat{v}_t \tag{1.22b}$$

The closer λ_0 is to zero, the less past observations are discounted in forming a current estimate of the level. Similarly, the closer λ_1 is to zero, the less they are discounted in estimating the slope. As with the EWMA, these smoothing constants can be fixed *a priori* or estimated by minimising the sum of squares function analogous to (1.17).

Another way of obtaining *ad hoc* forecasting procedures is by applying *discounted least squares* (DLS). While a global trend is fitted by ordinary least squares, DLS operates simply by introducing a discount factor, ω, into the sum of squares function to be minimised. Thus the DLS estimate of a level is based on finding the value of m which minimises

$$S(m;\omega) = \sum_{j=0}^{T-1} \omega^j (y_{T-j} - m)^2 \tag{1.23}$$

where $0 \leqslant \omega \leqslant 1$. Differentiating (1.23) with respect to m gives

$$m_T = \left(\sum_{j=0}^{T-1} \omega^j \right)^{-1} \sum_{j=0}^{T-1} \omega^j y_{T-j} \tag{1.24}$$

This reduces to the sample mean if ω equals one. For ω strictly less than one,

$$m_T = \frac{(1-\omega)}{1-\omega^T} \sum_{j=0}^{T-1} \omega^j y_{T-j} \tag{1.25}$$

On setting $\omega = 1 - \lambda$, expression (1.25) is seen to be the same as the EWMA (1.13) apart from the divisor $1 - (1 - \lambda)^T$.

If a slope term is to be introduced into the forecast function, discounted least squares amounts to finding values of the level, m, and the slope, b, which minimise

$$S(m, b; \omega) = \sum_{j=0}^{T-1} \omega^j (y_{T-j} - m + bj)^2 \tag{1.26}$$

It can be shown that these values, m_T and b_T, can be found from the Holt–Winters recursions, (1.21), by setting $\lambda_0 = 1 - \omega^2$ and $\lambda_1 = (1 - \omega)/(1 + \omega)$. They are then entered into the forecast function, (1.19). This is known as *double exponential smoothing*.

The discounted least squares principle may be extended further so as to cover a wide range of functions of time, including higher order polynomials and sinusoids. Further details may be found in the pioneering work by Brown (1963), and in various texts, such as Abraham and Ledolter (1983).

Random Walk

The random walk plays a central role in all the principal model-building procedures discussed in this chapter. At each point in time the series moves randomly away from its current position. Thus

$$y_t = y_{t-1} + \varepsilon_t, \qquad t = 1, \ldots, T \tag{1.27}$$

The model has the same form as an $AR(1)$ process, but since ϕ is one, it is not stationary. Repeatedly substituting for past values gives

$$y_t = y_0 + \sum_{j=0}^{t-1} \varepsilon_{t-j}, \qquad t = 1, 2, \ldots, T \tag{1.28}$$

If the initial value, y_0, is fixed, the mean of y_t is equal to it as $E(y_t) = y_0$. However, although the mean is constant over time, the variance and covariance are not since

$$\text{Var}(y_t) = t\sigma^2$$

and

$$\text{Cov}(y_t, y_{t-\tau}) = |t - \tau|\sigma^2 \tag{1.29}$$

The random walk therefore tends to meander away from its starting value but exhibits no particular direction or trend in doing so. On the other hand, the first difference of a random walk is stationary since it is just white noise, that is

$$\Delta y_t = y_t - y_{t-1} = \varepsilon_t \tag{1.30}$$

Adding a constant term to (1.27) gives the *random walk with drift*

$$y_t = y_{t-1} + \beta + \varepsilon_t, \qquad t = 1, \ldots, T \tag{1.31}$$

Repeatedly substituting for lagged values of y_t and taking expectations gives

$$E(y_t) = y_0 + \beta t \tag{1.32}$$

when y_0 is fixed. Thus the level of y_t is governed by a linear time trend, but unlike (1.6) it cannot be decomposed into a linear trend and a stationary disturbance term.

The difference between the random walk plus drift and a deterministic trend model is also brought out in the forecasts. The observation at time $T + l$ may be written as

$$y_{T+l} = y_T + \beta l + \sum_{j=1}^{l} \varepsilon_{T+j}$$

and so if the disturbances are independent, taking expectations conditional on the information at time T yields the MMSE

$$\tilde{y}_{T+l|T} = y_T + \beta l \qquad (1.33)$$

The forecast function is therefore a linear trend but, if β is known, it depends only on the last observation. In the case of a pure random walk, β is zero so the forecast function is a horizontal line starting at y_T.

If β is not known, it is clear from writing (1.31) as

$$\Delta y_t = \beta + \varepsilon_t, \qquad t = 2, \ldots, T \qquad (1.34)$$

that it may be estimated by the mean of the differenced observations, denoted b. This estimator can also be expressed in terms of the first and last observations since

$$b = \sum_{t=2}^{T} \Delta y_t / (T - 1) = (y_T - y_1) / (T - 1) \qquad (1.35)$$

Example 1 The logarithm of quarterly, seasonally adjusted US consumption appears to be a random walk plus drift. Hall (1978) gives an economic rationale as to why this should be the case.

5.2 Autoregressive-Integrated-Moving Average Models

The random walk model may be extended by replacing ε_t by a stationary and invertible ARMA(p, q) process. On the other side, y_t may be differenced more than once. When forecasting is carried out the differencing operation must be reversed, and Box and Jenkins (1976) call this operation integration. If d is the order of differencing needed to produce a stationary and invertible process, the original process is said to be *integrated of order d* and abbreviated as $y_t \sim I(d)$. Similarly the model

$$\phi(L) \Delta^d y_t = \theta(L)\varepsilon_t \qquad (2.1)$$

is called an *autoregressive-integrated-moving average process of order* (p, d, q), and denoted as ARIMA(p, d, q). In the case of the random walk we may write $y_t \sim$ ARIMA$(0, 1, 0)$. A stationary model has $d = 0$.

If a constant or drift term is brought into the ARIMA model it becomes

$$\phi(L) \Delta(L)y_t = \theta_0 + \theta(L)\varepsilon_t \qquad (2.2)$$

The issues involved in fitting ARMA models were studied in chapter 3. This leaves only two questions for the ARIMA methodology: how does d affect predictions, and how do we decide on its value?

Prediction

A basic feature of the predictions from stationary models is that they tend towards the mean of the series as the lead time, l, increases. If l is large, the structure of the model is irrelevant. This is no longer the case with integrated processes, where the forecast function contains a deterministic component which depends on the degree of differencing.

The mechanics of making predictions from ARIMA models are exactly the same as those involved in making predictions from ARMA models. The term $\phi(L)\,\Delta^d$ in (2.1) is expanded to yield an AR polynomial of order $p + d$,

$$\phi(L)\,\Delta^d = \varphi(L) = 1 - \varphi_1 L - \cdots - \varphi_{p+d} L^{p+d} \tag{2.3}$$

and predictions are made from the recursive equation

$$\tilde{y}_{T+l|T} = \varphi_1 \tilde{y}_{T+l-1|T} + \cdots + \varphi_{p+d}\tilde{y}_{T+l-p-d|T} + \tilde{\varepsilon}_{T+l|T} + \cdots + \theta_q \tilde{\varepsilon}_{T+l-q|T},$$
$$l = 1, 2, \ldots \tag{2.4}$$

where $\tilde{y}_{T+j|T}$ and $\tilde{\varepsilon}_{T+j}$ are defined as in (2.6.4).

Example 1 In the ARIMA$(0, 1, 1)$ model,

$$\Delta y_t = \varepsilon_t + \theta\varepsilon_{t-1} \tag{2.5}$$

forecasts are constructed from the equation

$$\tilde{y}_{T+l|T} = \tilde{y}_{T+l-1|T} + \tilde{\varepsilon}_{T+l|T} + \theta\tilde{\varepsilon}_{T+l-1|T}, \qquad l = 1, 2, \ldots \tag{2.6}$$

Since future values of ε_t are set to zero, it follows that

$$\tilde{y}_{T+1|T} = y_T + \theta\varepsilon_T \tag{2.7a}$$

while

$$\tilde{y}_{T+l|T} = \tilde{y}_{T+l-1|T}, \qquad l = 2, 3, \ldots \tag{2.7b}$$

Thus, for all lead times, the forecasts made at time T follow a horizontal straight line.

The disturbance term, ε_T, is constructed from the difference equation

$$\varepsilon_t = y_t - y_{t-1} - \theta\varepsilon_{t-1}, \qquad t = 2, \ldots, T \tag{2.8}$$

with $\varepsilon_1 = 0$; compare the CSS recursion given in (3.3.2). Substituting repeatedly for lagged values of ε_t in the equation for ε_T gives

$$\varepsilon_T = y_T - (1 + \theta)\sum_{j=1}^{T-1}(-\theta)^{j-1}y_{T-j} \tag{2.9}$$

The expression for the one-step ahead predictor, (2.7a), can therefore be written as

$$\tilde{y}_{T+1|T} = (1 + \theta)\sum_{j=0}^{T-1}(-\theta)^j y_{T-j} \tag{2.10}$$

This is just the EWMA of section 5.1 with $\lambda = 1 + \theta$. Furthermore since the ε_t's in (2.18) can be interpreted as prediction errors, $y_t - \tilde{y}_{t|t-1}$, a simple re-arrangement gives the EWMA recursion (1.16).

Example 2   The eventual forecast function in the ARIMA$(0, 2, 2)$ model,

$$\Delta^2 y_t = \varepsilon_t + \theta_1 \varepsilon_{t-1} + \theta_2 \varepsilon_{t-2} \tag{2.11}$$

is the solution of $(1 - L)^2 \tilde{y}_{T+l|T} = 0$. This is a straight line passing through the first two predictions, $\tilde{y}_{T+1|T}$ and $\tilde{y}_{T+2|T}$. It can be shown that, for certain values of θ_1 and θ_2, the forecast function is the same as that given by the Holt–Winters procedure, (1.19).

Example 3   In the ARIMA$(1, 1, 0)$ model,

$$\varphi(L) = (1 - \phi L)(1 - L) = 1 - (1 + \phi)L + \phi L^2$$

and forecasts are constructed from the difference equation

$$\tilde{y}_{T+l|T} = (1 + \phi)\tilde{y}_{T+l-1|T} - \phi \tilde{y}_{T+l-2|T}, \qquad l = 1, 2, \ldots$$

The corresponding forecast function is

$$\tilde{y}_{T+l|T} = y_T + (y_T - y_{T-1})\frac{\phi(1 - \phi^l)}{1 - \phi}, \qquad l = 1, 2, \ldots \tag{2.12}$$

As $l \to \infty$ this approaches the horizontal line

$$y_T + (y_T - y_{T-1})\phi/(1 - \phi) \tag{2.13}$$

In the ARIMA$(0, 1, 1)$ model the forecast function is horizontal, but its level depends on all past values as can be seen from (2.10). By way of contrast the eventual forecast function in (2.13) depends only on the last two points in the series. This is a feature of all ARIMA models in which there is no MA component.

The general point to emerge from these examples is that the eventual forecast function for an ARIMA(p, d, q) model is a polynomial of order $d - 1$. If the model has a non-zero mean, the eventual forecast function is a polynomial of order d.

Example 4   In the random walk plus drift the forecast function (1.33) is a linear trend. As was pointed out in example 2, the eventual forecast function for an ARIMA$(0, 2, 2)$ process *without* a constant term is also a linear trend. The distinguishing feature of the random walk plus drift is that the estimated slope, (1.35), gives equal weight to the first and last observations. In the ARIMA$(0, 2, 2)$ model, the later observations are relatively more important in determining the slope of the forecast function.

Adding a constant term to an integrated process introduces a deterministic component into the series. Box and Jenkins (1976, pp. 92–3) argue that this is unrealistic in most situations. They prefer to assume that θ_0 is zero 'unless such an assumption proves contrary to the facts presented by the data'.

The MSE of a prediction from an ARIMA model may be obtained from formula (2.6.11), the ψ_j coefficients being calculated by equating powers of L in the expression

$$\varphi(L)\psi(L) = \theta(L) \tag{2.14}$$

This yields

$$\psi_j = \sum_{i=1}^{\min(j,p+d)} \varphi_i\psi_{j-i} + \theta_j, \qquad 1 \leqslant j \leqslant q \tag{2.15a}$$

$$\psi_j = \sum_{i=1}^{\min(j,p+d)} \varphi_i\psi_{j-i}, \qquad j > q \tag{2.15b}$$

Note that $\psi_0 = 1$.

Example 5   In the ARIMA$(0, 2, 1)$ model

$$\Delta^2 y_t = \varepsilon_t + 0.5\varepsilon_{t-1} \tag{2.16}$$

the ψ_j's are calculated as follows:

$$\psi_1 = \varphi_1 + \theta_1 = 2.0 + 0.5 = 2.5$$

$$\psi_2 = \varphi_1\psi_1 + \phi_2 = 2(2.5) - 1.0 = 4.0$$

$$\psi_3 = \varphi_1\psi_2 + \varphi_2\psi_1 = 8.0 - 2.5 = 5.5$$

Thus for $l = 3$

$$\text{MSE}(\tilde{y}_{T+3|T}) = \sigma^2(1.0^2 + 2.5^2 + 4.0^2) = 23.25\sigma^2$$

and the 95% prediction interval for y_{T+3} is

$$\tilde{y}_{T+3|T} \pm 9.5\sigma$$

The MSEs of forecasts in ARIMA models tend to increase rapidly as the lead time becomes greater. This stresses that the main value of such models is in short-term forecasting.

A final point concerns differenced series which are stationary, but strictly non-invertible due to the presence of a unit root in the MA polynomial. Such series are said to be *overdifferenced*. If a finite sample prediction procedure is used, the predictions for any lead time are identical to the predictions which would have been obtained had the series not been over-differenced. This is in contrast to predictions based on the CSS recursion, which can be very inefficient in such circumstances.

Example 6*   Consider a white noise process with mean μ:

$$y_t = \mu + \varepsilon_t, \qquad t = 1, \ldots, T \tag{2.17}$$

The MMSLE of $y_{T+l|T}$ is $\bar{y}$ and this has an MSE of $(1 + T^{-1})\sigma^2$ for all l.

Now suppose that first differences are taken. If the resulting process is identified as ARIMA$(0, 1, 1)$, it may be put in state space form for $t = 2, \ldots, T$; compare with (4.1.9). Applying the Kalman filter yields

$$\mathbf{a}_T = \begin{bmatrix} \Delta y_T \\ \theta \tilde{\varepsilon}_T \end{bmatrix}, \qquad \mathbf{P}_T = \begin{bmatrix} 0 & 0 \\ 0 & f_{T+1} - 1 \end{bmatrix} \qquad (2.18)$$

where f_t is now defined as

$$f_t = 1 + \theta^{2(t-1)} / [1 + \theta^2 + \cdots + \theta^{2(t-2)}],$$

$$t = 2, \ldots, T + 1 \qquad (2.19)$$

Since predictions are needed for y_t, rather than Δy_t, the state space formulation must be modified. One way of doing this is to treat y_t as an ARMA$(1, 1)$ process in which $\phi = 1$. It can be shown that the new state vector at time $t = T$ is given by $\mathbf{a}_T^\dagger = (y_T, \theta \tilde{\varepsilon}_T)'$ with $\mathbf{P}_T$ defined by (2.18). The formulae for multi-step prediction, (4.2.5) and (4.2.6), then yield

$$\tilde{y}_{T+l|T} = y_T + \theta \tilde{\varepsilon}_T, \qquad l = 1, 2, \ldots \qquad (2.20a)$$

and

$$\mathbf{P}_{T+1|T} = \begin{bmatrix} f_{T+1} & \theta \\ \theta & \theta^2 \end{bmatrix},$$

$$\mathbf{P}_{T+2|T} = \begin{bmatrix} f_{T+1} + 2\theta + \theta^2 + 1 & \theta \\ \theta & \theta^2 \end{bmatrix}, \qquad (2.20b)$$

and so on. If $\theta = -1$, the top left hand element of $\mathbf{P}_{T+l|T}$ for all lead times is simply f_{T+1}, and so the MSE of any l-step ahead forecast is

$$\text{MSE}(\tilde{y}_{T+l|T}) = \sigma^2 (1 + T^{-1}), \qquad l = 1, 2, 3, \ldots \qquad (2.21)$$

This is identical to the MSE of $\bar{y}$ and, in fact, (2.20a) and $\bar{y}$ turn out to be identical.

In contrast, the predictions made by the CSS recursions will have a bigger MSE; see example 5 in section 2.6.

Model Selection

There are a number of ways of deciding on the appropriate degree of differencing. The most basic approach is to plot the data in levels and differences and to form a judgement according to which plots show trending movements. The eventual forecast functions implied by different degrees of differencing should also be borne in mind.

An examination of the correlogram can also be informative. For a stationary process, the autocorrelations tend towards zero as the lag increases, and this feature is reflected in the correlogram. The sample autocorrelations from a non-stationary process, on the other hand, do not typically damp down very rapidly as the lag increases. A simple illustration of why this is the case is provided by the AR(1) model. The closer ϕ is to 1, the more slowly the autocorrelation function, ϕ^τ, damps down. When $\phi = 1$, the process is a random walk and the theoretical autocorrelation function is not defined, but the sample autocorrelation function can still be computed. It follows that if an inspection of the correlogram for a series shows relatively large autocorrelations at high lags, differencing of the observations is probably appropriate. The strategy adopted by Box and Jenkins is to difference until a correlogram having the characteristics of a stationary process is obtained.

Example 7   The correlogram of the US rate of inflation, measured as the growth rate of the seasonally adjusted GNP deflator, is shown in figure 5.1(a) for data from 1952 Q1 to 1985 Q4. It gives a clear indication of non-stationarity. The correlogram of first differences shown in figure 5.1(b) is consistent with a stationary series.

Apart from $r(1)$, the sample autocorrelations in figure 5.1(b) are all very close to zero, and are statistically insignificant when judged against the standard errors computed using (3.6.2). The analysis therefore points to an ARIMA(0, 1, 1) model.

The problem with determining the degree of differencing from the correlogram is that in small samples the picture is often not clear cut. It was pointed out in section 2.8 that for a stationary process, the correlogram may sometimes not damp down as quickly as theoretical considerations would suggest because the sample autocorrelations themselves are correlated.

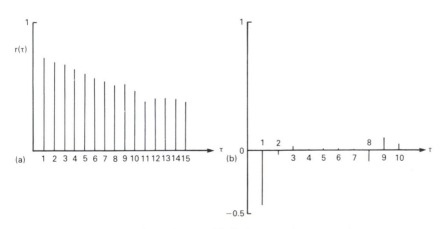

Figure 5.1 Correlograms for US rate of inflation: (a) levels; (b) first differences.

Conversely, the correlograms of non-stationary processes can damp down quite quickly. Some analytic results can be found in Hasza (1980).

The unit root tests described in section 5.4 provide a more formal approach to determining the degree of differencing. However, as we shall see, these tests can have quite severe limitations. If a preliminary analysis fails to resolve the differencing question adequately, there may be no alternative to fitting suitable models to observations in both levels and differences, and making a choice on the basis of goodness of fit.

Once the observations have been differenced, estimation and diagnostic checking may be carried out as for an ARMA model. Serial correlation in the residuals may be tested for using the methods described in section 3.6, and normality of the residuals may be assessed using the methods described in section 2.8. A simple test for heteroscedasticity, not described previously, is based on a statistic constructed as the ratio of the sum of squares of the last third of the residuals over the first third. If the ARMA parameters are known, this *H-statistic* has an F-distribution with $h = (T - d)/3$ degrees of freedom in both the numerator and the denominator. When they are unknown it can still be treated as having this distribution approximately, or a test may be based on the asymptotic distribution of hH, which is χ_h^2 under the null hypothesis.

Goodness of fit may be assessed by the estimated standard deviation of the disturbances, denoted s. The coefficient of multiple correlation, R^2, is not very useful for time series with strong upward or downward movements as any model which is able to pick up a trend reasonably well will give a value close to unity. A better measure is obtained by comparing the residual sum of squares with the sum of squares of the first differenced observations about their mean. Thus

$$R_D^2 = 1 - (T - d)s^2 \Big/ \sum_{t=2}^{T} (\Delta y_t - \overline{\Delta y})^2 \qquad (2.22)$$

The yardstick being adopted here is the random walk plus drift, (1.31). If the observations are in logarithms, the fit of the model is being compared with that achieved by simply estimating the average growth rate.

5.3 Structural Time Series Models

A structural time series model is one which is set up in terms of components which have a direct interpretation. Thus, for example, we may consider the classical decomposition in which a series is seen as the sum of trend, seasonal and irregular components. A model could be formulated as a regression with explanatory variables consisting of a time trend and a set of seasonal dummies. Typically, this would be inadequate. The necessary flexibility may be achieved by letting the regression coefficients change over time. A similar treatment may be accorded to other components such as cycles. The principal structural time series models are therefore nothing more than regression models in which the explanatory variables are functions of time and the parameters are time varying. Given this interpretation, the addition of observable explanatory variables is a natural extension. Furthermore, the use of a regression framework leads to a model selection methodology which has much in common with that employed in areas like econometrics.

The key to handling structural time series models is the state space form, with the state of the system representing the various unobserved components such as trends and seasonals. If the model is linear, the Kalman filter provides the means of updating the state as new observations become available. Predictions are made by extrapolating these components into the future, while the smoothing algorithms give the best estimate of the state at any point within the sample. A structural model can therefore not only provide forecasts, but also, through estimates of the components, present a set of stylised facts.

A thorough discussion of the methodological and technical ideas underlying structural time series models is contained in FSK (reference, Harvey, 1989). Sub-section 2.1.3 of FSK describes the way in which such models evolved through the work of, amongst others, Holt (1957), Muth (1960), Nerlove and Wage (1964), Rosenberg (1973), Harrison and Stevens (1976), Engle (1978a), Kitagawa (1981) and Harvey (1984a). A Bayesian viewpoint on structural models can be found in the book by West and Harrison (1989). Recent developments are discussed in Harvey and Shephard (1992).

Statistical Formulation

The simplest structural time series models consist of a trend component plus a random disturbance term. The random disturbance term may be interpreted as an irregular component in the time series or as a measurement error. Either way the model may be written as

$$y_t = \mu_t + \varepsilon_t, \qquad t = 1, \ldots, T \qquad (3.1)$$

where μ_t is the trend and ε_t is a zero mean white noise disturbance term, with variance σ_ε^2, which is assumed to be uncorrelated with any stochastic elements in μ_t.

The trend may take a variety of forms. The simplest is a random walk

$$\mu_t = \mu_{t-1} + \eta_t \qquad (3.2)$$

where η_t is a white noise disturbance, with variance σ_η^2, which is uncorrelated with ε_t. Thus the model may be thought of as having an underlying level which moves up and down over time. Although this is very simple, it fits a wide variety of time series. It is often referred to as the *local level* model. The crucial feature of the model is the *signal–noise ratio*, $q = \sigma_\eta^2 / \sigma_\varepsilon^2$.

Example 1   Reed (1978) collected a series of observations, 28 days apart over the period January 1968 to September 1973, on the number of purses snatched in the Hyde Park area of Chicago. As shown in FSK, the local level model provides a good fit, particularly if the square root transformation is applied. The signal–noise ratio in this case is $q = 0.13$.

The model may be extended by the introduction of a slope into the trend. The deterministic linear trend in (1.8) is

$$\mu_t = \alpha + \beta t, \qquad t = 1, \ldots, T \tag{3.3}$$

This trend could be made stochastic by letting α and β follow random walks. However, this would lead to a discontinuous pattern for μ_t. A more satisfactory model is obtained by working directly with the current level, μ_t, rather than with the intercept, α. Since μ_t may be obtained recursively from

$$\mu_t = \mu_{t-1} + \beta, \qquad t = 1, \ldots, T \tag{3.4}$$

with $\mu_0 = \alpha$, stochastic terms may be introduced as follows:

$$\mu_t = \mu_{t-1} + \beta_{t-1} + \eta_t \tag{3.5a}$$

$$\beta_t = \beta_{t-1} + \zeta_t \tag{3.5b}$$

where η_t and ζ_t are mutually uncorrelated white noise disturbances with zero means and variances, σ_η^2 and σ_ζ^2 respectively. Taken together, (3.1) and (3.5) form the *local linear trend* model. The effect of η_t is to allow the level of the trend to shift up and down, while ζ_t allows the slope to change. The larger the variances, the greater the stochastic movements in the trend. If $\sigma_\eta^2 = \sigma_\zeta^2 = 0$, (3.5) collapses to (3.4) showing that the deterministic trend is a limiting case.

Although the effect of (3.5) is to allow the parameters in the trend to change over time, the further assumption that all three disturbances are mutually and serially independent means that the forecast function still has the linear form

$$\tilde{\mu}_{T+l|T} = \tilde{\mu}_T + \tilde{\beta}_T l \tag{3.6}$$

where $\tilde{\mu}_T$ and $\tilde{\beta}_T$ are the conditional expectations of μ_T and β_T at time T. Since (3.1) specifies that the observations are equal to a trend plus a white noise disturbance term, (3.6) is also the forecast function for the series itself, that is

$$\tilde{y}_{T+l|T} = \tilde{\mu}_T + \tilde{\beta}_T l, \qquad l = 1, 2, \ldots \tag{3.7}$$

Many more structural models may be constructed. For example, a structural time series model for quarterly observations might consist of trend, cycle, seasonal and irregular components. Thus

$$y_t = \mu_t + \psi_t + \gamma_t + \varepsilon_t, \qquad t = 1, \ldots, T \tag{3.8}$$

where μ_t is the trend, ψ_t is the cycle, γ_t is the seasonal and ε_t is the irregular. All four components are stochastic and the disturbances driving them are mutually uncorrelated. The trend, seasonal and cycle are all derived from deterministic functions of time, and reduce to these functions as limiting cases. The irregular is white noise. Details of the seasonal component can be found in section 5.5, while the cycle is described in section 6.5.

Further generalisations are also possible. These may reflect prior knowledge concerning the way the data was collected or the type of features which are likely to be present. For example, the irregular component may be formulated so as to reflect the sampling scheme used to collect the data. If observations are collected on a daily basis, a slowly changing day of the week effect may be incorporated in the model, while for hourly observations an intra-day pattern may be modelled in a similar way to seasonality.

Properties in the Time Domain

The structural models set out above can be made stationary by differencing. The theoretical ACFs can then be found.

If the trend component in (3.1) is a random walk, the model can be made stationary by differencing once. This yields:

$$\Delta y_t = \eta_t + \Delta \varepsilon_t \tag{3.9}$$

from which it is easy to see that

$$E(\Delta y_t) = E(\eta_t) + E(\varepsilon_t) - E(\varepsilon_{t-1}) = 0$$

while

$$\gamma(0) = E[(\eta_t + \Delta \varepsilon_t)^2] = \sigma_\eta^2 + 2\sigma_\varepsilon^2$$

$$\gamma(1) = E[(\eta_t + \Delta \varepsilon_t)(\eta_{t-1} + \Delta \varepsilon_{t-1})] = -\sigma_\varepsilon^2$$

$$\gamma(\tau) = 0, \qquad \tau \geqslant 2 \tag{3.10}$$

Hence

$$\rho(\tau) = \begin{cases} -\sigma_\varepsilon^2/(\sigma_\eta^2 + 2\sigma_\varepsilon^2), & \tau = 1 \\ 0, & \tau \geqslant 2 \end{cases} \tag{3.11}$$

The only non-zero autocorrelation is therefore confined to the range, $-0.5 \leqslant \rho(1) \leqslant 0$.

In the local linear trend model, (3.1) and (3.5), differencing twice gives

$$\Delta^2 y_t = \zeta_{t-1} + \Delta\eta_t + \Delta^2\varepsilon_t \tag{3.12}$$

Evaluating the autocovariance function of (3.12) gives

$$\gamma(0) = \ 2\sigma_\eta^2 + \sigma_\zeta^2 + 6\sigma_\varepsilon^2$$
$$\gamma(1) = -\sigma_\eta^2 \qquad\quad - 4\sigma_\varepsilon^2$$
$$\gamma(2) = \qquad\qquad\qquad\ \ \sigma_\varepsilon^2$$
$$\gamma(\tau) = 0, \qquad \tau \geqslant 3 \tag{3.13}$$

Dividing the $\gamma(\tau)$s through by $\gamma(0)$ gives the autocorrelation function. The first two autocorrelations satisfy the restrictions

$$-0.667 \leqslant \rho(1) \leqslant 0 \qquad \text{and} \qquad 0 \leqslant \rho(2) \leqslant 0.167$$

Reduced Form ARIMA Models

A structural time series model normally contains several disturbance terms. Provided the model is linear, the components driven by these disturbances can be combined to give a model with a single disturbance. This is known as the *reduced form* or sometimes, as in Nerlove *et al.* (1979), the canonical form. The reduced form is an ARIMA model, and the fact that it is derived from a structural form will typically imply restrictions on the parameter space. If these restrictions are not imposed when an ARIMA model of the implied order is fitted, we are dealing with the *unrestricted* reduced form.

The terminology of reduced and structural form is used in a parallel fashion to the way it is used in econometrics, except that in structural time series models the restrictions come not from economic theory, but from a desire to ensure that the forecasts reflect features such as cycles and seasonals which are felt to be present in the data.

The autocorrelation function of first differences in the random walk plus noise model, (3.1) and (3.2), exhibits the cut-off at lag one characteristic of the MA(1) process. The reduced form is therefore the ARIMA(0, 1, 1) model

$$\Delta y_t = \xi_t + \theta\xi_{t-1}, \qquad t = 2, \ldots, T \tag{3.14}$$

where ξ_t is white noise with mean zero and variance σ^2; the notation ξ_t is used to stress that this disturbance term is not the same as ε_t in (3.1). Equating the autocorrelations at lag one in expressions (3.11) and (2.1.15) gives

$$\theta = [(q^2 + 4q)^{1/2} - 2 - q]/2 \tag{3.15}$$

where q is the signal–noise ratio $q = \sigma_\eta^2/\sigma_\varepsilon^2$. Furthermore $\sigma^2 = -\sigma_\varepsilon^2/\theta$.

In solving the quadratic equation to get (3.15), the negative of the square root is dropped as it implies a non-invertible MA parameter. With θ as defined in (3.15), $0 \leqslant q \leqslant \infty$ corresponds to $-1 \leqslant \theta \leqslant 0$. Thus the MA parameter in the ARIMA$(0, 1, 1)$ reduced form only covers half the usual parameter space for this model. Positive values of θ cannot be obtained from the random walk plus noise structural form. Finally note that the reduced form ARIMA$(0, 1, 1)$ model is strictly non-invertible when $\sigma_\eta^2 = 0$ since this corresponds to $\theta = -1$.

It can be seen from the autocovariance function in (3.13) that the reduced form of the local linear trend is an ARIMA$(0, 2, 2)$ process. The restrictions on the parameter space are even more severe than in the case of the random walk plus noise model; see figure 2.5.1 in FSK. In the special case when $\sigma_\zeta^2 = 0$, the trend component reduces to

$$\mu_t = \mu_{t-1} + \beta + \eta_t \qquad (3.16)$$

and so taking first differences yields

$$\Delta y_t = \beta + \eta_t + \Delta\varepsilon_{t-1} \qquad (3.17)$$

which is an ARIMA$(0, 1, 1)$ model plus constant. If second differences are taken

$$\Delta^2 y_t = (1 - L)(\eta_t + \varepsilon_t - \varepsilon_{t-1}) \qquad (3.18)$$

and it can be seen that the right hand side is a strictly non-invertible MA(2) process.

Estimation, Prediction and Smoothing

The state space form provides the key to the statistical treatment of structural models. It enables ML estimators of the unknown parameters in a Gaussian model to be computed via the Kalman filter and the prediction error decomposition. ML estimation can also be carried out in the frequency domain as described in section 6.8. However, even if this approach is used, the state space form is still needed for prediction and estimation of the unobserved components.

The random walk plus noise model goes immediately into state space form, with μ_t being the state. Following the discussion below equation (4.3.9), parameterising the model by setting the variance of η_t to $\sigma_\varepsilon^2 q$ enables the Kalman filter to be run independently of σ_ε^2. If m_t and $m_{t|t-1}$ denote the estimators of μ_t, corresponding to a_t and $a_{t|t-1}$ in section 4.2, and p_t and $p_{t|t-1}$ denote their corresponding MSEs divided by σ_ε^2, the Kalman filter prediction equations can be written as

$$m_{t|t-1} = m_{t-1} \quad \text{and} \quad p_{t|t-1} = p_{t-1} + q, \qquad t = 2, \ldots, T \quad (3.19)$$

while the updating equations are

$$m_t = m_{t|t-1} + p_{t|t-1}(y_t - m_{t|t-1})/(p_{t|t-1} + 1) \qquad (3.20a)$$

and

$$p_t = p_{t|t-1} - p_{t|t-1}^2/(p_{t|t-1} + 1), \qquad t = 2, \ldots, T \qquad (3.20b)$$

The starting values, as given by the argument below (4.2.12), are $m_1 = y_1$ and $p_1 = 1$. The parameter σ_ε^2 may be concentrated out of the likelihood function, since for a given value of q it is given by

$$\tilde{\sigma}_\varepsilon^2(q) = (T - 1)^{-1} \sum_{t=2}^{T} v_t^2/f_t \qquad (3.21)$$

where $f_t = p_{t|t-1} + 1$. This leaves a concentrated likelihood function of the form (4.3.13) to be maximised with respect to q.

The local linear trend model goes in state space form almost as easily once it is recognised that (3.5), the process generating μ_t and β_t, is a first-order vector autoregression. Thus

$$y_t = (1 \ \ 0)\alpha_t + \varepsilon_t, \qquad t = 1, \ldots, T \qquad (3.22a)$$

and

$$\alpha_t = \begin{bmatrix} \mu_t \\ \beta_t \end{bmatrix} = \begin{bmatrix} 1 & 1 \\ 0 & 1 \end{bmatrix} \begin{bmatrix} \mu_{t-1} \\ \beta_{t-1} \end{bmatrix} + \begin{bmatrix} \eta_t \\ \zeta_t \end{bmatrix} \qquad (3.22b)$$

In this case, the use of a diffuse prior for the state leads to initial conditions being formed from the first two observations.

Once the hyperparameters have been estimated, predictions of future observations, together with their MSEs, may be made by equations (4.2.5) and (4.2.6). The predictor of the state l steps ahead is

$$\mathbf{a}_{T+l|T} = \mathbf{T}^l \mathbf{a}_T, \qquad l = 1, 2, 3, \ldots$$

and so for the local linear trend, expression (3.6), and consequently the forecast function in (3.7), follow almost immediately. Smoothing algorithms may be used to extract the trend.

Structural Models and Ad Hoc Forecasting

It was shown in (2.10) that the optimal forecast from an ARIMA$(0, 1, 1)$ model is an EWMA with smoothing constant, λ, equal to $1 + \theta$. Given that the random walk plus noise model is equivalent to ARIMA$(0, 1, 1)$, it follows that it must also yield forecasts similar to those produced by an EWMA. This can be shown directly by examining the Kalman filter for the local level model. Combining equations (3.19) and (3.20) gives

$$m_t = (1 - \lambda_t)m_{t-1} + \lambda_t y_t \qquad (3.23a)$$

and

$$p_t = p_{t-1} + q - (p_{t-1} + q)^2/(p_{t-1} + q + 1), \qquad t = 2, \ldots, T \qquad (3.23b)$$

where

$$\lambda_t = (p_{t-1} + q)/(p_{t-1} + q + 1) \qquad (3.23c)$$

with starting values $m_1 = y_1$ and $p_1 = 1$. In a steady state, p_t converges to a constant $\bar{p}$; see FSK, section 3.3. Equation (3.23b) therefore becomes

$$\bar{p} = \bar{p} + q - (\bar{p} + q)^2/(\bar{p} + q + 1)$$

Solving the resulting quadratic equation

$$\bar{p}^2 + \bar{p}q - q = 0$$

gives

$$\bar{p} = (-q + \sqrt{q^2 + 4q})/2 \qquad (3.24)$$

the other root being inappropriate since it is negative. In the steady state, therefore, the estimator of the level satisfies the recursion

$$m_t = (1 - \lambda)m_{t-1} + \lambda y_t \qquad (3.25a)$$

with

$$\lambda = \frac{\bar{p} + q}{\bar{p} + q + 1} = \frac{q + \sqrt{q^2 + 4q}}{2 + q + \sqrt{q^2 + 4q}} \qquad (3.25b)$$

provided that q is strictly positive. This recursion corresponds to the EWMA of (1.14) and, with $q > 0$, the smoothing constant in (3.25b) must lie in the range $0 < \lambda \leqslant 1$. The Kalman filter of (3.23) therefore converges to the EWMA. Note, however, that it works even if $q = 0$, whereas the EWMA cannot be applied when λ takes the corresponding value of zero.

A similar exercise can be carried out with the local linear trend model. Provided σ_ζ^2 is strictly positive, the Kalman filter converges to the Holt–Winters recursions (1.21) with suitably defined smoothing constants; see FSK, pp. 175–7. The actual relationship is

$$q_\eta = (\lambda_0^2 + \lambda_0^2\lambda_1 - 2\lambda_0\lambda_1)/(1 - \lambda_0) \qquad (3.26a)$$

$$q_\zeta = \lambda_0^2\lambda_1^2/(1 - \lambda_0) \qquad (3.26b)$$

where q_η and q_ζ are the relative variances $\sigma_\eta^2/\sigma_\varepsilon^2$ and $\sigma_\zeta^2/\sigma_\varepsilon^2$ respectively. Expressions linking λ_0 and λ_1 to the discount factor, ω, in discounted least squares were given below (1.26) and so it follows from (3.26) that forecasts corresponding to those obtained by double exponential smoothing are given by setting

$$q_\zeta = (q_\eta/2)^2 = (1 - \omega)^2/\omega^2$$

Model Selection

The attraction of the structural framework is that it enables the researcher to formulate, at the outset, a model which is explicitly designed to pick up the salient characteristics of the data. Once the model has been estimated, its suitability can be assessed, not only by carrying out diagnostic tests, but also by checking whether the estimated components are consistent with any prior knowledge which might be available. Thus if a cyclical component is used to model the trade cycle, a knowledge of the economic history of the period should enable one to judge whether the estimated parameters are reasonable. This is in the same spirit as assessing the plausibility of a regression model by reference to the sign and magnitude of its estimated coefficients.

Classical time series analysis is based on the theory of stationary stochastic processes, and this is reflected in the ARIMA approach, where non-stationarity is handled by differencing and a model selected on the basis of an analysis of the differenced series. The fact that the principal structural time series models can be made stationary by differencing provides an important link with classical time series analysis. However, the analysis of series which it is hoped have been transformed to stationarity does not play a fundamental role in structural model selection.

Once a structural model has been estimated, it is subjected to diagnostic checking in much the same way as an ARIMA model. The residuals are the standardised one-step ahead prediction errors defined in (4.3.16). The degrees of freedom of the Box–Ljung Q-statistic are taken to be the number of hyperparameters minus one.

Example 2   The US rate of inflation, measured as the first difference of the logarithm of the seasonally adjusted GNP deflator, is graphed in figure 5.2 from 1952 Q1 to 1985 Q4. There appears to be no sustained upward or downward movement, and a random walk plus noise seems to be a plausible model. The ML estimates of the variances of ε_t and η_t are

$$\tilde{\sigma}_\varepsilon^2 = 0.123 \quad \text{and} \quad \tilde{\sigma}_\eta^2 = 0.028$$

respectively, the goodness of fit statistics are

$$s = 0.446, \quad R^2 = 0.62 \quad \text{and} \quad R_D^2 = 0.28$$

while the diagnostics include

$$Q(12) = 7.35, \quad N = 4.96 \quad \text{and} \quad H = 0.85$$

As can be seen by the diagnostics, the model fits well. The degrees of freedom for the Q-statistic is eleven, and so the value of 7.35 is clearly not significant.

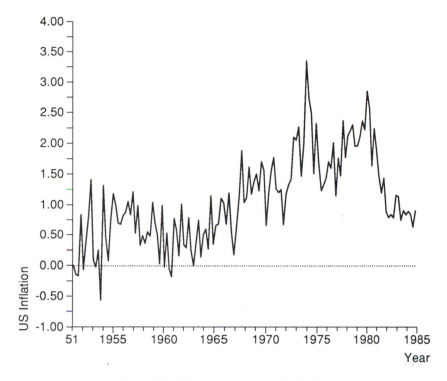

Figure 5.2 US quarterly rate of inflation.

If μ_t is interpreted as the underlying rate of inflation, the filtered estimate at the end of the series provides useful information to policymakers as the current estimate to be projected into the future. The smoothed estimates give the best indication of how inflation has evolved over the period.

In example 7 at the end of section 5.2, an analysis of correlograms led to the identification of an ARIMA(0, 1, 1) model for the inflation series. This model is the reduced form of the random walk plus noise.

5.4 Autoregressive Models

The attraction of autoregressions is that they are easy to specify and estimate. They can be expected to yield good short-term forecasts in many situations, and generalisation to multivariate series is straightforward. As was observed in section 3.6, model selection can be carried out in a systematic way by fitting a general model and then 'testing down' until a suitably parsimonious specification has been found.

The modelling of non-stationary series by autoregressions raises some interesting issues. Differencing need not be imposed and this in turn leads on to an approach for testing non-stationarity by means of *unit root tests*.

Consider an ARIMA$(1, 1, 0)$ model

$$\Delta y_t = \phi \, \Delta y_{t-1} + \varepsilon_t, \qquad |\phi| < 1 \tag{4.1}$$

Such a model generates a stationary series in first differences, Δy_t, but the corresponding levels, y_t, are non-stationary. On replacing Δ by $1 - L$ and re-arranging, as was done earlier for prediction purposes in (2.3), equation (4.1) can be expressed as,

$$y_t = (1 + \phi)y_{t-1} - \phi y_{t-2} + \varepsilon_t \tag{4.2}$$

This is an AR(2) process, but the fact that it is non-stationary is reflected in the presence of a unit root in the autoregressive polynomial in the lag operator, that is

$$\varphi(L) = 1 - (1 + \phi)L + \phi L^2 = (1 - \phi L)(1 - L) \tag{4.3}$$

What happens if a unit root is not imposed on a model for a series when one is present? The simplest case to analyse is fitting an AR(1) to a random walk. For a stationary AR(1) process, it was shown in section 3.2 that the least squares estimator of ϕ obtained by regressing y_t on y_{t-1} is asymptotically normal with mean ϕ and variance $(1 - \phi^2)/T$. This result does not hold when the true model is a random walk. Indeed, it clearly makes no sense to set ϕ equal to unity in the formula for the asymptotic variance. In fact it turns out that there is a limiting distribution for the OLS estimator, $\hat{\phi}$, but it is for $T(\hat{\phi} - 1)$ rather than for $T^{\frac{1}{2}}(\hat{\phi} - 1)$. This means that convergence to the limiting distribution is much faster than for a stationary process, the intuitive reason being that the denominator of $\hat{\phi}$ increases at a much faster rate because the series does not hover around a constant level. The fast convergence is also the reason why the estimator is said to be *superconsistent*. Unfortunately, the limiting distribution of $T(\hat{\phi} - 1)$ is not Gaussian; see, for example, Phillips (1987). Furthermore, the typical estimate likely to be obtained in small samples will be well below unity, and if this point is not recognised one may well erroneously conclude that the series is stationary.

Dickey–Fuller Test

Despite the non-standard properties of the OLS estimator in a non-stationary AR(1) model, a test of the hypothesis that the process is a random walk against the alternative that it is stationary can be carried out using the standard regression 't-statistic' and comparing its value with tables constructed by Dickey and Fuller. These tables are given in Table 8.5.2 of the book by Fuller (1976), and are reproduced in EATS. Formally stated, the model is

$$y_t = \phi y_{t-1} + \varepsilon_t, \qquad t = 2, \ldots, T$$

and the test statistic is

$$\hat{\tau} = (\hat{\phi} - 1)/\{\operatorname{avar}(\hat{\phi})\}^{1/2} \tag{4.4}$$

where

$$\operatorname{avar}(\hat{\phi}) = s^2 \Big/ \left(\sum_{t=2}^{T} y_{t-1}^2 \right)$$

with

$$s^2 = \sum_{t=2}^{T} (y_t - \hat{\phi} y_{t-1})^2/(T-2)$$

The test is of $H_0: \phi = 1$ against $H_1: \phi < 1$.

The distribution of $\hat{\phi}$ is shifted further to the left if a constant term is included in the model, and further still if there is a time trend, so that

$$y_t = \alpha + \beta t + \phi y_{t-1} + \varepsilon_t \tag{4.5}$$

The critical values for the statistic obtained when there is a constant in the model, $\hat{\tau}_\mu$, and when there is a constant and a time trend, $\hat{\tau}_\tau$, are also given in the Dickey–Fuller tables. Note that the t-statistic obtained from model (4.5) is the same as the t-statistic obtained when the observations are first detrended by regressing on time, and an AR(1) model is fitted to the residuals.

Another way of formulating the AR(1) model is as

$$\Delta y_t = \phi^\dagger y_{t-1} + \varepsilon_t, \qquad t = 2, \ldots, T \tag{4.6}$$

where $\phi^\dagger = \phi - 1$. The parameter $\phi^\dagger$ is zero when the process is a random walk and it follows from the previous discussion that its estimator will tend to be negative. The t-statistic for testing $\phi^\dagger$ equal to zero is identical to the statistic (4.4). The attraction of setting up the AR(1) model in such a way that the unit root test is the test that a particular parameter is zero, is that it generalises to higher order autoregressive processes. Thus the AR(p) model may be reformulated as

$$\Delta y_t = \phi^\dagger y_{t-1} + \sum_{j=1}^{p-1} \phi_j^\dagger \Delta y_{t-j} + \varepsilon_t \tag{4.7}$$

where

$$\phi_j^\dagger = -\sum_{k=j+1}^{p} \phi_k, \qquad j = 1, 2, \ldots, p-1 \tag{4.8a}$$

and

$$\phi^{\dagger} = \sum_{k=1}^{p} \phi_k - 1 \tag{4.8b}$$

When $\phi^{\dagger}$ is zero, the model reduces to an AR$(p-1)$ in first differences, that is ARIMA$(p-1, 1, 0)$. Thus a test of the hypothesis that $\phi^{\dagger}$ is zero is the test of a unit root. The test could also be carried out by regressing y_t on y_{t-1} to y_{t-p} and testing the restriction that the coefficients sum to one. However, the formulation in (4.7) is not only more convenient, but it is also more stable numerically.

The asymptotic distribution of the 't-statistic' associated with y_{t-1} in (4.7) is the same as that of (4.4). This suggests the use of the critical values given in the Dickey–Fuller tables. This generalisation of the test for a unit root is known as the *augmented Dickey–Fuller* test. It can further be shown that the t-statistics associated with the differenced variables in (4.7) are asymptotically standard normal, so that inference on the lags can be conducted in the usual way. The intuition behind this result is that when $\phi^{\dagger}$ is zero, the superconsistency of its estimator means that this also effectively takes a value of zero when the limiting distribution of $T^{1/2}$ times the estimators of $\phi_1^{\dagger}$ to $\phi_{p-1}^{\dagger}$ is considered.

Example 1   Carrying out a regression of the form (4.7), with a constant and time trend included, using data on seasonally adjusted US real GNP gives

$$\widehat{\Delta y_t} = 1.654 + 0.0134t - 0.374y_{t-1} + 0.052\,\Delta y_{t-1} \tag{4.9}$$
$$(0.837)\ (0.0072)\ (0.196)\qquad(0.243)$$

where the observations on Δy_t run from 1950 to 1971. The t-statistic for y_{t-1} is -1.91. A one-sided test of the null hypothesis of a unit root against the alternative of a stationary autoregressive process would lead to a rejection of the unit root at the 5% level if the t-statistic were treated as being asymptotically normal and -1.64 were taken to be the critical value. The Dickey–Fuller table, on the other hand, gives a 5% critical value of -3.60 for $T = 25$. Inference on the coefficient of Δy_{t-1} can be carried out in the usual way, and it is clear that it is not statistically significant. Dropping this variable from the regression gives

$$\widehat{\Delta y_t} = 1.574 + 0.0127t - 0.355y_{t-1}$$
$$(0.705)\ (0.0062)\ (0.165)$$

where the observations on Δy_t now start at 1949. The t-statistic for y_{t-1} is -2.15, but, as before, the null hypothesis of a unit root cannot be rejected at any reasonable level of significance when the Dickey–Fuller tables are used. Note that if the above equation is re-arranged so that y_t is the dependent variable, the coefficient of y_{t-1} is 0.645, a value which one might quite reasonably have supposed was comfortably within the stationarity region. Note also that the '*t*-statistic' of the time trend is 2.07, a value which would normally be thought of as significant. However, in this situation standard asymptotic theory does not apply to the coefficient of the time trend, and the significance tends to be overstated.

Autoregressions as Approximations

How well an AR model will be able to approximate a mixed process will depend on how close the MA part is to the boundary of the invertibility region, in other words how close the roots of the MA polynomial are to the unit circle. This is demonstrated quite clearly in the case of an MA(1) model. As can be seen from (2.3.5), the AR coefficient for y_{t-j} is $(-\theta)^j$ and if θ is close to ± 1, a high order autoregression will be needed to provide a reasonable approximation.

Example 2   Fitting an AR(3) model to the US rate of inflation as defined in example 2 of section 5.3 gives coefficients of 0.38, 0.24 and 0.23 respectively. These sum to 0.85 which is close enough to one to arouse suspicions of a unit root. Re-arranging the model with the difference of the rate of inflation as the dependent variable, and including a constant, gives

$$\widehat{\Delta y}_t = 0.154 - 0.136 y_{t-1} - 0.476 \, \Delta y_{t-1} - 0.234 \, \Delta y_{t-2} \quad (4.10)$$
$$\phantom{\widehat{\Delta y}_t = } (0.075) \ (0.059) \qquad (0.088) \qquad\quad (0.083)$$

The '*t*-statistic' on y_{t-1} is 2.31 and since the 5% critical value in the Dickey–Fuller tables for $T = 100$ is -2.89, the null hypothesis of a unit root cannot be rejected.

The connection with the local level model fitted in section 5.3 is as follows. The reduced form of this model is the ARIMA(0, 1, 1) process (3.14) and the value of the MA parameter implied by (3.15) and the estimated structural parameters is $\theta = -0.62$. The implied coefficients in the AR representation

$$\Delta y_t = \theta \, \Delta y_{t-1} - \theta^2 \, \Delta y_{t-2} + \theta^3 \, \Delta y_{t-3} - \cdots + \xi_t$$

are therefore -0.62, -0.38, -0.24, -0.15 and so on. If the constant term and the level, y_{t-1}, are dropped from (4.10) and another lag is added, the estimated coefficients of the lagged differences are -0.58, -0.35 and -0.14 respectively.

The use of AR models as approximations raises the question of the applicability of the augmented Dickey–Fuller test. In theory the test is only valid if the underlying process is indeed a finite autoregression. When an MA part is present, a bias is introduced into the test statistics. Despite this difficulty, Said and Dickey (1984) showed that the augmented Dickey–Fuller test could still be justified on asymptotic grounds, if, in (4.7), p increases with the sample size in such a way that it is of order $T^{1/2}$. Phillips and Perron (1988) suggested a modified test statistic which employed a correction constructed from the residuals in (4.6), while Hall (1989) proposed an instrumental variable test statistic based on an estimator of ϕ in an AR(1) model using y_{t-2} as an instrument for y_{t-1}. However, the Monte Carlo evidence in Schwert (1989) and the analysis in Pantula (1991) indicates that these modifications may not be very successful. For example, in the ARIMA (0, 1, 1) model, a negative value of θ close to minus one means that the series is not too far from being stationary white noise. In these circumstances, all the above tests reject the null hypothesis of a unit root much more frequently than they should. Thus for $T = 100$ and $\theta = -0.8$, Pantula (1991, p. 67) shows that for a nominal test size of 0.05, the augmented Dickey–Fuller tests based on AR models with $p = 4$ and $p = 8$ have empirical sizes of 0.36 and 0.11 respectively, Hall's IV test has a size of 0.22, while the Phillips–Perron tests have sizes of over 0.85. Both Pantula and Schwert end up recommending the augmented Dickey–Fuller test, while conceding that the question of how to decide on an appropriate value of p is a difficult one to resolve.

Situations in which the MA part of a non-stationary model is close to non-invertibility may easily arise in practice. This is particularly likely to be the case for I(2) processes. For example, in the local linear trend model, the variance of the slope disturbance, ζ_t, is generally small in relation to the other variances, and this corresponds to a reduced form ARIMA(0, 2, 2) model in which the MA part is close to non-invertibility. The net result is that distinguishing between I(1) and I(2) processes is likely to be very difficult in practice, with the AR based unit root tests tending to favour I(1) specifications, even when I(2) models are appropriate.

5.5 Seasonality

When observations are available on a monthly or a quarterly basis, some allowance must be made for seasonal effects. One approach would be to work with seasonally adjusted data, but for the reasons discussed in the final sub-section this is not generally desirable. The bulk of this section is therefore concerned with ways in which seasonality can be incorporated into time series models.

There are two aspects to seasonality. The first is concerned with patterns in the observations which are repeated more or less regularly from year to year. These features are permanent, and they may be regarded as stemming from factors such as the weather. Modelling such effects involves considerations similar to those which arise in modelling trends. A deterministic seasonal component is appropriate if it is felt that the seasonal pattern is constant from year to year, while a stochastic component can be introduced if it is felt that the pattern is slowly changing. Both models project a regular seasonal pattern into the future, but when a stochastic model is used this pattern depends more heavily on the later observations in the series. There is a direct parallel with the concept of a local trend in a non-seasonal series.

The other aspect of seasonality concerns effects which arise in the absence of, or in addition to, the type of seasonality described in the previous paragraph. For example, a dock strike in March of last year could influence production targets in March of this year if firms believe that there is a high probability of such an event happening again. However, unless dock strikes in March turn out to be a regular occurrence, the effect of the original strike will be transitory. Thus, while it is likely that observations in the same seasons of different years will be correlated, these correlations can be expected to be small if the years are a long way apart. These considerations suggest a stationary model, in which any seasonal pattern tends to disappear as the lead time of a forecast increases. Models of this kind are discussed in the first sub-section below. This is followed by a description of models with deterministic and slowly changing seasonal effects.

Seasonal Autoregressive-Moving Average Processes

Consider a stationary series of quarterly observations. A very simple way of capturing a seasonal effect is by a fourth-order seasonal autoregressive process of the form

$$y_t = \phi_4 y_{t-4} + \varepsilon_t, \qquad |\phi_4| < 1 \tag{5.1}$$

This model is a special case of an $AR(4)$ process, but with the constraint that $\phi_1 = \phi_2 = \phi_3 = 0$. The properties of (5.1) are very similar to those of a stationary $AR(1)$ process and using the techniques developed in section 2.2, it is not difficult to show that the autocorrelation function is given by

$$\rho(\tau) = \begin{cases} \phi_4^{\tau/4}, & \tau = 0, 4, 8, \ldots \\ 0, & \text{otherwise} \end{cases} \tag{5.2}$$

The closer $|\phi_4|$ is to unity, the stronger the seasonal pattern. However, as long as ϕ_4 remains within the unit circle, the seasonal effect is non-deterministic, with the seasonal pattern gradually dying away as predictions are made further and further ahead.

Model (5.1) may be extended to allow for both AR and MA terms at other seasonal lags. If s denotes the number of seasons in the year, a general formulation is as follows:

$$\Phi(L^s)y_t = \Theta(L^s)\zeta_t \qquad (5.3)$$

where

$$\Phi(L^s) = 1 - \Phi_1 L^s - \cdots - \Phi_P L^{Ps} \qquad (5.4a)$$

$$\Theta(L^s) = 1 + \Theta_1 L^s + \cdots + \Theta_Q L^{Qs} \qquad (5.4b)$$

and ζ_t is a white noise disturbance term. The value of s will typically be either four or twelve in economic applications, corresponding to quarterly and monthly observations respectively.

Expression (5.3) defines a pure seasonal ARMA process of order $(P, Q)_s$. As in the case of (5.1), the autocorrelation function will contain 'gaps' at non-seasonal lags. However, unless seasonal movements are felt to be the only predictable feature of the series, such a model will not be appropriate. With monthly data, for example, it seems reasonable to suppose that an observation in March will be related to the observation in February, as well as to the observation in March of the previous year.

There are basically two ways of constructing models which make allowance for both seasonal and non-seasonal movements. The first is simply to fill in the gaps in the seasonal process. Thus a first-order lag might be incorporated into (5.1) to yield

$$y_t = \phi_1 y_{t-1} + \phi_4 y_{t-4} + \varepsilon_t \qquad (5.5)$$

A second approach is to replace the white noise disturbance term in (5.3) by a non-seasonal ARMA(p, q) process, that is

$$\phi(L)\zeta_t = \theta(L)\varepsilon_t \qquad (5.6)$$

where $\phi(L)$ and $\theta(L)$ are the associated polynomials defined in (2.1.26). Combining (5.3) and (5.6) produces

$$\Phi(L^s)\phi(L)y_t = \Theta(L^s)\theta(L)\varepsilon_t \qquad (5.7)$$

This is a *multiplicative seasonal* ARMA process of order $(p, q) \times (P, Q)_s$. As a simple example, consider seasonal and non-seasonal AR(1) processes so that

$$(1 - \phi L)(1 - \Phi L^4) = \varepsilon_t \qquad (5.8)$$

This can be re-written as

$$y_t = \phi_1 y_{t-1} + \phi_4 y_{t-4} + \phi_5 y_{t-5} + \varepsilon_t \qquad (5.9)$$

where $\phi_1 = \phi$, $\phi_4 = \Phi$, $\phi_5 = -\phi\Phi$.

Multiplicative forms are widely used in time series modelling. However, there is nothing in the development so far to indicate why, for example,

(5.9) should be preferred to (5.5). It will be argued later that multiplicative models arise most naturally when differencing has taken place.

Although the methods described above are the two most common ways of formulating stationary seasonal models, there is a third possibility. This is to construct an unobserved components model

$$y_t = \gamma_t + v_t \tag{5.10}$$

in which v_t is an ARMA(p, q) process and γ_t is a seasonal ARMA process of order $(P, Q)_s$ as in (5.3). The disturbance terms deriving the two processes are assumed to be independent. As an example consider

$$y_t = \frac{\zeta_t}{1 - \Phi L^4} + \frac{\varepsilon_t}{1 - \phi L} \tag{5.11}$$

This can be re-written as

$$(1 - \phi L)(1 - \Phi L^4)y_t = \zeta_t + \varepsilon_t - \phi\zeta_{t-1} - \Phi\varepsilon_{t-4} \tag{5.12}$$

The right hand side of (5.12) is an MA(4) process, but the parameters are subject to restrictions determined by ϕ and Φ.

Deterministic Seasonality

A model consisting of a stationary stochastic process, u_t, superimposed on a fixed seasonal pattern may be written as

$$y_t = \sum_{j=1}^{s} \gamma_j z_{jt} + u_t, \qquad t = 1, \ldots, T \tag{5.13}$$

where z_{jt} is a dummy variable taking the value one in season j and zero otherwise. The model may be reformulated as

$$y_t = \mu + \sum_{j=1}^{s-1} \gamma_j z_{jt} + u_t, \qquad t = 1, \ldots, T \tag{5.14}$$

where μ is the mean and the γ_js are now seasonal coefficients constrained to sum to zero. This constraint is effected by setting up the z_{jt}'s as dummy variables defined such that for $j = 1, \ldots, s - 1$,

$$z_{jt} = \begin{cases} 1, & t = j, j + s, j + 2s, \ldots \\ 0, & t \neq j, j + s, j + 2s, \ldots \\ -1, & t = s, 2s, 3s, \ldots \end{cases} \tag{5.15}$$

The point about this representation is that the seasonal pattern is eliminated if the series is aggregated over s consecutive time periods. Thus there is a separation of the level and the seasonal. Adding a slope term gives the more general deterministic trend plus seasonal model

$$y_t = \alpha + \beta t + \sum_{j=1}^{s-1} \gamma_j z_{jt} + u_t, \qquad t = 1, \ldots, T \qquad (5.16)$$

An alternative way of modelling a seasonal pattern is by a set of trigonometric terms at the seasonal frequencies. Thus (5.16) becomes

$$y_t = \alpha + \beta t + \sum_{j=1}^{[s/2]} (\gamma_j \cos \lambda_j t + \gamma_j^* \sin \lambda_j t) + u_t, \qquad t = 1, \ldots, T \qquad (5.17)$$

where $[s/2]$ is $s/2$ if s is even and $(s-1)/2$ if s is odd, and $\lambda_j = 2\pi j/s$, $j = 1, \ldots, [s/2]$. When s is even, the sine term disappears for $j = s/2$ and so the number of trigonometric parameters, the γ_j's and γ_j^*'s, is always $(s-1)/2$, which is the same as the number of coefficients in the seasonal dummy formulation of (5.15). The equivalence of the seasonal patterns can be shown using standard trigonometric identities. Trigonometric seasonality is discussed further in section 6.6.

It is worth noting the effects of the various operations described in section 5.1. The aggregation referred to below (5.15) is accomplished by the seasonal summation operator, $S(L)$ of (1.3). Applying this operator to (5.14) yields

$$S(L)y_t = s\mu + S(L)u_t, \qquad t = s, \ldots, T \qquad (5.18)$$

the term $s\mu$ being obtained because $S(L)\mu = S(1)\mu$, and $S(1) = s$. Applying the first difference operator to (5.18) removes $s\mu$ leaving only a term involving u_t. The same result is achieved by a single operation of seasonal differencing. This can be seen very easily if the model is in the original form (5.13). The fact that this happens is a reflection of the identity (1.5). Finally note that the deterministic components can be removed from (5.16) by the combined first and seasonal difference operations, $\Delta\Delta_s$.

Estimation of (5.13) is straightforward, since it can be shown that the seasonal means are efficient estimators of the γ_j's for u_t following any stationary stochastic process. Taking seasonal means is the same as carrying out an OLS regression with the z_{jt}'s as explanatory variables. An OLS regression based on (5.14) gives an equivalent result.

Ad Hoc Forecasting by Holt–Winters

The Holt–Winters local linear trend forecasting procedure introduced in section 5.1 may be extended to allow for seasonality. There are two versions, depending on whether the trend and seasonal components are thought to combine in an additive or multiplicative fashion. Only the additive version will be described here.

There are three smoothing constants, λ_0, λ_1 and λ_s, all of which lie between zero and one. The first two play a similar role to the smoothing constants in the local linear trend forecasting procedure. The recursions for the level, slope and seasonal components, m_t, b_t, and c_t respectively, are as follows:

$$m_t = \lambda_0(y_t - c_{t-s}) + (1 - \lambda_0)(m_{t-1} + b_{t-1}) \tag{5.19a}$$

$$b_t = \lambda_1(m_t - m_{t-1}) + (1 - \lambda_1)b_{t-1} \tag{5.19b}$$

$$c_t = \lambda_s(y_t - m_t) + (1 - \lambda_s)c_{t-s} \tag{5.19c}$$

The forecast function is of the form

$$\hat{y}_{T+l|T} = m_T + b_T l + c_{T+l|T}, \qquad l = 1, 2, \ldots \tag{5.20}$$

where $c_{T+l|T}$ is the latest estimate of the relevant seasonal component. Note that the first two recursions are the same as the recursions in (1.21) but with y_t corrected for the seasonal effect. Similarly, (5.19c) is a weighted average of the seasonal effect s periods ago and the current detrended observation. An obvious weakness is that each seasonal component is only updated every s periods and the deseasonalising in (5.19a) is carried out using an estimate of the seasonal component which is s periods out of date. Nevertheless, the method seems to work quite well in practice.

5.6 Seasonal ARIMA and Structural Models

We now consider how the ideas set out in the previous section may be developed to provide practical models for seasonal time series. As we have seen the Holt–Winters procedure provides a means of projecting a trend and seasonal pattern with more weight put on the most recent observations. This section shows how the ARIMA and structural classes of models can be extended to allow for evolving seasonal patterns.

Seasonal Autoregressive-Integrated-Moving Average Models

The ARIMA class of models is based on the idea that non-stationary trend movements can be captured implicitly by fitting an ARMA model to differenced observations. This idea may be extended by supposing that evolving seasonality can be handled by the use of seasonal differences. The first step is to generalise (5.3) to

$$\Phi(L^s) \Delta_s^D y_t = \Theta(L^s) \zeta_t \tag{6.1}$$

where D is the degree of seasonal differencing.

Example 1   A simple seasonal MA(1) process is

$$\Delta_s y_t = \zeta_t + \Theta \zeta_{t-s} \qquad (6.2)$$

The forecast function is

$$\tilde{y}_{T+l|T} = \tilde{y}_{T+l-s|T} + \Theta \zeta_{T+l-s}, \qquad l = 1, 2, \ldots \qquad (6.3)$$

where the residuals are obtained from the CSS recursion

$$\zeta_t = y_t - y_{t-s} - \Theta \zeta_{t-s}$$

with the initial disturbances set to zero. Repeatedly substituting for past disturbances, as in (2.9), shows that each of the predictions in (6.3) is an EWMA of the seasonally differenced observations corresponding to the season in question, that is

$$\tilde{y}_{T+l|T} = (1 + \Theta) \sum_{j \geqslant 1} (-\Theta)^{j-1} y_{T+l-sj}, \qquad l = 1, 2, \ldots, s \quad (6.4)$$

For $l \geqslant s + 1$, $\tilde{y}_{T+l|T} = \tilde{y}_{T+l-s|T}$, and so the forecast function projects out a fixed seasonal pattern which depends more on the later observations than the early ones.

The white noise disturbance term in (6.1) can be replaced by an ARIMA(p, d, q) process yielding a generalisation of the model in (5.7):

$$\Phi(L^s)\phi(L)\,\Delta^d\,\Delta_s^D y_t = \theta_0 + \Theta(L^s)\theta(L)\varepsilon_t,$$

$$t = d + sD + 1, \ldots, T \qquad (6.5)$$

This is known as a *multiplicative seasonal* ARIMA model of order $(p, d, q) \times (P, D, Q)_s$.

The most important model within the seasonal ARIMA class has subsequently become known as the 'airline model' since it was originally fitted to a monthly series on UK airline passenger totals. The model is of order $(0, 1, 1) \times (0, 1, 1)_s$ with no constant and is written as

$$\Delta\Delta_s y_t = (1 + \theta L)(1 + \Theta L^s)\varepsilon_t \qquad (6.6)$$

where θ and Θ are MA parameters which, if the model is to be invertible, must have modulus less than one. Setting $\theta = \Theta = -1$ yields a model which is equivalent to the deterministic trend and seasonal of (5.16) when u_t is equal to a white noise disturbance ε_t. This may be seen by observing that the $\Delta\Delta_s$ operator removes both deterministic components to give

$$\Delta\Delta_s y_t = (1 - L)(1 - L^s)\varepsilon_t$$

Since $\Delta\Delta_s$ is equal to $\Delta^2 S(L)$, the trend can be thought of as being annihilated by Δ^2, while the seasonal is averaged out by the summation operator, $S(L)$.

Box and Jenkins (1976, pp. 305–6) gave a rationale for the airline model in terms of EWMA forecasts. The forecasts from an ARIMA$(0, 1, 1)$ model take the form of an EWMA, (2.20). Denote this as $\text{EWMA}(y_t; \theta)$ where y_t is the last observation. Similarly the forecasts in the seasonal MA model (6.2) are a seasonal EWMA as given in (6.4). Denote this as $\text{SEWMA}(y_t; \Theta)$. Combining the two models gives the airline model, for which, as shown by Box and Jenkins (1976, p. 312), the one-step ahead forecast is given by

$$\tilde{y}_{t+1|t} = \text{EWMA}(y_t; \theta) + \text{SEWMA}\{y_{t-s+1} - \text{EWMA}(y_{t-s}; \theta); \Theta\}$$

Thus the forecast is the EWMA taken over previous observations, modified by a second EWMA of discrepancies between EWMAs and actual values in the same season of previous years.

Like all models in the class, the airline model is handled by first multiplying out the polynomials in the lag operator. Thus

$$\Delta\Delta_s y_t = \varepsilon_t - \theta\varepsilon_{t-1} - \Theta\varepsilon_{t-s} + \theta\Theta\varepsilon_{t-s-1}, \qquad t = s+2, \ldots, T$$

Viewed in this way, the right hand side is an $\text{MA}(s+1)$ process with gaps at lags 2 to $s-1$ and the coefficient at lag $s+1$ equal to the product of the coefficients at lags 1 and s. Such restrictions are, in principle, testable. The CSS recursion is

$$\varepsilon_t = \Delta\Delta_s y_t + \theta\varepsilon_{t-1} + \Theta\varepsilon_{t-s} - \theta\Theta\varepsilon_{t-s-1}, \qquad t = s+2, \ldots, T$$

Forecasts are built up recursively, as for an ARIMA model.

Example 2 The actual airline passenger data consists of monthly totals over the period January 1949 to December 1960; see Box and Jenkins (1976, p. 531) or FSK, p. 518. Figure 5.3 shows a plot of the logarithms

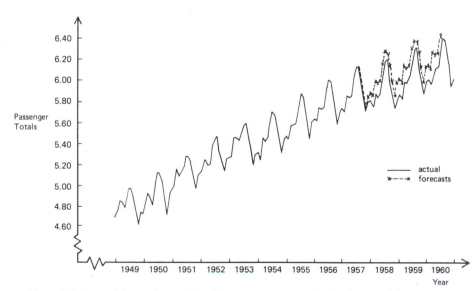

Figure 5.3 Logarithms of monthly airline passenger totals (in thousands). *Source of data:* Box and Jenkins (1976, p. 531).

of these figures (in thousands) together with forecasts made from July 1957. The parameter estimates, obtained by exact ML, based on the full set of observations are

$$\tilde{\theta} = -0.40 \qquad \tilde{\Theta} = -0.55$$
$$(0.09) \qquad\qquad (0.07)$$

The figures in parentheses are asymptotic standard errors. The Box–Ljung Q-statistic based on the first 48 residual autocorrelations is 44.12. This gives no indication of misspecification.

The seasonal ARIMA class is very general. However, D is rarely set to a value greater than one, and $D = 1$ is usually combined with $d = 0$ or 1. When $d = D = 1$ and $\theta_0 = 0$, as in the airline model, the eventual forecast function is a fixed seasonal pattern superimposed upon a linear trend. The same is true when $d = 0$ and $\theta_0 \neq 0$; if $\theta_0 = 0$, the slope of the trend is zero. A fixed seasonal pattern can be modelled by setting $D = 0$ and introducing into (6.5) a set of seasonal dummies defined as in (5.15).

The autocovariance function for $\Delta\Delta_s y_t$ from the airline model is

$$\gamma(0) = (1 + \theta^2)(1 + \Theta^2)\sigma^2$$
$$\gamma(1) = \theta(1 + \Theta^2)\sigma^2$$
$$\gamma(\tau) = 0, \qquad\qquad\qquad \tau = 2, \ldots, s - 2$$
$$\gamma(s - 1) = \theta\Theta\sigma^2 \tag{6.7}$$
$$\gamma(s) = \Theta(1 + \theta^2)\sigma^2$$
$$\gamma(s + 1) = \theta\Theta\sigma^2$$
$$\gamma(\tau) = 0, \qquad\qquad\qquad \tau \geqslant s + 2$$

Thus the salient features of the ACF are non-zero autocorrelations at lags one, $s - 1$, s and $s + 1$. The ACFs of other models may be similarly obtained. However, the presence of autoregressive effects together with seasonal and non-seasonal polynomials can make model identification very difficult. In practice, attention is often restricted to the airline model and specifications close to it.

Structural Models

A fixed seasonal pattern has the property that the seasonal effect at time t, denoted γ_t, is equal to the seasonal effect at time $t - s$, γ_{t-s}. This suggests that a possible way to model changing seasonality is

$$\gamma_t = \gamma_{t-s} + \omega_t \tag{6.8}$$

where ω_t is a white noise disturbance term. The model

$$y_t = \gamma_t + u_t \tag{6.9}$$

then collapses to (5.13) when the disturbance in (6.8) has zero variance. However, just as (5.13) confounds the level and seasonal effects, so does (6.8). A better approach is to set up a model for stochastic seasonality based on the formulation in (5.14). Here the seasonal effects are constrained to sum to zero over a year, that is

$$\gamma_t + \gamma_{t-1} + \cdots + \gamma_{t-s+1} = 0 \tag{6.10}$$

The pattern can be allowed to evolve over time by setting this sum equal to a random disturbance term, so that

$$\sum_{j=0}^{s-1} \gamma_{t-j} = \omega_t \quad \text{or} \quad \gamma_t = -\sum_{j=1}^{s-1} \gamma_{t-j} + \omega_t \tag{6.11}$$

Using this form of stochastic seasonality, (5.14) can be generalised to

$$y_t = \mu_t + \gamma_t + u_t, \qquad t = 1, \ldots, T \tag{6.12}$$

where the level, μ_t, can also be allowed to evolve over time by modelling it as a random walk. Unlike (6.9), the level and seasonal components are separate in (6.12). The non-stationarity in μ_t derives from the first difference operator, while the seasonal component depends on the $S(L)$ operator and is reduced to a random disturbance when it is applied. The combined effect of the two operators is the seasonal difference, Δ_s, which is the operator implied by (6.8).

For many quarterly and monthly time series, the *basic structural model* (BSM) is appropriate. This is of the form (6.12), except that μ_t is generalised to include a slope, as in (3.5), while u_t reduces to white noise, ε_t. Thus

$$y_t = \mu_t + \gamma_t + \varepsilon_t, \qquad t = 1, \ldots, T \tag{6.13}$$

The model may be handled statistically by putting it in state space form. Thus for $s = 4$:

$$y_t = (1 \ 0 \ 1 \ 0 \ 0)\alpha_t + \varepsilon_t \tag{6.14a}$$

$$\alpha_t = \begin{bmatrix} \mu_t \\ \beta_t \\ \cdots \\ \gamma_t \\ \gamma_{t-1} \\ \gamma_{t-2} \end{bmatrix} = \begin{bmatrix} 1 & 1 & \vdots & & \mathbf{0} & \\ 0 & 1 & \vdots & & & \\ \cdots & & \cdots & \cdots & \cdots & \cdots \\ & & \vdots & -1 & -1 & -1 \\ & \mathbf{0} & \vdots & 1 & 0 & 0 \\ & & \vdots & 0 & 1 & 0 \end{bmatrix} \begin{bmatrix} \mu_{t-1} \\ \beta_{t-1} \\ \cdots \\ \gamma_{t-1} \\ \gamma_{t-2} \\ \gamma_{t-3} \end{bmatrix} + \begin{bmatrix} \eta_t \\ \zeta_t \\ \cdots \\ \omega_t \\ 0 \\ 0 \end{bmatrix}$$

$$\tag{6.14b}$$

The third element in the state vector therefore represents the current seasonal effect.

Example 3   The UK consumption of gas by 'Other final users', a category which includes offices, shops and agriculture, is shown in figure 5.4; see appendix 2 in FSK for the data. There are clear trend and seasonal movements. Fitting a BSM and applying a smoothing algorithm gives the trend shown by the dotted line in figure 5.4(a) and the seasonal in figure 5.4(b). The rapid growth in the early 1970s follows the introduction of cheaper natural gas from the North Sea. The seasonal pattern becomes more pronounced at the same time. This is because most of the increased gas usage went on heating, and hence the main effect is on consumption in the winter.

Comparison of Airline and Basic Structural Models

The properties of the BSM are captured by the autocovariance function for the stationary form of the model,

$$\Delta\Delta_s y_t = S(L)\zeta_{t-1} + \Delta_s \eta_t + \Delta^2 \omega_t + \Delta\Delta_s \varepsilon_t \tag{6.15}$$

Thus

$$
\begin{aligned}
\gamma(0) &= 2\sigma_\eta^2 + s\sigma_\zeta^2 + 6\sigma_\omega^2 + 4\sigma_\varepsilon^2 \\
\gamma(1) &= (s-1)\sigma_\zeta^2 - 4\sigma_\omega^2 - 2\sigma_\varepsilon^2 \\
\gamma(2) &= (s-2)\sigma_\zeta^2 + \sigma_\omega^2 \\
\gamma(\tau) &= (s-\tau)\sigma_\zeta^2, && \tau = 3, \ldots, s-2 \\
\gamma(s-1) &= \sigma_\zeta^2 + \sigma_\varepsilon^2 \\
\gamma(s) &= -\sigma_\eta^2 - 2\sigma_\varepsilon^2 \\
\gamma(s+1) &= \sigma_\varepsilon^2 \\
\gamma(\tau) &= 0, && \tau \geqslant s+2
\end{aligned}
\tag{6.16}
$$

The form of the ACF in (6.16) implies that the BSM is such that $\Delta\Delta_s y_t \sim \text{MA}(s+1)$. The same is true for the airline model, although, as can be seen from (6.7), the constraints on the MA parameters are not the same. This then raises the question as to the relationship between the BSM and the airline model. Both appear to be relatively successful at modelling time series which exhibit trend and seasonal movements and so one would expect them to be fairly close. The table in Maravall (1985) compares the autocorrelation functions of the two models for some typical values of the parameters; see also FSK, p. 73. They are quite similar, particularly when the seasonal MA parameter, Θ, is close to minus one. In fact in the limiting

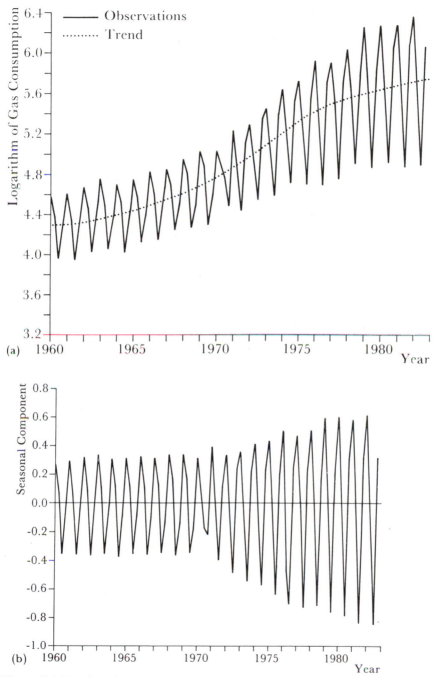

Figure 5.4 Trend and seasonal components for UK gas consumption: (a) observations and trend; (b) seasonal.

case when Θ is equal to minus one, the airline model is equivalent to a BSM in which σ_ζ^2 and σ_ω^2 are both zero. It is straightforward to see that this is true from the stationary form of the BSM given in (6.15): removing the terms in ω_t and ζ_t gives

$$\Delta\Delta_s y_t = \Delta_s \eta_t + \Delta\Delta_s \varepsilon_t = \Delta_s(\eta_t + \varepsilon_t - \varepsilon_{t-1})$$

Following the argument in section 5.3, the term in parentheses is equivalent to an MA(1) process with disturbance term ξ_t, and so

$$\Delta\Delta_s y_t = (1 + \theta L)(1 - L^s)\xi_t \tag{6.17}$$

with θ given by (3.15). An example of such a situation can be found in the models fitted by Harvey and Durbin (1986) to car drivers killed and seriously injured in Great Britain.

In terms of the BSM, the airline model provides a close approximation when σ_ω^2 and σ_ζ^2 are close to zero. In relatively short time series, consisting of only a few years, it is difficult to detect a change in the seasonal pattern which suggests that σ_ω^2 will be zero or close to zero. Changes in the slope may also be difficult to detect in a short time series. For longer stretches of data, non-negligible values for either σ_ω^2 or σ_ζ^2 may lead to the airline model being relatively less satisfactory since there is effectively only one parameter to pick up changes in the slope and the seasonal pattern.

Seasonal Adjustment

Official statistics are often published as seasonally adjusted series. It is tempting to work with seasonally adjusted data on the grounds that this removes the need to make allowance for seasonal effects and therefore makes model building easier. Unfortunately, the seasonal adjustment procedures adopted by statistical agencies can severely distort the properties of a series. Wallis (1974), for example, studied the effects of the widely used Bureau of the Census X-11 procedure on a quarterly white process and found that it would induce marked negative autocorrelation at the seasonal lags; see the theoretical ACF shown in figure 5.5. Thus it is conceivable that one would end up fitting a seasonal ARMA model to the adjusted series.

There have been a number of other studies showing the distorting effects of the standard seasonal adjustment procedures used by statistical agencies. Frequency domain analysis is particularly useful in this respect. The techniques used are described in section 6.6.

If seasonal adjustment is to be carried out, it would seem preferable to base it on a statistical model. The structural time series approach is ideal for this purpose, since one can fit a model such as the BSM of (6.13), and then remove the seasonal component by smoothing. Such model-based seasonal adjustment can also be carried out within an ARIMA framework,

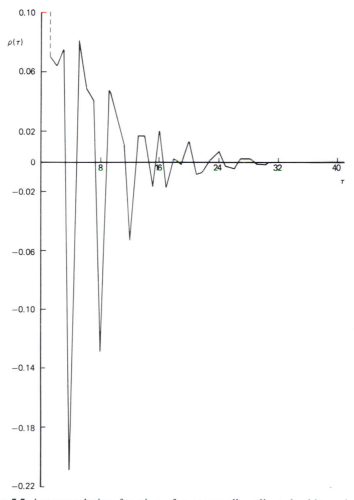

Figure 5.5 Autocorrelation function of a seasonally adjusted white noise process.
Source: Wallis (1974).

generally using the airline model; see Hillmer and Tiao (1982). However, if
the ultimate objective is to construct a model for analysing and forecasting
a series, there would appear to be little point in doing this in two stages.
Further discussion can be found in FSK, section 6.2.

5.7 Long Memory and Growth Curves

So far the long run movements in a series have been modelled in such a way
that the eventual forecasts are around a polynomial function of time. There
are other ways in which the long term movements in a series may be captured.

Long Memory and Fractional Integration

The ARIMA class of models can be generalised by allowing the order of differencing, d, to take non-integer values. Such models are said to be *fractionally integrated* and are denoted ARFIMA (p, d, q). If d is positive but less than one-half the model is stationary, but exhibits what is known as long memory or persistence. The simplest case is fractionally integrated white noise

$$\Delta^d y_t = \varepsilon_t \qquad (7.1)$$

where ε_t is white noise and the fractional difference operator is defined by the binomial expansion

$$\Delta^d = (1 - L)^d = 1 + \sum_{k=1}^{\infty} \frac{\Gamma(k - d)}{\Gamma(-d)\Gamma(k + 1)} L^k$$

where $\Gamma(x)$ is the gamma function. Since $\Gamma(x) = (x - 1)\Gamma(x - 1)$ for positive x,

$$\Delta^d = 1 - dL - \tfrac{1}{2}d(1 - d)L^2 - \tfrac{1}{6}d(1 - d)(2 - d)L^3 - \cdots \qquad (7.2)$$

For k large, the coefficients of L^k are proportional to $k^{-(1+d)}$. Thus the coefficients die away very slowly, and so a very large number of lags is needed if y_t is to be approximated by an autoregressive model.

It is shown in Granger and Joyeux (1980) and Hosking (1981) that if $|d| < \tfrac{1}{2}$, y_t is stationary and invertible, with variance

$$\mathrm{Var}(y_t) = \Gamma(1 - 2d)/[\Gamma(1 - d)]^2 \qquad (7.3a)$$

and ACF

$$\rho(\tau) = \frac{\Gamma(1 - d)\Gamma(\tau + d)}{\Gamma(d)\Gamma(\tau + 1 - d)}, \qquad \tau = 1, 2, \ldots \qquad (7.3b)$$

It can be seen that $\rho(1) = d/(1 - d)$. If d is positive, the autocorrelations are positive, and the ACF declines monotonically and hyperbolically towards zero as the lag increases. This contrasts with the exponential decay exhibited by a stationary AR(1) process, and it means that the correlation between observations some distance apart can be relatively high. As with the slow decline in the autoregressive weights given by (7.2), this is a reflection of the long memory of the model. The long memory phenomenon has been well documented in hydrology, and there is some evidence that it may be relevant for certain economic and financial time series.

When $d \geqslant \tfrac{1}{2}$, the variance of y_t is infinite and the process is non-stationary. Such processes can be differenced in the usual way until they are stationary and invertible. When the model in (7.1) is generalised by letting $\Delta^d y_t$ be an ARMA (p, q) process, a model-building strategy ideally requires a method of estimating d independently of the rest of the model. A frequency domain procedure for doing this is described in section 6.8. Once a tentative value of d has been found, an ARMA model may be selected in the usual way using the fractionally differenced observations calculated approximately by means of the expansion in (7.2).

A model which has been fully specified in terms of p, d and q may be estimated by maximum likelihood. The likelihood function of a stationary and invertible model may be obtained in the form (3.1.23) by evaluating the autocovariances and constructing the $T \times T$ covariance matrix, $\mathbf{V}$. For fractionally integrated white noise this means using the expressions in (7.3). Unfortunately there is no way of decomposing the likelihood function into prediction errors, and so the need repeatedly to construct and invert the $\mathbf{V}$ matrix makes the whole procedure quite time consuming. Carrying out ML estimation in the frequency domain, as described in section 6.8, may be more appealing.

Growth Curves

Certain non-linear trend functions, like the logistic and Gompertz functions, may be attractive in situations where there is thought to be a saturation level to the series. Such situations arise where a new product is entering a market. Typically penetration into the market is slow at first, after which there follows a period of acceleration, and finally a slowing down as sales reach a saturation level. The trend used to model such a process is known as a *growth curve*. Growth curves may equally well apply to the stock of a good, such as the total number of telephones in a country, or to proportion of households owning that good.

The traditional formulation of a growth curve model is:

$$y_t = \mu_t + \varepsilon_t, \qquad t = 1, \ldots, T \tag{7.4}$$

where μ_t is a deterministic function of time. In the logistic case

$$\mu_t = \alpha/(1 + \beta \, e^{\gamma t}) \tag{7.5}$$

where α, β and γ are parameters such that $\alpha, \beta > 0$ and $\gamma < 0$. A constant term is sometimes added. Even though μ_t is deterministic, the model is intrinsically non-linear and ML estimation has to be carried out by non-linear least squares.

The properties of growth curves are best presented by regarding them as continuous functions of time. As such they will be denoted by $\mu(t)$. For the logistic curve, it can be seen that as $t \to \infty$, $\mu(t)$ tends asymptotically to its saturation level of α, while as $t \to -\infty$ it goes towards zero. The slope is always positive, while the growth rate is

$$d \log \mu(t)/dt = (-\gamma/\alpha)\{\alpha - \mu(t)\} \tag{7.6}$$

showing it to be proportional to the distance below the saturation level. Evaluating the second derivative and setting it equal to zero indicates a point of inflexion at $t = (-1/\gamma) \log \beta$ with $\mu(t)$ equal to $\alpha/2$.

The general modified exponential function takes the form

$$\mu(t) = \alpha(1 + \beta \, e^{\gamma t})^{\kappa} \tag{7.7}$$

When κ is equal to minus one, this becomes the logistic, while setting κ equal to one gives the simple modified exponential. The logarithm of a Gompertz curve, a function which has been used quite widely in demography, is also obtained by setting κ equal to one. The slope of (7.7) is given by

$$d\mu(t)/dt = \mu(t)^{\rho} \exp(\delta + \gamma t) \tag{7.8}$$

where $\delta = -\beta\gamma/\alpha$.

The model in (7.4) may be easily extended by allowing the disturbance to follow a stationary ARMA process. However, the more interesting issue is whether it is possible to introduce some discounting of past observations into the estimation of the trend. A detailed discussion of how the trend may be made stochastic can be found in FSK, section 6.6.1. Here attention is restricted to two approaches. The first is based on the observation that the growth rate in the logistic trend (7.6) is a linear function of $\mu(t)$, that is

$$d \log \mu(t)/dt = -\gamma + \gamma^{\dagger}\mu(t) \tag{7.9}$$

where $\gamma^{\dagger} = \gamma/\alpha$. This expression is used in Levenbach and Reuter (1976) as the basis for the model

$$\Delta \log y_t = -\gamma + \gamma^{\dagger}y_t + \eta_t \tag{7.10}$$

where η_t is a disturbance term. Levenbach and Reuter also suggest a generalisation which includes the reciprocal of y_t as an additional term, so that

$$\Delta \log y_t = -\gamma + \gamma^{\dagger}y_t + \gamma^* y_t^{-1} + \eta_t \tag{7.11}$$

and the resulting path of y_t is known as a *Riccati growth curve*. If η_t is white noise, estimation of (7.11) can be carried out by OLS.

In the second approach, it is supposed that Y_t, $t = 1, \ldots, T$, is the stock of a variable and that this stock is subject to an unknown saturation level. The corresponding flow, or net increase, in the stock is $y_t = \Delta Y_t$, $t = 2, \ldots, T$. Attention is focused on the way in which y_t may be modelled and forecasts constructed for it. Forecasts for the stock, Y_t, then emerge as a by-product. The method can only be applied if y_t is always strictly positive.

Taking logarithms in the expression (7.8) for the slope of $\mu(t)$ in a general modified exponential function and assuming an additive disturbance term suggests the model

$$\log y_t = \rho \log \mu_{t-1} + \delta + \gamma t + \varepsilon_t, \qquad t = 2, \ldots, T \tag{7.12}$$

The inclusion of μ_{t-1} means that the long-term movements in y_t are affected by the build-up in the total stock. Since μ_{t-1} is unobservable, it may be replaced by Y_{t-1} to yield

$$\log y_t = \rho \log Y_{t-1} + \delta + \gamma t + \varepsilon_t \tag{7.13}$$

This model may then be estimated by OLS. If ρ is given, then $\log(y_t/Y_{t-1}^{\rho})$ is simply regressed on t. The l-step ahead forecasts, $\tilde{y}_{T+l|T}$ and $\tilde{Y}_{T+l|T}$, can be computed from the recursion

$$\tilde{y}_{T+l|T} = \tilde{Y}_{T+l-1|T}^{\rho} \exp\{\delta + \gamma(T + l)\} \tag{7.14a}$$

$$\tilde{Y}_{T+l|T} = \tilde{Y}_{T+l-1|T} + \tilde{y}_{T+l|T}, \qquad l = 1, 2, \ldots \tag{7.14b}$$

where $\tilde{Y}_{T|T} = Y_T$. The forecast function for the stock takes the form of a general modified exponential and gradually approaches the saturation level, α. Although model (7.13) contains a deterministic linear trend component, it yields a local trend predictor for the growth curve for the stock variable, Y_t.

Example 1 Estimating (7.13) using figures on tractor ownership in Spain over the period 1951–1976 gives

$$\widehat{\log y}_t = 1.799 \log Y_{t-1} - 1.509 - 0.1612t \tag{7.15}$$
$$(0.421) \qquad\qquad (0.143)\ (0.0623)$$

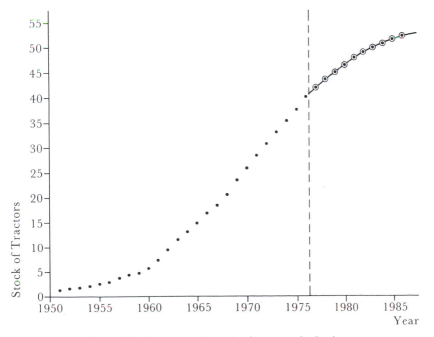

Figure 5.6 Forecasts of stock of tractors in Spain.

The coefficient of log Y_{t-1} is not significantly different from two, which suggests that a model corresponding to the logistic curve is appropriate. Re-estimating the parameters δ and γ by regressing $\log(y_t/Y_{t-1}^2)$ on time yields

$$\widehat{\log y_t} = 2 \log Y_{t-1} - 1.535 - 0.1907t \qquad (7.16)$$
$$\qquad\qquad\qquad (0.130)\ (0.0083)$$

The residuals are reasonably well behaved, although there is some indication of serial correlation with a Durbin–Watson d-statistic of 1.33.

The predictions for the stock of tractors, Y_t, are shown in figure 5.6. A comparison of these predictions with predictions based on a global logistic model (7.4) can be found in Harvey (1984b).

5.8 Explanatory Variables

Suppose observations are available on a variable, x_t, which is able to explain some of the movements in the variable of interest, y_t. It will be supposed that y_t can be modelled, either directly or indirectly, as an ARIMA process, although the ideas to be presented easily extend to more general processes, for example those which take account of seasonality. Incorporating x_t into the model, possibly with some lag structure to capture the dynamic response of y_t, still leaves some non-stationarity in y_t to be picked up by a time series component. This is in contrast to a dynamic regression model where the disturbance term is taken to be stationary, or even to be white noise. In other words we are attempting to build a model which only partially accounts for the movements in y_t, rather than a model which attempts to provide a full behavioural explanation. To do so would take us into the details of subjects such as econometrics; see EATS, chapters 7 and 8.

The next two sub-sections describe how dynamic models may be constructed within the ARIMA and structural time series frameworks. The last sub-section explains how such models fit in with a class of dynamic regression models called autoregressive distributed lags. The models will be described for a single explanatory variable, although they may all be generalised.

Forecasts of y_t are made on values of the explanatory variable. In general these values will be unknown as they are future values. A model relating y_t and x_t is therefore only useful if the explanatory variable is exogenous in the sense that it is not subject to any feedback from past values of y_t. This is sometimes referred to as *strong exogeneity*; see EATS, chapter 8 or, for a full discussion of the whole issue of exogeneity, Engle *et al.* (1983). Note that if lagged values of an exogenous variable enter into the equation, the variable is said to be a *leading indicator*. In this case some of the lagged values of the exogenous variables will be known for a limited number of future time periods. The gains from leading indicators are discussed in Box and Jenkins (1976) and EATS, pp. 253–7.

Transfer Function Models

A lag structure may be represented by the ratio of two polynomials in the lag operator. This is sometimes referred to as a *rational distributed lag*. The idea of having the lag structure represented by the ratio of two polynomials in the lag operator parallels the representation of an ARIMA model. Thus

$$y_t = \frac{\omega(L)}{\lambda(L)} x_t + \frac{\theta(L)}{\Delta^d \phi(L)} \varepsilon_t, \qquad t = 1, \ldots, T \qquad (8.1)$$

where $\omega(L)$ and $\lambda(L)$ are finite order polynomials in the lag operator. Models of this kind are widely used, particularly in the engineering literature and are advocated in Box and Jenkins (1976). Differencing both variables d times makes the disturbance term stationary, that is

$$\Delta^d y_t = \frac{\omega(L)}{\lambda(L)} \Delta^d x_t + \frac{\theta(L)}{\phi(L)} \varepsilon_t, \qquad t = d + 1, \ldots, T \qquad (8.2)$$

Example 1   Box and Jenkins (1976, pp. 409–12) construct the following model for sales of a company

$$\Delta y_t = \theta_0 + \frac{\omega}{1 - \lambda L} \Delta x_{t-3} + (1 + \theta L) \varepsilon_t \qquad (8.3)$$

and estimate the parameters as $\tilde{\theta}_0 = 0.035$, $\tilde{\omega} = 4.82$, $\tilde{\lambda} = 0.72$ and $\tilde{\theta} = -0.54$. The explanatory variable is a leading indicator as y_t can be forecast up to three steps ahead using actual values of x_t.

The lag structure of the explanatory variable is infinite, except when $\lambda(L)$ is just a constant. For example, the lag in (8.3) is of the form

$$\frac{\omega}{1 - \lambda L} x_t = \omega \sum_{j=0}^{\infty} \lambda^j x_{t-j}$$

This is a geometric distributed lag. More generally, if $\delta(L)$ denotes the infinite polynomial giving the coefficients of x_{t-j}, these lag coefficients can be found in the same way as the coefficients of the infinite MA representation of an $\text{ARMA}(p, q)$ model; see (2.4.6).

The CSS approach described for the approximate ML estimation of ARIMA models can be generalised to transfer function models. The model is re-arranged so that the disturbance term, ε_t, can be calculated recursively. The sum of squares function is then minimised with respect to the unknown parameters in $\omega(L)$, $\lambda(L)$, $\theta(L)$ and $\phi(L)$. Analytic derivatives are easily constructed.

Example 2   The CSS recursion in (8.3) is

$$\varepsilon_t = \Delta y_t - \lambda \, \Delta y_{t-1} - \omega \, \Delta x_{t-3} + (\lambda - \theta)\varepsilon_{t-1} + \theta\lambda\varepsilon_{t-2} - \theta_0(1 - \lambda),$$

$$t = 3, \ldots, T$$

with the initial values, ε_1 and ε_2, set to zero.

A model selection procedure was developed by Box and Jenkins. However, the transfer function formulation is not particularly amenable to a systematic approach to model selection, particularly when there is more than one explanatory variable; see the discussion in EATS, sub-section 7.5.

Structural Time Series Models

In order to introduce the ideas of structural time series modelling, we first suppose that there are no lags on the explanatory variable and that there is a *stochastic trend component*, μ_t, defined as in (3.5). Thus

$$y_t = \mu_t + \delta x_t + \varepsilon_t, \qquad t = 1, \ldots, T \tag{8.4}$$

with

$$\mu_t = \mu_{t-1} + \beta_{t-1} + \eta_t$$
$$\beta_t = \qquad \beta_{t-1} + \zeta_t$$

Other components such as seasonals, cycles or daily effects could be employed as well as, or instead of, the trend component, but such generalisations raise no new issues of principle. The rationale for the stochastic trend component is that it is picking up the long-run movements in y_t which are not accounted for by x_t.

If $\sigma_\eta^2 = \sigma_\zeta^2 = 0$, the stochastic trend collapses to a deterministic trend and the models may be written as

$$y_t = \alpha + \beta t + \delta x_t + \varepsilon_t, \qquad t = 1, \ldots, T \tag{8.5}$$

A model of this kind may be estimated by regressing y_t on x_t and a time trend. Alternatively, the same estimator of δ may be obtained by first detrending the dependent and explanatory variables by regressing each of them individually on time, and then regressing the detrended dependent variable on the detrended explanatory variables. However, if the trend is not a deterministic one, treating it as such can lead to poor forecasts and misleading inferences about δ; see Nelson and Kang (1984).

The disturbance term in (8.4) can be made stationary by taking second differences to give

$$\Delta^2 y_t = \delta \, \Delta^2 x_t + w_t, \qquad t = 3, \ldots, T \tag{8.6a}$$

where

$$w_t = \Delta\eta_t + \zeta_{t-1} + \Delta^2\varepsilon_t \tag{8.6b}$$

The reduced form of (8.6b) is an MA(2) process, and so the reduced form of the model as a whole is a transfer function (8.1) with an ARIMA(0, 2, 2) disturbance. This is simply a reflection of the fact that the reduced form of a local linear trend model is an ARIMA(0, 2, 2) process. In the special case when σ_ζ^2 is zero, it is only necessary to difference once in order to obtain a stationary disturbance term, since then

$$\Delta y_t = \beta + \delta\,\Delta x_t + w_t, \qquad t = 2, \ldots, T \tag{8.7a}$$

where

$$w_t = \eta_t + \Delta\varepsilon_t \tag{8.7b}$$

corresponds to an MA(1) process. If σ_ε^2 is equal to zero, the model is

$$\Delta y_t = \beta + \delta\Delta x_t + \eta_t, \qquad t = 2, \ldots, T$$

and a simple OLS regression of Δy_t on Δx_t and a constant term gives efficient estimators of β and δ.

Structural model can be handled by state space methods without differencing the variables. One approach is to incorporate δ into the state. This gives an augmented state vector $\boldsymbol{\alpha}_t^\dagger = (\mu_t\,\beta_t\,\delta_t)'$ which satisfies the state space model

$$y_t = (1\ \ 0\ \ x_t)\boldsymbol{\alpha}_t^\dagger + \varepsilon_t, \qquad t = 1, \ldots, T \tag{8.8a}$$

and

$$\boldsymbol{\alpha}_t^\dagger = \begin{bmatrix} \mu_t \\ \beta_t \\ \delta_t \end{bmatrix} = \begin{bmatrix} 1 & 1 & 0 \\ 0 & 1 & 0 \\ 0 & 0 & 1 \end{bmatrix}\begin{bmatrix} \mu_{t-1} \\ \beta_{t-1} \\ \delta_{t-1} \end{bmatrix} + \begin{bmatrix} \eta_t \\ \zeta_t \\ 0 \end{bmatrix} \tag{8.8b}$$

The lower part of the transition equation simply reflects the fact that $\delta = \delta_t$ is time invariant. Including it in the state vector allows it to be estimated simultaneously with μ_t and β_t. In addition it opens up the generalisation to a time-varying parameter model in which δ_t evolves over time according to a random walk as in section 4.5.

Example 3   The per capita consumption of spirits in the UK from 1870 to 1938 can be explained, at least partly, by per capita income and relative price; see Prest (1949). However, estimating a double-log regression model with these two explanatory variables and a deterministic time trend leaves considerable serial correlation in the residuals. The traditional solution is to fit an AR(1) model to the disturbances. Thus Fuller (1976, p. 426) reports results for models with a quadratic time trend and an AR(1) term with ϕ estimated to be 0.76.

A stochastic trend model of the form (8.4) provides a good fit in many respects. It is more parsimonious than the model reported by Fuller and the movements in the stochastic trend component can be interpreted as reflecting changes in tastes. Estimating the model using observations up to and including 1930 gives the following results:

$$y_t = m_{t|T} + 0.69x_{1t} - 0.95x_{2t} + e_{t|T} \qquad (8.9)$$
$$(0.13) \qquad (0.07)$$

where y_t is the logarithm of per capita spirit consumption, x_{1t} is the logarithm of per capita income, x_{2t} is the logarithm of relative price and $m_{t|T}$ and $e_{t|T}$ are the smoothed estimates of the trend and irregular components respectively. The estimates of the hyperparameters are

$$\tilde{\sigma}_\eta^2 = 69 \times 10^{-6}, \qquad \tilde{\sigma}_\zeta^2 = 37 \times 10^{-6} \qquad \text{and} \qquad \tilde{\sigma}_\varepsilon^2 = 161 \times 10^{-6}$$

while the estimate of the standard deviation of the one-step ahead prediction errors is $s = 0.023$. The coefficients of the explanatory variables appear to be plausible in terms of sign and magnitude. The asymptotic standard errors shown in parentheses indicate that both variables are highly significant.

Figure 5.7 shows the predictions of the dependent variable which would have been made in 1930 had the values of the explanatory variable been

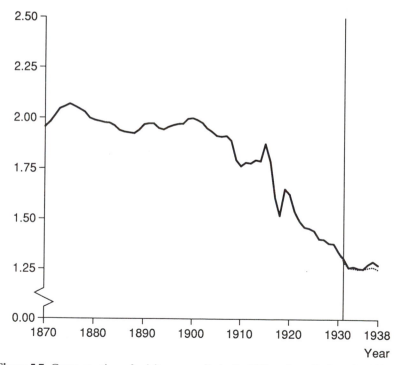

Figure 5.7 Consumption of spirits per capita in the UK and predictions for 1931–8.

known. The results are impressive, and the role of the explanatory variables emerges clearly in that it is not difficult to see that a straightforward univariate extrapolation would under-predict quite considerably.

Introducing lagged values of the explanatory variable into (8.4) gives

$$y_t = \mu_t + \sum_{\tau=0}^{h} \delta_\tau x_{t-\tau} + \varepsilon_t, \qquad t = 1, \dots, T \tag{8.10}$$

However, if the object of the exercise is to obtain a reasonably precise estimate of the lag structure, a formulation of this kind may not always be satisfactory. The reason is that economic time series are typically slowly changing and so the various lagged values of each explanatory variable will tend to be highly correlated with each other. There are various ways of tackling this multicollinearity problem. However, they all have the same objective, which is to impose constraints on the lag structure, thereby reducing the number of parameters to be estimated. Techniques which fit well into the structural framework include Almon distributed lags. Rational lags could also be used, although they are less convenient for both estimation and specification.

Example 1 (*contd*) The model fitted in (8.3) can be interpreted as a model with a stochastic trend component taking the form of a random walk with drift. On comparing (8.3) with (8.7), it can be seen that the estimated drift parameter is 0.035, while the ratio of the variance of η_t to ε_t is

$$q = -(1 + \theta^2)/\theta = (1 + 0.54^2)/0.54 = 0.39$$

If constraints are not to be introduced into the lag structure, it may be desirable to re-parameterise the lag structure. The model in (8.10) may be rewritten as

$$y_t = \mu_t + \delta x_t + \sum_{\tau=0}^{h-1} \delta_\tau^\dagger \Delta x_{t-\tau} + \varepsilon_t \tag{8.11}$$

where

$$\delta_\tau^\dagger = - \sum_{j=\tau+1}^{h} \delta_j, \qquad \tau = 0, 1, \dots, h-1 \tag{8.12a}$$

and

$$\delta = \sum_{j=0}^{h} \delta_j \tag{8.12b}$$

Thus δ is the *total multiplier*. This formulation is more stable numerically because the multicollinearity between the transformed variables $x_t, \Delta x_t, \dots, \Delta x_{t-h+1}$ will typically be considerably less than the multicollinearity between the original variables. The fact that x_t will not usually be strongly correlated with its first differences makes it clear why its coefficient, δ, may be estimated reasonably accurately even though the shape of the lag distribution may be difficult to determine precisely.

Lagged values of the dependent variable may also be introduced into (8.4) so that

$$y_t = \mu_t + \sum_{j=1}^{r} \phi_j y_{t-j} + \sum_{i=0}^{s} \omega_i x_{t-i} + \varepsilon_t \qquad (8.13)$$

Model selection proceeds on the basis that the researcher has some prior idea of the components to be put in a model. Thus a stochastic trend would normally be included, and for monthly or quarterly observations a seasonal is usually appropriate. Lags and additional explanatory variables can be brought into a more general specification, and tested for significance as in econometric model building; see the discussion in FSK, section 7.5.

Example 4   Economic theory concerning the relationship between employment and output suggests that a trend component is needed to account for changes in the capital stock and technical progress; see Ball and St. Cyr (1966). A stochastic trend model of the form (8.13) is therefore appropriate. The theory specifies only one lag on employment, but if second-order lags are included on both dependent variables, the coefficients are found to be small and statistically insignificant. The preferred model, estimated by ML, is

$$y_t = m_{t|T} + 0.775 y_{t-1} + 0.112 x_t + 0.058 x_{t-1} + e_{t|T} \qquad (8.14)$$

$$(0.041) \qquad (0.014) \qquad (0.016)$$

with

$$\tilde{\sigma}_\varepsilon^2 = 1.505 \times 10^{-6}, \qquad \tilde{\sigma}_\eta^2 = 4.831 \times 10^{-6}, \qquad \tilde{\sigma}_\zeta^2 = 0$$

where y_t and x_t are, respectively, the logarithms of UK manufacturing employment and output. Furthermore

$$s = 2.76 \times 10^{-3} \qquad \text{and} \qquad Q(8) = 4.39$$

A plot of $m_{t|T}$, the smoothed estimate of the trend, is informative about the changes in productivity over the period in question; see Harvey *et al.* (1986) and FSK, p. 397.

Autoregressive Distributed Lags

Autoregressive distributed lag models are of the form

$$y_t = \sum_{j=1}^{r} \phi_j y_{t-j} + \sum_{i=0}^{s} \omega_i x_{t-i} + \varepsilon_t \qquad (8.15)$$

and can be estimated by OLS regression since the disturbance is assumed to be white noise. Models of this kind could be used to approximate the kind of situations envisaged by (8.1) and (8.4) by working with differences and letting the lags be long enough to account for any MA terms. Such models would not necessarily be very parsimonious. However, autoregressive distributed lags are usually used with the variables in levels. When the variables are non-stationary, the lag structure can be re-parameterised as

$$\Delta y_t = (\phi - 1)y_{t-1} + \sum_{j=1}^{r-1} \phi_j^\dagger \Delta y_{t-j} + \omega_0 \Delta x_t + \omega x_{t-1} + \sum_{i=1}^{s-1} \omega_i^\dagger \Delta x_{t-i} + \varepsilon_t$$

(8.16)

where $\omega, \omega_1^\dagger, \ldots, \omega_{s-1}^\dagger$ are defined analogously to $\delta, \delta_1^\dagger, \ldots, \delta_{s-1}^\dagger$ in (8.13) and

$$\phi_j^\dagger = -\sum_{k=j+1}^{r} \phi_k, \qquad j = 1, 2, \ldots, r-1$$

(8.17a)

$$\phi = \sum_{k=1}^{r} \phi_k$$

(8.17b)

This parameterisation has the attraction of numerical stability, and, in addition, the long-run effects are associated with the levels variables, y_{t-1} and x_{t-1}. The total multiplier is $\omega/(1 - \phi)$. When (8.16) is estimated by OLS it is estimated as the coefficient of x_{t-1} divided by minus the coefficient of y_{t-1}.

The arrangement of the dependent variable lag structure in (8.16) parallels equation (4.7). If the relationship is one which is in first differences, the coefficients of y_{t-1} and x_{t-1} are theoretically zero, though their estimators will be subject to the kind of behaviour noted for y_{t-1} in section 5.4. Thus it is not easy to determine whether a first difference formulation is appropriate. This issue is taken up in the more general framework of a multivariate model in section 7.7.

Example 3 (contd) A regression of the logarithm of per capita consumption of spirits on its lagged value, a time trend, and current and lagged per capita income and price (in logarithms) gave an estimate of 0.74 for the coefficient of lagged consumption, with a standard error of 0.074.

The main appeal of autoregressive distributed lags lies in modelling situations where there is a long-run relationship between the levels of the variables, thereby making the inclusion of a stochastic trend component unnecessary. If the contributions from the levels variables in (8.16) are put together as

$$(\phi - 1)y_{t-1} + \omega x_{t-1} = (\phi - 1)\{y_{t-1} - \delta x_{t-1}\}$$

the model can be expressed in the form

$$\Delta y_t = \sum_{j=1}^{r} \phi_j^{\dagger} \Delta y_{t-j} + \omega_0 \Delta x_t + \sum_{i=1}^{s-1} \omega_i^{\dagger} \Delta x_{t-i} + (\phi - 1)\{y_{t-1} - \delta x_{t-1}\} + \varepsilon_t$$

(8.18)

This is an *error correction* model with the long-run relationship between y and x given by the error correction term in the braces. As a rule the variables are in logarithms, in which case δ is the long-run elasticity of y with respect to x. If δ is known to take some particular value, the error correction term can be treated as an explanatory variable. For example, in modelling the relationship between income and consumption, Davidson *et al.* (1978) argued that δ should be unity and so $y_{t-1} - x_{t-1}$ is included as an explanatory variable in an equation which would otherwise be entirely in differences. Further discussion will be found in EATS, chapter 8.

5.9 Intervention Analysis

Intervention analysis is concerned with making inferences about the effects of known events. The effects are measured by including intervention, or dummy, variables as explanatory variables. Other explanatory variables may or may not be present.

The intervention model may be set up within the framework of (8.1) or (8.4). In order to focus attention on the main issues, we may drop any lag structure and write both models as

$$y_t = \delta x_t + \lambda w_t + u_t, \qquad t = 1, \ldots, T \tag{9.1}$$

where w_t is the intervention variable, λ is its coefficient and u_t is an ARIMA process which is either modelled explicitly, as in a transfer function model, or implicitly, as in a structural time series model.

The definition of w_t depends on the form which the intervention effect is assumed to take. There are a number of different possibilities, but in all cases it will be supposed that the intervention takes place at time $t = \tau$.

If the intervention has an effect only in time period τ, w_t is a *pulse* variable of the form

$$w_t = \begin{cases} 0, & t \neq \tau \\ 1, & t = \tau \end{cases} \tag{9.2}$$

Examples might include the effects of a strike, or indeed any event which leads to the observation at time τ being classed as an outlier. On the other hand, a shift in the level of the series will be captured by a *step* variable

$$w_t = \begin{cases} 0, & t < \tau \\ 1, & t \geq \tau \end{cases} \tag{9.3}$$

This represents an underlying change or structural break. The same is true of a change in the slope of the trend component. This can be modelled by defining the variable

$$w_t = \begin{cases} 0, & t < \tau \\ t - \tau, & t \geqslant \tau \end{cases} \tag{9.4}$$

Within the framework of a structural time series model in which u_t is a stochastic trend plus error, step and slope changes can be interpreted as pulse changes to the level and slope equations respectively. For example, (9.4) is equivalent to

$$\beta_t = \beta_{t-1} + \lambda w_t + \zeta_t$$

where w_t is as in (9.2).

Intervention variables may also be used to model a sudden change in the seasonal pattern. An example of such a change would be the change in the system of registering cars in the UK a few years ago. The last letter on a UK number plate indicates the year in which the car was registered, and when the first month in the 'year' was changed from January to August there was a marked effect on the seasonal pattern of new car sales.

Finally, an intervention variable might be used to account for a shift from one period to another, as might happen if consumers bring forward their purchases of a particular good in anticipation of an increase in tax on it. In this case

$$w_t = \begin{cases} 1, & t = \tau \\ -1, & t = \tau + 1 \\ 0, & t \neq \tau, \tau + 1 \end{cases} \tag{9.5}$$

Example 1 In a study of the effects of the car seat belt law in Great Britain, Harvey and Durbin (1986) constructed a structural time series model for the number of car drivers killed and seriously injured using monthly data from January 1969 to December 1984. The model contained stochastic trend and seasonal components, and two explanatory variables, a car mileage index, x_{1t}, and the real price of petrol, x_{2t}. All variables were in logarithms.

The seat belt law was introduced on 31 January 1983, and the wearing rate rose to 95 per cent immediately. The most straightforward hypothesis is that the law induced a once and for all downward shift in the level of the series. This implies a step intervention variable, so that

$$y_t = \mu_t + \gamma_t + \delta_1 x_{1t} + \delta_2 x_{2t} + \lambda w_t + \varepsilon_t \tag{9.6}$$

Actually, since the seat belt wearing rate rose from 40% in December 1982 to 50% in January 1983 in anticipation of the introduction of the law, (9.3) was modified slightly by setting w_t equal to 0.18 in January

1983. The relative variances of the stochastic components estimated using data up to the end of 1982 were used when the intervention parameter, λ, was estimated using the data up to and including December 1984. The resulting estimate of λ was -0.262 with a standard error of 0.053. The 't-statistic' is about five and so the intervention is clearly statistically significant. Since $\exp(-0.262) = 0.770$, the estimated reduction in drivers killed and seriously injured is 23.0%. The 50% confidence interval for this reduction is 20.2 to 25.8% while the 95% confidence interval is 14.7% to 30.6%.

Figure 5.8 shows the predictions for 1983 to 1984. These are made using the actual values of the explanatory variables for 1983 and 1984 but not using the corresponding observations for the car drivers series itself. Including the intervention variable, which was subsequently estimated from the 1983 data, gives very accurate results.

It is quite possible for an intervention to give rise to several of the effects listed above. There is also the possibility of a dynamic response to the intervention. Thus if a transitory effect dies away gradually it might be appropriate to model it by the intervention variable

$$
w_t = \begin{cases} 0, & t < \tau \\ \phi^{t-\tau}, & \tau \geqslant t \end{cases} \tag{9.7}
$$

with ϕ between zero and one. An interesting property of this specification is that w_t becomes a pure pulse variable when ϕ is zero and a pure step

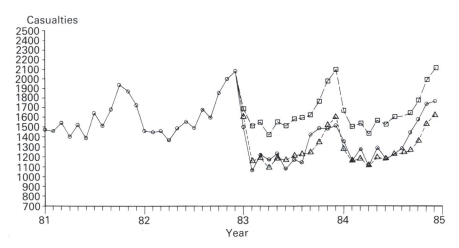

Figure 5.8 Car drivers killed and seriously injured in Great Britain: predictions for 1983 and 1984 with and without the estimated intervention for the seat belt law: $\bigcirc$, actual values of series; $\triangle$, predictions with intervention effect included; $\square$, predictions with intervention effect removed. *Source:* Harvey and Durbin (1986).

when ϕ is one. More generally, Box and Tiao (1975) suggest that an intervention may be modelled by the kind of dynamics employed in transfer function.

The specification of intervention models is not usually easy because the dynamics following an intervention are rarely known. There is also the question of determining whether the intervention is a pulse, a step or a slope change. This is crucial to any evaluation of the effects of the intervention, since a pulse means that there are no permanent effects, whereas a step or slope change does. When the dynamics of the intervention are unknown as well, determining whether it is a pulse, a step or a slope change can become extremely difficult.

A large part of the specification problem in intervention analysis arises from the fact that because a time series model typically involves discounting, the period during which an intervention makes itself felt on the series is limited. Hence elaborate nested models incorporating all types of change and dynamics are rarely a viable proposition. Even a very simple model may be very difficult to estimate with any degree of accuracy. The only reasonable strategy may therefore be to use as much prior knowledge as possible to construct an intervention model and then to submit it to diagnostic checking. The usual diagnostics, such as the Box–Ljung test, are of limited value in this respect since any distortion in the residuals immediately after the intervention will be diluted in the full set of residuals. Intervention misspecification diagnostics should therefore concentrate on the period immediately after the intervention. Some methods of testing whether the generalised recursive residuals immediately after an intervention are bigger than before the intervention are developed in Harvey and Durbin (1986). A *post-intervention test* statistic is suggested, the rationale for this being similar to that underlying the Chow statistic for post-sample predictive testing. A CUSUM plot of the post-intervention residuals is also proposed.

Exercises

1. The following model was fitted to the logarithm of US GNP by Nelson (1972):

$$\widehat{\Delta y_t} = 2.76 + 0.615\,\Delta y_{t-1}$$

   Determine the form of the forecast function and the eventual GNP projections.

2. Find expressions for forecasts one, two and three time periods ahead for an ARMA(0, 2, 3) model. Show that the forecast function for $l > 1$ is based on a second-order difference equation with solution,

$$\tilde{y}_{T+l|T} = \alpha + \beta l$$

   where α and β depend on $\tilde{y}_{T+2|T}$ and $\tilde{y}_{T+3|T}$.
   If $y_T = 10$, $y_{T-1} = 9$, $\theta_1 = -1.0$, $\theta_2 = 0.2$, $\theta_3 = -0.5$, $\varepsilon_T = 0.5$, $\varepsilon_{T-1} = 1.0$ and $\varepsilon_{T-2} = -0.2$, determine the values of $\tilde{y}_{T+l|T}$ for $l = 1, 2$ and 3 and find α and β.

3. (a) It is sometimes argued that the appropriate degree of differencing for a series can be determined by choosing the variance to be a minimum. Comment on this argument by deriving the variance of a stationary $AR(1)$ process and comparing it with the variance of its first differences.

   (b) Find the ACF for the first differences of an $AR(1)$ process with $\phi = 0.5$.

4. If the local level model were amended so that the correlation between the two disturbances was ρ rather than zero, show that the first-order autocorrelation can be positive. Is it possible to estimate the signal–noise ratio, q, and ρ in this model if both are unknown?

5. Consider the damped trend model in which (5.3.5b) of the local linear trend is amended to $\beta_t = \phi \beta_{t-1} + \zeta_t$, with $|\phi| < 1$.

   (a) Find the ACF of the stationary form of the model.

   (b) Determine the values of p, d and q in the corresponding reduced form $ARIMA(p, d, q)$ model.

   (c) Put the model in state space form and obtain the distribution of the state vector at time $t = 1$ conditional on the first observation. Explain briefly how you would construct the likelihood function.

   (d) Obtain an expression for the optimal predictor of y_{T+l} based on the information at time T. What is the form of the eventual forecast function?

6. Consider the $ARIMA(0, 2, 1)$ model, $\Delta^2 y_t = \varepsilon_t - \theta \varepsilon_{t-1}$, with $var(\varepsilon_t) = 4$. If $y_T = 10$, $y_{T-1} = 8$ and $\varepsilon_T = -1$, make forecasts up to three periods ahead and find the coefficients of the polynomial which the eventual forecast function satisfies. Construct a 95% prediction interval for y_{T+4}. Write down an equivalent structural time series model and obtain the values of its parameters.

7. In the model

$$y_t = \alpha + \beta t + u_t, \qquad t = 1, \ldots, T$$

   u_t is a stationary $AR(1)$ process. Find an expression for the variance of the kth differences $\Delta_k = y_t - y_{t-k}$. Show that dividing this variance by k yields an expression which tends towards zero as k increases. How does this behaviour differ if y_t is a random walk with drift?

8. Construct the ACFs for the following stationary processes:

   (a) $y_t = \varepsilon_t + \theta_1 \varepsilon_{t-1} + \theta_{12} \varepsilon_{t-12}$;

   (b) $(1 - \Phi L^4) y_t = (1 + \Theta L^4) \varepsilon_t$.

9. Construct an LM test for testing $H_0: \phi_4 = 0$ in (5.5). Construct a test of $H_0: \Phi = 0$ in (5.8).

10. Write down recursive expressions for the derivatives of ε_t in (6.6.). Hence derive an expression for the asymptotic covariance matrix of the ML estimators of θ and Θ. Show that if $|\theta|$ is not too close to unity, these estimators are approximately uncorrelated, while their asymptotic variances are approximately equal to $(1 - \theta^2)/T$ and $(1 - \Theta^2)/T$ respectively.

11. Given the sample autocorrelations $r(1) = -0.34$ and $r(12) = -0.39$ for $\Delta\Delta_{12} y_t$ estimate θ and Θ in the airline model, (6.6).

12. (a) Let p_t, $t = 1, \ldots, T$, be a series of observations on the logarithm of the price level in month t. Another researcher has fitted an $ARIMA(0, 2, 1)$ model to these data and estimated the moving average parameter to be -0.5 and the variance of the disturbance to be 4. Using these results, construct estimates of the parameters σ_ε^2 and q in a random walk plus noise model applied to the rate of inflation, r_t ($= \Delta p_t$).

   (b) How would you compute an estimate of the current underlying rate of inflation, μ_T? Assuming T is large, find an expression for the root mean square error (RMSE) of this estimate in terms of σ_ε^2 and q.

(c) Suppose that the government estimates the underlying rate of inflation as the growth rate over the previous year, that is $g_T = (y_T - y_{T-12})/12$. If the model in (a) is correct, find the RMSE of g_T as an estimator of μ_T. Compare with the expression you derived in (b) and comment.

(d) Find an expression for the RMSE of the optimal predictor of the rate of inflation one year ahead based on the random walk plus noise model.

13. (a) The correlogram for a very long quarterly series after taking first and seasonal differences is

τ	1	2	3	4	5	6
$r(\tau)$	-0.4	0	0.2	-0.5	0.2	0

Estimate the parameters in a seasonal $\text{ARIMA}(0, 1, 1) \times (0, 1, 1)_s$ model (i.e. an 'airline' model). Are there any features of the fitted model you wish to comment on? Write down an equivalent structural time series model, and estimate the variances of the disturbances in the trend and seasonal components relative to the variance of the irregular term.

14. Explain how you would obtain approximate ML estimates in a regression model with MA(1) disturbances by using the CSS algorithm. Write down recursive expressions for computing the first derivatives.

Derive the large sample covariance matrix of the estimators.

15. Explain how you would make predictions of future values of the dependent variable in a regression model with ARMA(1, 1) disturbances, given the appropriate values of the explanatory variables. Write down an expression for computing the MSE of the predictions conditional on the estimated parameters in the model.

16. Suppose that the parameters ϕ and θ in a regression model with ARMA(1, 1) disturbances are known. Show how the GLS estimator of β can be computed by setting up the model in state space form. Explain how the state space model can be used to make predictions for future values of y_t, given the corresponding values of x_t. Set up 95% prediction intervals. Are these intervals exact, given that β had to be estimated?

17. A regression model with a slowly changing seasonal component may be written in the form

$$y_t = \gamma_t + x_t'\beta + \varepsilon_t, \qquad t = 1, \ldots, T$$
$$\gamma_t = -\gamma_{t-1} - \gamma_{t-2} - \cdots - \gamma_{t-s+1} + \omega_t$$

where ε_t and ω_t are independent, normally distributed white noise processes. Explain how you would estimate a model of this form, and how you would make predictions of future values of y_t, given knowledge of the relevant x_t's.

6

The Frequency Domain

6.1 Introduction

In the frequency domain interest is centred on the contributions made by various periodic components in the series. Such components need not be identified with regular cycles. In fact, regular cycles are unusual in economic time series, and in talking of a period component what is usually meant is a tendency towards cyclical movements centred around a particular frequency.

In order to gain some insight into the rather vaguely defined concept of an irregular cycle, it is first necessary to see how regular cycles are analysed. This is done in section 6.2, where it is shown how cycles may be extracted from a time series using Fourier analysis. Section 6.3 then establishes the link between Fourier and spectral analysis. The first step is to convert a model consisting of fixed cyclical components into a stationary process by re-interpreting the coefficients as random variables. The second step is to permit an infinite number of cyclical components in the model. It is then possible to give a frequency domain interpretation to the properties of ARMA processes. This is done in section 6.4, while section 6.5 formulates a linear stochastic process which is specifically designed to model irregular cyclical behaviour.

The properties of linear filters are examined in section 6.6. Frequency domain analysis gives some important insights which would not be apparent in the time domain. Furthermore, the concepts introduced form the basis for cross-spectral analysis. The cross-spectrum characterises the relationship between two series in the frequency domain, and is discussed in section 7.2 of the next chapter.

The estimation of the spectrum raises a number of issues which are not encountered in estimating the autocovariance function. These are examined in section 6.7. Section 6.8 shows how spectral methods may be used as the basis for estimating time series models, even though cyclical behaviour may not be a feature of the models concerned. Finally, the construction of tests in the frequency domain is considered.

The Spectrum

The power spectrum of any indeterministic process of the form (2.1.23) is defined by the continuous function

$$f(\lambda) = (2\pi)^{-1} \left[\gamma(0) + 2 \sum_{\tau=1}^{\infty} \gamma(\tau) \cos \lambda\tau \right] \qquad (1.1)$$

where λ, the frequency in radians, may take any value in the range $[-\pi, \pi]$. However, since $f(\lambda)$ is symmetric about zero, all the information in the power spectrum is contained in the range $[0, \pi]$.

If y_t is white noise, $\gamma(\tau) = 0$ for $\tau \neq 0$, and so

$$f(\lambda) = \sigma^2/2\pi \qquad (1.2)$$

where σ^2 is the variance of y_t. Thus the spectrum, which is shown in figure 6.1, is flat. The process may be regarded as consisting of an infinite number of cyclical components all of which have equal weight. In fact, this effectively provides a definition of white noise in the frequency domain.

Looking at (1.2), it will be seen that the area under the power spectrum over the range $[-\pi, \pi]$ is equal to the variance, σ^2. More generally,

$$\int_{-\pi}^{\pi} f(\lambda) \, d\lambda = \gamma(0) \qquad (1.3)$$

This result will be demonstrated in section 6.3, but for the moment it is its interpretation which is important. Expression (1.3) shows that the power spectrum of a linear process may be viewed as a decomposition of the variance of the process in terms of frequency.

The power spectrum is sometimes standardised by dividing by $\gamma(0)$. The same effect is achieved by replacing the autocovariances in (1.1) by the corresponding autocorrelations. The standardised function is known as the

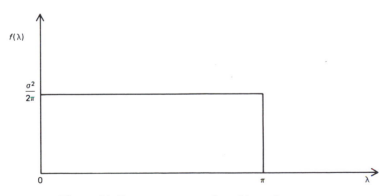

Figure 6.1 Power spectrum of a white noise process.

spectral density, although the same term may also be used to denote the power spectrum. To add to the confusion, many authors multiply the power spectrum and spectral density by a factor of two, so that the areas under them are respectively $\gamma(0)$ and unity, when λ is defined over the range $[0, \pi]$. This usage will not be adopted here, and the discussion throughout the book will be based on the definition (1.1). The terms power spectrum and spectral density will, however, be used interchangeably, since, from the practical point of view, standardisation is not particularly important.

Defining the power spectrum over the range $[-\pi, \pi]$ when it is symmetric perhaps requires some explanation. The implicit assumption made in the discussion so far is that the series y_t is real. If y_t were complex, the power spectrum would have to be defined by the complex Fourier transform,

$$f(\lambda) = (2\pi)^{-1} \sum_{\tau = -\infty}^{\infty} \gamma(\tau) e^{-i\lambda\tau} \tag{1.4}$$

for λ in the range $[-\pi, \pi]$. When y_t is real, (1.4) collapses to (1.1), but this will not be true in general and $f(\lambda)$ need not be symmetric around zero. This is the reason for defining $f(\lambda)$ over the range $[-\pi, \pi]$, and although this book is restricted to real processes, it is useful to retain the more general definition for comparability with other work. Furthermore, the complex Fourier transform (1.4) is often easier to work with when deriving theoretical results. This provides an even more important reason for its adoption.

Example 1   The MA(1) model defined in (2.1.1) has $\gamma(0) = (1 + \theta^2)\sigma^2$, $\gamma(1) = \theta\sigma^2$, and $\gamma(\tau) = 0$ for $\tau \geqslant 2$; see (2.1.14). Substituting into (1.1) gives

$$f(\lambda) = (\sigma^2/2\pi)(1 + \theta^2 + 2\theta \cos \lambda) \tag{1.5}$$

If $\theta = 0.5$

$$f(\lambda) = \sigma^2(5 + 4 \cos \lambda)/8\pi \tag{1.6}$$

and this is sketched in figure 6.2. Because y_t is a weighted average of current and lagged disturbance terms, the series is rather smoother than white noise. In other words, it changes 'more slowly' than white noise. In the time domain this is reflected in the positive first-order autocovariance, while in the frequency domain the same property shows up in the higher values of the power spectrum at the lower frequencies. Had the process been defined with a negative sign for θ, the spectrum would have been greater at the higher frequencies, indicating a process more irregular than white noise.

It should be clear from the above example that the power spectrum and the autocovariance function are complementary rather than competitive. They highlight the properties of the series in different ways. The power

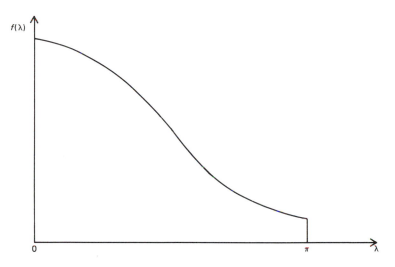

Figure 6.2 Power spectrum for an MA(1) process with $\theta = 0.5$.

spectrum contains no information which is not present in the autocovariance function, since it is simply a linear combination of the autocovariances.

6.2 Fixed Cycles

This section introduces the concept of fixed cycles, and shows how such cycles may be fitted by regression methods. A straightforward extension of these results then leads naturally into Fourier analysis and the definition of the periodogram. In discussing this material, it is necessary to draw on certain standard results relating to trigonometric functions. These results are grouped together in appendix B.

Cyclical Functions

The trigonometric function

$$y = \cos x \qquad (2.1)$$

is defined in terms of an angle, x, which is measured in radians. Since there are 2π radians in a circle, y goes through its full complement of values as x moves from 0 to 2π. This pattern is then repeated and so for any integer, k, $\cos(x + 2k\pi) = \cos x$. The sine function exhibits a similar property, and figure 6.3 shows both $\sin x$ and $\cos x$ plotted against x. It will be observed that the cosine function is symmetric about zero. This is a reflection of the

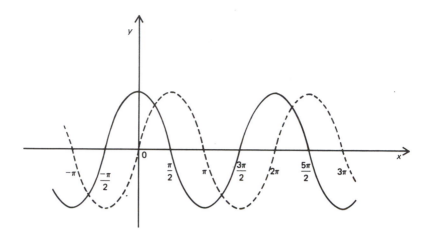

Figure 6.3 Sine (– – –) and cosine (——) functions.

fact that it is an even function, i.e. $\cos x = \cos(-x)$. The sine function, on the other hand, is odd as $\sin x = -\sin(-x)$.

The variable y may be expressed as a cyclical function of time by defining a parameter, λ, which is measured in radians and is known as the (angular) *frequency*. The variable x is then replaced by λt. By assigning different values to λ, the function can be made to expand or contract along the horizontal axis, t. The *period* of the cycle, which is the time taken for y to go through its complete sequence of values, is equal to $2\pi/\lambda$. Thus a trigonometric function which repeated itself every five time periods would have a frequency of $2\pi/5$.

Further flexibility may be introduced into a cyclical function by multiplying the cosine, or sine, function by a parameter, ρ, known as the *amplitude*. Finally, there remains the problem that the position of the function is fixed with respect to the horizontal axis. This may be remedied by the introduction of an angle, θ, which is again measured in radians, and is known as the *phase*. Expression (2.1) therefore becomes

$$y = \rho \cos(\lambda t - \theta) = \rho \cos \lambda(t - \xi) \qquad (2.2)$$

The parameter $\xi = \theta/\lambda$ gives the shift in terms of time.

Example 1 Suppose that a cosine function has a period of five, but that we wish to shift it so that its peaks are at $t = 2, 7, 12, \ldots$ rather than at $t = 0, 5, 10, \ldots$. Then $\xi = 2$ and so $\theta = \lambda \xi = (2\pi/5) \cdot 2 = 4\pi/5 = 2.513$ radians. Whether this movement actually represents a forward or backward shift, however, is somewhat problematic, since the same effect could have been accomplished by setting $\xi = -3$. This would have meant $\theta = (2\pi/5)(-3) = -3.770$ radians. The ambiguity surrounding the phase has some important implications in cross-spectral analysis.

A lateral shift in a trigonometric function may be induced in a different way. Rather than introducing a phase into the sine or cosine function, it is expressed as a mixture of a sine and a cosine function. Thus (2.2) becomes

$$y = \alpha \cos \lambda t + \beta \sin \lambda t \qquad (2.3)$$

where $\alpha = \rho \cos \theta$ and $\beta = \rho \sin \theta$, and so in the example above,

$$y = \cos(\lambda t - 2.513) = -0.809 \cos \lambda t + 0.588 \sin \lambda t$$

The transformation is often made in reverse, in which case

$$\rho^2 = \alpha^2 + \beta^2 \qquad (2.4a)$$

$$\theta = \tan^{-1}(\beta/\alpha) \qquad (2.4b)$$

Fourier Analysis

At the end of the previous sub-section it was observed that trigonometric terms could be imposed, one on the other, to produce a consolidated cyclical pattern. Now suppose that T points, $y_1, \ldots, y_T$, are available, and that we wish to construct a function, $y(t)$, which passes through every point. One way of achieving this objective is to let $y(t)$ be a linear function of T trigonometric terms.

If $y_1, \ldots, y_T$ have the usual interpretation as a set of time series observations, the easiest way to fit T trigonometric terms is by Fourier analysis. Let

$$n = \begin{cases} T/2, & \text{if } T \text{ is even} \\ (T-1)/2, & \text{if } T \text{ is odd} \end{cases} \qquad (2.5)$$

and define the frequencies

$$\lambda_j = 2\pi j/T, \qquad j = 1, \ldots, n \qquad (2.6)$$

The first step in constructing the appropriate function, $y(t)$, is to take a pair of trigonometric terms, $\cos \lambda_j t$ and $\sin \lambda_j t$, at each of these frequencies. If T is even, there will only be one term at $j = n$ for $t = 1, \ldots, T$, since $\sin \pi t = 0$ when t is an integer. This gives exactly $T - 1$ trigonometric terms, irrespective of whether T is odd or even. The full complement of T terms is then made up by the addition of a constant.

When T is even, the *Fourier representation* of the time series, y_t, is

$$y_t = T^{-1/2} a_0 + \sqrt{2/T} \sum_{j=1}^{n-1} (a_j \cos \lambda_j t + b_j \sin \lambda_j t) + T^{-1/2} a_n (-1)^t \qquad (2.7)$$

If T is odd, the last term in (2.7), which is based on $\cos \pi t$, does not appear, and the summation runs from $j = 1, \ldots, n$. Everything else remains the same.

If these rules are borne in mind, the appropriate results for an odd number of observations may be obtained directly from those presented for T even. Note that in neither case is a frequency defined at less than π radians. The frequency $\lambda = \pi$ is known as the *Nyquist* frequency, and it corresponds to a period of two time units. To involve shorter periods would introduce an element of ambiguity into the proceedings, since no meaningful information on such cycles could be extracted from the observations. The introduction of the factors involving $T^{-1/2}$ is rather arbitrary, but the rationale underlying this will become clear at a later stage.

The reason for the choice of the frequencies defined by (2.6) is essentially computational. It enables the orthogonality relations in appendix B to be exploited, thereby producing simple expressions for the Fourier coefficients, the a_js and b_js. Multiplying both sides of (2.7) by $\sin(2\pi it/T)$, summing from $t = 1$ to T and using (B.3b) and (B.3c) yields

$$\sum_{t=1}^{T} y_t \sin \frac{2\pi i}{T} t = (T/2)^{1/2} b_i, \qquad i = 1, \ldots, n-1 \tag{2.8}$$

Re-arranging and setting i equal to j then gives

$$b_j = (2/T)^{1/2} \sum_{t=1}^{T} y_t \sin(2\pi j/T)t, \qquad j = 1, \ldots, n-1 \tag{2.9a}$$

In a similar way, multiplying through by $\cos(2\pi it/T)$ produces the following expressions:

$$a_j = (2/T)^{1/2} \sum_{t=1}^{T} y_t \cos(2\pi j/T)t, \qquad j = 1, \ldots, n-1 \tag{2.9b}$$

$$a_0 = T^{-1/2} \sum_{t=1}^{T} y_t \tag{2.9c}$$

and

$$a_n = T^{-1/2} \sum_{t=1}^{T} y_t(-1)^t \tag{2.9d}$$

Example 2 Suppose four observations are available and that these take values $y_1 = 1$, $y_2 = 3$, $y_3 = 5$ and $y_4 = 7$. The Fourier representation is

$$y_t = T^{-1/2} a_0 + (2/T)^{1/2} a_1 \cos \frac{2\pi}{4} t + (2/T)^{1/2} b_1 \sin \frac{2\pi}{4} t$$

$$+ T^{-1/2} a_2 (-1)^t, \qquad t = 1, \ldots, 4 \tag{2.10}$$

Calculating the Fourier coefficients from (2.9) gives

$$y_t = 4 + 2\cos\frac{\pi}{2}t - 2\sin\frac{\pi}{2}t + (-1)^t$$

$$= 4 + \sqrt{8}\cos(\lambda t - \tfrac{1}{4}\pi) + (-1)^t \tag{2.11}$$

Whether a cyclical representation is sensible in these circumstances depends on whether the observed pattern will repeat itself over subsequent sets of T observations. This implies that

$$y_{t+4k} = y_t, \qquad t = 1, 2, 3, 4, \qquad k = 1, 2, \ldots$$

thereby leading to the pattern depicted in figure 6.4. Such a pattern seems rather unlikely, and faced with these data, a more reasonable course of action is simply to fit a linear trend.

Since each pair of sine and cosine terms in (2.7) can be represented by a single translated term, the relative importance of each frequency can be measured by a single quantity. Expression (2.4a) suggests the use of

$$p_j = a_j^2 + b_j^2, \qquad j = 1, \ldots, n - 1 \tag{2.12}$$

The sum of squared deviations of the observations may be decomposed in terms of these quantities by writing

$$\sum_{t=1}^{T} (y_t - \bar{y})^2 = \sum_{j=1}^{n} p_j \tag{2.13}$$

where $p_n = a_n^2$. This is *Parseval's theorem*. The proof, which is based on the orthogonality relations, is straightforward. If the mean is not subtracted, $p_0 = a_0^2$ is added to the right hand side.

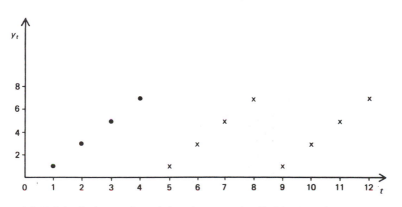

Figure 6.4 Original observations ($\bullet$) and pattern implied by Fourier representation ($\times$) in example 2.

A diagram showing each p_j plotted against the corresponding period, $2\pi/\lambda_j$, is known as the *periodogram*. However, it is generally more convenient to plot p_j against λ_j. This is known as the spectrogram, although the term periodogram is also employed in this context. In fact, the most common usage of the term periodogram is for a plot of p_j against λ_j, and it is in this sense that it will be used throughout the book.

The periodogram ordinates are often defined in complex terms as

$$p_j = (2/T)\left|\sum_{t=1}^{T} y_t\, e^{-i\lambda_j t}\right|^2, \qquad j = 1, \ldots, n-1 \qquad (2.14)$$

On expanding the exponential term using the identity (A.5), imaginary quantities drop out, leaving

$$p_j = (2/T)\left[\left(\sum_{t=1}^{T} y_t \cos \lambda_j t\right)^2 + \left(\sum_{t=1}^{T} y_t \sin \lambda_j t\right)^2\right] \qquad (2.15)$$

This expression follows immediately from the formulae in (2.9).

Equations (2.14) and (2.15) may be written with y_t replaced by $(y_t - \bar{y})$. An alternative form for (2.14) is therefore

$$p_j = \frac{2}{T}\left|\sum_{t=1}^{T} (y_t - \bar{y})\, e^{-i\lambda_j t}\right|^2, \qquad j = 1, \ldots, n-1 \qquad (2.16)$$

This can be verified directly by noting that

$$\sum_{t=1}^{T} (y_t - \bar{y})\, e^{-i\lambda_j t} = \sum_{t=1}^{T} y_t\, e^{-i\lambda_j t} - \bar{y} \sum_{t=1}^{T} e^{-i\lambda_j t}$$

and observing that the second term is zero in view of the identity in (B.5). For $j = 0$, the use of formula (2.16) leads to $p_0 = 0$. This makes sense, since in (2.14) p_0 is just a function of the mean.

Cyclical Regression Models

The value of the Fourier representation (2.7) can only be assessed by relating it to some underlying model. Consider the cyclical regression model,

$$y_t = T^{-1/2}\alpha_0 + \sqrt{2/T} \sum_{j=1}^{n-1} (\alpha_j \cos \lambda_j t + \beta_j \sin \lambda_j t) + T^{-1/2}\alpha_n(-1)^t + \varepsilon_t,$$

$$t = 1, \ldots, T \qquad (2.17)$$

where $\varepsilon_t \sim \text{NID}(0, \sigma^2)$. Within this framework, the Fourier coefficients (2.9) are seen to be the OLS estimators of the parameters in (2.17). By defining the $T \times 1$ vector, $\gamma = (\alpha_0, \alpha_1, \beta_1, \alpha_2, \ldots, \alpha_{T/2})'$, (2.17) may be written in matrix notation as

$$\mathbf{y} = \mathbf{Z}\gamma + \varepsilon \qquad (2.18)$$

where $\mathbf{Z}$ is the $T \times T$ *Fourier matrix*

$$\mathbf{Z} = \begin{bmatrix} \dfrac{1}{\sqrt{T}} & \sqrt{\dfrac{2}{T}}\cdot\cos\dfrac{2\pi}{T} & \sqrt{\dfrac{2}{T}}\cdot\sin\dfrac{2\pi}{T} & \sqrt{\dfrac{2}{T}}\cdot\cos\dfrac{4\pi}{T} & \cdots & -\sqrt{\dfrac{1}{T}} \\[2ex] \dfrac{1}{\sqrt{T}} & \sqrt{\dfrac{2}{T}}\cdot\cos\dfrac{2\pi}{T}2 & \sqrt{\dfrac{2}{T}}\cdot\sin\dfrac{2\pi}{T}2 & \sqrt{\dfrac{2}{T}}\cdot\cos\dfrac{4\pi}{T}2 & \cdots & \sqrt{\dfrac{1}{T}} \\[2ex] \vdots & \vdots & \vdots & \vdots & & \vdots \\[2ex] \dfrac{1}{\sqrt{T}} & \sqrt{\dfrac{2}{T}}\cdot\cos\dfrac{2\pi}{T}(T-1) & \sqrt{\dfrac{2}{T}}\cdot\sin\dfrac{2\pi}{T}(T-1) & \sqrt{\dfrac{2}{T}}\cdot\cos\dfrac{4\pi}{T}(T-1) & \cdots & -\sqrt{\dfrac{1}{T}} \\[2ex] \dfrac{1}{\sqrt{T}} & \sqrt{\dfrac{2}{T}} & 0 & \sqrt{\dfrac{2}{T}} & \cdots & \sqrt{\dfrac{1}{T}} \end{bmatrix}$$

$$(2.19)$$

It follows from (B.3) that $\mathbf{Z}$ is an orthogonal matrix, and so the OLS estimator of γ is given by

$$\mathbf{c} = (\mathbf{Z}'\mathbf{Z})^{-1}\mathbf{Z}'\mathbf{y} = \mathbf{Z}'\mathbf{y} \tag{2.20}$$

This is exactly the result in (2.9). Because of the orthogonality of the regressors, the individual OLS estimators are independent of each other. Explanatory variables may therefore be removed from (2.17) without affecting the estimates of the parameters which remain.

The distributional properties of the Fourier coefficients may be derived immediately from standard least squares theory. Thus

$$\text{Var}(\mathbf{c}) = \sigma^2(\mathbf{Z}'\mathbf{Z})^{-1} = \sigma^2\mathbf{I} \tag{2.21}$$

and so the elements of $\mathbf{c} - \gamma$ are normally and independently distributed with zero mean and variance σ^2. It follows that when $\alpha_j = \beta_j = 0$,

$$\sigma^{-2}p_j \sim \chi_2^2, \qquad j = 1, \ldots, n-1 \tag{2.22}$$

Unless the model is fitted with the full complement of T regressors, an estimate of σ^2 can be computed from the residuals. The usual formula for s^2 is applicable, and so the statistics $s^{-2}p_j/2$ may be tested against an F-distribution. The interpretation of the null hypothesis is that there is no component of frequency λ_j in the model.

6.3 Spectral Representation of a Stochastic Process

Consider the model

$$y_t = \alpha \cos \lambda t + \beta \sin \lambda t, \qquad t = 1, \ldots, T \tag{3.1}$$

where α and β are fixed parameters and λ takes a particular value between 0 and π. This can be regarded as one of the deterministic components in a cyclical trend model of the form (2.17). It is clearly not stationary, as $E(y_t)$ is a function of t, but this state of affairs can be remedied by replacing α and β by two random variables, u and v, which are uncorrelated and have mean zero and variance σ^2. It then follows that

$$E(y_t) = E(u) \cos \lambda t + E(v) \sin \lambda t = 0 \qquad (3.2a)$$

$$\mathrm{Var}(y_t) = E[(u \cos \lambda t + v \sin \lambda t)^2]$$

$$= \sigma^2 (\cos^2 \lambda t + \sin^2 \lambda t) = \sigma^2 \qquad (3.2b)$$

and

$$\gamma(\tau) = E(y_t y_{t-\tau}) = \sigma^2 [\cos \lambda t \cos \lambda (t-\tau) + \sin \lambda t \sin \lambda (t-\tau)]$$

$$= \sigma^2 \cos \lambda \tau, \qquad \tau = 1, 2, 3, \ldots \qquad (3.2c)$$

Although u and v are random variables, they are fixed in any particular realisation. Thus, although it is stationary, the model is still deterministic; only two observations are necessary to determine u and v exactly, and once this has been done the remaining points in the series can be forecast with zero mean square error. In practice, therefore, the only difference between the non-stationary model (3.1) and the corresponding stationary model is in the interpretation of the parameters.

The stationary model can be extended to include terms at more than one frequency. If J frequencies, $\lambda_1, \ldots, \lambda_J$, are included then

$$y_t = \sum_{j=1}^{J} (u_j \cos \lambda_j t + v_j \sin \lambda_j t) \qquad (3.3)$$

If

$$E(u_j) = E(v_j) = 0, \qquad j = 1, \ldots, J \qquad (3.4a)$$

$$\mathrm{Var}(u_j) = \mathrm{Var}(v_j) = \sigma_j^2, \qquad j = 1, \ldots, J \qquad (3.4b)$$

$$E(u_i u_j) = E(v_i v_j) = 0, \qquad i \neq j \qquad (3.4c)$$

and

$$E(u_i v_j) = 0, \qquad \text{for all } i, j \qquad (3.4d)$$

the mean of the series is zero while

$$\gamma(0) = \sum_{j=1}^{J} \sigma_j^2 \qquad (3.5)$$

and

$$\gamma(\tau) = \sum_{j=1}^{J} \sigma_j^2 \cos \lambda \tau \qquad (3.6)$$

Expression (3.5) shows that the variance of the process can be regarded as the sum of the variances of the u_j's and v_j's. If the set of frequencies in (3.3) corresponded to the set of frequencies defined by (2.6), this result would be similar to (2.13), but with the important difference that in (2.13) it is the variance in the sample which is being decomposed into estimates of fixed quantities, namely the amplitudes of the various trigonometric components.

Now consider the white noise process, defined by (2.1.12). Since this is completely random, all of its frequency components are of equal importance, but this immediately raises the question of what is meant by 'all' in this context. It makes no sense to consider a particular set of frequencies and say that they all make an equal contribution to the variance of the process, since there are an infinite number of frequencies in the range 0 to π. In order to extend equation (3.3) to cover this type of situation, it is necessary to allow an infinite number of trigonometric terms to be included in the range 0 to π. This is achieved by letting $J \to \infty$ and replacing the summation sign by an integral. The u_j's and v_j's are then replaced by continuous functions of λ denoted by $u(\lambda)$ and $v(\lambda)$ and the resulting *spectral representation* is given by

$$y_t = \int_0^\pi u(\lambda) \cos \lambda t \, d\lambda + \int_0^\pi v(\lambda) \sin \lambda t \, d\lambda \tag{3.7}$$

This is often referred to as *Cramér's representation*.

The functions $u(\lambda)$ and $v(\lambda)$ are stochastic, with properties somewhat analogous to those of the u_j's and v_j's in the discrete representation, (3.3). Consider any small interval, $d\lambda$, and let

$$E[u(\lambda) \, d\lambda] = E[v(\lambda) \, d\lambda] = 0 \tag{3.8a}$$

for all such intervals in the range $[0, \pi]$. If this assumption holds, applying the expectation operator to (3.7) yields $E(y_t) = 0$. In a similar way let

$$\text{Var}[u(\lambda) \, d\lambda] = \text{Var}[v(\lambda) \, d\lambda] = 2f(\lambda) \, d\lambda \tag{3.8b}$$

where $f(\lambda)$ is a continuous function, and suppose that

$$E[u(\lambda_1) \, d\lambda_1 u(\lambda_2) \, d\lambda_2] = E[v(\lambda_1) \, d\lambda_1 v(\lambda_2) \, d\lambda_2] = 0 \tag{3.8c}$$

where $d\lambda_1$ and $d\lambda_2$ are non-overlapping intervals, centred on λ_1 and λ_2 respectively, and (3.8c) is true for all possible non-overlapping intervals in the range $[0, \pi]$. Finally let

$$E[u(\lambda) \, d\lambda_1 v(\lambda) \, d\lambda_2] = 0 \tag{3.8d}$$

for all intervals, including cases where $d\lambda_1 = d\lambda_2$. From the spectral representation, (3.7),

$$\gamma(\tau) = E(y_t y_{t-\tau}) = E\left\{ \left[\int_0^\pi u(\lambda) \cos \lambda t \, d\lambda + \int_0^\pi v(\lambda) \sin \lambda t \, d\lambda \right] \right.$$
$$\left. \times \left[\int_0^\pi u(\lambda) \cos \lambda(t-\tau) \, d\lambda + \int_0^\pi v(\lambda) \sin \lambda(t-\tau) \, d\lambda \right] \right\} \tag{3.9}$$

but in view of assumption (3.8d) all cross-product terms involving sines and cosines disappear on expanding this expression out. Taking expectations of the remaining terms and using the trigonometric addition formulae (A.1) and (A.2) yields

$$\gamma(\tau) = 2 \int_0^\pi f(\lambda) \cos \lambda\tau \, d\lambda, \qquad \tau = 0, \pm 1, \pm 2, \dots \qquad (3.10)$$

All indeterministic processes have a spectral representation. Setting $\tau = 0$ in (3.10) gives

$$\gamma(0) = 2 \int_0^\pi f(\lambda) \, d\lambda \qquad (3.11)$$

showing that the power spectrum may be interpreted as a decomposition of the variance into cyclical components over the continuum $[0, \pi]$. In order to determine $f(\lambda)$ from the autocovariances, a Fourier transform of (3.10) is taken; see appendix C. This gives the formula stated in (1.1).

Complex Spectral Representation

The complex spectral representation is more compact than (3.7) and easier to handle mathematically. Let i be defined such that $i^2 = -1$. For a purely indeterministic process

$$y_t = \int_{-\pi}^\pi e^{i\lambda t} z(\lambda) \, d\lambda \qquad (3.12)$$

where for any small interval, $d\lambda$, in the range $-\pi \leqslant \lambda \leqslant \pi$

$$E[z(\lambda) \, d\lambda] = 0 \qquad (3.13a)$$

and

$$E[z(\lambda) \, d\lambda \cdot \overline{z(\lambda) \, d\lambda}] = f(\lambda) \, d\lambda \qquad (3.13b)$$

while for any two non-overlapping intervals, $d\lambda_1$ and $d\lambda_2$, centred on λ_1 and λ_2 respectively,

$$E[z(\lambda_1) \, d\lambda_1 \cdot \overline{z(\lambda_2) \, d\lambda_2}] = 0 \qquad (3.13c)$$

These properties are analogous to those set out in (3.8). As before, it follows almost immediately that $E(y_t) = 0$ for all t, while

$$\gamma(\tau) = E[y_t \overline{y_{t-\tau}}] = E\left[\int_{-\pi}^\pi e^{i\lambda t} z(\lambda) \, d\lambda \cdot \int_{-\pi}^\pi e^{-i\lambda(t-\tau)} \overline{z(\lambda) \, d\lambda} \right]$$

In view of (3.13b) and (3.13c), this becomes

$$\gamma(\tau) = \int_{-\pi}^{\pi} e^{i\lambda\tau} f(\lambda)\, d\lambda \tag{3.14}$$

The inverse Fourier transform of (3.14) is (1.4).

Wold Decomposition Theorem

In moving from (3.3) to (3.7), a strong distinction was drawn between deterministic and indeterministic processes. However, it is possible to conceive of a process containing both deterministic and indeterministic components. In fact, a general result known as the *Wold decomposition theorem* states that any covariance stationary process can be represented as

$$y_t = y_t^* + y_t^\dagger$$

where y_t^* is a deterministic component, as in the right hand side of (3.3), and $y_t^\dagger$ is a linear process as defined by (2.1.23). Since the spectrum of y_t^* is discrete, the frequency domain properties of the process as a whole must be described in terms of the *spectral distribution function*; this shows a jump at each of the frequencies, λ_j, appearing in (3.3).

Seasonal effects aside, perfectly regular period components are unusual in economic time series. To the extent that such a component were present in a series, it would tend to show up as a sharp spike in the estimated spectrum. Irregular cycles emerge as broad peaks; see section 6.5.

6.4 Properties of Autoregressive-Moving Average Processes

In the time domain, the properties of ARMA processes are characterised by their autocovariance, or equivalently autocorrelation, functions. While the autocovariance function may highlight certain features of the process, there may be other aspects which emerge less clearly. In particular, the cyclical properties of the series may not be well characterised by the autocovariances, especially if this behaviour is at all complex. For this reason, it is often desirable to examine the power spectrum of the process, as well as the autocovariance function.

The power spectrum of a stationary process may be obtained by evaluating the autocovariances and then substituting in (1.1) or (1.4). However, it is not necessary to evaluate the autocovariances. Replacing the lag operator by $\exp(-i\lambda)$ in the ACGF (2.4.14) yields the *spectral generating function* (SGF). Comparing this expression with (1.4) shows that dividing by 2π

gives the spectrum, that is

$$f(\lambda) = (2\pi)^{-1} g(e^{-i\lambda}) \tag{4.1}$$

For an ARMA(p, q) model it follows from (2.4.16) that

$$f(\lambda) = \frac{\sigma^2}{2\pi} \frac{|\theta(e^{-i\lambda})|^2}{|\phi(e^{-i\lambda})|^2} \tag{4.2}$$

Thus for an MA(1) model

$$g(e^{-i\lambda}) = (1 + \theta e^{-i\lambda})(1 + \theta e^{i\lambda})$$

$$= 1 + \theta^2 + \theta(e^{-i\lambda} + e^{i\lambda})$$

$$= 1 + \theta^2 + 2\theta \cos \lambda$$

Dividing by 2π gives the expression obtained earlier in (1.5).

Autoregressive Processes

For an AR(1) model, $\phi(L) = 1 - \phi L$ and so

$$g(e^{-i\lambda}) = \sigma^2/|1 - \phi e^{-i\lambda}|^2 = \sigma^2/(1 + \phi^2 - 2\phi \cos \lambda) \tag{4.3}$$

The spectrum of an AR(1) process with $\phi > 0$ is similar to the MA(1) spectrum shown in figure 6.2. The positive series correlation is reflected in the high values of $f(\lambda)$ at the low frequencies. As ϕ tends towards one, the contribution of these lower frequencies to the variance of the process increases as the series becomes more 'slowly changing'.

For an AR(2) process, evaluating $|1 - \phi_1 e^{-i\lambda} - \phi_2 e^{-i2\lambda}|^2$ yields

$$f(\lambda) = \left(\frac{\sigma^2}{2\pi}\right)\left(\frac{1}{1 + \phi_1^2 + \phi_2^2 - 2\phi_1(1 - \phi_2)\cos \lambda - 2\phi_2 \cos 2\lambda}\right) \tag{4.4}$$

The shape of the spectrum depends crucially on the values taken by the parameters. A spectrum in which $f(\lambda)$ monotonically decreases or increases could obviously arise as the AR(1) model is a special case of AR(2). However, in section 2.2, attention was drawn to AR(2) processes in which the roots of the characteristic equation were complex. This led to a damped cyclical pattern in the autocorrelation function and it was pointed out that this was an indication of some kind of cyclical behaviour in the series. The nature of these movements emerges clearly in the frequency domain. Figure 6.5 shows the spectrum for the AR(2) process of figure 2.4 in which $\phi_1 = 0.7$ and $\phi_2 = -0.5$. The peak indicates a tendency towards a cycle at a frequency around λ^*. This may be termed *pseudo-cyclical* behaviour, since the movements are not regular. A deterministic cycle, say of the form (3.1), would show up as a sharp spike.

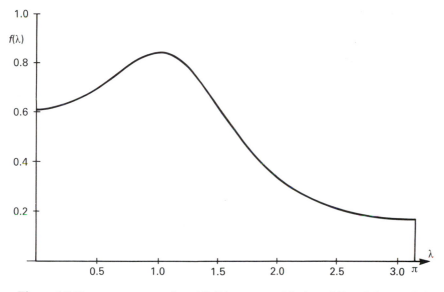

Figure 6.5 Power spectrum of an AR(2) process with $\phi_1 = 0.7$ and $\phi_2 = -0.5$.

When the spectrum contains a peak within the range $0 < \lambda < \pi$, its exact position may be determined by setting the derivative of (4.4) equal to zero. Solving the resulting equation yields

$$\lambda_0^* = \cos^{-1}[-\phi_1(1 - \phi_2)/4\phi_2] \qquad (4.5)$$

For the process in figure 6.5, $\lambda_0^* = \cos^{-1}(0.5250) = 1.018$, which coincides with a period of 6.172. This is not the same as the period of the autocorrelation function, which is determined from (2.2.15), although the two figures are quite close. On a related point, it is not true to say that complex roots necessarily imply a peak in the spectrum in the range $0 < \lambda < \pi$, although this will generally be the case.

The type of pseudo-cyclical behaviour exhibited by the AR(2) process is attractive from the point of view of economic modelling. Seasonal movements aside, regular cyclical patterns are unlikely to occur in economics, yet series generated by AR(2) processes can easily exhibit the kind of fluctuations often observed in practice.

Unobserved Components

Corresponding to the result noted for the ACGF in (2.5.4), the SGF of a sum of uncorrelated stationary ARMA processes is given by the sum of the individual SGF's. Thus for the unobserved component ARMA model defined in (2.5.1),

$$g(e^{-i\lambda}) = g_\mu(e^{-i\lambda}) + g_\xi(e^{-i\lambda}) \qquad (4.6)$$

Example 1   For the model, (2.5.2), the AR(1) process observed with error,

$$g(e^{-i\lambda}) = \frac{\sigma_\eta^2}{1 + \phi^2 - 2\phi \cos \lambda} + \sigma_\varepsilon^2 \qquad (4.7)$$

6.5 Stochastic Cycles

Deterministic cycles are inappropriate for many time series. This section shows how a stochastic cycle may be formulated and used as a model or as a component in a structural time series model. A similar approach is used to formulate a model for a slowly changing seasonal pattern based on trigonometric terms.

Stochastic Cycle

Let ψ_t be a cyclical function of time with frequency λ_c, which is measured in radians. Adopting the parameterisation in (2.3) gives

$$\psi_t = \alpha \cos \lambda_c t + \beta \sin \lambda_c t \qquad (5.1)$$

where $(\alpha^2 + \beta^2)^{1/2}$ is the amplitude and $\tan^{-1}(\beta/\alpha)$ is the phase. If the observations were given by

$$y_t = \psi_t + \varepsilon_t, \qquad t = 1, \ldots, T \qquad (5.2)$$

where ε_t is a white noise disturbance term and ψ_t is as defined in (5.1) with λ_c known, OLS would be an appropriate estimation technique. However, the deterministic cycle may be made stochastic by allowing the parameters α and β to evolve over time. As with the local linear trend model described in section 5.3, continuity must be preserved when time variation is introduced into the parameters. The first step is to write down a recursion for ψ_t:

$$\begin{bmatrix} \psi_t \\ \psi_t^* \end{bmatrix} = \begin{bmatrix} \cos \lambda_c & \sin \lambda_c \\ -\sin \lambda_c & \cos \lambda_c \end{bmatrix} \begin{bmatrix} \psi_{t-1} \\ \psi_{t-1}^* \end{bmatrix}, \qquad t = 1, \ldots, T \qquad (5.3)$$

with $\psi_0 = \alpha$ and $\psi_0^* = \beta$. That this recursion gives the current values of the cycle as in (5.1) can be checked by using the trigonometric identities in (A.1) and (A.2) of appendix A. Note that ψ_t^* only appears by construction to form ψ_t, and is of no intrinsic importance.

Introducing two white noise disturbances, κ_t and κ_t^*, into (5.3) yields

$$\begin{bmatrix} \psi_t \\ \psi_t^* \end{bmatrix} = \begin{bmatrix} \cos \lambda_c & \sin \lambda_c \\ -\sin \lambda_c & \cos \lambda_c \end{bmatrix} \begin{bmatrix} \psi_{t-1} \\ \psi_{t-1}^* \end{bmatrix} + \begin{bmatrix} \kappa_t \\ \kappa_t^* \end{bmatrix} \qquad (5.4)$$

For the model to be identifiable it must be assumed either that the two disturbances have the same variance or that they are uncorrelated. In practice both of these assumptions are usually imposed for reasons of parsimony.

Further flexibility can be introduced into (5.4) by bringing in a damping factor, ρ, to give

$$\begin{bmatrix} \psi_t \\ \psi_t^* \end{bmatrix} = \rho \begin{bmatrix} \cos \lambda_c & \sin \lambda_c \\ -\sin \lambda_c & \cos \lambda_c \end{bmatrix} \begin{bmatrix} \psi_{t-1} \\ \psi_{t-1}^* \end{bmatrix} + \begin{bmatrix} \kappa_t \\ \kappa_t^* \end{bmatrix} \tag{5.5}$$

where $0 \leqslant \rho \leqslant 1$.

The reduced form for ψ_t, and therefore y_t, can be obtained by first noting that $(\psi_t, \psi_t^*)'$ is a vector AR(1) process and writing

$$\begin{bmatrix} \psi_t \\ \psi_t^* \end{bmatrix} = \begin{bmatrix} 1 - \rho \cos \lambda_c \cdot L & -\rho \sin \lambda_c \cdot L \\ \rho \sin \lambda_c \cdot L & 1 - \rho \cos \lambda_c \cdot L \end{bmatrix}^{-1} \begin{bmatrix} \kappa_t \\ \kappa_t^* \end{bmatrix} \tag{5.6}$$

where L is the lag operator. Substituting the resulting expression for ψ_t in (5.2) gives

$$y_t = \frac{(1 - \rho \cos \lambda_c L)\kappa_t + (\rho \sin \lambda_c L)\kappa_t^*}{1 - 2\rho \cos \lambda_c L + \rho^2 L^2} + \varepsilon_t, \qquad t = 1, \dots, T \tag{5.7}$$

Re-arranging this expression as

$$y_t - (2\rho \cos \lambda_c)y_{t-1} + \rho^2 y_{t-2}$$

$$= \kappa_t - (\rho \cos \lambda_c)\kappa_{t-1} + (\rho \sin \lambda_c)\kappa_{t-1}^* + \varepsilon_t - (2\rho \cos \lambda_c)\varepsilon_{t-1} + \rho^2 \varepsilon_{t-2}$$

shows y_t to be an ARMA(2, 2) process. The cycle by itself is ARMA(2, 1). The MA part is subject to restrictions but the more interesting constraints are on the AR parameters. The AR polynomial, $\phi(L) = 1 - \phi_1 L - \phi_2 L^2$ has $\phi_1 = 2\rho \cos \lambda_c$ and $\phi_2 = -\rho^2$ and so its roots are

$$m_1, m_2 = [2\rho \cos \lambda_c \pm \sqrt{4\rho^2 \cos^2 \lambda_c - 4\rho^2}]/2\rho^2 = \rho^{-1} \exp(\pm i\lambda_c) \tag{5.8}$$

Thus, for $0 < \lambda_c < \pi$, the roots are a pair of complex conjugates with modulus ρ^{-1} and phase λ_c. When $0 \leqslant \rho \leqslant 1$ they lie outside the unit circle and the process is stationary. Since the roots of an AR(2) polynomial can be either real or complex, the formulation of the cyclical model effectively restricts the admissible region of the autoregressive coefficients to that part which is capable of giving rise to pseudo-cyclical behaviour.

Note that in the special case when $\lambda_c = 0$ or π, ψ_t collapses to an AR(1) process. This arises because $\sin \lambda_c$ is zero when $\lambda_c = 0$ or π and so the equation generating ψ_t^* is redundant. The first equation in (5.5) is therefore

$$\psi_t = \rho \psi_{t-1} + \kappa_t \tag{5.9a}$$

when $\lambda_c = 0$ and

$$\psi_t = -\rho \psi_{t-1} + \kappa_t \tag{5.9b}$$

when $\lambda_c = \pi$. Thus although ρ is non-negative the autoregressive parameter in the AR(1) model can be either positive or negative.

Spectrum

The properties of the stochastic cycle model emerge very clearly in the frequency domain. It can be seen from (5.7) that ψ_t is the sum of two uncorrelated ARMA components. Applying (4.6) the SGF is

$$g_\psi(e^{-i\lambda}) = \frac{|1 - \rho \cos \lambda_c \cdot e^{-i\lambda}|^2 + |\rho \sin \lambda_c \cdot e^{-i\lambda}|^2}{|1 - 2\rho \cos \lambda_c \cdot e^{-i\lambda} + \rho^2 e^{-i2\lambda}|^2} \sigma_\kappa^2$$

$$= \frac{1 + \rho^2 - 2\rho \cos \lambda_c \cdot \cos \lambda}{1 + \rho^4 + 4\rho^2 \cos^2 \lambda_c - 4\rho(1 + \rho^2) \cos \lambda_c \cdot \cos \lambda + 2\rho^2 \cos 2\lambda} \sigma_\kappa^2$$

(5.10)

As can be seen from the formula, the shape of the spectrum depends on λ_c and ρ, while σ_κ^2 is simply a scale parameter. Figure 6.6 shows the power spectrum of a cycle with λ_c equal to $\pi/4$ and ρ taking the values 0.7, 0.9 and 0.99 respectively; compare with figure 6.5 for the spectrum of the AR(2) model given in (4.4). As can be seen, the peak in the spectrum becomes sharper as ρ tends towards unity. When ρ is unity the cyclical process is non-stationary and the spectrum is no longer defined. If, on the other hand, σ_κ^2 is zero when ρ is unity, the assumption that ψ_0 and ψ_0^* are mutually uncorrelated random variables with zero mean and common variance means that ψ_t can be regarded as a stationary deterministic process of the kind described at the beginning of section 6.3. Its frequency domain properties can then be captured by the spectral distribution function.

The ACF of ψ_t can be shown to be

$$\rho(\tau) = \rho^\tau \cos \lambda_c \tau, \qquad \tau = 0, 1, 2, \ldots \qquad (5.11)$$

see exercise 7.5. This is a damped cycle and so quite informative about the nature of the process. However, when there is more than one cycle present, the autocorrelations from the two components become mixed up with each other giving a confusing message. By contrast, the information presented in the spectrum is clear. Figure 6.6(d) shows the spectrum for the model

$$y_t = \psi_{1t} + \psi_{2t} \qquad (5.12)$$

where the frequencies in the two cycles are $\pi/2$ and $\pi/10$, the former with ρ equal to 0.9 and the latter with ρ equal to 0.8.

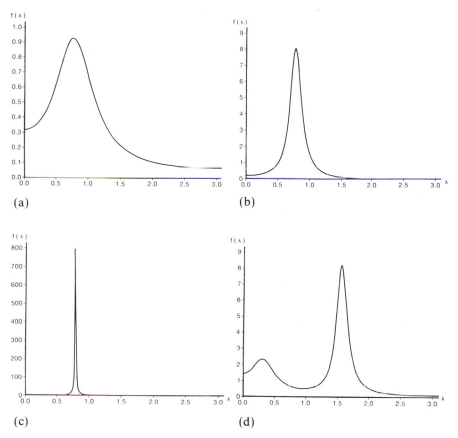

Figure 6.6 Power spectra for stochastic cycles: (a) $\lambda_c = \pi/4$, $\rho = 0.7$; (b) $\lambda_c = \pi/4$, $\rho = 0.9$; (c) $\lambda_c = \pi/4$, $\rho = 0.99$; (d) $\lambda_c = \pi/10$, $\rho = 0.8$ and $\lambda_c = \pi/2$, $\rho = 0.9$.

Statistical Treatment

The stochastic cycle model can be handled in state space form. Equation (5.5) is the transition equation for the state vector $(\psi_t, \psi_t^*)'$ and the measurement equation simply extracts ψ_t to give (5.2). The Kalman filter gives the optimal estimators of ψ_T and ψ_T^* at time T, and if these are denoted by $\tilde{\psi}_T$ and $\tilde{\psi}_T^*$ respectively, the l-step ahead predictor of ψ_t, and therefore y_t, is

$$\tilde{\psi}_{T+l|T} = \rho^l(\tilde{\psi}_T \cos \lambda_c l + \tilde{\psi}_T^* \sin \lambda_c l), \qquad l = 1, 2, \ldots \qquad (5.13)$$

If $0 < \rho < 1$, the forecast function is a damped sine, or cosine, wave. If $\rho = 1$ the forecast function is again a sine or cosine wave but no damping is present. The situation is analogous to that of the AR(1) forecast function in (2.6.6), and illustrates the point that ρ must be strictly less than unity for stationarity.

The cycle can be combined with other components, thereby enriching the class of structural time series models. A particularly useful model for macroeconomic time series is

$$y_t = \mu_t + \psi_t + \varepsilon_t \qquad (5.14)$$

where μ_t is a stochastic trend component (5.3.5) and ψ_t and ε_t are as in (5.2). The state space formulation is straightforward. The measurement equation is

$$y_t = (1 \ 0 \ 1 \ 0)\boldsymbol{\alpha}_t + \varepsilon_t, \qquad t = 1, \dots, T \qquad (5.15a)$$

while the transition equation is

$$\boldsymbol{\alpha}_t = \begin{bmatrix} \mu_t \\ \beta_t \\ \cdots \\ \psi_t \\ \psi_t^* \end{bmatrix} = \begin{bmatrix} 1 & 1 & \vdots & 0 & 0 \\ 0 & 1 & \vdots & 0 & 0 \\ \cdots & & \vdots & \cdots & \cdots \\ 0 & 0 & \vdots & \rho\cos\lambda_c & \rho\sin\lambda_c \\ 0 & 0 & \vdots & -\rho\sin\lambda_c & \rho\cos\lambda_c \end{bmatrix} \begin{bmatrix} \mu_{t-1} \\ \beta_{t-1} \\ \cdots \\ \psi_{t-1} \\ \psi_{t-1}^* \end{bmatrix} + \begin{bmatrix} \eta_t \\ \zeta_t \\ \cdots \\ \kappa_t \\ \kappa_t^* \end{bmatrix}$$

$$(5.15b)$$

The covariance matrix of the vector of disturbances in (5.15b) is a diagonal matrix with diagonal elements $\{\sigma_\eta^2, \sigma_\zeta^2, \sigma_\kappa^2, \sigma_\kappa^2\}$.

Example 1 Fitting a model of the form (5.15) to seasonally adjusted quarterly observations on US GNP, 1947 Q1 to 1988 Q2, yields smoothed estimates of the trend and cycle as shown in figure 6.7. The estimated values of the variance parameters σ_η^2, σ_ζ^2, σ_κ^2 and σ_ε^2 were 0, 0.0015, 0.0664 and 0 respectively, while the estimate of ρ was 0.92. The estimate of λ_c was 0.30, corresponding to a period of 20.82 quarters. Thus the length of the business cycle is around five years.

Seasonality

The model for a deterministic seasonal pattern based on a set of trigonometric terms at the seasonal frequencies, $\lambda_j = 2\pi j/s$, $j = 1, \dots, s/2$, or $(s-1)/2$ if odd, was introduced briefly in section 5.6. In what follows it will be assumed that the number of seasons in a year, s, is even, and so the seasonal effect at time t is

$$\gamma_t = \sum_{j=1}^{1/2 s - 1} (\gamma_j \cos\lambda_j t + \gamma_j^* \sin\lambda_j t) + \gamma_{s/2} \cos\lambda_{s/2} t \qquad (5.16)$$

This is just a Fourier representation, as in (2.7), of a set of points which sum to zero over s time periods. The same pattern repeats itself every year.

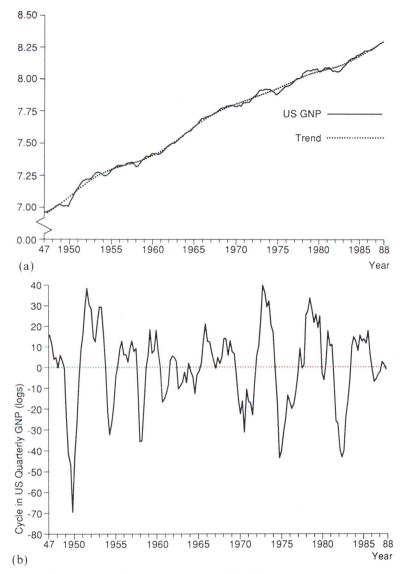

Figure 6.7 Trend and cyclical components in US GNP: (a) observations and trend; (b) cycle.

The period of the first frequency, $\lambda_1 = 2\pi/s$, is one year. This is known as the *fundamental* frequency, while the other frequencies are called *harmonics*.

If the trigonometric terms of (5.16) are included as explanatory variables in a regression model, the γ_j and γ_j^* parameters can be estimated by OLS. The resulting seasonal effect is identical to that which would be obtained by a dummy variable specification, as in (5.6.13). However, seasonal patterns sometimes change quite smoothly throughout the year. In such cases the lower frequencies dominate and it may be possible to drop the higher frequencies.

Example 2   Figure 6.8 shows the periodogram ordinates at the seasonal frequencies for a three-year series of monthly observations of sales in a butter market; see Anderson (1971, pp. 106–7). The first two frequencies, corresponding to periods of twelve and six months respectively, account for a high proportion of the seasonal variation. The remaining components are not statistically significant at the 5 per cent level of significance when tested within the framework of a model of the form (2.17).

A seasonal pattern based on (5.16) is the sum of cyclical components, and so each component may be allowed to evolve over time as in (5.4). Thus

$$\gamma_t = \sum_{j=1}^{s/2} \gamma_{j,t} \tag{5.17}$$

where

$$\gamma_{j,t} = \gamma_{j,t-1} \cos \lambda_j + \gamma_{j,t-1}^* \sin \lambda_j + \omega_{jt}, \qquad j = 1, \ldots, \tfrac{1}{2}s - 1$$

$$\gamma_{j,t}^* = -\gamma_{j,t-1} \sin \lambda_j + \gamma_{j,t-1}^* \cos \lambda_j + \omega_{jt}^*, \qquad j = 1, \ldots, \tfrac{1}{2}s - 1$$

and

$$\gamma_{j,t} = \gamma_{j,t-1} \cos \lambda_j + \omega_{jt}, \qquad j = s/2$$

with the ω_{jt}'s and ω_{jt}^*'s being zero mean white noise processes which are uncorrelated with each other and have a common variance σ_ω^2. The larger this variance, the more rapidly the seasonal pattern can change.

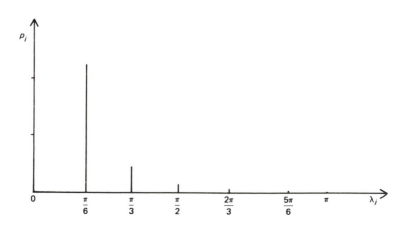

Figure 6.8 Periodogram ordinates for seasonal frequencies in example 2.

Because the damping factor in each of the trigonometric seasonal components is unity, γ_t is non-stationary. This is reflected in the forecasts. The Kalman filter gives estimators of the γ_{jt}'s and γ_{jt}^*'s at the end of the sample and the seasonal pattern based on these estimators remains constant, without damping down, just as the forecasted seasonal pattern from the stochastic dummy variable formulation (5.6.11) does.

As with the evolving dummy variable seasonal model, γ_t can be made stationary by the seasonal summation operator, and it is shown in FSK that $S(L)\gamma_t$ is an $MA(s-2)$ process. The spectrum of γ_t itself is not defined. If we were to introduce a damping factor, ρ, into the model generating each cyclical component, as in (5.5), the spectrum would be defined for $\rho < 1$. The closer ρ is to one the more sharply defined the peaks at the seasonal frequencies. As ρ goes to one, all the power becomes concentrated at the seasonal frequencies and the spectrum at these points goes to infinity.

6.6 Linear Filters

Suppose a series, y_t, is constructed as a weighted average of another series, x_t. Thus

$$y_t = \sum_{j=-r}^{s} w_j x_{t-j} \tag{6.1}$$

where the weights, $w_{-r}, \ldots, w_0, \ldots, w_s$, are fixed and real. Such an operation is called a *linear time-invariant filter*. Time invariance simply means that the weights are independent of t. When the weights sum to one, a filter is sometimes referred to as a 'moving average', though this term should be used with some care to avoid confusion with a moving average *process*.

Analysing the effect of a filter in the frequency domain can often provide valuable insight. Suppose that x_t is an indeterministic stationary process of the form (2.1.23). It may be written in terms of a polynomial in the lag operator, $\psi(L)$, and the filter can similarly be expressed as a polynomial

$$W(L) = w_{-r}L^{-r} + \cdots + w_{-1}L^{-1} + w_0 + w_1L + \cdots + w_sL^s \tag{6.2}$$

Thus (6.1) can be written as

$$y_t = W(L)x_t = W(L)\psi(L)\varepsilon_t \tag{6.3}$$

If the MA coefficients in (1.2.23) satisfy the condition (1.2.24b), and the weights in the filter satisfy a similar condition, namely $\sum |w_j| < \infty$, then y_t is also a stationary indeterministic process; see Fuller (1976, chapter 2). From (4.2) the SGF of y_t is

$$g_y(L) = |W(e^{-i\lambda})\psi(e^{-i\lambda})|^2\sigma^2 = |W(e^{-i\lambda})|^2|\psi(e^{-i\lambda})|^2\sigma^2$$

from which it can be seen that the spectrum of y_t is related to that of x_t by the expression

$$f_y(\lambda) = |W(e^{-i\lambda})|^2 f_x(\lambda) \tag{6.4}$$

The term

$$W(e^{-i\lambda}) = \sum_{j=-r}^{s} w_j e^{-i\lambda j} \tag{6.5}$$

is known as the *frequency response function*, and it is this which provides the basis for the analysis in the frequency domain. Note that if two filters, $W_1(L)$ and $W_2(L)$, are applied consecutively so that

$$y_t = W_2(L)W_1(L)x_t \tag{6.6}$$

their combined effect is just given by the product of the respective frequency response functions, that is

$$W(e^{-i\lambda}) = W_2(e^{-i\lambda})W_1(e^{-i\lambda}) \tag{6.7}$$

Gain and Phase

The effect of a linear filter on a series is twofold. The first effect is to change the relative importance of the various cyclical components. This becomes clear in an examination of the spectrum of the process before and after the filter is applied. It can be seen from (6.4) how this effect is captured in the term $|W(e^{-i\lambda})|^2$, which is known as the *power transfer function*. The factor by which the amplitude of a cyclical component is enhanced or diminished is given by the modulus of the frequency response function, $|W(e^{-i\lambda})|$. This quantity, which will be denoted by $G(\lambda)$, is termed the *gain*.

The other property of a filter concerns the extent to which it induces a shift in the series with regard to its position in time. Suppose that

$$y_t = x_{t-3} \tag{6.8}$$

The effect of this rather trivial filtering operation is to shift the series back by three time periods. If x_t were generated by a cyclical process, say

$$x_t = \cos \lambda t \tag{6.9}$$

the filtered series would be

$$y_t = \cos \lambda(t-3) = \cos(\lambda t - 3\lambda) \tag{6.10}$$

The *phase* shift, in radians, is given by $\text{Ph}(\lambda) = 3\lambda$. Thus a lateral shift of three periods in the time domain becomes a phase change of 3λ in the frequency domain.

A graph of $\mathrm{Ph}(\lambda)$ against λ is termed the *phase diagram*. For the pure delay given in (5.4), $\mathrm{Ph}(\lambda)$ is a straight line through the origin with a slope equal to the time lag; see figure 6.9.

The phase may be obtained from the frequency response function. This is, in general, a complex quantity, and if we write $W(e^{-i\lambda}) = W^*(\lambda) + iW^\dagger(\lambda)$, where $W^*(\lambda)$ and $W^\dagger(\lambda)$ are both real, then

$$\mathrm{Ph}(\lambda) = \tan^{-1}[-W^\dagger(\lambda)/W^*(\lambda)], \qquad 0 \leqslant \lambda \leqslant \pi \qquad (6.11)$$

The rationale behind this formula is best explained by reference to the Cramér representation of a stochastic process. This is discussed in the next sub-section. For a given $\mathrm{Ph}(\lambda)$, the shift in time units is $\mathrm{Ph}(\lambda)/\lambda$. Except when $\mathrm{Ph}(\lambda)$ is a linear function of λ, as in the example above, the time shift will be different for different values of λ.

The definition of the phase is subject to a fundamental ambiguity which can sometimes give rise to problems. This is because adding or subtracting a complete cycle from an angle will not change its tangent. Thus if a particular angle, denoted, say, by $\mathrm{Ph}^*(\lambda)$, emerges as a solution to (6.11), any angle satisfying the relationship $\mathrm{Ph}(\lambda) = \mathrm{Ph}^*(\lambda) \pm 2h\pi$, where h is an integer, is also a valid solution of (6.11). In the case of the simple filter (6.8), the general solution is $\mathrm{Ph}(\lambda) = 3\lambda \pm 2h\pi$. Therefore, at a frequency of $\lambda = \pi/2$, for example, the phase could be interpreted not as a lag of 3, but as a lead of $-3 + 2\pi/(\pi/2) = 1$. However, taking a solution other than $\mathrm{Ph}(\lambda) = 3\lambda$ in this case would result in a non-linear phase function which would not have the interpretation of a constant lag in the time domain.

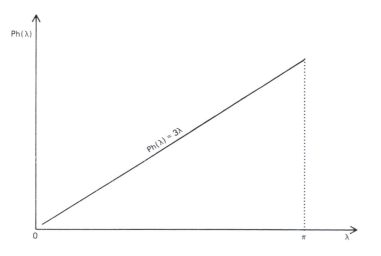

Figure 6.9 Phase diagram for $y_t = x_{t-3}$.

A final point to note is that a filter which is symmetric does not exhibit a phase shift. The result follows because the sine function is odd and so

$$\sum_{j=-r}^{r} w_j e^{-i\lambda j} = \sum_{j=-r}^{r} w_j \cos \lambda j - i \sum_{j=-r}^{r} w_j \sin \lambda j$$

$$= w_0 + 2 \sum_{j=1}^{r} w_j \cos \lambda j$$

Hence the frequency response function is real and it is clear from (6.11) that there is no phase shift.

The Frequency Response Function and the Spectral Representation

The spectral representation of x_t in complex terms is

$$x_t = \int_{-\pi}^{\pi} e^{i\lambda t} z_x(\lambda) \, d\lambda \tag{6.12}$$

where

$$E[z_x(\lambda_1) \, d\lambda_1 \cdot \overline{z_x(\lambda_2) \, d\lambda_2}] = \begin{cases} f_x(\lambda) \, d\lambda, & \text{for } \lambda_1 = \lambda_2 \\ 0, & \text{for } \lambda_1 \neq \lambda_2 \end{cases}$$

Substituting the spectral representation of x_t in (6.1) gives

$$y_t = \sum_{-r}^{s} w_j \int_{-\pi}^{\pi} e^{i(t-j)\lambda} z_x(\lambda) \, d\lambda$$

$$= \int_{-\pi}^{\pi} e^{i\lambda t} (\Sigma w_j e^{-i\lambda j}) z_x(\lambda) \, d\lambda$$

$$= \int_{-\pi}^{\pi} e^{i\lambda t} W(e^{-i\lambda}) z_x(\lambda) \, d\lambda \tag{6.13}$$

Expression (6.13) is the spectral representation of y_t, with $z_y(\lambda) = W(\lambda)z_x(\lambda)$. Since by definition,

$$f_y(\lambda) \, d\lambda = E[z_y(\lambda) \cdot \overline{z_y(\lambda) \, d\lambda}]$$

it is clear that (6.4) holds.

Writing the frequency response function in polar form,

$$W(e^{-i\lambda}) = G(\lambda) e^{-i\text{Ph}(\lambda)} \tag{6.14}$$

and substituting in (6.13), yields

$$y_t = \int_{-\pi}^{\pi} e^{i\lambda t} G(\lambda) e^{-iPh(\lambda)} z_x(\lambda) \, d\lambda$$

$$= \int_{-\pi}^{\pi} e^{i\lambda(t - Ph(\lambda)/\lambda)} G(\lambda) z_x(\lambda) \, d\lambda \qquad (6.15)$$

The interpretation of the gain and phase should now be clear. At each frequency the amplitude component, $z_x(\lambda)$, is multiplied by $G(\lambda)$, while the nature of the phase shift emerges in the term $(t - Ph(\lambda)/\lambda)$; that is, for periodic components of frequency λ, y lags x by $Ph(\lambda)/\lambda$ periods.

Averaging and Differencing

Filters may be applied for a number of reasons. At the simplest level is the idea that a time series may consist of a long-term movement, a trend, upon which is superimposed an irregular component. A moving average filter will smooth the series, reducing the irregular movements and revealing the trend more clearly. Suppose the filter is a simple moving average of length $m = 2r + 1$, in which the weights are equal and sum to unity, that is

$$y_t = \frac{1}{m} \sum_{j=-r}^{r} x_{t-j} \qquad (6.16)$$

Using (A.9) and (A.10) it can be seen that the frequency response function is given by

$$W(e^{-i\lambda}) = \frac{\sin(m\lambda/2)}{m \sin(\lambda/2)} \qquad (6.17)$$

This is real, reflecting the fact that the filter is symmetric. Its effect can be seen in figure 6.10(a), which is a graph of the gain, the absolute value of (6.17), for a five-period moving average. Smoothing takes place because the gain at high frequencies is relatively small, thereby dampening irregular movements in any series to which it is applied. In addition the power at the fundamental frequency of a five-period cycle, $\lambda = 2\pi/5$, is removed completely, as is the power at the harmonic, $4\pi/5$.

The five-period differencing operation

$$y_t = x_t - x_{t-5} \qquad (6.18)$$

also removes power at the frequencies $2\pi/5$ and $4\pi/5$. Using (A.7), the gain is easily seen to be

$$G(\lambda) = |1 - e^{-i5\lambda}| = 2^{1/2}(1 - \cos 5\lambda)^{1/2} \qquad (6.19)$$

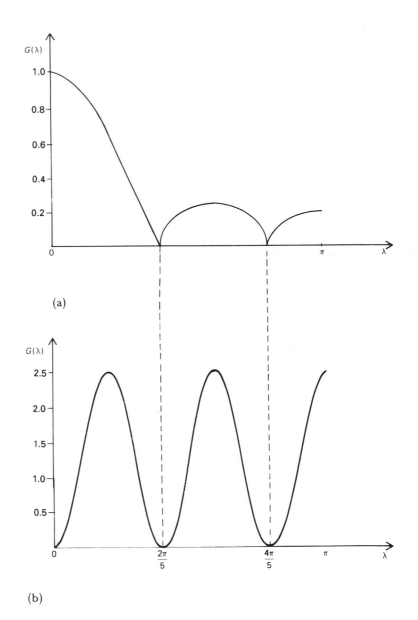

Figure 6.10 Graphs showing the gain for (a) a five-year moving average and (b) a five-year differencing filter.

The graph of the gain, shown in figure 6.10(b), provides an interesting contrast to the one in (a). While it again removes power at the fundamental and harmonic frequencies of a five-period cycle, it is also zero at frequency zero and there is no smoothing of the high frequencies. Furthermore it induces a phase shift since

$$Ph(\lambda) = \tan^{-1}[(-\sin 5\lambda)/(1 - \cos 5\lambda)]$$

The formal relationship between the moving average and differencing filters can be established quite easily. Write the moving average as

$$M_5(L) = (L^{-2} + L^{-1} + 1 + L + L^2)/5$$

Then, following (5.1.5), the fifth difference filter is

$$\Delta_5 = 5L^2 M_5(L)(1 - L) \qquad (6.20)$$

so we could, in principle, evaluate its gain from the product of the frequency response functions of the moving average and the first difference filters.

Spurious Cyclical Behaviour

Over half a century ago, it was observed that certain operations on a time series could produce a curious distorting effect. In particular, it was found that applying a set of summing operations could induce a spurious cycle in the data if a certain amount of differencing had already taken place. This phenomenon is known as the *Yule–Slutsky effect*. The manner in which it arises shows up quite clearly when the problem is analysed in the frequency domain.

Consider the power transfer function associated with the first difference operator, $1 - L$. This is given by

$$|W_1(e^{-i\lambda})|^2 = 2(1 - \cos \lambda) \qquad (6.21)$$

In view of (6.7), the application of the first difference operator d times produces the power transfer function

$$\prod_{i=1}^{d} |W_1(e^{-i\lambda})|^2 = |W_1(e^{-i\lambda})|^{2d} = 2^d(1 - \cos \lambda)^d \qquad (6.22)$$

In a similar way, if the summation filter $1 + L$ is applied s times, we obtain the power transfer function

$$|W_2(e^{-i\lambda})|^{2s} = 2^s(1 + \cos \lambda)^s \qquad (6.23)$$

The overall effect of d differencing operations followed by s summations is therefore

$$|W(e^{-i\lambda})|^2 = 2^{s+d}(1 - \cos \lambda)^d(1 + \cos \lambda)^s \qquad (6.24)$$

The differencing operations attenuate the low frequencies, while the summations attenuate the high frequencies. The combined effect can be to emphasise certain of the intermediate frequencies. This shows up insofar as the transfer function has a peak. Differentiating (6.24) with respect to λ shows it to have a turning point at the frequency

$$\lambda_0 = \cos^{-1}[(s-d)/(s+d)] \tag{6.25}$$

and taking the second derivative confirms that this is a maximum. By a suitable choice of d and s, λ_0 may be made arbitrarily close to any desired frequency, and the larger d and s are, the sharper the peak in the transfer function.

An interesting example of what is essentially the Yule–Slutsky effect is described by Fishman (1969, pp. 45–9). This is important in that it illustrates some of the pitfalls that may be encountered in analysing time series data. The study in question, by Kuznets (1961), was an investigation of the long swing hypothesis, which postulates the existence of a cycle of around 20 years in certain economic time series. Before proceeding to examine the data for evidence of a long-run cycle, Kuznets first decided to remove some of the cyclical components at higher frequencies. He therefore applied two filters. The first, a simple five-year moving average, was presumably aimed at attenuating the effects of the five-year trade cycle. This filter has a frequency response function given by (6.17) with $m = 5$. The frequency response function of the second filter, a differencing operation of the form

$$y_t = x_{t+5} - x_{t-5} \tag{6.26}$$

is simply $2\mathrm{i}\sin 5\lambda$. Combining these two results through (6.7) gives an overall transfer function of

$$|W(\mathrm{e}^{-\mathrm{i}\lambda})|^2 = \left[\frac{2\sin 5\lambda \sin(5\lambda/2)}{5\sin(\lambda/2)}\right]^2 \tag{6.27}$$

This has a very high peak centred at a frequency corresponding to a period of 20.3 years. Kuznets concluded that the average period of the cycle he was observing was about 20 years, but as (6.27) shows, these movements could correspond to a spurious cycle induced by the two filtering operations!

Trends and Seasonals

The analysis as applied so far has been restricted to stationary time series. Not all the conclusions carry over straightforwardly to non-stationary models. Consider a simplified version of the basic structural model, described in section 5.6, in which the trend component, μ_t, follows a random walk. Thus

$$y_t = \mu_t + \gamma_t + \xi_t \tag{6.28}$$

where γ_t is the stochastic seasonal dummy process, (5.6.11), and ξ_t is any indeterministic stationary process, such as a stochastic cycle or simply white noise. The model can be conveniently written in the form

$$y_t = \frac{\eta_t}{\Delta} + \frac{\omega_t}{S(L)} + \xi_t \qquad (6.29)$$

We can now examine the effects of various filtering operations on the different components. For example, a simple first differencing operation will remove all the power at zero frequency in the spectrum of ξ_t, but its effect on the trend is to cancel out the non-stationary Δ operator in the denominator leaving η_t, which has a flat spectrum.

Seasonal effects may be removed by a simple moving average. For monthly observations a suitable set of weights is

$$w_j = \begin{cases} 1/12, & j = 0, \pm 1, \ldots, \pm 5 \\ 1/24, & j = \pm 6 \end{cases} \qquad (6.30)$$

The frequency response function of this filter is

$$W(e^{-i\lambda}) = \frac{\sin 6\lambda \cos(\lambda/2)}{12 \sin(\lambda/2)} \qquad (6.31)$$

This expression may be derived in much the same way as (6.17) was obtained from (6.16), although the algebra is a little more complicated because of the unequal weights. As might be expected from the earlier discussion, the gain at high frequencies is relatively small, representing a smoothing effect, while at the fundamental seasonal frequency, $\pi/6$, and at the harmonics, $2\pi j/12$, $j = 2, \ldots, 6$, the gain is zero; see Fishman (1969, p. 86). This latter feature of the filter explains why it removes the seasonal component. Writing the filter in terms of a polynomial in the lag operator, $M(L)$, it can be seen to be related to the seasonal summation operator since

$$M(L) = [\{L^{-6} + \cdots + L^5\} + \{L^{-5} + \cdots + L^6\}]/24$$
$$= [\{L^{-6} + L^{-5}\}/24]S(L) \qquad (6.32)$$

Thus the summation operator in the seasonal component is cancelled out, leaving a stationary process. The same thing happens with trigonometric seasonality of the form (5.17). On the other hand, the effect of the filter on the stationary component ξ_t is that the otherwise smooth shape of its spectrum becomes punctuated by dips at the seasonal frequencies. This has created some concern, as discussed in Nerlove et al. (1979), because filters like (6.30) play a key role in seasonal adjustment procedures, and the implied distortion in the properties of the stationary part of a series appears to be an unfortunate side efffect.

The seasonal difference operator has essentially the same effect as the seasonal summation operator and the first difference operator combined;

compare (6.20). Multiplying (6.29) by $\Delta_{12} = 1 - L^{12}$ gives

$$\Delta_{12} y_t = S(L)\eta_t + (1 - L)\omega_t + (1 - L^{12})\xi_t \qquad (6.33)$$

The effect of the filter on each component can be analysed using the appropriate frequency response function. The spectrum of the trend will exhibit the dips at seasonal frequencies noted in the previous paragraph, while the stationary component has these dips combined with an attenuation of the low frequencies. The overall conclusion is that while differencing and seasonal moving averages are effective for removing trend and seasonal components, the resulting distortion may obscure important features of the original series. This is also true of more complex detrending and seasonal adjustment procedures which are *ad hoc* in the sense of not being based on a model fitted to the series in question. Harvey and Jaeger (1993) discuss this issue and conclude that the best way of obtaining 'stylised facts' is to fit a structural time series model and then extract the components of interest by the optimal smoother.

6.7 Estimation of the Spectrum

The power spectrum of a stochastic process was defined in (1.1). An obvious estimator, given a set of T observations, is therefore

$$I(\lambda) = \frac{1}{2\pi}\left[c(0) + 2\sum_{\tau=1}^{T-1} c(\tau)\cos\lambda\tau\right], \qquad 0 \leqslant \lambda \leqslant \pi \qquad (7.1)$$

The theoretical autocovariances in (1.1) are replaced by the sample autocovariances in (7.1). Since T is finite, the summation is no longer infinite. Autocovariances can only be estimated up to a lag of $T - 1$, with $c(T - 1)$ being a function of a single pair of observations, the first and the last.

Expression (7.1) defines the *sample spectral density*. It is closely related to the periodogram. From (2.16)

$$p_j = \frac{2}{T}\left|\sum_{t=1}^{T} (y_t - \bar{y})e^{-i\lambda_j t}\right|^2$$

$$= \frac{2}{T}\sum_{t=1}^{T}\sum_{s=1}^{T} (y_t - \bar{y})(y_s - \bar{y})e^{-i\lambda_j(t-s)}$$

Letting $\tau = t - s$, and noting the definition of $c(\tau)$ in (2.1.11), gives

$$p_j = 2\sum_{\tau=-(T-1)}^{T-1} c(\tau)e^{-i\lambda_j\tau}$$

$$= 2\left[c(0) + 2\sum_{\tau=1}^{T-1} c(\tau)\cos\lambda\tau\right] \qquad (7.2)$$

The last equality follows from the symmetry of $c(\tau)$. Comparing (7.2) with (7.1) then shows that

$$I(\lambda_j) = (1/4\pi)p_j \tag{7.3}$$

for λ_j defined by (2.6). If T is even, $I(\lambda_n) = p_n/2\pi$.

There is nothing to prevent $I(\lambda)$ from being computed for any value of λ in the range $[-\pi, \pi]$. However, it is generally convenient to consider it as being defined at the same frequencies for which the periodogram is calculated. This will be implicitly assumed throughout the ensuing discussion.

Since the sample spectral density, $I(\lambda)$, is proportional to the periodogram, it is often referred to as the periodogram in the literature. This usage will sometimes be adopted here when the distinction is unimportant.

Properties of the Sample Spectral Density

If the observations, $y_1, \ldots, y_T$, are drawn from a normally distributed white noise process, the properties of the sample spectral density may be derived very easily using the results in section 6.2. If all the α and β parameters in (2.17) are zero, it follows from (2.22) and (6.3) that

$$I(\lambda_j) \sim (\sigma^2/4\pi)\chi_2^2 \tag{7.4}$$

for all λ_j as defined by (2.6).

The theoretical power spectrum of a white noise process is $f(\lambda) = \sigma^2/2\pi$ for all λ. Since the mean and variance of a χ_f^2 distribution are f and $2f$ respectively,

$$E[I(\lambda_j)] = (\sigma^2/4\pi)E(\chi_2^2) = \sigma^2/2\pi = f(\lambda) \tag{7.5}$$

while

$$\mathrm{Var}[I(\lambda_j)] = \frac{\sigma^4}{16\pi^2}\,\mathrm{Var}(\chi_2^2) = \left(\frac{\sigma^2}{2\pi}\right)^2 = f^2(\lambda) \tag{7.6}$$

For a given λ_j, the sample spectral density is an unbiased estimator of $f(\lambda)$. However, its variance does not depend on T and so it does not give a consistent estimator of the power spectrum at a given frequency. Furthermore, since the estimators of the parameters in (2.17) are mutually uncorrelated, it follows that

$$\mathrm{Cov}[I(\lambda_j), I(\lambda_i)] = 0, \qquad \text{for } j \neq i \tag{7.7}$$

Thus, with normally distributed observations, the ordinates of the sample spectral density are independent. As a result of these properties, a graph of the sample spectral density calculated at the points defined by (2.6) has a jagged and irregular appearance. This is illustrated in figure 6.11. Such a pattern persists no matter how large the sample.

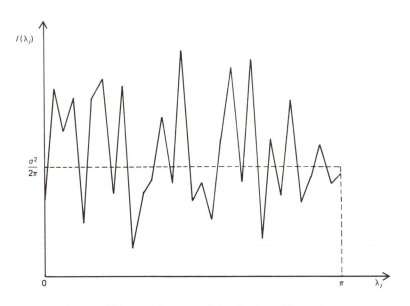

Figure 6.11 Sample spectral density for white noise.

If the observations are generated by any stationary stochastic process with a continuous spectrum, it can be shown that $2I(\lambda)/f(\lambda)$ has a limiting χ_2^2 distribution for $0 \leqslant \lambda \leqslant \pi$. Thus the limiting distribution of $I(\lambda)$ has a mean of $f(\lambda)$ and a variance of $f^2(\lambda)$. The ordinates of the sample spectral density at different frequencies are asymptotically independent. This suggests that $I(\lambda)$ will continue to have the irregular appearance noted in the white noise model. The empirical evidence confirms that this is indeed the case.

Spectrum Averaging

For a white noise process, the independence of the ordinates of the sample spectral density at the frequencies defined by (2.6) suggests smoothing $I(\lambda_j)$ by averaging over adjacent frequencies. Thus a possible estimator of $f(\lambda)$ at $\lambda = \lambda_j$ is

$$\hat{f}(\lambda_j) = m^{-1} \sum_{i = -m^*}^{m^*} I(\lambda_{j-i}) \tag{7.8}$$

where $m = 2m^* + 1$. In view of the additive properties of the χ^2 distribution it follows from (7.4) that

$$\hat{f}(\lambda_j) \sim (\sigma^2/4\pi m)\chi_{2m}^2 \tag{7.9}$$

The expectation of $\hat{f}(\lambda_j)$ is $\sigma^2/2\pi$, and so it is unbiased. Its variance is

$$\text{Var}[\hat{f}(\lambda_j)] = (\sigma^2/2\pi)^2/m = f^2(\lambda_j)/m \qquad (7.10)$$

and although T does not enter directly into (7.10), it could be made to do so by allowing m to increase as T increases. To formalise this, set $m = \kappa T$, where κ is a constant. Expression (7.10) then becomes

$$\text{Var}[\hat{f}(\lambda_j)] = [f^2(\lambda_j)/\kappa]/T \qquad (7.11)$$

Since the variance of $\hat{f}(\lambda_j)$ is $0(T^{-1})$, it is a consistent estimator of $f(\lambda_j)$.

A convenient way of computing (7.8) at all the points defined by (2.6) is by a simple moving average. This yields estimates at n points, although only those estimates which are at least m points apart will be independent.

The estimator defined by (7.8) uses what is known as a rectangular *window*. The term 'window' conveys the notion that only some of the sample spectral ordinates are taken account of, or 'seen', in the weighting procedure. In this case the window is rectangular, as all the ordinates which are 'seen' are given equal weight in the construction of $\hat{f}(\lambda_j)$.

The *width* of the window is simply the length of its base. The width may be measured in two ways. The first measure is the *range*, which is the number of spectral points used in each weighted average. Thus the range is equal to m. There are n points in the spectrum, and so dividing this figure by m gives the number of completely independent estimators. The second measure is the *bandwidth*, which is the width of the window in radians. If $T = 200$ and $m = 5$, it is possible to construct 20 independent estimators of the spectrum in the range $[0, \pi]$ and so the width of each window is $\pi/20$. In general, the bandwidth is equal to $2\pi m/T$.

For a white noise spectrum, any weighted average will be an unbiased estimator of $f(\lambda)$. Furthermore, it is apparent from (7.10) that for a given sample size, the variance of the estimator will be smaller the larger is m. This inverse relationship between m and the variance of the estimator holds, irrespective of whether or not the series is generated by a white noise process. However, once we relax the assumption that the underlying spectrum is flat, it is no longer the case that an estimator like (7.8) will always be unbiased. Furthermore, a trade-off now emerges with respect to the choice of m, since the wider the bandwidth, the greater the possibility of a large bias emerging. A large value of m also leads to sharp peaks in the spectrum being 'smudged' over a much greater number of spectral points than should ideally be the case. Hence a sharp cyclical pattern may not emerge very clearly. The problems associated with too wide a bandwidth are captured by the term *resolution*. Poor resolution implies a good deal of smudging and bias.

The discussion so far has been with respect to the simple weighted average, (7.8). Other weighting schemes may also be considered, and (7.8) may be generalised to

$$\hat{f}(\lambda_j) = \sum_{i=-m^*}^{m^*} h_i I(\lambda_{j-i}) \qquad (7.12)$$

where the weights, h_i, sum to unity. One possible scheme is to choose the weights in such a way that the window is triangular. This gives more weight to the ordinates closest to the frequency of interest.

The estimator given by (7.12) is an unbiased estimator of the spectrum of a white noise series, and its variance is not difficult to obtain in this case. The bandwidth for such an estimator is generally defined as being equal to the width of a rectangular window which would produce an estimator with the same variance.

Weighting in the Time Domain

An alternative approach to spectral estimation is to weight the auto-covariances. The sample spectral density, (7.1), is modified by a series of weights $k(0), k(1), \ldots, k(T-1)$, to give

$$\tilde{f}(\lambda) = (2\pi)^{-1} \left[k(0)c(0) + 2 \sum_{\tau=1}^{T-1} k(\tau)c(\tau) \cos \lambda\tau \right],$$

$$0 \leqslant \lambda \leqslant \pi \qquad (7.13)$$

These weights are known as the *lag window*.

The simplest weighting scheme consists of truncating the weights beyond a certain lag length, N. For $|\tau| \leqslant N$, the weights are set equal to unity and so the lag window is effectively rectangular. This is intuitively sensible, since it cuts out the higher order sample autocovariances and these are the ones which are most unstable. Unfortunately, an estimator constructed in this way exhibits certain undesirable properties. This may be demonstrated by seeing what this particular weighting scheme implies in the frequency domain. Corresponding to any lag window there is a spectral window. This is exactly the same as the window described in the previous section, except that it may be regarded as a continuous function of λ. It is convenient to define λ in terms of the difference between the frequency of interest and a particular adjacent frequency, so that the expression

$$h(\lambda) = (2\pi)^{-1} \left[k(0) + 2 \sum_{\tau=1}^{T-1} k(\tau) \cos \lambda\tau \right],$$

$$-\pi \leqslant \lambda \leqslant \pi \qquad (7.14)$$

defines the *spectral window* centred on $\lambda = 0$. Since $h(\lambda)$ is symmetric, it need only be defined for positive λ, and it is almost invariably plotted on this basis. The derivation of (7.14) is carried out by replacing $c(\tau)$ in (7.13) by its Fourier transform and re-arranging the resulting expression.

For the truncated estimator

$$h(\lambda) = (2\pi)^{-1} \left[1 + 2 \sum_{\tau=1}^{N} \cos \lambda\tau \right]$$

$$= \frac{\sin[(N + 1/2)\lambda]}{2\pi \sin(\lambda/2)} \tag{7.15}$$

The last equality follows from (A.9). Figure 6.12 shows the spectral window for $N = 6$. A larger value of N would result in $h(\lambda)$ being more concentrated around $\lambda = 0$, but at the expense of increasing the variance. As in the direct averaging of the sample spectral density, there is a trade-off between bias and variance. However, the fluctuating shape of the window in figure 6.12 means that the nature of the bias is rather different from that induced, say, by a rectangular window in the frequency domain. In the latter case the peaks and troughs in the spectrum tend to be smoothed out, but with the truncated estimator the existence of subsidiary peaks in the window means that an estimate may reflect important cycles in another part of the spectrum. This is known as *leakage*. When a relatively large peak corresponds to a negative part of the window, it is even possible for $\tilde{f}(\lambda)$ itself to be negative.

By suitably modifying the weighting scheme, the problems inherent in the truncated estimator can, to a large extent, be overcome. A number of estimation procedures have been suggested, two of the most widely used being due to Blackman and Tukey, and Parzen. Both truncate the

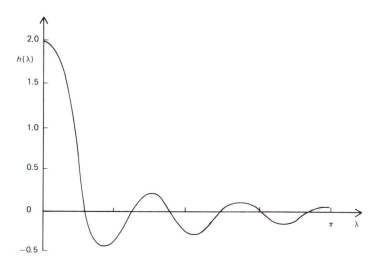

Figure 6.12 Spectral window (7.15) for the truncated estimator with $N = 6$.

weights beyond some pre-specified lag, N, but the values of $k(\tau)$ decline as τ moves from zero to N. For example, in the Blackman–Tukey window

$$k(\tau) = 1 - 2a + 2a \cos(\pi\tau/N) \tag{7.16}$$

with $a = 0.23$ ('hamming') or $a = 0.25$ ('hanning'). Giving less emphasis to the higher order autocovariances tends to produce an estimator with better resolution; see Priestley (1981, pp. 432–71).

Fast Fourier Transform

Direct averaging of the sample spectral density is conceptually the most straightforward way of computing a consistent estimator of the spectrum. Unfortunately, the task of computing all n periodogram ordinates is, at first sight, a relatively time-consuming one, and historically this led to a shift in emphasis towards weighting the sample autocovariance function in the time domain. Since the mid-1960s, however, a technique known as the *fast Fourier transform* has become increasingly popular. This reduces the computing time for Fourier coefficients from $0(T^2)$ to $0(T \log_2 T)$, a reduction which can be considerable for a moderately large value of T. The availability of the fast Fourier transform algorithm has tended to re-establish periodogram averaging, although time domain weighting is still widely used.

Autoregressive Spectral Estimation

Any linear process can be approximated by an AR process, and this has led Parzen (1969) to suggest a technique known as *autoregressive spectral estimation*. The first step in this procedure is to estimate the coefficients of an $AR(P)$ process by OLS. These estimates are then substituted for the parameters $\phi_1, \phi_2, \ldots, \phi_P$ in expression (4.2), thereby yielding an estimator of the power spectrum, $f(\lambda)$. In other words, an $AR(P)$ model is fitted to the data, and the estimator of the power spectrum is taken as the theoretical spectrum of the fitted process.

Just as the lag length, N, is allowed to increase with T when estimation is based on the weighted autocovariance function, so P may be allowed to increase with T, and for large T, Parzen shows that

$$\text{Var}[\hat{f}(\lambda)] \simeq [2Pf^2(\lambda)]/T \tag{7.17}$$

The fact that the variance is proportional to P suggests that P be made no larger than is necessary for the AR model to be an adequate approximation to the underlying data generation process. The difficulty lies in deciding on a value for P, since if it is made too small the estimated spectrum may be badly biased, with the result that the salient frequency domain characteristics of the series will be seriously distorted. The trade-off is therefore similar to that encountered in other types of spectral estimation. One solution is to determine actively the order of the model on a goodness of fit criterion, rather than employ an automatic rule, which, say, sets $P = \sqrt{T}$. Criteria which have been adopted for determining the value of P include the AIC, defined in (3.6.13). Such methods have been used in autoregressive spectral estimation with some success. Because the estimator is a theoretical spectrum, it will tend to be smoother than a spectrum produced by standard methods. However, although the procedure gives a smooth spectrum, it also seems to have high resolution, in that it is able to pick out narrow peaks; see, for example, Griffiths and Prieto-Diaz (1977) and Beamish and Priestley (1981). This is important, since the main *raison d'être* of spectral analysis is in the description it provides of the cyclical movements in a series. Nevertheless, great care must be taken in determining the value of P, since setting it too low could result in a failure of the spectrum to show the narrow peaks indicative of strong cyclical movements.

6.8 Maximum Likelihood Estimation of Time Series Models

The frequency domain approach to the ML estimation of unknown parameters in stationary Gaussian processes is based on a Fourier transform which converts serial correlation into heteroscedasticity. This enables the likelihood function to be written as

$$\log L = -\frac{1}{2} T \log 2\pi - \frac{1}{2} \sum_{j=0}^{T-1} \log g_j - \pi \sum_{j=0}^{T-1} \frac{I(\lambda_j)}{g_j} \tag{8.1}$$

where $I(\lambda_j)$ is the sample spectrum

$$I(\lambda_j) = \frac{1}{2\pi T} \left| \sum_{t=1}^{T} y_t e^{-i\lambda_j t} \right|^2 \tag{8.2}$$

and g_j is the spectral generating function, $g[\exp(-i\lambda_j)]$, defined at the points $\lambda_j = 2\pi j/T$, $j = 0, \ldots, T-1$. If preferred, (8.1) can be written in terms of the spectrum by substituting $2\pi f(\lambda_j)$ for g_j. Strictly speaking, the expression in (8.1) is only equal to the likelihood function if the stationary process in question has the characteristics of a *circular* process, meaning that the first observation is treated as though it follows the last. This assumption is unrealistic. Nevertheless (8.1) is approximately equal to the likelihood function for any stationary, invertible process and any results which can be shown to hold exactly under the circularity assumption will, in general, hold asymptotically when it is relaxed.

The unknown parameters, ψ, appear in the spectral generating function and so ML estimation involves iterating with different values of ψ, and hence

g_j, until (8.1) is maximised. The periodogram ordinates are independent of ψ and so are only calculated once. The method of scoring is a particularly attractive iterative procedure in this context since the information matrix depends only on first derivatives.

Example 1   In the AR(1) plus noise model, (2.5.2),

$$g_j = \frac{\sigma_\eta^2}{1 + \phi^2 - 2\phi \cos \lambda_j} + \sigma_\varepsilon^2$$

Thus $\psi = (\sigma_\eta^2, \phi, \sigma_\varepsilon^2)'$.

For ARMA models, the second term on the right hand side of (8.1) reduces to $[-T/2] \log \sigma^2$, the maximising $\log L$ with respect to σ^2 gives

$$\tilde{\sigma}^2(\phi, \theta) = \frac{2\pi}{T} \sum_{j=0}^{T-1} \frac{I(\lambda_j)}{g_j(\phi, \theta)} \tag{8.3}$$

where $g_j(\phi, \theta) = g_j/\sigma^2$. Thus σ^2 may be concentrated out of the likelihood function, with the result that maximising $\log L$ is equivalent to minimising

$$S(\phi, \theta) = \sum_{j=0}^{T-1} \frac{I(\lambda_j)}{g_j(\phi, \theta)} \tag{8.4}$$

with respect to ϕ and θ. Although the $\sum \log g_j$ term does not disappear for unobserved components models, the relative appeal of the frequency domain approach is even greater because there is no simple time domain procedure based on minimising the conditional sum of squares. As well as providing a means of computing ML estimators, the form of the information matrix provides a viable means of obtaining asymptotic standard errors.

Fourier Transforms and the Spectral Likelihood

Consider a stationary stochastic process with mean zero and a strictly positive spectral density. The log–likelihood function for T normally distributed observations, denoted by the $T \times 1$ vector $\mathbf{y}$, is

$$\log L(\mathbf{y}) = -\tfrac{1}{2}T \log 2\pi - \tfrac{1}{2}\log|\mathbf{V}| - \tfrac{1}{2}\mathbf{y}'\mathbf{V}^{-1}\mathbf{y} \tag{8.5}$$

where $\mathbf{V}$ is the $T \times T$ covariance matrix of the observations, that is $E(\mathbf{yy}') = \mathbf{V}$. If the process is circular, then $\gamma(\tau) = \gamma(T - \tau)$ and so $\mathbf{V}$ is a Toeplitz matrix, that is one in which the elements on each of the diagonals are the same.

The complex $T \times T$ Fourier matrix, $\mathbf{W}$, has as its jtth element

$$w_{jt} = T^{-1/2}[\exp\{-i\lambda_{j-1}t\}], \qquad j, t = 1, \dots, T \tag{8.6}$$

This matrix has the property that it diagonalises a Toeplitz matrix, so that

$$\mathbf{WVW}^{\dagger} = \mathbf{G} \tag{8.7}$$

where $\mathbf{W}^{\dagger}$ is the complex conjugate transpose of $\mathbf{W}$ and $\mathbf{G}$ is a $T \times T$ diagonal matrix with jth diagonal element g_{j-1}, $j = 1, \ldots, T$.

It can be seen from (B.5) that the Fourier matrix is a unitary matrix, that is $\mathbf{W}^{\dagger}\mathbf{W}$ is an identity matrix. It therefore follows from (8.7) that

$$\mathbf{V} = \mathbf{W}^{\dagger}\mathbf{GW} \tag{8.8}$$

and so

$$|\mathbf{V}| = |\mathbf{W}^{\dagger}||\mathbf{G}||\mathbf{W}| = |\mathbf{G}||\mathbf{W}^{\dagger}\mathbf{W}| = |\mathbf{G}| \tag{8.9}$$

from which

$$-\frac{1}{2}\log|\mathbf{V}| = -\frac{1}{2}\sum_{j=0}^{T-1} \log g_j \tag{8.10}$$

Furthermore

$$\mathbf{V}^{-1} = \mathbf{W}^{\dagger}\mathbf{G}^{-1}\mathbf{W} \tag{8.11}$$

and so, bearing in mind the definition of the sample spectral density, (8.2),

$$\tfrac{1}{2}\mathbf{y}'\mathbf{V}^{-1}\mathbf{y} = \tfrac{1}{2}\mathbf{y}'\mathbf{W}^{\dagger}\mathbf{G}^{-1}\mathbf{W}\mathbf{y} = \pi \sum_{j=0}^{T-1} \frac{I(\lambda_j)}{g_j} \tag{8.12}$$

since the $(j+1)$th element of $\mathbf{Wy}$ is

$$\frac{1}{\sqrt{T}}\sum_{t=1}^{T} y_t\, e^{-i\lambda_j t}, \qquad j = 0, \ldots, T-1$$

Substituting (8.10) and (8.12) in (8.5) gives (8.1).

The reason for defining $I(\lambda_j)$ over the range $[0, 2\pi]$ is for convenience of presentation. However, since $I(\pi + \lambda) = I(\pi - \lambda)$ there is no point in actually computing almost twice as many periodogram ordinates as are necessary. Indeed an alternative expression to (8.1) is

$$\log L = \frac{-T}{2}\log 2\pi - \sum_{j=0}^{n} \delta_j \log g_j - 2\pi \sum_{j=0}^{n} \delta_j \frac{I(\lambda_j)}{g_j} \tag{8.13}$$

where n is as defined in (2.5) and δ_j is the Kronecker delta

$$\delta_j = \begin{cases} 1/2, & j = 0, n \text{ (when } T \text{ is even)} \\ 1, & \text{elsewhere} \end{cases} \tag{8.14}$$

The Fourier transform can also be carried out in real terms, by letting $\mathbf{W}$ be the transpose of the matrix $\mathbf{Z}$ defined in (2.19). The diagonalisation of (8.8) still holds, but with the difference that the elements on the diagonal of **G** are such that the frequencies from zero to π are grouped together in pairs. Thus, if T is even, $\mathbf{G} = \text{diag}(g_0\ g_1\ g_1\ g_2\ g_2 \cdots g_{n-1}\ g_{n-1}\ g_n)$. Corresponding to (8.10),

$$-\tfrac{1}{2}\log|\mathbf{V}| = -\tfrac{1}{2}\log|\mathbf{G}| = -\sum_{j=0}^{n} \delta_j \log g_j \tag{8.15}$$

while

$$\frac{1}{2}\mathbf{y}'\mathbf{V}^{-1}\mathbf{y} = \frac{1}{2}\mathbf{y}'\mathbf{W}'\mathbf{G}^{-1}\mathbf{W}\mathbf{y} = \frac{1}{2}\sum_{j=0}^{n}\frac{p_j}{g_j} \tag{8.16}$$

where the p_j's are the periodogram ordinates. Noting (7.3) and substituting (8.15) and (8.16) in (8.5) gives (8.13).

A final point to note is that the general results on the distribution of the sample spectral density ordinates, $I(\lambda_j)$, quoted in section 6.7, follow immediately if (8.13) is taken to be the expression for their joint density function. Thus, for T even,

$$\begin{aligned} 4\pi I(\lambda_j)/g_j &\sim \chi_2^2 \quad \text{for } j \neq 0, n \\ 2\pi I(\lambda_j)/g_j &\sim \chi_1^2 \quad \text{for } j = 0, n \end{aligned} \tag{8.17}$$

and the $I(\lambda_j)$s are mutually independent for $j = 0, \ldots, n$. An immediate corollary is that, since the mean and variance of a χ_k^2 are k and $2k$ respectively, $I(\lambda_j)$ has a mean of g_j and a variance of g_j^2 for $j = 0, \ldots, n$.

The Information Matrix and the Method of Scoring

Differentiating the log–likelihood function in (8.1) with respect to the $n \times 1$ vector of parameters, $\boldsymbol{\psi}$, gives

$$\begin{aligned} \frac{\partial \log L}{\partial \boldsymbol{\psi}} &= -\frac{1}{2}\sum_{j=0}^{T-1}\frac{1}{g_j}\frac{\partial g_j}{\partial \boldsymbol{\psi}} + \pi\sum_{j=0}^{T-1}\frac{I(\lambda_j)}{g_j^2}\frac{\partial g_j}{\partial \boldsymbol{\psi}} \\ &= \frac{1}{2}\sum_{j=0}^{T-1}\left[\frac{2\pi I(\lambda_j)}{g_j} - 1\right]\frac{1}{g_j}\frac{\partial g_j}{\partial \boldsymbol{\psi}} \end{aligned} \tag{8.18}$$

Differentiating a second time gives

$$\begin{aligned} \frac{\partial^2 \log L}{\partial \boldsymbol{\psi}\, \partial \boldsymbol{\psi}'} &= \sum_{j=0}^{T-1}\left(\frac{2\pi I(\lambda_j)}{g_j} - 1\right)\frac{1}{2g_j}\frac{\partial^2 g_j}{\partial \boldsymbol{\psi}\, \partial \boldsymbol{\psi}'} \\ &\quad -2\sum_{j=0}^{T-1}\left(\frac{4\pi I(\lambda_j)}{g_j} - 1\right)\left(\frac{1}{2g_j}\right)^2\frac{\partial g_j}{\partial \boldsymbol{\psi}}\frac{\partial g_j}{\partial \boldsymbol{\psi}'} \end{aligned} \tag{8.19}$$

If expectations are taken in (8.19) the first term disappears since, as noted below (8.17),

$$E[I(\lambda_j)] = g_j/2\pi, \qquad j = 0, \ldots, T-1 \qquad (8.20)$$

The information matrix is therefore

$$\mathbf{I}(\boldsymbol{\psi}) = \frac{1}{2} \sum_{j=0}^{T-1} \frac{1}{g_j^2} \frac{\partial g_j}{\partial \boldsymbol{\psi}} \frac{\partial g_j}{\partial \boldsymbol{\psi}'} \qquad (8.21a)$$

$$= \sum_{j=0}^{n} \frac{\delta_j}{g_j^2} \frac{\partial g_j}{\partial \boldsymbol{\psi}} \frac{\partial g_j}{\partial \boldsymbol{\psi}'} \qquad (8.21b)$$

This expression may be regarded as a large sample approximation to the information matrix if the process is not circular.

The simple form taken by the information matrix makes the method of scoring an attractive procedure for computing ML estimates of $\boldsymbol{\psi}$. The method of scoring is an iterative optimisation procedure of the form

$$\boldsymbol{\psi}^* = \hat{\boldsymbol{\psi}} + [\mathbf{I}(\hat{\boldsymbol{\psi}})]^{-1} \{\partial \log L / \partial \boldsymbol{\psi}\} \qquad (8.22)$$

where $\hat{\boldsymbol{\psi}}$ is the current estimate of $\boldsymbol{\psi}$ and $\boldsymbol{\psi}^*$ is the updated estimator. Both the information matrix, $\mathbf{I}(\boldsymbol{\psi})$, and the score vector, $\partial \log L / \partial \boldsymbol{\psi}$, are evaluated at $\boldsymbol{\psi} = \hat{\boldsymbol{\psi}}$. Substituting from (8.18) and (8.12) yields the following algorithm

$$\boldsymbol{\psi}^* = \hat{\boldsymbol{\psi}} + \left(\sum_{j=0}^{T-1} \frac{1}{g_j^2} \frac{\partial g_j}{\partial \boldsymbol{\psi}} \frac{\partial g_j}{\partial \boldsymbol{\psi}'} \right)^{-1} \sum_{j=0}^{T-1} \frac{1}{g_j^2} \frac{\partial g_j}{\partial \boldsymbol{\psi}} \{2\pi I(\lambda_j) - g_j\} \qquad (8.23)$$

where g_j and its derivatives are evaluated at $\boldsymbol{\psi} = \hat{\boldsymbol{\psi}}$. The scoring algorithm therefore takes the form of a weighted Gauss–Newton algorithm as described, for example, in EATS, chapter 4. At each iteration the estimate of $\boldsymbol{\psi}$ is updated by a weighted regression of $2\pi I(\lambda_j) - g_j$ on the elements of $\partial g_j / \partial \boldsymbol{\psi}$.

Tapering

There is some evidence to suggest that the small sample properties of the FD estimator may be improved by tapering. Tapering consists of introducing a weighting function into the sample spectrum, (8.2), which becomes

$$I(\lambda_j) = \frac{1}{2\pi H} \left| \sum_{t=1}^{T} y_t h_t e^{-i\lambda_j t} \right|^2 \qquad (8.24)$$

where

$$H = \sum_{t=1}^{T} h_t^2$$

The taper, h_t, normally decreases as t goes to one or T. Dahlhaus (1988) has provided a theoretical justification for the technique and argued that it is likely to be particularly effective when the parameters in a model are such as to put it close to being non-stationary or non-invertible.

Asymptotic Properties

When the observations are generated by a stationary Gaussian linear process, $T^{1/2}(\tilde{\psi} - \psi)$ has a limiting normal distribution with mean vector zero and covariance matrix $\mathbf{IA}^{-1}(\psi)$, where $\mathbf{IA}(\psi)$ is given by

$$\mathbf{IA}(\psi) = \frac{1}{4\pi} \int_{-\pi}^{\pi} \frac{\partial \log g(e^{-i\lambda j})}{\partial \psi} \frac{\partial \log g(e^{-i\lambda j})}{\partial \psi'} d\lambda \qquad (8.25)$$

The regularity conditions under which this result is valid are summarised in Walker (1964). It is particularly important to note that the spectral density, and hence the SGF, $g(e^{-i\lambda})$, must always be strictly positive in the range $[-\pi, \pi]$.

The rationale behind (8.25) is as follows. The information matrix was given in (8.21a), and, when divided by T, we would expect this to converge to a fixed matrix as $T \to \infty$. However, as $T \to \infty$ the frequencies become closer and closer together, and, by an appropriate limiting argument, the summation over T points is replaced by an integral over the range $[-\pi, \pi]$. Correspondingly, the divisor of T is replaced by a divisor of 2π. Expression (8.25) then follows immediately on noting that $\partial \log g / \partial \psi$ is $\partial g / \partial \psi$ divided by g.

Estimating the Mean and Other Deterministic Functions of Time

It was shown in section 3.2 that in large samples the mean of a stationary AR process can be estimated efficiently by the sample mean. The same result can be shown in the frequency domain, and generalised to certain other functions of time in the sense that it can be demonstrated that they can be estimated independently of the stochastic part of the model.

Consider a stationary and invertible series with a non-zero, unknown mean, μ. Writing the model as

$$y_t = \mu + w_t \qquad (8.26)$$

where w_t has an SGF, g_j, which is continuous and strictly positive everywhere in the range $[-\pi, \pi]$, the likelihood function may be written as in (8.1) but with

$$I(\lambda_j) = \frac{1}{2\pi T} \left| \sum_{t=1}^{T} (y_t - \mu) e^{-i\lambda_j t} \right|^2 \qquad (8.27)$$

Using (B.5) in appendix B, it follows that μ can be omitted from the expression for $I(\lambda_j)$ except in the case of λ_0 when

$$I(\lambda_0) = \frac{1}{2\pi T}\left(\sum_{t=1}^{T} y_t - T\mu\right)^2 \tag{8.28}$$

Since g_j does not depend on μ, differentiating the log–likelihood function with respect to μ yields

$$\frac{\partial \log L}{\partial \mu} = \left(\sum_{t=1}^{T} y_t - T\mu\right)\bigg/ g_0 \tag{8.29}$$

and so the ML estimator of μ is

$$\tilde{\mu} = \bar{y} \tag{8.30}$$

This result is exact if the circularity assumption is true, but only approximate otherwise.

Substituting $\bar{y}$ for μ in the likelihood function gives a concentrated likelihood function which takes the form of (8.1) but with $I(\lambda_j)$ defined in terms of deviations of the observations from the mean. This makes no difference to the values of $I(\lambda_j)$ except at λ_0 where $I(\lambda_0)$ is now zero. Hence ML estimators of the hyperparameters, ψ, can be computed without actually computing $\bar{y}$. Note that the term $\log g_0$ should also be dropped from the likelihood when $I(\lambda_0)$ is zero.

As a corollary to the above result, consider estimating the parameter β in a model which is stationary and invertible in first differences, that is

$$\Delta y_t = \beta + w_t, \qquad t = 2, \ldots, T \tag{8.31}$$

The parameter β is the slope in the final forecast function and it follows from (8.30) that its ML estimator is

$$\tilde{\beta} = \sum_{t=2}^{T} \Delta y_t/(T-1) = (y_T - y_1)/(T-1) \tag{8.32}$$

Frequency domain methods can also be used to show that in a model with a fixed mean and deterministic seasonality, (5.5.14), seasonal sample means provide efficient estimators of the parameters.

The asymptotic variance of the same mean can be obtained from the inverse of the information matrix. It is easy to check that the information matrix is block diagonal with respect to μ and ψ. Differentiating (8.29) yields

$$\frac{\partial^2 \log L}{\partial \mu^2} = \frac{-T}{g_0}$$

Hence

$$\text{Avar}(\bar{y}) = g_0/T \tag{8.33}$$

It follows almost immediately from the definition of the spectrum, (1.2) or (1.4), that this expression is the same as the time domain formula (2.7.4). However, it is very easy to evaluate.

Example 2 In the AR(1) plus noise model (2.5.2),

$$\text{Avar}(\bar{y}) = \{\sigma_\eta^2/(1 - \phi)^2 + \sigma_\varepsilon^2\}/T \tag{8.34}$$

More generally, if w_t in (8.26) is any unobserved components model of the form (2.5.1),

$$\text{Avar}(\bar{y}) = [\sigma_\eta^2\{\theta_\mu(1)/\phi_\mu(1)\}^2 + \sigma_\varepsilon^2\{\theta_\xi(1)/\phi_\xi(1)\}^2]/T \tag{8.35}$$

The asymptotic variance of the estimator of β in a model of the form (8.31) can be found in a similar way.

Example 3 For the fixed slope local linear trend model (5.3.16) it follows immediately from (8.33) that

$$\text{Avar}(\tilde{\beta}) = \sigma_\eta^2/(T - 1) \tag{8.36}$$

The irregular component, ε_t, makes no contribution to this expression even if it follows a more general process than white noise. The reason is that the SGF of $\Delta\varepsilon_t$ is zero at $\lambda = 0$.

Structural Time Series Models

The frequency domain approach to ML estimation is particularly attractive for unobserved components models, since there is no simple approximate ML procedure in the time domain corresponding to the CSS algorithm for ARMA models. The FD approach simplifies even further for what may be termed pure variance components models. In such models g_j is a linear function of the unknown parameters of ψ, and so may be written in the form

$$g_j = \mathbf{z}_j'\psi \tag{8.37}$$

where all the elements of $\mathbf{z}_j$ are independent of ψ. Substituting (8.37) in (8.23) and replacing $\partial g_j/\partial\psi$ by $\mathbf{z}_j$ gives

$$\begin{aligned}
\psi^* &= \hat{\psi} + [\textstyle\sum g_j^{-2}\mathbf{z}_j\mathbf{z}_j']^{-1} \sum g_j^{-2}\mathbf{z}_j 2\pi I(\lambda_j) \\
&\quad - [\textstyle\sum g_j^{-2}\mathbf{z}_j\mathbf{z}_j']^{-1} \sum g_j^{-2}\mathbf{z}_j\mathbf{z}_j' \cdot \hat{\psi} \\
&= [\textstyle\sum g_j^{-2}\mathbf{z}_j\mathbf{z}_j']^{-1} \sum g_j^{-2}\mathbf{z}_j 2\pi I(\lambda_j)
\end{aligned} \tag{8.38}$$

This is just a weighted least squares regression of $2\pi I(\lambda_j)$ on $\mathbf{z}_j$. The initial estimate is usually constructed by setting g_j equal to one, so that (8.38) is OLS.

Several of the principal structural time series models are pure variance components models, and so can be estimated using (8.38). They must first be made stationary by differencing.

Example 4 Taking first differences in the local level model, (3.1) and (3.2), gives

$$\Delta y_t = \eta_t + \varepsilon_t - \varepsilon_{t-1}, \qquad t = 2, \ldots, T$$

and so

$$g_j = \sigma_\eta^2 + 2(1 - \cos \lambda_j)\sigma_\varepsilon^2 \qquad (8.39)$$

Thus g_j is of the form (8.37) with $z_j = [1, 2(1 - \cos \lambda_j)]'$. The information matrix is therefore

$$\mathbf{I}(\psi) = \frac{1}{2} \sum_{j=0}^{T-2} \frac{1}{\{\sigma_\eta^2 + 2(1 - \cos \lambda_j)\sigma_\varepsilon^2\}^2} \begin{bmatrix} 1 & 2(1 - \cos \lambda_j) \\ 2(1 - \cos \lambda_j) & 4(1 - \cos \lambda_j)^2 \end{bmatrix}$$

$$(8.40)$$

Fractionally Integrated Models

Fractionally integrated models were introduced in section 5.6 and it was pointed out that estimation in the time domain (TD) is quite cumbersome since there is no way of breaking down the $T \times T$ covariance matrix of the observations. By contrast, the frequency domain likelihood can be obtained very easily. Suppose that

$$\Delta^d y_t = w_t \qquad (8.41)$$

where w_t follows a stationary and invertible linear model with spectrum $f_w(\lambda)$, and that d is in the range $-\frac{1}{2} < d < \frac{1}{2}$. Writing

$$y_t = (1 - L)^{-d} w_t \qquad (8.42)$$

the spectrum of y_t is seen to be

$$\begin{aligned} f(\lambda) &= |1 - e^{-i\lambda}|^{-2d} f_w(\lambda) \\ &= 2^{-d}(1 - \cos \lambda)^{-d} f_w(\lambda) \\ &= 4^{-d} \sin^{-2d}(\lambda/2) f_w(\lambda) \end{aligned} \qquad (8.43)$$

The likelihood function can therefore be constructed as in (8.1), with the term at frequency zero omitted to allow for a non-zero mean. The evidence in Cheung and Diebold (1990) suggests that the time domain estimator has a lower MSE than the frequency domain estimator in small samples. For larger samples, the frequency domain estimator performs almost as well as the time domain estimator, particularly when the mean has to be estimated, and is far more attractive computationally. Note that the scoring algorithm could be used to compute the ML estimators.

An initial estimator of d, independent of the parameters determining w_t, has been proposed by Geweke and Porter-Hudak (1983). Taking logarithms in (8.43) gives

$$\log f(\lambda) = -d \log\{4 \sin^2(\lambda/2)\} + \log f_w(\lambda) \tag{8.44}$$

Adding $I(\lambda_j)$ to each side of (8.44) at the frequencies $2\pi j/T, j = 0, \ldots, T - 1$, and re-arranging, gives

$$\log I(\lambda_j) = \log\{f_w(0)\} - d \log\{4 \sin^2(\lambda_j/2)\} + \log\{f_w(\lambda_j)/f_w(0)\}$$
$$+ \log\{I(\lambda_j)/f(\lambda_j)\} \tag{8.45}$$

This suggests treating (8.45) as a regression model in which the last term is the disturbance. The penultimate term is roughly constant if attention is restricted to the lower frequencies. Kunsch (1986) argues that frequencies around the origin also need to be excluded to get a consistent estimator of d from regressing $\log I(\lambda_j)$ on $\log\{4 \sin^2(\lambda_j/2)\}$. As regards the higher frequencies, he suggests excluding those for which $j > T^{1/2}$.

6.9 Testing

Specification tests and diagnostics may be constructed in the frequency domain. This approach sometimes has advantages compared with the time domain.

Cumulative Periodogram

The cumulative periodogram is a frequency domain alternative to the portmanteau test described in section 2.8. The periodogram ordinates are used to construct a series of statistics,

$$s_i = \sum_{j=1}^{i} p_j \Big/ \sum_{j=1}^{n} p_j, \qquad i = 1, \ldots, n \tag{9.1}$$

The test procedure is based on a plot of s_i against i, which is known as the cumulative periodogram. This differs from the periodogram itself, in that the highly unstable behaviour of the p_j's is, to a large extent, ironed out by the process of accumulation. Thus, although a visual inspection of the periodogram is of limited value, the cumulative periodogram is a useful diagnostic tool.

For a white noise series, the s_i's will lie close to the 45° line on the graph of s_i against i. On the other hand, the cumulative periodogram for a process with an excess of low frequency will tend to lie above the 45° line. By way of contrast, a process with an excess of high frequency components will tend to have a cumulative periodogram which lies below the 45° line.

A formal test departure from randomness is obtained by constructing two lines parallel to the 45° line, $s = i/n$. These are defined by

$$s = \pm c_0 + i/n \qquad (9.2)$$

where c_0 is a significance value which depends on n and may be read off directly from a table given in Durbin (1969). This table is reproduced at the end of EATS as table C, and the appropriate significance value is obtained by entering the table at $n - 1$. For a two-sided test of size α, c_0 is read from the column headed $\alpha/2$. The null hypothesis is rejected at the α level of significance if the sample path, $s_1, \ldots, s_n$, crosses either of the lines in (9.2); compare figure 6.13 in section 6.10.

In certain circumstances a one-sided test may be appropriate. For example, if the alternative hypothesis is that there is an excess of low frequency, only the upper line is relevant. Since an excess of low frequency corresponds to positive serial correlation, such an alternative will often be very reasonable. The significance value is found in exactly the same way as for a one-sided test, except that the column headed 'α' is now the one to be consulted.

When T is odd, the one-sided test is exact. However, the approximations involved in carrying out two-sided tests, or one-sided tests with T even, are likely to be negligible in practice. Note that the test can be carried out without actually graphing the s_i's. The rule for a two-sided procedure is to reject H_0 if

$$\max_i |s_i - i/n| > c_0$$

Wald and Lagrange Multiplier Tests

Classical tests can be carried out in the frequency domain, just as in the time domain.

Wald tests can be based on the asymptotic covariance matrix of the ML estimators, $\tilde{\psi}$. This is obtained by dividing the inverse of $\mathbf{IA}(\tilde{\psi})$, as given in (8.25), by T. That is

$$\text{Avar}(\tilde{\psi}) = T^{-1}\mathbf{IA}^{-1}(\tilde{\psi}) \qquad (9.3)$$

Alternatively, the asymptotic information matrix can be approximated by the expression for the inverse of the information matrix given in (8.21a),

$$
\text{avar}(\tilde{\psi}) = 2\left[\sum_{j=0}^{T-1} \frac{1}{g_j^2} \frac{\partial g_j}{\partial \psi} \frac{\partial g_j}{\partial \psi'}\right]^{-1}
$$

$$
= 2\left[\sum_{j=0}^{T-1} \frac{\partial \log g_j}{\partial \psi} \frac{\partial \log g_j}{\partial \psi'}\right]^{-1} \tag{9.4}
$$

where g_j and its derivatives are evaluated at $\tilde{\psi}$. It is usually easier to evaluate the asymptotic covariance matrix from the finite summation in (9.4) than it is by working out the integrals in (8.25). In any case, (9.4) is computed anyway as part of a scoring algorithm. As with the use of (3.1.12) in the time domain, there is no reason to suppose that the small sample properties of (9.4) are in any way inferior.

As regards Lagrange multiplier tests, substituting the expressions for the first derivatives, (8.18), and the information matrix, (8.21a), in the general expression for the LM statistic, (3.4.5), gives

$$
\text{LM} = \frac{1}{2}\left[\sum_{j=0}^{T-1} \frac{1}{g_j^2} \frac{\partial g_j}{\partial \psi} v_j\right]'\left[\sum_{j=0}^{T-1} \frac{1}{g_j^2} \frac{\partial g_j}{\partial \psi} \frac{\partial g_j}{\partial \psi'}\right]^{-1}\left[\sum_{j=0}^{T-1} \frac{1}{g_j^2} \frac{\partial g_j}{\partial \psi} v_j\right] \tag{9.5}
$$

where g_j and its derivatives are evaluated at $\psi = \tilde{\psi}_0$ and

$$
v_j = 2\pi I(\lambda_j) - g_j, \qquad j = 0, \ldots, T-1 \tag{9.6}
$$

As in the time domain, LM is asymptotically χ_m^2 under the null hypothesis.

An alternative form of the test statistic is obtained by dividing (9.5) through by $T^{-1}\sum v_j^2/g_j^2$. Since, from (8.17), the variance of v_j is g_j^2, it follows that

$$
p\lim T^{-1}\sum_{j=0}^{T-1} v_j^2/g_j^2 = 1 \tag{9.7}
$$

and so the asymptotic distribution of the test statistic is unaltered. The amended test statistic may be written as

$$
\text{LM}^* = \frac{T}{2}\cdot\frac{\left(\sum_{j=0}^{T-1} g_j^{-2}\mathbf{z}_j v_j\right)'\left[\sum_{j=0}^{T-1} g_j^{-2}\mathbf{z}_j\mathbf{z}_j'\right]^{-1}\left(\sum_{j=0}^{T-1} g_j^{-2}\mathbf{z}_j v_j\right)}{\sum_{j=0}^{T-1}(v_j^2/g_j^2)} \tag{9.8}
$$

where

$$
\mathbf{z}_j = \left.\frac{\partial g_j}{\partial \psi}\right|_{\psi = \tilde{\psi}_0} \tag{9.9}
$$

Despite the definition of z_j in (9.9) it will, on occasion, be more convenient to define an element of z_j as being proportional to, rather than equal to, the corresponding first derivative. This is one of the reasons for the change in notation from (9.5). The other reason for the change in notation is that it makes it clearer that LM can be expressed as

$$LM^* = \tfrac{1}{2}TR^2 \tag{9.10}$$

where R^2 is the coefficient of determination in a weighted regression of v_j on the elements z_j; compare with (3.4.6). A constant term is not included unless it is already in z_j. Note that it follows from (8.3) and (2.13) that the mean of the v_j/g_j's is zero.

The appearance of the one-half in (9.10) may at first sight seem rather strange to those familiar with the TR^2 form of the LM statistic. The explanation lies in the fact that each observation is effectively counted twice when the summation in (9.8) is over T points. Re-defining the summation from $j = 0, \ldots, [\tfrac{1}{2}T]$ leaves the value of LM^* unchanged but perhaps makes the appearance of $T/2$ rather than T more plausible.

Some examples of the frequency domain LM test are given in FSK, chapter 5. For ARMA models the frequency domain tests turn out to be essentially the same as the corresponding time domain tests. For example, the frequency domain test statistic for white noise against AR(1) is approximately equal to $Tr^2(1)$. However, the frequency domain approach makes the construction of tests for unobserved components models considerably easier.

Cycles

A test for the presence of a deterministic cycle at a given frequency when the null hypothesis is that the series is Gaussian white noise with variance σ^2 can be constructed straightforwardly within the framework established by (2.17). As noted below (2.22), the test statistic based on the appropriate periodogram ordinate has an F-distribution with $(2, T-2)$ degrees of freedom. A rather different test, again within the framework of (2.17), does not specify the frequency in advance, but instead focuses attention on the largest periodogram ordinate, $\max(p_j)$, $j = 1, \ldots, [T/2]$. For a null hypothesis of Gaussian white noise, the exact distribution of the statistic

$$g = \max(p_j) \Bigg/ \sum_{j=1}^{[T/2]} p_j \tag{9.11}$$

was derived by Fisher in 1929; see Priestley (1981, pp. 406–15). Given the comments earlier about the relevance of deterministic cycles for many types of time series, it would perhaps be unwise to interpret a significant value of Fisher's g-statistic as evidence for the existence of such a cycle at the frequency corresponding to the largest periodogram ordinate. One could, of course, always interpret the test as a pure significance test, but it is not clear that, when used in this way, it would have any advantages over other tests for randomness, such as the von Neumann ratio or the cumulative periodogram.

A test against a stochastic cycle can be constructed using the LM principle. The model is $y_t = \psi_t$, where ψ_t is defined by (5.5), and the null hypothesis is $H_0: \rho = 0$. Using a frequency domain argument, as in FSK, pp. 244–5, it can be shown that the LM test of $H_1: \rho \neq 0$ can be carried out by treating $T^{1/2} r(1)$ as asymptotically $N(0, 1)$ under the null. This test does not require that λ_c be specified. An exact test may be based on the von Neumann ratio, and if the sign of $\cos \lambda_c$ is known to be positive (negative), a one-sided test against positive (negative) serial correlation is appropriate. The LM test can be extended to testing for a stochastic cycle in a model where another component, such as stochastic trend, is present. It can also be used to test for a further stochastic cycle when one has already been fitted.

6.10 Regression in the Frequency Domain

The classical linear regression model may be set up in the frequency domain by applying a finite Fourier transform to the dependent and independent variables. This creates T sets of observations which are indexed not by time, but by frequency. *Spectral regression* is then carried out by regressing the transformed dependent variable on the transformed independent variables. There are a number of reasons for doing this. One is to permit the application of the technique known as *band spectrum regression*, in which regression is carried out in the frequency domain with certain wavelengths omitted. This has a number of interesting applications with regard to dealing with seasonality and errors in the explanatory variables. For example, if the observations show a strong seasonal pattern, it may be advantageous to try to discount any seasonal effects in the relationship by omitting the transformed observations which lie on and around the seasonal frequencies. With respect to the errors in variables problem, it has been suggested that the adverse effects on the least squares estimator might be mitigated by deleting the high frequency observations from a frequency domain regression. Since economic variables tend to be slowly changing, whereas errors of measurement are typically taken to be 'white noise', the distortion in the variables will be relatively more severe at higher frequencies. The lower frequencies, on the other hand, are relatively robust to this type of measurement error, and so restricting spectral regression to these frequencies may prove to be advantageous. Further discussion of these ideas will be found in Engle (1974, 1978b).

The second reason for being interested in spectral regression is that serial correlation in the original disturbances is converted into heteroscedasticity in the transformed disturbances. The generalised least squares (GLS) estimator can therefore be computed by weighted least squares in the frequency domain. The weights are given by the spectral density of the disturbances and this opens up the possibility of constructing a *non-parametric* feasible GLS estimator in which the spectral density is estimated without specifying a model for the disturbances. On the other hand, if we wish to specify a model for the process generating the disturbances, frequency domain ML estimation can be carried out by extending the methods described in section 6.8. Again this approach is particularly appealing for models with unobserved components. Furthermore it has advantages for dealing with other features of time series regression, such as distributed lags.

In order to develop the frequency domain estimators, we will consider a model with a $k \times 1$ vector of exogenous variables, $\mathbf{x}_t$, and a disturbance term, u_t, which is generated by a stationary stochastic process with zero mean and a continuous power spectrum, $f(\lambda)$, which is everywhere positive in the interval $[0, \pi]$. Such a model may be written as

$$y_t = \mathbf{x}_t'\boldsymbol{\delta} + u_t, \qquad t = 1, \ldots, T \tag{10.1}$$

where $\boldsymbol{\delta}$ is a $k \times 1$ vector of unknown parameters. For models with non-stationary disturbances, the observations will need to be differenced in some way before (10.1) is appropriate. The matrix form of (10.1) is

$$\mathbf{y} = \mathbf{X}\boldsymbol{\delta} + \mathbf{u} \tag{10.2}$$

where $\mathbf{u}$ is a $T \times 1$ vector of disturbances with covariance matrix $\sigma^2\mathbf{V}$.

As noted in section 6.8, frequency domain methods are exact when applied to circular processes, but are asymptotically valid even when this assumption does not hold. In the context of (10.1) it is important to stress that it is the circularity of the disturbance term, u_t, which is relevant. The question of whether the elements of $\mathbf{x}_t$ are circular does not enter into the discussion at all except in the special methods described for distributed lags. More importantly there is no reason, in general, for $\mathbf{x}_t$ to be stationary. It is the stationarity of u_t which is crucial. Conditions on $\mathbf{x}_t$ are needed in order to derive asymptotic properties of the estimators, but these conditions can be much weaker than a requirement of stationarity.

Spectral Regression with Uncorrelated Disturbances

The transformation to the frequency domain can be made by pre-multiplying the observation matrices in (10.2) by the $T \times T$ Fourier matrix defined in (8.6). This matrix is complex, but the transformation can also be carried out using a real matrix which is the transpose of the $\mathbf{Z}$ matrix defined in

(2.19). Either way the transformed model may be written as

$$\dot{\mathbf{y}} = \dot{\mathbf{X}}\delta + \dot{\mathbf{u}} \tag{10.3}$$

where $\dot{\mathbf{y}} = \mathbf{Wy}$, $\dot{\mathbf{X}} = \mathbf{WX}$ and $\dot{\mathbf{u}} = \mathbf{Wu}$.

When the disturbances are serially uncorrelated, we have a classical linear regression model. In this case

$$\mathrm{Var}(\dot{\mathbf{u}}) = E(\dot{\mathbf{u}}\dot{\mathbf{u}}^\dagger) = E(\mathbf{Wuu'W}^\dagger) = \sigma^2 \mathbf{WW}^\dagger = \sigma^2 \mathbf{I} \tag{10.4}$$

where † denotes the complex conjugate transpose, or simply the transpose if the real transformation is used. Since the covariance matrix of the transformed disturbances is scalar, OLS applied to the transformed observations will yield the BLUE of δ. Not surprisingly, this estimator is identical to the OLS estimator, $\mathbf{d}$, computed from the original observations. A formal demonstration is straightforward:

$$\mathbf{d} = (\dot{\mathbf{X}}^\dagger\dot{\mathbf{X}})^{-1}\dot{\mathbf{X}}^\dagger\dot{\mathbf{y}} = (\mathbf{X'W}^\dagger\mathbf{WX})^{-1}\mathbf{X'W}^\dagger\mathbf{Wy} = (\mathbf{X'X})^{-1}\mathbf{X'y} \tag{10.5}$$

The transformed observations correspond to different frequencies. Certain frequency components may therefore be omitted simply by dropping the appropriate transformed observations from the data set. This is band spectral regression. Various tests can be carried out within the regression framework. In particular, analysis of covariance tests can be used to test whether the transformed observations corresponding to certain frequencies obey the same model as the remaining observations.

To see exactly how band spectral regression works, we explore the transformation in more detail for the case of a single explanatory variable, x_t, and show how the least squares estimator can be expressed in terms of the sample spectral density of x_t and a quantity relating x_t and y_t, known as the cross-spectrum. The same result is obtained irrespective of whether the real or complex Fourier transformation is applied. The complex transformation is more elegant mathematically, but the real transformation has the practical advantage that estimation and testing can be carried out using a standard regression package.

For the complex Fourier transform (8.6) the jth element of $\dot{\mathbf{y}}$ is

$$\dot{y}_j = \frac{1}{\sqrt{T}} \sum_{t=1}^{T} y_t \, e^{-i\lambda_j - \imath t}, \qquad j = 1, \ldots, T \tag{10.6}$$

and similarly for the jth transformed observation on the explanatory variable, $\dot{x}_j$. The OLS estimator can therefore be written as

$$
\begin{aligned}
d &= \left[\sum_{j=0}^{T-1} \dot{x}_j \bar{\dot{x}}_j \right]^{-1} \sum_{j=0}^{T-1} \dot{x}_j \bar{\dot{y}}_j \\
&= \left[\sum_{j=0}^{T-1} I_x(\lambda_j) \right]^{-1} \sum_{j=0}^{T-1} I_{xy}(\lambda_j)
\end{aligned} \tag{10.7}
$$

since $\dot{x}_j$ multiplied by its complex conjugate is 2π times the sample spectral density of x_t, $I_x(\lambda_j)$, while $\dot{x}_j$ multiplied by the complex conjugate of $\dot{y}_j$ is the cross-spectrum between x_t and y_t, $I_{xy}(\lambda_j)$. The interpretation of this quantity is discussed in section 7.2, but in the present context this interpretation is not important. It should, however, be noted that $I_{xy}(\lambda_j)$ is complex, but the complex part cancels out under the summation in (10.7). Thus $I_{xy}(\lambda_j)$ can be replaced in (10.7) by its real part

$$I_{xy}^*(\lambda_j) = (2\pi T)^{-1}[(\sum x_t \cos \lambda_j t)(\sum y_t \cos \lambda_j t)$$
$$+ (\sum x_t \sin \lambda_j t)(\sum y_t \sin \lambda_j t)] \qquad (10.8)$$

with all summations running from $t = 1$ to T.

The real Fourier transform yields

$$\dot{y}_s = \delta\dot{x}_s + \dot{u}_s, \qquad s = 1, \ldots, T \qquad (10.9)$$

In this case successive pairs of transformed observations correspond to particular frequencies for $s = 2, \ldots, T - 1$ (assuming T is even). Furthermore if $p_{j,x}$ denotes the periodogram of x_t, it follows from (2.12) that

$$p_{j,x} = \dot{x}_{2j}^2 + \dot{x}_{2j+1}^2, \qquad j = 1, \ldots, n - 1$$
$$p_{0,x} = \dot{x}_0^2 \qquad \text{and} \qquad p_{n,x} = \dot{x}_n^2$$

Thus

$$\sum_{s=1}^{T} \dot{x}_s^2 = \sum_{j=0}^{n} p_{j,x} = 4\pi \sum_{j=0}^{n} \delta_j I_x(\lambda_j) = 2\pi \sum_{j=0}^{T-1} I_x(\lambda_j) \qquad (10.10)$$

In a similar way, the terms involving the transformed values of x_t and y_t yield the real part of the cross-spectrum, that is

$$I_{xy}^*(\lambda_j) = (\dot{x}_{2j}\dot{y}_{2j} + \dot{x}_{2j+1}\dot{y}_{2j+1})/4\pi$$

Thus the OLS estimator obtained by regressing y_s on x_s in (10.9) is identical to the estimator derived in (10.7).

In the general case when the model contains k exogenous variables, $\mathbf{I}_{xy}(\lambda_j)$ is a $k \times 1$ vector of the sample cross-spectra between y_t and the elements of $\mathbf{x}_t$, and $\mathbf{I}_{xx}(\lambda_j)$ denotes a $k \times k$ matrix containing the sample spectra of the exogenous variables on the main diagonal and the sample cross-spectra in the off-diagonal positions. The matrix is Hermitian, that is equal to its complex conjugate transpose, and hence the complex parts cancel in the summation over T frequencies. Thus we need only consider its real part, $\mathbf{I}_{xx}^*(\lambda_j)$, and so

$$\mathbf{d} = \left[\sum_{j=0}^{T-1} \mathbf{I}_{xx}^*(\lambda_j) \right]^{-1} \sum_{j=0}^{T-1} \mathbf{I}_{xy}^*(\lambda_j) \qquad (10.11)$$

Cumulative Periodogram

When a regression model is estimated by OLS a general test against serial correlation can be based on the portmanteau statistic. If attention is to be focused primarily on the first autocorrelation, $r(1)$, a bounds test based on the Durbin–Watson statistic can be carried out; see EATS, section 6.3.

The use of the cumulative periodogram as a general test against serial correlation was described in section 6.9. When the periodogram ordinates in (9.1) are constructed from OLS residuals, Durbin (1969) has shown that a bounds test is possible. If the regression is carried out in the frequency domain, the periodogram ordinates can be computed almost immediately, directly from the residuals.

The bounds test is implemented as follows. In place of a single line, $s = c_0 + i/n$, two lines are drawn. When the path of s_i crosses the upper line, the null hypothesis is rejected against the alternative of an excess of low frequency. If it fails to cross the lower line, the null hypothesis is not rejected, while crossing the lower line but not the upper line is taken to be inconclusive. Carried out in this way the test corresponds to a Durbin–Watson bounds test against positive serial correlation. A two-sided bounds test may also be carried out by constructing a corresponding pair of lines below the 45° line.

If $n^* = \frac{1}{2}(T - k)$, the two outer lines are

$$s = \pm c_0 + i/n^*$$

while the inner lines are

$$s = \pm c_0 + [i - \tfrac{1}{2}(k - 1)]/n^*$$

for $\frac{1}{2}k - \frac{1}{2} \leqslant i \leqslant n^*$. Thus the only tables needed are those for carrying out the standard cumulative periodogram test. No additional tables of upper and lower bounds are needed since the difference between the inner and outer lines depends only on $k - 1$, the number of degrees of freedom attributable to the regression. The bounds are exact when T and k are both odd, but if this is not the case Durbin (1969, p. 10) notes that '... the amount of approximation is slight and should be negligible in practice unless n^* is small'.

Example 1 Figure 6.13 shows the cumulative periodogram for the OLS residuals from the regression of consumption on profits and wages as originally carried out by Klein (1950, pp. 74–5, 135). In this case $T = 21$ and $k = 3$ and so $n^* = 9$. For a one-sided test at the 5% level of significance $c_0 = 0.32538$, and this figure is used in constructing the lines on the diagram. On inspecting figure 6.13 it will be observed that s_i rises initially, indicating that low frequencies are dominant in the residuals. However, although s_i crosses the lower line, it fails to cross the upper line, and the test is inconclusive.

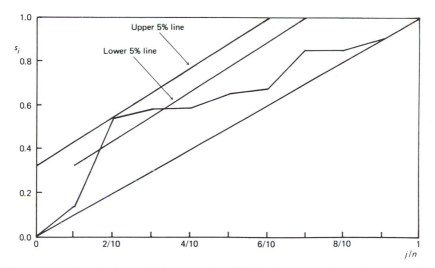

Figure 6.13 Cumulative periodogram of residuals from regression of consumption on wages and profits for USA 1921–41. *Source:* Durbin (1969, p. 13).

Serial Correlation and Generalised Least Squares

When the disturbances in (10.1) are serially correlated, with spectrum $f(\lambda)$, the effect of the transformation in (10.3) is to yield a disturbance term with diagonal covariance matrix; see (8.7). Again a single explanatory variable is assumed to simplify the exposition. Irrespective of whether the transformation matrix is real or complex, the frequency domain GLS estimator is

$$\tilde{\delta} = \left[\sum_{j=0}^{T-1} I_x(\lambda_j)/f(\lambda_j) \right]^{-1} \sum_{j=0}^{T-1} I_{xy}^*(\lambda_j)/f(\lambda_j) \qquad (10.12)$$

If u_t is circular, this estimator has a mean of δ and a variance

$$\mathrm{Var}(\tilde{\delta}) = \left[\sum_{j=0}^{T-1} I_x(\lambda_j)/f(\lambda_j) \right]^{-1} \qquad (10.13)$$

When u_t is normally distributed, $\tilde{\delta}$ has a normal distribution. If the circularity assumption for u_t does not hold, (10.12) must be regarded as an approximation to the GLS estimator, but it has the same asymptotic distribution. In this case a limiting argument of the kind needed to obtain (8.25) is needed to derive an expression for the asymptotic variance of $\tilde{\delta}$. If we assume that x_t is stationary with a continuous spectrum, $f_x(\lambda)$, then

$$\mathrm{Avar}(\tilde{\delta}) = \frac{1}{T} \left[\frac{1}{2\pi} \int_{-\pi}^{\pi} f^{-1}(\lambda) f_x(\lambda)\, d\lambda \right]^{-1} \qquad (10.14)$$

The above discussion has assumed that the spectrum of the disturbance term, $f(\lambda)$, is known. When it is unknown, a non-parametric estimator of δ, denoted $\tilde{d}$, can be obtained by replacing $f(\lambda_j)$ in (10.12) by a consistent estimator, $\hat{f}(\lambda_j)$, computed from the OLS residuals using one of the standard procedures, for example a Blackman–Tukey or Parzen window. The resulting estimator, $\tilde{d}$, has the same asymptotic distribution as the GLS estimator. Its asymptotic variance will normally be estimated by

$$\mathrm{avar}(\tilde{d}) = \left[\sum_{j=0}^{T-1} I_x(\lambda_j)/\hat{f}(\lambda_j) \right]^{-1} \qquad (10.15)$$

Since $f(\lambda)$ is estimated by smoothing, it is also legitimate to consider smoothing $I_x(\lambda_j)$ and $I_{xy}(\lambda_j)$. Furthermore, a continuity argument suggests that a reduction in the number of points at which spectra and cross-spectra are estimated will have little effect on estimates of δ. If N is the lag length employed in the spectral estimator and $\lambda_i = 2\pi i/N$, an alternative to the estimator based on (10.12), $\tilde{d}$, is

$$\tilde{d}^{\dagger} = \left[\sum_{i=0}^{N-1} I_x(\lambda_i)/f(\lambda_i) \right]^{-1} \sum_{i=0}^{N-1} I_{xy}^*(\lambda_i)/f(\lambda_i) \qquad (10.16)$$

Under suitable regularity conditions, $\tilde{d}^{\dagger}$ has the same asymptotic distribution as $\tilde{d}$. However, although $\tilde{d}^{\dagger}$ may be slightly easier to compute, the fact that $\tilde{d}$ is the exact GLS estimator when $f(\lambda)$ is known and u_t is circular, seems to be a strong argument in its favour.

Non-parametric GLS estimators can also be constructed in the time domain. For example, the disturbance could be modelled by an AR(P) process where P/T remains constant as $T \to \infty$. This *autoregressive least squares* procedure, referred to as ALS(P), is easy to implement; consistent estimators of the AR parameters are obtained by regressing OLS residuals on their lagged values, and these are used to transform the observations so that a feasible GLS estimator is obtained.

Although non-parametric estimators are asymptotically efficient, they may not be effective in small samples. The Monte Carlo results presented in Engle and Gardner (1976) suggest that for $T = 100$, the variance of the spectral estimator will, at best, be twice that of the asymptotic variance. This leaves plenty of scope for a more efficient small sample estimator based on a suitably parsimonious representation of the disturbance term. In fact, even if the disturbance is mis-specified, it is still quite possible for the resulting estimator to be more efficient in small samples than a non-parametric estimator. Engle and Gardner again provide evidence on this point, with one particular set of experiments showing ALS(1) dramatically out-performing the spectral estimator for $T = 100$, even though the disturbance was actually generated by an AR(2) model. Supporting evidence comes from Gallant and Goebel (1976), where for a particular non-linear regression model, the ALS(2) estimator has a smaller MSE than the spectral estimator for an underlying MA(4) disturbance term.

Maximum Likelihood

Suppose now that a particular stochastic process is specified for u_t so that $f(\lambda)$ depends on a set of unknown parameters, ψ. Both sets of parameters, ψ and δ, may be estimated by maximum likelihood. If u_t is assumed to be normally distributed, the log–likelihood function is of the form given in (8.1), that is

$$\log L(\delta, \psi) = -\frac{1}{2}T \log 2\pi - \frac{1}{2} \sum_{j=0}^{T-1} \log g_j - \pi \sum_{j=0}^{T-1} \frac{I(\lambda_j)}{g_j} \quad (10.17)$$

where $I(\lambda_j)$ is now the sample spectrum of $y_t - x_t'\delta$, that is

$$I(\lambda_j) = \frac{1}{2\pi T} \left| \sum_{t=1}^{T} y_t \, e^{-i\lambda_j t} - \delta \sum_{t=1}^{T} x_t \, e^{-i\lambda_j t} \right|^2 \quad (10.18)$$

For a given value of ψ, the ML estimator of δ is the GLS estimator, (10.12). (Since the likelihood is expressed in terms of g_j rather than $f(\lambda_j)$, it may be more convenient to write the GLS estimator with $f(\lambda_j)$ replaced by g_j.) As regards asymptotic properties, it is not difficult to show that the information matrix is block diagonal with respect to ψ and δ. The asymptotic variance of $\tilde{\psi}$ is as given in (8.25), while for $\tilde{\delta}$ it is as in (10.14).

A way of computing ML estimates is by the method of scoring. Since the information matrix is block diagonal with respect to δ and ψ in large samples, the scoring algorithm consists of two parts: one for ψ and one for δ. The part for δ consists simply of the repeated computation of the GLS estimator, while the part for ψ is of the same form as for a model without exogenous variables, that is, (8.23). A variant on this procedure is to iterate the part for ψ to convergence at each step, before the feasible GLS estimate is re-computed. In fact doing this once, using the sample spectral density from an initial OLS regression, will result in the subsequent GLS estimator being asymptotically efficient.

Example 2 Consider a regression model with a stochastic trend component, (8.5.4), in which the slope is fixed, that is $\sigma_\zeta^2 = 0$. This is estimated in the frequency domain by first taking differences to give (5.8.7). An initial estimator of δ is obtained by an OLS regression of Δy_t on Δx_t, and the ML estimators are obtained by iterating to convergence using scoring or some other algorithm.

The asymptotic variance of the ML estimator of δ can be computed from (10.13) or (10.14). In the latter case, an assumption about the process generating the single explanatory variable x_t can lead to a simple expression. Thus if x_t follows a random walk with disturbance variance, σ_x^2,

$$\text{Avar}(\tilde{\delta}) = T^{-1}\sigma_\varepsilon^2 \sigma_x^{-2}(q^2 + 4q)^{1/2}$$

Distributed Lags

Suppose that the model consists of an unconstrained distributed lag in a single explanatory variable, that is

$$y_t = \sum_{\tau=0}^{h} \delta_\tau x_{t-\tau} + u_t \qquad (10.19)$$

where u_t is a stationary disturbance term. The model is therefore a special case of (10.1) with the x_t vector consisting of the $(h+1) \times 1$ vector of current and lagged variables, $(x_t, x_{t-1}, \ldots, x_{t-h})'$. Although the estimator of δ in (10.11) is perfectly valid, its computation can be simplified by observing that the transformation to the frequency domain of x_{t-k} is

$$\sum_{t=1}^{T} x_{t-k}\, e^{-i\lambda_j t} \simeq e^{-i\lambda_j k} \sum_{t=1}^{T} x_t\, e^{-i\lambda_j t} \qquad (10.20)$$

The spectral distributed lag estimator is then

$$\mathbf{d} = \left[\sum_{j=0}^{T-1} \mathbf{e}_j \mathbf{e}_j^\dagger \cdot \frac{I_x(\lambda_j)}{f(\lambda_j)} \right]^{-1} \sum_{j=0}^{T-1} \frac{1}{f(\lambda_j)} \text{Re}\{\mathbf{e}_j I_{xy}(\lambda_j)\} \qquad (10.21)$$

where $\mathbf{e}_j$ is an $(h+1) \times 1$ vector with $\exp(-i\lambda_j p)$ in the $(t+1)$th position for $p = 0, \ldots, h$, and $\text{Re}\{\cdot\}$ denotes real part. Thus a direct calculation of the periodogram quantities involving the lagged explanatory variable is avoided.

For $k = 1$, the approximation in (10.20) entails the omission of $e^{-i\lambda_j}(x_0 - x_T)$. Compared with the other terms, this term will normally be negligible in large samples. In fact, if $x_0 = x_T$, it disappears completely, irrespective of the sample size. A similar argument holds for any lag. Any distortion induced by the approximation will be relatively minor if the sample is large and/or the differences between the last h observations and the initial observations, $x_{-h+1}, \ldots, x_0$, are small. The use of this approximation may therefore not be advisable in a small sample when x_t has a strong trend. On the other hand, when x_t is a circulant, (10.20) becomes an equality.

The above device can also be applied to lagged dependent variables, and it is particularly useful for computing estimators of the parameters in a rational distributed lag model.

Appendix A Trigonometric Identities

The *addition formulae* are

$$\sin(x \pm y) = \sin x \cos y \pm \cos x \sin y \tag{A.1}$$

$$\cos(x \pm y) = \cos x \cos y \mp \sin x \sin y \tag{A.2}$$

The addition formulae form the basis for deriving many results. For example, setting $x = y$ in (A.2) and using the fundamental identity

$$\sin^2 x + \cos^2 x = 1$$

yields, after some re-arrangement,

$$\cos^2 x = \tfrac{1}{2} + \tfrac{1}{2} \cos 2x \tag{A.3}$$

Such results are often useful in the calculus. For example

$$\int \cos^2 x \, dx = \int (\tfrac{1}{2} + \tfrac{1}{2} \cos 2x) \, dx$$

$$= \tfrac{1}{2}x + \tfrac{1}{4} \sin 2x = \tfrac{1}{2}(x + \sin x \cos x) \tag{A.4}$$

The identity

$$e^{\pm ix} = \cos x \pm i \sin x \tag{A.5}$$

plays a particularly important role in spectral analysis, one of the main reasons being that the exponential function is relatively easy to manipulate. Thus, given (A.5), the first addition formula may be shown to hold directly by expanding both sides of the equation

$$e^{i(x+y)} = e^{ix} e^{iy} \tag{A.6}$$

and equating real and complex parts.

Because of the convenience of working with exponential terms, the sine and cosine functions are often expressed in the form

$$\cos x = (e^{ix} + e^{-ix})/2 \tag{A.7}$$

and

$$\sin x = (e^{ix} - e^{-ix})/2i \tag{A.8}$$

Both results follow almost directly from (A.5).

An example of the use of these formulae is given by the proof of the identity

$$y_n(\lambda) = \frac{1}{2} + \sum_{x=1}^{n} \cos \lambda x = \frac{\sin(n + 1/2)\lambda}{2 \sin(\lambda/2)} \tag{A.9}$$

The first step is to use (A.7) to construct

$$y_n(\lambda) = \frac{1}{2} \sum_{x=-n}^{n} e^{i\lambda x} = \frac{1}{2} e^{-in\lambda}[1 + e^{i\lambda} + e^{i2\lambda} + \cdots + e^{i2n\lambda}] \qquad \text{(A.10)}$$

The term in square brackets may be summed as a finite geometric progression. This yields

$$y_n(\lambda) = \frac{1}{2} e^{-in\lambda} \frac{1 - e^{i\lambda(2n+1)}}{1 - e^{i\lambda}} = \frac{1}{2} \frac{e^{-in\lambda} - e^{i(n+1)\lambda}}{1 - e^{i\lambda}}$$

Multiplying the numerator and denominator of this expression by $-e^{-i\lambda/2}$ and using (A.8) gives the required result.

Appendix B Orthogonality Relationships

The trigonometric orthogonality relationships between pairs of sines and cosines may be expressed concisely in the form

$$\int_{-\pi}^{\pi} e^{inx} e^{-imx} \, dx = \begin{cases} 0, & n \neq m \\ 2\pi, & n = m \end{cases} \qquad \text{(B.1)}$$

where n and m are integers. When $n = m$ this result follows directly, while for $n - m = k \neq 0$,

$$\int_{-\pi}^{\pi} e^{ikx} = \left[\frac{1}{ik} e^{ikx} \right]_{-\pi}^{\pi} = 0 \qquad \text{(B.2)}$$

since

$$e^{ik\pi} = e^{-ik\pi} = \begin{cases} 1 & \text{for } k \text{ even} \\ -1 & \text{for } k \text{ odd} \end{cases}$$

The orthogonality relationships used in deriving the Fourier representation of section 6.2 are, for integer k and j, and T even,

$$\sum_{t=1}^{T} \cos \frac{2\pi j}{T} t \cdot \cos \frac{2\pi k}{T} t = \begin{cases} 0, & 0 \leqslant k \neq j \leqslant T/2 \\ T/2, & 0 < k = j < T/2 \\ T, & k = j = 0, T/2 \end{cases} \qquad \text{(B.3a)}$$

$$\sum_{t=1}^{T} \sin \frac{2\pi j}{T} t \cdot \sin \frac{2\pi k}{T} t = \begin{cases} 0, & 0 \leqslant k \neq j \leqslant T/2 \\ T/2, & 0 < k = j < T/2 \\ 0, & k = j = 0, T/2 \end{cases} \qquad \text{(B.3b)}$$

$$\sum_{t=1}^{T} \cos \frac{2\pi j}{T} t \cdot \sin \frac{2\pi k}{T} t = 0, \qquad k, j = 0, 1, \ldots, T/2 \qquad \text{(B.3c)}$$

Setting $j = 0$ in (B.3a) and (B.3c) yields

$$\sum_{t=1}^{T} \cos \frac{2\pi k}{T} t = 0, \qquad k = 1, \ldots, T/2 \tag{B.4a}$$

and

$$\sum_{t=1}^{T} \sin \frac{2\pi k}{T} t = 0, \qquad k = 0, 1, \ldots, T/2 \tag{B.4b}$$

respectively. Using these results together with (A.5) shows that

$$\sum_{t=1}^{T} \exp\left(\pm \frac{2\pi k}{T} t \right) = \begin{cases} 0, & 0 < k \leqslant T/2 \\ T, & k = 0 \end{cases} \tag{B.5}$$

Appendix C Fourier Transforms

The results in (B.1) and (B.2) form the basis for the *Fourier transform* of a continuous function. The expression

$$f(x) = \frac{\alpha_0}{2} + \sum_{k=1}^{n} (\alpha_k \cos kx + \beta_k \sin kx) \tag{C.1}$$

is a trigonometric polynomial of order n, with $2n + 1$ Fourier coefficients, $\alpha_0, \alpha_1, \ldots, \alpha_n, \beta_1, \ldots, \beta_n$. Since $f(x)$ is a linear combination of sines and cosines of period 2π, it follows that it is a continuous function over any range of x of length 2π. By defining

$$\delta_k = (\alpha_k + i\beta_k)/2, \qquad \delta_{-k} = (\alpha_k - i\beta_k)/2 \qquad \text{and} \qquad \delta_0 = \alpha_0/2$$

expression (C.1) may be written in complex notation as

$$f(x) = \sum_{k=-n}^{n} \delta_k e^{-ikx} \tag{C.2}$$

Suppose now that $f(x)$ is given, and that we wish to find the δ_k's or, equivalently, the α_k's and β_k's. Multiplying both sides of (C.2) by e^{ijx} and integrating over a range of 2π, say $-\pi$ to π, yields

$$\int_{-\pi}^{\pi} f(x) e^{ijx} \, dx = \sum_{k=1}^{n} \delta_k \int_{-\pi}^{\pi} e^{-i(k-j)x} \, dx, \qquad j = 0, 1, \ldots, n \tag{C.3}$$

Using (B.1) then gives

$$\delta_k = \frac{1}{2\pi} \int_{-\pi}^{\pi} f(x) e^{ikx} \, dx \tag{C.4}$$

Expressions (C.2) and (C.4) are often referred to as Fourier transform pairs.

If $f(x)$ is an even function, (C.2) contains only cosine terms and δ_k is real with $\delta_k = \delta_{-k}$. The Fourier transform pair may then be written:

$$f(x) = \delta_0 + 2 \sum_{k=1}^{n} \delta_k \cos kx \tag{C.5}$$

and

$$\delta_k = \frac{\alpha_k}{2} = \frac{1}{\pi} \int_0^\pi f(x) \cos kx \, dx \tag{C.6}$$

It is always possible to approximate a continuous function by a trigonometric polynomial. As an example consider the function

$$f(x) = \begin{cases} 1/2b, & |x| \leqslant b \\ 0, & \text{elsewhere} \end{cases} \tag{C.7}$$

Applying (C.6) yields

$$2\delta_k = \alpha_k = (2\pi b)^{-1} \int_{-b}^{b} \cos kx \, dx = \frac{\sin bk}{\pi bk} \tag{C.8}$$

and $\alpha_0 = 1/\pi$. Therefore

$$f(x) = \frac{1}{2\pi} + \frac{1}{b\pi} \sum_{k=1}^{\infty} \frac{\sin bk}{k} \cos kx \tag{C.9}$$

Exercises

1. Derive the spectrum for an MA(2) process. Can this give rise to cyclical behaviour of the form exhibited by the AR(2) process?
2. Find the spectrum for $y_t = \phi y_{t-4} + \varepsilon_t$, where $|\phi| < 1$, and comment on its shape when $\phi = 0.9$. What happens as ϕ gets closer to one?
3. Suppose that the filter (6.16) is applied with $r = 2$ and the filtered series is then subtracted from the original series. Find the gain and compare this with the gain of (6.18).
4. Write down an expression for the phase, $\text{Ph}(\lambda)$, in terms of the co-spectrum and quadrature spectrum.
5. Derive (6.27).
6. Draw the power spectra for AR(1) processes with $\phi = 0.5$, $\phi = 0.99$ and $\phi = -0.5$. Comment.
7. Derive an expression for the power spectrum of an ARMA(1, 1) process. Sketch the spectra of the processes whose autocorrelation functions are shown in figure 2.5.
8. By calculating the appropriate gain and phase functions, explain the advantages and disadvantages of using a difference filter of the form

$$y_t^* = y_t - y_{t-7}$$

as opposed to a simple seven-year moving average, to remove a seven-year cycle.

9. Determine the forms of the autocorrelation function and power spectrum of the stochastic process which results when first differences are taken in the model,

$$y_t = \alpha + \beta t + u_t$$

$$u_t = \phi u_{t-4} + \varepsilon_t$$

where α, β and ϕ are parameters and $|\phi| < 1$.

10. The following figures are quarterly observations on an economic time series:

Year	Q1	Q2	Q3	Q4
1	2	5	9	3
2	1	3	6	5
3	3	4	8	6
4	4	4	7	6

Estimate the seasonal pattern in this series by fitting an appropriate number of trigonometric terms.

If the model is of the form (2.17), test whether the individual trigonometric coefficients are significantly different from zero, *given* that the variance of the disturbance term, ε_t, is known to be 2.25. Comment on the implications of your result. How would you modify the above testing procedure if σ^2 were unknown?

11. (a) What is the relationship between a spectral window and a lag window? Why might some lag windows have undesirable properties?

(b) Suppose that

$$y_t = \beta t + v_t, \qquad t = 1, \ldots, T$$

where β is an unknown parameter and v_t is an ARIMA$(p, 1, q)$ process. Derive an expression for the maximum likelihood estimator of β, b, in the frequency domain. What assumptions are you making?

Find an expression for the large sample variance of b in terms of the spectrum of v_t and show that it may be estimated consistently by

$$\text{avar}(b) = \sum_{t=M+1}^{T} (M^{-1} \Delta_M y_t - b)^2 / (T-1)$$

where $\Delta_M y_t = y_t - y_{t-M}$. Should there be any relationship between M and T? Hint: $\Delta_M = \Delta \cdot S(L)$.

12. If, in the local linear trend model, (3.3.5), the variance of η_t, σ_η^2, is zero write down an expression for the information matrix in the frequency domain. Show that a Lagrange multiplier test of the hypothesis that $\sigma_\eta^2 = 0$ can be set up in terms of the coefficient of determination from a certain regression.

13. Show how scoring algorithms can be set up for (a) a random walk plus noise; (b) a stationary AR(1) plus noise; and (c) fractionally integrated white noise, (5.7.1).

14. Consider the stationary, Gaussian, fractionally integrated white noise process, (5.7.1). Obtain a frequency domain expression for the asymptotic covariance matrix of the ML estimators of d and σ^2. Conditional on a given value of d, find a frequency domain expression for estimating σ^2. Hence explain how d could be estimated by concentrating σ^2 out of the likelihood function.

15. Consider the model

$$y_t = \delta x_t + u_t, \qquad t = 1, \ldots, T$$

where u_t is a stationary stochastic process with spectrum $\sigma^2 g^*(\lambda)/2\pi$. If $g^*(\lambda)$ is known, find frequency domain expressions for the ML estimators of δ and σ^2. If the model is extended to include a lagged explanatory variable, show that ML estimators of the coefficients of x_t and x_{t-1} can be computed without explicitly computing the periodogram of x_{t-1}.

If the disturbance term in the geometric distributed lag model

$$y_t = \beta \sum_{j=0}^{\infty} \alpha^j x_{t-j} + \varepsilon_t, \qquad 0 < \alpha < 1$$

is Gaussian white noise, find an expression for the likelihood function in the frequency domain.

16. How would you estimate the model in question 17 of chapter 5 in the frequency domain?

7

Multivariate Time Series

7.1 Stationary Series and their Properties in the Time Domain

The concepts involved in analysing univariate time series may be extended to multivariate series. Attention is focused on the joint behaviour of the elements in the $N \times 1$ vector $\mathbf{y}_t = (y_{1t}, \ldots, y_{Nt})'$, observed over the period $t = 1, \ldots, T$. If the series is stationary, its properties may be analysed in the time and frequency domains.

Stationarity and Autocovariance Matrices

It may be assumed, without any loss of generality, that $E(\mathbf{y}_t) = \mathbf{0}$. The covariance matrix between $\mathbf{y}_t$ and $\mathbf{y}_{t-\tau}$ is then defined by $E(\mathbf{y}_t\mathbf{y}'_{t-\tau})$. The ijth element in this matrix is equal to $E(y_{it}y_{j,t-\tau})$ and the vector process $\mathbf{y}_t$ is covariance stationary only if all such elements are independent of t for all values of τ. This is a stronger condition than simply requiring that each individual series be covariance stationary. This would merely constrain the diagonal elements in the covariance matrices to be independent of t, without imposing a similar constraint on the off-diagonal elements. These off-diagonal elements denote the *cross-covariances* between different series at particular lags, and the two stationary series will only be *jointly stationary* if these quantities are independent of t.

For a weakly stationary vector process, the covariance between $\mathbf{y}_t$ and $\mathbf{y}_{t-\tau}$ will be denoted by

$$E(\mathbf{y}_t\mathbf{y}'_{t-\tau}) = \mathbf{\Gamma}(\tau), \qquad \tau = 0, 1, 2, \ldots \qquad (1.1)$$

and $\mathbf{\Gamma}(\tau)$ will generally be referred to as the *autocovariance matrix* at lag τ. The *covariance* matrix is obtained when $\tau = 0$; this matrix is symmetric.

In the univariate case the autocovariance function has the property that $\gamma(-\tau) = \gamma(\tau)$, but for multivariate models the matrices $\mathbf{\Gamma}(\tau)$ and $\mathbf{\Gamma}(-\tau)$

will not, in general, be identical. However, taking the ijth element in $\mathbf{\Gamma}(\tau)$ and setting $t = t^* + \tau$ gives

$$\gamma_{ij}(\tau) = E(y_{it}y_{j,t-\tau}) = E(y_{i,t^*+\tau}y_{j,t^*}) = E(y_{jt^*}y_{i,t^*+\tau}) = \gamma_{ji}(-\tau) \qquad (1.2)$$

and so the ijth element in $\mathbf{\Gamma}(\tau)$ is equal to the jith element in $\mathbf{\Gamma}(-\tau)$. Thus the autocovariance matrix of a stationary vector process satisfies the relation

$$\mathbf{\Gamma}(\tau) = \mathbf{\Gamma}'(-\tau), \qquad \tau = 0, 1, 2, \ldots \qquad (1.3)$$

Autocovariance matrices are estimated in an analogous fashion to autocovariances in univariate series. Thus, if allowance is made for a non-zero mean,

$$\mathbf{C}(\tau) = \hat{\mathbf{\Gamma}}(\tau) = T^{-1} \sum_{t=\tau+1}^{T} (\mathbf{y}_t - \bar{\mathbf{y}})(\mathbf{y}_{t-\tau} - \bar{\mathbf{y}})', \qquad \tau = 0, 1, 2, \ldots \qquad (1.4)$$

Autocorrelation Matrices and the Cross-Correlation Function

An autocovariance matrix may be standardised to yield the corresponding *autocorrelation matrix*. The ijth element in $\mathbf{\Gamma}(\tau)$ is simply divided by the square roots of the variances of y_i and y_j to give the corresponding autocorrelation or cross-correlation. In matrix terms the autocorrelation matrix at lag τ, $\mathbf{P}(\tau)$, is defined by

$$\mathbf{P}(\tau) = \mathbf{D}_0^{-1}\mathbf{\Gamma}(\tau)\mathbf{D}_0^{-1}, \qquad \tau = 0, \pm 1, \pm 2, \ldots \qquad (1.5)$$

where $\mathbf{D}_0^2 = \text{diag}\{\gamma_{11}(0), \ldots, \gamma_{NN}(0)\}$. The ijth element of $\mathbf{P}(\tau)$ gives the cross-correlation between y_i and y_j at lag τ, that is

$$\rho_{ij}(\tau) = \gamma_{ij}(\tau)/\sqrt{\gamma_{ii}(0)\gamma_{jj}(0)}, \qquad \tau = 0, \pm 1, \pm 2, \ldots \qquad (1.6)$$

The information on the relationship between different variables in $\mathbf{y}_t$ is contained in the cross-correlations. A plot of these quantities against both negative and positive values of τ displays the *cross-correlation function*.

Example 1 Suppose that ε_t and x_t are uncorrelated white noise processes with mean zero and variances σ^2 and σ_x^2 respectively. A third variable, y_t, is defined by the equation

$$y_t = \beta x_{t-1} + \varepsilon_t \qquad (1.7)$$

The vector process $(y_t, x_t)'$ is covariance stationary with the cross-correlation function given by

$$\rho_{yx}(\tau) = \begin{cases} \beta\sigma_x/(\beta^2\sigma_x^2 + \sigma^2)^{1/2}, & \tau = 1 \\ 0, & \tau \neq 1 \end{cases} \qquad (1.8)$$

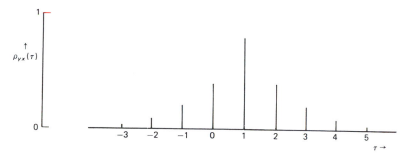

Figure 7.1 Cross-correlation function defined in (1.10).

Example 2 If, in the above example, x_t is generated by a stationary AR(1) process,

$$x_t = \phi x_{t-1} + \eta_t, \qquad |\phi| < 1 \tag{1.9}$$

where η_t is white noise with mean zero and variance, σ_η^2, the cross-correlation function is more complicated. Given that ε_t and η_t are independent, multiplying (1.7) by $x_{t-\tau}$ and taking expectations yields

$$\gamma_{yx}(\tau) = \beta \gamma_x(\tau - 1), \qquad \tau = 0, \pm 1, \pm 2, \dots \tag{1.10}$$

Thus

$$\rho_{yx}(\tau) = \beta \phi^{|\tau - 1|} \sigma_x / \sigma_y, \qquad \tau = 0, \pm 1, \dots \tag{1.11}$$

where $\sigma_x^2 = \sigma_\eta^2/(1 - \phi^2)$ and $\sigma_y^2 = \beta^2 \sigma_x^2 + \sigma^2$; see figure 7.1. Although the relationship between x_t and y_t shows up quite clearly in (1.8), this is no longer the case when x_t is serially correlated. As (1.11) shows, the cross-correlation function depends not only on the relationship between x_t and y_t, but also on the nature of the process generating x_t.

7.2 Cross-Spectral Analysis

The frequency domain analogue of the autocovariance matrix, $\mathbf{\Gamma}(\tau)$, is the $N \times N$ *multivariate spectrum*

$$\mathbf{F}(\lambda) = (2\pi)^{-1} \sum_{\tau = -\infty}^{\infty} \mathbf{\Gamma}(\tau) e^{-i\lambda\tau}, \qquad -\pi \leqslant \lambda \leqslant \pi \tag{2.1}$$

The diagonal elements of $\mathbf{F}(\lambda)$ are the power spectra of the individual processes. The *ij*th element of $\mathbf{F}(\lambda)$ is the *cross-spectrum* between the *i*th and the *j*th variable for $j > i$. It is the cross-spectrum which contains all the information concerning the relationship between two series in the frequency domain. The *ji*th element of $\mathbf{F}(\lambda)$ is simply the complex conjugate of the *ij*th element.

Gain, Phase and Coherence

The relationship between two series is normally characterised by the gain and the phase. These two quantities are derived from the cross-spectrum, but they are real rather than complex. Suppose that y_t and x_t are jointly stationary stochastic processes, with continuous power spectra $f_y(\lambda)$ and $f_x(\lambda)$ respectively. The cross-spectrum between y_t and x_t is defined by

$$f_{yx}(\lambda) = (2\pi)^{-1} \sum_{\tau = -\infty}^{\infty} \gamma_{yx}(\tau) e^{-i\lambda\tau} \tag{2.2}$$

for $-\pi \leqslant \lambda \leqslant \pi$. The *gain* is

$$G(\lambda) = |f_{yx}(\lambda)|/f_x(\lambda) \tag{2.3}$$

while the *phase* is

$$Ph(\lambda) = \tan^{-1}\{-Im[f_{yx}(\lambda)]/Re[f_{yx}(\lambda)]\} \tag{2.4}$$

The concepts of gain and phase were introduced in section 6.5 to describe the properties of a linear filter. Their interpretation in cross-spectral analysis is similar. Suppose that the linear filter in (6.6.1) is modified by adding to the right hand side a stochastic disturbance term which is distributed independently of x_t. This yields the model

$$y_t = \sum_{j=-r}^{s} w_j x_{t-j} + u_t, \qquad t = 1, \ldots, T \tag{2.5}$$

If, for convenience, x_t is assumed to have zero mean, multiplying both sides of (2.5) by $x_{t-\tau}$ and taking expectations gives the cross-covariance function

$$\gamma_{yx}(\tau) = \sum_{j=-s}^{r} w_j \gamma_x(\tau - j), \qquad \tau = 0, \pm 1, \pm 2, \ldots \tag{2.6}$$

Substituting (2.6) into (2.2) gives

$$f_{yx}(\lambda) = (2\pi)^{-1} \sum_{\tau = -\infty}^{\infty} \sum_{j=-r}^{s} w_j \gamma_x(\tau - j) e^{-i\lambda\tau}$$

Setting $k = \tau - j$ and reversing the order of the summation signs then yields

$$f_{yx}(\lambda) = (2\pi)^{-1} \sum_{j=-r}^{s} w_j e^{-i\lambda j} \sum_{k = -\infty}^{\infty} \gamma_x(k) e^{-i\lambda k}$$

which on comparing with (6.6.5) is seen to be

$$f_{yx}(\lambda) = W(e^{-i\lambda}) f_x(\lambda) \tag{2.7}$$

Having established (2.7), the link between (2.3) and (2.4) and the formulae given in section 6.6 is clear. The gain and phase characterise the relationship between y_t and x_t just as they do for the linear filter, (6.6.1). The only difference is that the relationship is no longer an exact one. This suggests the need for a third quantity which somehow measures the strength of the relationship between y_t and x_t at different frequencies.

Let z_t denote the systematic part of y_t, that is

$$z_t = \sum_{j=-r}^{s} w_j x_{t-j}, \qquad t = 1, \ldots, T \qquad (2.8)$$

Since $E(x_t u_\tau) = 0$ for all t and τ

$$\gamma_y(\tau) = \gamma_z(\tau) + \gamma_u(\tau), \qquad \tau = 0, 1, 2, \ldots \qquad (2.9)$$

and so

$$f_y(\lambda) = f_z(\lambda) + f_u(\lambda) \qquad (2.10)$$

The *coherence*,

$$\text{Coh}(\lambda) = f_z(\lambda)/f_y(\lambda) = 1 - f_u(\lambda)/f_y(\lambda), \qquad 0 \leqslant \lambda \leqslant \pi \qquad (2.11)$$

is a measure of the fraction of $f_y(\lambda)$ which can be systematically accounted for by movements in x. Since

$$f_z(\lambda) = |W(e^{-i\lambda})|^2 f_x(\lambda) \qquad (2.12)$$

the coherence can be expressed in an alternative form by substituting from (2.7) to give

$$\text{Coh}(\lambda) = \frac{|f_{yx}(\lambda)|^2}{f_x(\lambda)f_y(\lambda)} \qquad (2.13)$$

Example 1 Consider the model defined by (1.7) and (1.9). Since

$$W(e^{-i\lambda}) = \beta e^{-i\lambda} \qquad (2.14)$$

it follows immediately from the definition of the frequency response function in (6.6.14) that $G(\lambda) = \beta$ at all frequencies while $\text{Ph}(\lambda) = \lambda$. After some re-arrangement, the coherence function may be written as

$$\text{Coh}(\lambda) = \left[1 + \frac{f_u(\lambda)}{|W(e^{-i\lambda})|^2 f_x(\lambda)}\right]^{-1} \qquad (2.15)$$

and so in this case

$$\text{Coh}(\lambda) = [1 + \sigma^2 \beta^{-2} \sigma_\eta^{-2}(1 + \phi^2 - 2\phi \cos \lambda)]^{-1} \qquad (2.16)$$

This function is shown in figure 7.2 for $\phi = 0.8$, $\beta = 1$ and $\sigma^2 = \sigma_\eta^2 = 1$. Since x_t is slowly changing, its spectrum has relatively high power at the lower frequencies and this is reflected in the high coherence around $\lambda = 0$. On the other hand, the disturbance term has a much greater effect at the higher frequencies, and the relationship between x and y is correspondingly

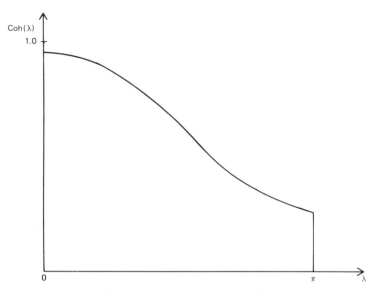

Figure 7.2 Coherence in example 1.

weaker. Note that ϕ is the crucial parameter in determining the overall shape of the coherence function, and that a positive value is likely to be more characteristic of actual time series than a negative one. The pattern shown in figure 7.2 is probably not atypical.

Example 2 The Koyck, or geometric, distributed lag model,

$$y_t = \beta \sum_{j=0}^{\infty} \alpha^j x_{t-j} + \varepsilon_t, \qquad 0 < \alpha < 1 \tag{2.17}$$

imposes an exponentially declining pattern on the lag coefficients. In terms of (2.5), $w_j = \beta\alpha^j$, and the frequency response function is given by

$$W(e^{-i\lambda}) = \beta \sum_{j=0}^{\infty} \alpha^j e^{-i\lambda j} = \beta/(1 - \alpha e^{-i\lambda}) \tag{2.18}$$

If x_t is generated by the AR(1) process in (1.9), the coherence is given by

$$\text{Coh}(\lambda) = [1 + \sigma^2\beta^{-2}\sigma_\eta^{-2}(1 + \phi^2 - 2\phi\cos\lambda)(1 + \alpha^2 - 2\alpha\cos\lambda)] \tag{2.19}$$

When ϕ is positive, the salient characteristic of figure 7.2, namely the relatively high coherence at low frequencies, is reproduced by (2.19). This feature becomes more exaggerated the closer α is to one.

Estimation

Given data on two time series, the gain, phase and coherence functions may all be estimated. As they stand, they provide a description of the relationship between the two series in the frequency domain. There need be no assumption that the series are linked by the kind of linear relationships which have featured in the discussions so far; these were introduced merely to illustrate certain aspects of the theoretical cross-spectrum. Indeed, one of the attractions of cross-spectral analysis is that it may permit the characterisation of cyclical relationships which are difficult to model in the time domain.

Since the cross-spectrum is a complex quantity, it is normally broken down into two real quantities, the *co-spectrum*, $c(\lambda)$, and the *quadrature spectrum*, $q(\lambda)$. Thus

$$f_{yx}(\lambda) = c(\lambda) + iq(\lambda) \tag{2.20}$$

where

$$c(\lambda) = (2\pi)^{-1} \sum_{\tau=-\infty}^{\infty} \gamma_{yx}(\tau) \cos \lambda\tau \tag{2.21a}$$

and

$$q(\lambda) = -(2\pi)^{-1} \sum_{\tau=-\infty}^{\infty} \gamma_{yx}(\tau) \sin \lambda\tau \tag{2.21b}$$

A direct interpretation of $c(\lambda)$ and $q(\lambda)$ will be found in Granger and Hatanaka (1964, pp. 74–6). However, the information in the cross-spectrum is more easily analysed in terms of gain, phase and coherence and these quantities can be readily obtained from $c(\lambda)$ and $q(\lambda)$.

The main considerations which arise in estimating the cross-spectrum are essentially the same as those which arise with the spectrum. The sample co-spectrum and quadrature spectrum are obtained by replacing the theoretical cross-covariances in (2.21) by the corresponding sample cross-covariances. However, consistent estimators of the gain, phase and coherence can only be obtained if some smoothing is carried out. This may be done directly in the frequency domain by averaging over adjacent frequencies, or in the time domain by using an appropriate lag window to weight the sample cross-covariances.

The sampling distributions of the gain, phase and coherence are discussed at some length in Fishman (1969, pp. 131–8) and Priestley (1981, pp. 702–6). An important point concerns the dependence of the large sample variances of these statistics on the population coherence. The closer $\text{Coh}(\lambda)$ is to unity at a particular frequency, the smaller the variance of the corresponding sample statistics. On the other hand when the coherence is small, the estimated gain, phase and coherence may all be unreliable. This may not be surprising once it is realised that the sample coherence can be interpreted as a measure of the 'correlation' between the two series at different frequencies.

7.3 Vector Autoregressive-Moving Average Processes

An indeterministic vector process, $\mathbf{y}_t$, can always be written as a vector MA process of infinite order, that is

$$\mathbf{y}_t = \sum_{j=0}^{\infty} \mathbf{\Psi}_j \boldsymbol{\varepsilon}_{t-j} \tag{3.1}$$

where $\mathbf{\Psi}_j$ is an $N \times N$ matrix of parameters, $\boldsymbol{\psi}_0 = \mathbf{I}$, and $\boldsymbol{\varepsilon}_t$ is an $N \times 1$ vector of white noise variables with mean zero. The properties of $\boldsymbol{\varepsilon}_t$, which is sometimes known as a *multivariate white noise process*, may be summarised as follows:

$$E(\boldsymbol{\varepsilon}_t) = \mathbf{0}$$

and

$$E(\boldsymbol{\varepsilon}_t \boldsymbol{\varepsilon}_s') = \begin{cases} \mathbf{\Omega}, & t = s \\ \mathbf{0}, & t \neq s \end{cases} \tag{3.2}$$

where $\mathbf{\Omega}$ is an $N \times N$ covariance matrix. Thus the elements of $\boldsymbol{\varepsilon}_t$ may be contemporaneously correlated.

The moving average representation in (3.1) is a direct generalisation of (2.1.23). As in the univariate case, $\mathbf{y}_t$ may be modelled parsimoniously by a mixed process of the form

$$\mathbf{y}_t = \mathbf{\Phi}_1 \mathbf{y}_{t-1} + \cdots + \mathbf{\Phi}_p \mathbf{y}_{t-p} + \boldsymbol{\varepsilon}_t + \mathbf{\Theta}_1 \boldsymbol{\varepsilon}_{t-1} + \cdots + \mathbf{\Theta}_q \boldsymbol{\varepsilon}_{t-q} \tag{3.3}$$

where $\mathbf{\Phi}_i$'s are $N \times N$ matrices of AR parameters and the $\mathbf{\Theta}_j$'s are $N \times N$ matrices of MA parameters. This model is known as a multivariate, or vector, ARMA(p, q) process. Purely autoregressive processes are known as *vector autoregressions*, and denoted VAR(p).

Autocovariance and Autocorrelation Functions

The time domain properties of vector ARMA processes may be derived using similar techniques to those employed for univariate processes. The vector MA(1) process,

$$\mathbf{y}_t = \boldsymbol{\varepsilon}_t + \mathbf{\Theta} \boldsymbol{\varepsilon}_{t-1} \tag{3.4}$$

is stationary, irrespective of the values of the parameters in $\boldsymbol{\Theta}$. Since $E(\mathbf{y}_t) = \mathbf{0}$, the covariance matrix of $\mathbf{y}_t$ is

$$\boldsymbol{\Gamma}(0) = E(\mathbf{y}_t \mathbf{y}_t') = \boldsymbol{\Omega} + \boldsymbol{\Theta}\boldsymbol{\Omega}\boldsymbol{\Theta}' \tag{3.5}$$

while the autocovariance matrices are given by

$$\boldsymbol{\Gamma}(\tau) = E(\mathbf{y}_t \mathbf{y}_{t-\tau}') = \begin{cases} \boldsymbol{\Theta}\boldsymbol{\Omega}, & \tau = 1 \\ \boldsymbol{\Omega}\boldsymbol{\Theta}', & \tau = -1 \\ \mathbf{0}, & |\tau| \geqslant 2 \end{cases} \tag{3.6}$$

Note that $\boldsymbol{\Gamma}'(-1) = \boldsymbol{\Gamma}(1)$, but that there is an abrupt cut-off for $|\tau| \geqslant 2$. This behaviour exactly parallels that in the univariate MA(1) process.

The conditions under which the first-order vector autoregressive process,

$$\mathbf{y}_t = \boldsymbol{\Phi}\mathbf{y}_{t-1} + \boldsymbol{\varepsilon}_t \tag{3.7}$$

is stationary are derived in the next sub-section. Given that these conditions are satisfied, the autocovariance matrices may be derived by post-multiplying $\mathbf{y}_t$ by $\mathbf{y}_{t-\tau}$ and taking expectations. Thus

$$E(\mathbf{y}_t \mathbf{y}_{t-\tau}') = \boldsymbol{\Phi} E(\mathbf{y}_{t-1} \mathbf{y}_{t-\tau}') + E(\boldsymbol{\varepsilon}_t \mathbf{y}_{t-\tau}') \tag{3.8}$$

For $\tau \geqslant 1$, the last term is a matrix of zeros, and so

$$\boldsymbol{\Gamma}(\tau) = \boldsymbol{\Phi}\boldsymbol{\Gamma}(\tau - 1), \qquad \tau \geqslant 1 \tag{3.9}$$

This is a vector difference equation with a solution corresponding to (2.2.29), namely

$$\boldsymbol{\Gamma}(\tau) = \boldsymbol{\Phi}^\tau \boldsymbol{\Gamma}(0), \qquad \tau \geqslant 0 \tag{3.10}$$

When $\tau = 0$, the last term in (3.8) is given by

$$E[\boldsymbol{\varepsilon}_t(\boldsymbol{\Phi}\mathbf{y}_{t-1} + \boldsymbol{\varepsilon}_t)'] = E(\boldsymbol{\varepsilon}_t \boldsymbol{\varepsilon}_t') = \boldsymbol{\Omega}$$

Furthermore, in view of (1.3) and (3.10), the first term on the right hand side of (3.8) becomes

$$\boldsymbol{\Phi}\boldsymbol{\Gamma}(-1) = \boldsymbol{\Phi}\boldsymbol{\Gamma}'(1) = \boldsymbol{\Phi}\boldsymbol{\Gamma}(0)\boldsymbol{\Phi}'$$

and so

$$\boldsymbol{\Gamma}(0) = \boldsymbol{\Phi}\boldsymbol{\Gamma}(0)\boldsymbol{\Phi}' + \boldsymbol{\Omega} \tag{3.11}$$

There are a number of ways of solving these equations in order to evaluate $\boldsymbol{\Gamma}(0)$. One possibility is to adopt an iterative procedure in which successive approximations are computed using an initial guess for $\boldsymbol{\Gamma}(0)$. Alternatively, a direct solution can be obtained from the identity

$$\text{vec}\{\boldsymbol{\Gamma}(0)\} = [\mathbf{I} - \boldsymbol{\Phi} \otimes \boldsymbol{\Phi}]^{-1} \text{vec}\{\boldsymbol{\Omega}\} \tag{3.12}$$

The symbol $\otimes$ denotes a Kronecker product while the vec($\cdot$) operator indicates that the columns of an $n \times m$ matrix are being stacked, one on top of the other, to form a vector of length nm.

Finally it is worth noting that in the model defined by (1.7) and (1.9), $(y_t\ x_t)'$ is a vector AR(1) process with

$$\mathbf{\Phi} = \begin{bmatrix} 0 & \beta \\ 0 & \phi \end{bmatrix}$$

Although the variances and cross-variances can be derived directly in this case, obtaining them from the general formulae above is a useful exercise.

Stationarity and Invertibility for Multivariate Autoregressive-Moving Average Processes

Repeatedly substituting for lagged values of y_t in the vector AR(1) process, (3.7) gives

$$\mathbf{y}_t = \sum_{j=0}^{J-1} \mathbf{\Phi}^j \varepsilon_{t-j} + \mathbf{\Phi}^J \mathbf{y}_{t-J} \qquad (3.13)$$

By analogy with the argument set out for the univariate case, $\mathbf{y}_t$ ceases to depend on $\mathbf{y}_{t-J}$ if the elements of $\mathbf{\Phi}^J$ tend to zero as J becomes large. In order to determine the conditions under which this holds, we will attempt to diagonalise the matrix $\mathbf{\Phi}$, by trying to find a non-singular $N \times N$ matrix, $\mathbf{Q}$, such that

$$\mathbf{\Phi} = \mathbf{Q}\mathbf{\Lambda}\mathbf{Q}^{-1} \qquad (3.14)$$

where $\mathbf{\Lambda} = \text{diag}\{\lambda_1, \ldots, \lambda_N\}$. The elements $\lambda_1, \ldots, \lambda_N$ are obtained by solving the *determinantal equation*

$$|\mathbf{\Phi} - \lambda\mathbf{I}| = 0 \qquad (3.15)$$

Thus if $N = 2$ and ϕ_{ij} is the ijth element in $\mathbf{\Phi}$, the determinantal equation is

$$\begin{vmatrix} \phi_{11} - \lambda & \phi_{12} \\ \phi_{21} & \phi_{22} - \lambda \end{vmatrix} = 0 \qquad (3.16)$$

and the two roots are obtained by solving the quadratic

$$\lambda^2 - (\phi_{11} + \phi_{22})\lambda + (\phi_{11}\phi_{22} - \phi_{12}\phi_{21}) = 0 \qquad (3.17)$$

The roots may be real or a pair of complex conjugates.

The diagonalisation implied by (3.14) is only possible if all N roots are distinct. Assuming this to be the case,

$$\mathbf{\Phi}^J = \mathbf{Q}\mathbf{\Lambda}\mathbf{Q}^{-1} \cdot \mathbf{Q}\mathbf{\Lambda}\mathbf{Q}^{-1} \cdots \mathbf{Q}\mathbf{\Lambda}\mathbf{Q}^{-1} = \mathbf{Q}\mathbf{\Lambda}^J\mathbf{Q}^{-1}$$

Since $\mathbf{Q}$ is independent of J while $\boldsymbol{\Lambda}^J = \mathrm{diag}(\lambda_1^J, \ldots, \lambda_N^J)$, it follows that

$$\lim_{J \to \infty} \boldsymbol{\Phi}^J = \lim_{J \to \infty} \mathbf{Q}\boldsymbol{\Lambda}^J\mathbf{Q}^{-1} = \mathbf{0} \tag{3.18}$$

provided that the roots of the determinantal equation are less than one in absolute value. Thus the condition

$$|\lambda_i| < 1, \qquad i = 1, \ldots, N \tag{3.19}$$

is necessary for (3.7) to be stationary.

This result generalises to a process with a pth-order autoregressive component. The model can be shown to be stationary if the roots of

$$|\lambda^p\mathbf{I} - \lambda^{p-1}\boldsymbol{\Phi}_1 - \cdots - \boldsymbol{\Phi}_p| = 0 \tag{3.20a}$$

are less than one in absolute value. Similarly, it is invertible if the roots of

$$|\lambda^q\mathbf{I} + \lambda^{q-1}\boldsymbol{\Theta}_1 + \cdots + \boldsymbol{\Theta}_q| = 0 \tag{3.20b}$$

are less than one in absolute value.

The lag operator representation of (3.3) is

$$\boldsymbol{\Phi}_p(L)\mathbf{y}_t = \boldsymbol{\Theta}_q(L)\boldsymbol{\varepsilon}_t \tag{3.21}$$

where

$$\boldsymbol{\Phi}_p(L) = \mathbf{I} - \boldsymbol{\Phi}_1 L - \cdots - \boldsymbol{\Phi}_p L^p \tag{3.22a}$$

and

$$\boldsymbol{\Theta}_q(L) = \mathbf{I} + \boldsymbol{\Theta}_1 L + \cdots + \boldsymbol{\Theta}_q L^q \tag{3.22b}$$

The stationarity and invertibility conditions may be expressed in terms of the *determinantal polynomials*, $|\boldsymbol{\Phi}_p(L)|$ and $|\boldsymbol{\Theta}_q(L)|$, although the conditions must now be stated in terms of roots lying *outside* the unit circle, just as in the univariate case.

Identifiability

In section 2.4 attention was drawn to the implications of common factors for the identifiability of univariate ARMA models. Similar considerations arise in multivariate models, although the whole issue is much more complex. Indeed it is even possible to have identifiability problems with a pure autoregression or moving average, as the following example shows.

Example 1   The VAR(1) model

$$\begin{aligned} y_{1t} &= \phi y_{2,t-1} + \varepsilon_{1t} \\ y_{2t} &= \phantom{\phi y_{2,t-1} + {}} \varepsilon_{2t} \end{aligned} \tag{3.23}$$

can be written as a vector MA(1) simply by substituting for $y_{2,t-1}$ in the first equation so that

$$y_{1t} = \varepsilon_{1t} + \phi\varepsilon_{2,t-1}$$
$$y_{2t} = \varepsilon_{2t}$$

$$(3.24)$$

The full identifiability conditions are complicated. However, a sufficient condition is that

$$\text{rank}[\boldsymbol{\Phi}_p \; \boldsymbol{\Theta}_q] = N \qquad (3.25)$$

This is easy to understand, but it can only be checked in advance if there is prior knowledge concerning $\boldsymbol{\Phi}_p$ and $\boldsymbol{\Theta}_q$. Such knowledge is unlikely to be available. This suggests that standard multivariate ARMA models are not an ideal class. An alternative approach is based on what is known as the *echelon form*. A detailed study of this and other forms, together with a full treatment of the identifiability issue, can be found in Hannan and Deistler (1988). A good introduction is in Lütkepohl (1991, chapters 7 and 8).

Prediction

Prediction for a vector ARMA model may be carried out by the same mechanism as in the univariate case. The recursion in (2.6.4) generalises directly simply by replacing scalars by the corresponding vectors and matrices. Covariance matrices for the prediction errors can be computed from the matrices in the MA representation.

Example 2   In the VAR(1) model the *l*-step ahead predictor is

$$\tilde{\mathbf{y}}_{T+l|T} = \boldsymbol{\Phi}^l\mathbf{y}_T, \qquad l = 1, 2, \ldots \qquad (3.26)$$

and since

$$\mathbf{y}_{T+l} = \boldsymbol{\Phi}^l\mathbf{y}_T + \sum_{j=0}^{l-1} \boldsymbol{\Phi}^j\boldsymbol{\varepsilon}_{T+l-j}, \qquad l = 1, 2, \ldots \qquad (3.27)$$

the MSE of $\tilde{\mathbf{y}}_{T+l|T}$ is

$$\text{MSE}(\tilde{\mathbf{y}}_{T+l|T}) = \sum_{j=0}^{l-1} \boldsymbol{\Phi}^j\boldsymbol{\Sigma}\boldsymbol{\Phi}'^j \qquad (3.28)$$

Estimating $\boldsymbol{\Phi}$ introduces a term of $0(T^{-1})$ into this expression; see Baillie (1979).

Multivariate and Univariate Models

Any stationary vector ARMA process may be written in the form (3.1) by inverting the matrix polynomial $\boldsymbol{\Phi}(L)$. This yields

$$\mathbf{y}_t = \boldsymbol{\Phi}^{-1}(L)\boldsymbol{\Theta}(L)\boldsymbol{\varepsilon}_t \qquad (3.29)$$

The power series expansion of $\mathbf{\Phi}^{-1}(L)$ is

$$\mathbf{\Phi}^{-1}(L) = \mathbf{\Phi}^{\dagger}(L)/|\mathbf{\Phi}(L)| \qquad (3.30)$$

where $\mathbf{\Phi}^{\dagger}(L)$ is the adjoint matrix of $\mathbf{\Phi}(L)$. Substituting into (3.29) and re-arranging gives the *autoregressive final form*,

$$|\mathbf{\Phi}(L)|\mathbf{y}_t = \mathbf{\Phi}^{\dagger}(L)\mathbf{\Theta}(L)\mathbf{\varepsilon}_t \qquad (3.31)$$

The right hand side of each of the N equations in (3.31) consists of a linear combination of MA processes each of order $p + q$. However, each of these linear combinations can be expressed as an MA process of order $(N - 1)p + q$; see section 2.5. Thus the equations in (3.31) can be written as

$$\phi_i^*(L)y_{it} = \theta_i^*(L)\eta_{it}, \qquad i = 1, \dots, N \qquad (3.32)$$

where η_{it} is white noise, $\theta_i^*(L)$ is an MA polynomial in the lag operator of order $p + q$ and $\phi_i^*(L) = |\mathbf{\Phi}(L)|$ is an AR polynomial of order Np.

The implication of this result is that each variable in $\mathbf{y}_t$ can be modelled as a univariate ARMA process. However, if the variables are considered together, (3.32) also implies that the disturbances in the different ARMA models will be correlated and the autoregressive components will be identical. In practice, though, common AR components may not be observed because of common factors in $\phi_i^*(L)$ and $\theta_i^*(L)$ in some equations.

7.4 Estimation

The methods available for estimating multivariate ARMA models of the form (3.3) are basically generalisations of the procedures developed in the univariate case. Exact ML estimation may, in principle, be carried out. However, the extra parameters introduced to link the series together pose more complex computational problems. Fortunately the generalisation of the CSS procedure is straightforward. The multivariate Gauss–Newton algorithm may be employed, and, as for univariate models, the efficiency of this approach is considerably enhanced by the fact that analytic derivatives are relatively easy to compute.

The discussion below will be confined to the vector AR(1) and MA(1) models. The first of these models is important insofar as it is the simplest multivariate process from the point of view of estimation. Once this model can be handled, the extension to higher order autoregressive processes is relatively straightforward. Similarly, the vector MA(1) process illustrates most of the difficulties involved in estimating the general multivariate ARMA(p, q) process.

Estimation of the Vector AR(1) Process

Because of its relative simplicity the first-order vector autoregressive process

$$\mathbf{y}_t = \mathbf{\Phi}\mathbf{y}_{t-1} + \mathbf{\varepsilon}_t, \qquad t = 1, \dots, T \qquad (4.1)$$

has received considerable attention, particularly in the econometric literature. However, it still contains a large number of unknown parameters. The autoregressive matrix, $\mathbf{\Phi}$, contains N^2 parameters, while the symmetric covariance matrix, $\mathbf{\Omega}$, contributes a further $N(N+1)/2$ distinct terms.

The likelihood function for (4.1) may be derived exactly as in the scalar case. Given the vector $\mathbf{y}_{t-1}$, the distribution of $\mathbf{y}_t$ is multivariate normal with a mean of $\mathbf{\Phi}\mathbf{y}_{t-1}$ and a covariance matrix $\mathbf{\Omega}$, and so

$$\log L(\mathbf{y}_T, \mathbf{y}_{T-1}, \ldots, \mathbf{y}_2 | \mathbf{y}_1) = -\frac{N(T-1)}{2} \log 2\pi$$

$$-\frac{1}{2}(T-1)\log|\mathbf{\Omega}|$$

$$-\frac{1}{2}\sum_{t=2}^{T}(\mathbf{y}_t - \mathbf{\Phi}\mathbf{y}_{t-1})'\mathbf{\Omega}^{-1}(\mathbf{y}_t - \mathbf{\Phi}\mathbf{y}_{t-1})$$

$$(4.2)$$

This is the log–likelihood function conditional on the first observation, $\mathbf{y}_1$. The full log–likelihood function is obtained by taking account of the unconditional distribution of $\mathbf{y}_1$. This is multivariate normal with a mean of zero and a covariance matrix, $\mathbf{\Sigma}$, which, from (3.11), is given by

$$\mathbf{\Sigma} = \mathbf{\Phi}\mathbf{\Sigma}\mathbf{\Phi}' + \mathbf{\Omega} \qquad (4.3)$$

Combining the distribution of $\mathbf{y}_1$ with (4.2) yields the full log–likelihood function:

$$\log L(\mathbf{y}_T, \ldots, \mathbf{y}_1) = -\frac{NT}{2}\log 2\pi - \frac{1}{2}\log|\mathbf{\Sigma}| - \frac{(T-1)}{2}\log|\mathbf{\Omega}|$$

$$-\frac{1}{2}\sum_{t=2}^{T}(\mathbf{y}_t - \mathbf{\Phi}\mathbf{y}_{t-1})'\mathbf{\Omega}^{-1}(\mathbf{y}_t - \mathbf{\Phi}\mathbf{y}_{t-1})$$

$$-\frac{1}{2}\mathbf{y}_1'\mathbf{\Sigma}^{-1}\mathbf{y}_1 \qquad (4.4)$$

The maximisation of (4.4) with respect to $\mathbf{\Omega}$ and $\mathbf{\Phi}$ may be carried out by a general numerical optimisation routine. However, it is considerably easier to treat $\mathbf{y}_1$ as fixed, and work with the conditional log–likelihood function, (4.2). Given $\mathbf{\Omega}$, the ML estimator of $\mathbf{\Phi}$ is then obtained by minimising

$$S(\mathbf{\Phi}) = \sum_{t=2}^{T}(\mathbf{y}_t - \mathbf{\Phi}\mathbf{y}_{t-1})'\mathbf{\Omega}^{-1}(\mathbf{y}_t - \mathbf{\Phi}\mathbf{y}_{t-1}) \qquad (4.5)$$

This is precisely the criterion function which is minimised by the multivariate least squares estimator; see EATS, section 2.10. In other words, the ML estimator of $\mathbf{\Phi}$ does not depend on $\mathbf{\Omega}$, the ith row in $\tilde{\mathbf{\Phi}}$ being given by a straightforward OLS regression of the ith element in $\mathbf{y}_t$ on the vector $\mathbf{y}_{t-1}$, i.e.

$$\tilde{\mathbf{\Phi}}' = \left[\sum_{t=2}^{T} \mathbf{y}_{t-1} \mathbf{y}_{t-1}' \right]^{-1} \sum_{t=2}^{T} \mathbf{y}_{t-1} \mathbf{y}_t' \tag{4.6}$$

The ML estimator of $\mathbf{\Omega}$ may be calculated directly from the residuals, $\mathbf{e}_t = \mathbf{y}_t - \tilde{\mathbf{\Phi}} \mathbf{y}_{t-1}$, $t = 2, \ldots, T$. Thus

$$\tilde{\mathbf{\Omega}} = T^{-1} \sum_{t=2}^{T} \mathbf{e}_t \mathbf{e}_t' \tag{4.7}$$

Asymptotic Distribution of the ML Estimator and Associated Test Statistics

Let $\phi = \text{vec}(\mathbf{\Phi}')$. The ML estimator of ϕ is then asymptotically normally distributed with mean ϕ and covariance matrix

$$\text{Avar}(\tilde{\phi}) = T^{-1}(\mathbf{\Omega} \otimes \mathbf{\Sigma}^{-1}) \tag{4.8}$$

The easiest way to estimate $\mathbf{\Sigma}$ is from the formula

$$\hat{\mathbf{\Sigma}} = T^{-1} \sum_{t=2}^{T} \mathbf{y}_t \mathbf{y}_t' \tag{4.9}$$

Tests of hypotheses concerning $\mathbf{\Phi}$ may be carried out using the Wald principle. The statistic for testing $H_0: = \mathbf{0}$ against $H_1: \mathbf{\Phi} \neq \mathbf{0}$ is

$$W = \tilde{\phi}' [\text{Avar}(\tilde{\phi})]^{-1} \tilde{\phi} \tag{4.10}$$

When H_0 is true, W has a χ^2 distribution with N^2 degrees of freedom in large samples.

An alternative approach to testing hypotheses is to use the LR statistic. For a test of $\mathbf{\Phi} = \mathbf{0}$,

$$\text{LR} = T \log(|\hat{\mathbf{\Sigma}}|/|\tilde{\mathbf{\Omega}}|) \tag{4.11}$$

Wald and LR statistics may also be used to test whether $\mathbf{\Phi}$ is diagonal. In fact it may be useful first to test $\mathbf{\Phi}$ for diagonality and, if this hypothesis is not rejected, then to test whether the diagonal elements are zero. These hypotheses are nested, and so if W_1 is the Wald statistic for testing the diagonality of $\mathbf{\Phi}$, and W is the test statistic (7.11), W_1 and $W - W_1$ are asymptotically distributed as independent χ^2 variates with $N(N-1)$ and N degrees of freedom respectively; see EATS, section 5.8. Note that if $\mathbf{\Phi}$ is taken to be diagonal, the ML estimates of $\mathbf{\Phi}$ will no longer be independent of $\mathbf{\Omega}$, and so a sequence of Wald tests involves less computation than a corresponding sequence of LR tests.

The Vector MA(1) Process

The vector $MA(1)$ was defined in (3.4). If $\varepsilon_t \sim NID(0, \Omega)$ and $\varepsilon_0 = 0$, the log–likelihood function is of the form

$$\log L = -\frac{TN}{2} \log 2\pi - \frac{T}{2} \log|\Omega| - \frac{1}{2} \sum_{t=1}^{T} \varepsilon_t' \Omega^{-1} \varepsilon_t \qquad (4.12)$$

The ε_t's may be obtained from the recursion

$$\varepsilon_t = \mathbf{y}_t - \mathbf{\Theta}\varepsilon_{t-1}, \qquad t = 1, \ldots, T \qquad (4.13)$$

while Ω is estimated by a formula analogous to (4.7). The likelihood function may be maximised with respect to $\mathbf{\Theta}$ by the multivariate Gauss–Newton algorithm; see Tunnicliffe-Wilson (1973). Let $\hat{\boldsymbol{\theta}}$ be an initial estimator of the $N^2 \times 1$ vector $\boldsymbol{\theta} = \text{vec}(\mathbf{\Theta}')$. For a given value of Ω, this may be updated by

$$\boldsymbol{\theta}^* = \hat{\boldsymbol{\theta}} + \left[\sum_{t=1}^{T} \mathbf{Z}_t \Omega^{-1} \mathbf{Z}_t' \right]^{-1} \sum_{t=1}^{T} \mathbf{Z}_t \Omega^{-1} \varepsilon_t \qquad (4.14)$$

where $\mathbf{Z}_t$ is the $N^2 \times N$ matrix of derivatives defined by $\mathbf{Z}_t = -\partial \varepsilon_t'/\partial \boldsymbol{\theta}$. This is repeated until convergence with the estimate of Ω updated after each iteration.

The derivatives may be calculated recursively just as in the univariate case. The residual recursion in (4.13) may be written as

$$\varepsilon_t = \mathbf{y}_t - \mathbf{\Theta}\varepsilon_{t-1} = \mathbf{y}_t - [\mathbf{I} \otimes \varepsilon_{t-1}']\boldsymbol{\theta}, \qquad t = 1, \ldots, T \qquad (4.15)$$

and so

$$\mathbf{Z}_t' = [\mathbf{I} \otimes \varepsilon_{t-1}'] + \mathbf{\Theta}\mathbf{Z}_{t-1}', \qquad t = 1, \ldots, T \qquad (4.16)$$

with $\mathbf{Z}_0 = \mathbf{0}$.

An estimator of the asymptotic covariance matrix of the ML estimator is given automatically by the multivariate Gauss–Newton algorithm. This is

$$\text{avar}(\tilde{\boldsymbol{\theta}}) = \left[\sum_{t=1}^{T} \mathbf{Z}_t \tilde{\Omega}^{-1} \mathbf{Z}_t' \right]^{-1} \qquad (4.17)$$

all the elements in $\mathbf{Z}_t$ being evaluated at $\boldsymbol{\theta} = \tilde{\boldsymbol{\theta}}$. Hence Wald tests can be carried out just as in the vector $AR(1)$ model.

Seemingly Unrelated ARMA Processes*

Specifying diagonal coefficient matrices and employing a two-step estimation procedure leads to considerable simplification for MA and mixed processes. Consistent estimates of the ARMA parameters may be obtained by treating each of the N processes separately, while an estimate of Ω may be constructed from the residuals. One iteration of the multivariate Gauss–Newton scheme yields an asymptotically efficient estimator of the full set of ARMA parameters. This estimator has the form of a feasible GLS estimator in a system of seemingly unrelated regression equations.

The Monte Carlo experiments reported in Nelson (1976) examine the small sample gains which can be expected by treating individual ARMA processes as a system. For a vector $AR(1)$ process with $N = 2$,

$$\begin{bmatrix} y_{1t} \\ y_{2t} \end{bmatrix} = \begin{bmatrix} \phi_1 & 0 \\ 0 & \phi_2 \end{bmatrix} \begin{bmatrix} y_{1,t-1} \\ y_{2,t-1} \end{bmatrix} + \begin{bmatrix} \varepsilon_{1t} \\ \varepsilon_{2t} \end{bmatrix} \tag{4.18}$$

the relative efficiency of the single series estimator of one of the parameters, say ϕ_1, may be obtained analytically for large samples. If $\hat{\phi}_1$ and $\tilde{\phi}_1$ denote the single series and joint ML estimators respectively, and ρ is the correlation between ε_{1t} and ε_{2t}, the relative efficiency of $\hat{\phi}_1$ is

$$\mathrm{Eff}(\hat{\phi}_1) = \frac{\mathrm{Avar}(\tilde{\phi}_1)}{\mathrm{Avar}(\hat{\phi}_1)} = (1 - \rho^2)\left[1 - \frac{\rho^4 (1 - \phi_1^2)(1 - \phi_2^2)}{(1 - \phi_1 \phi_2)^2} \right]^{-1} \tag{4.19}$$

For samples of size 30, (4.19) gives a very good guide to the gains in efficiency actually obtained. As might be expected, the higher the correlation between the series, the greater the gain in efficiency from estimating the parameters jointly. Furthermore, on examining (4.19) further it can be seen that significant gains in efficiency are associated with large differences in the parameter values. As $|\phi_1 - \phi_2|$ goes to its maximum of 2, $\mathrm{Eff}(\hat{\phi}_1)$ tends to its minimum value of $1 - \rho^2$.

A similar analysis may be carried out for two $MA(1)$ processes. Again Nelson's results show the gains in efficiency to be approximately as predicted by asymptotic theory, even though the small sample distribution of the MA parameters is much more dispersed than asymptotic theory would suggest.

7.5 Multivariate ARIMA Modelling

While many of the techniques applicable to univariate model building can be extended straightforwardly to the multivariate case, a number of additional problems do arise. In particular, model specification becomes much more complex. Rather than attempting to give a definitive summary of multivariate model building, this section will focus on a particular application, and the various aspects of the problem will be discussed as they arise.

The study chosen is by Chan and Wallis (1978). The data relate to the number of skins of mink and muskrat traded annually by the Hudson Bay Company in Canada from 1848 to 1909. The reason a multivariate analysis is called for is that there is known to be a prey–predator relationship between the two species, and this directly affects the population dynamics of both of them.

Identification, Estimation and Diagnostic Checking

A preliminary analysis of the data suggests that the muskrat observations are stationary in first differences, while the mink are stationary in levels. Chan and Wallis argue that differencing each of a pair of series a different number of times distorts the phase relationship between them. Rather than differencing the mink series as well, they carry out a quadratic regression on both series, and analyse the relationship between the residuals.

Letting y_{1t} and y_{2t} denote the detrended muskrat and mink series respectively, Chan and Wallis fit the following univariate models:

(a)
$$(1 - 1.03L + 0.68L^2 - 0.39L^3 + 0.34L^4)y_{1t} = \eta_{1t} \tag{5.1}$$
$$(0.12)\quad(0.17)\quad(0.17)\quad(0.13)$$

$$\tilde{\sigma}_1^2 = 0.0789, \qquad Q(16) = 19.12$$

(b)
$$(1 - 1.36L + 0.67L^2)y_{2t} = (1 - 0.70L)\eta_{2t} \tag{5.2}$$
$$(0.13)\quad(0.09)\qquad\qquad(0.15)$$

$$\tilde{\sigma}_2^2 = 0.0605, \qquad Q(17) = 15.86$$

These models suggest a number of possible specifications for a multivariate process. Although the model chosen for y_{1t} was a pure AR process, the vector ARMA$(2, 1)$ was found to be the most satisfactory formulation on the basis of LR tests. The fitted model is

$$
\begin{bmatrix}
1 - 1.22L + 0.61L^2 & 0 \\
(0.16)\quad(0.12) & \\
& 1 - 1.29L + 0.62L^2 \\
0 & (0.15)\quad(0.13)
\end{bmatrix}
\begin{bmatrix}
y_{1t} \\
y_{2t}
\end{bmatrix}
$$

$$
=
\begin{bmatrix}
1 - 0.15L & -0.83L \\
(0.22) & (0.16) \\
0.37L & 1 - 0.81L \\
(0.14) & (0.14)
\end{bmatrix}
\begin{bmatrix}
\varepsilon_{1t} \\
\varepsilon_{2t}
\end{bmatrix}
\tag{5.3}
$$

with

$$
\tilde{\Omega} =
\begin{bmatrix}
0.061 & 0.022 \\
0.022 & 0.053
\end{bmatrix}, \qquad
Q(30) =
\begin{bmatrix}
28.05 & 18.15 \\
15.73 & 22.45
\end{bmatrix}
$$

Joint estimation reduces the residual variances below those obtained in the separate univariate models. Furthermore, $|\tilde{\Omega}| = 0.00275$, while for the two univariate models $|\tilde{\Omega}_0| = \tilde{\sigma}_1^2 \times \tilde{\sigma}_2^2 = 0.0789 \times 0.0605 = 0.00477$. For the multivariate case, the AIC suggests a comparison based on

$$\text{AIC}^\dagger = |\tilde{\Omega}| \exp(2n/T) \tag{5.4}$$

The multivariate model is clearly superior on this criterion since $n = 11$ and $AIC^\dagger = 0.00397$, while for the univariate models $n = 9$ and $AIC^\dagger = 0.00643$. (Chan and Wallis do not consider the AIC in their analysis.)

The **Q** matrix given in (5.3) is a generalisation of the Box–Pierce statistic, the off-diagonal elements being constructed from residual cross-correlations. A rough indication of goodness of fit is obtained by testing each individual statistic against a χ^2_{P-p-q} distribution. A single 'multivariate portmanteau statistic' has now been proposed by Hosking (1980). This is given by

$$Q(P) = T^2 \sum_{\tau=1}^{P} \text{tr}\{\mathbf{C}(\tau)'\mathbf{C}(0)\mathbf{C}(\tau)\mathbf{C}^{-1}(0)\} \qquad (5.5)$$

where $\mathbf{C}(\tau)$ is the autocovariance matrix computed from the residuals, as in (1.5). For a correctly specified model, $Q(P)$ is asymptotically χ^2 with $N^2(P - p - q)$ degrees of freedom.

The two AR polynomials in (5.3) are very similar, and estimating the model subject to the restriction that they are identical, as implied by (3.31), yields

$$(1 - 1.28L + 0.63L^2)\mathbf{y}_t = \begin{bmatrix} 1 - 0.27L & -0.79L \\ (0.16) & (0.14) \\ \\ 0.34L & 1 - 0.75L \\ (0.11) & (0.12) \end{bmatrix} \begin{bmatrix} \varepsilon_{1t} \\ \\ \varepsilon_{2t} \end{bmatrix} \qquad (5.6)$$
$$(0.13) \quad (0.11)$$

with

$$\tilde{\mathbf{\Omega}} = \begin{bmatrix} 0.061 & 0.023 \\ 0.023 & 0.054 \end{bmatrix}$$

The null hypothesis that the AR operators are the same is not rejected by an LR test.

The relationship between (3.30) and (3.32) suggests that the only vector ARMA process which has as its solution a set of final equations of the form (5.6) is a first-order autoregression. The fitted model is

$$\begin{bmatrix} 1 - 0.79L & 0.68L \\ (0.07) & (0.09) \\ \\ -0.29L & 1 - 0.51L \\ (0.07) & (0.09) \end{bmatrix} \mathbf{y}_t = \mathbf{\varepsilon}_t \qquad (5.7)$$

with

$$\tilde{\mathbf{\Omega}} = \begin{bmatrix} 0.061 & 0.022 \\ 0.022 & 0.058 \end{bmatrix}, \qquad \mathbf{Q}(30) = \begin{bmatrix} 29.11 & 21.02 \\ 18.41 & 26.38 \end{bmatrix}$$

Although $|\tilde{\mathbf{\Omega}}| = 0.00305$, which is greater than the corresponding figure for (5.6), model (5.7) has fewer parameters. The reason for this is that the polynomials $|\mathbf{\Phi}(L)|$ and $\mathbf{\Phi}^\dagger(L)$ are both derived from $\mathbf{\Phi}(L)$, yet the implicit restrictions imposed on their coefficients are not taken account of in estimating (5.6). Thus, two fewer parameters are contained in (5.7) and the AIC† is lower.

It is a useful exercise to derive the final equations corresponding to (5.7). Since

$$\mathbf{\Phi}(L) = \begin{bmatrix} 1 - 0.79L & 0.68L \\ -0.29L & 1 - 0.51L \end{bmatrix} \tag{5.8}$$

the determinantal polynomial is

$$|\mathbf{\Phi}(L)| = (1 - 0.79L)(1 - 0.51L) - (0.68L)(-0.29L)$$
$$= 1 - 1.30L + 0.60L^2 \tag{5.9}$$

This is fairly close to the fitted AR polynomial in (5.6). The adjoint matrix is

$$\mathbf{\Phi}^\dagger(L) = \begin{bmatrix} 1 - 0.51L & -0.68L \\ 0.29L & 1 - 0.79L \end{bmatrix} \tag{5.10}$$

This may be compared directly with the MA matrix in (5.6), since in terms of (3.32), $\mathbf{\Theta}(L) = \mathbf{I}$ in (5.7). The parameters are quite similar.

The Q-statistic in (5.7) appears to be satisfactory, and in addition Chan and Wallis report that the model, despite its simplicity, passes various 'overfitting tests'. They observe that it provides '... a direct account of the interactions of the series, and in doing so captures the essential phenomena noted by biologists'. The off-diagonal coefficients imply that an increase in muskrat is followed by an increase in mink a year later, and an increase in mink is followed by a decrease in muskrat a year later.

Properties of the Models and Predictions

The roots of the AR polynomial in (5.6) are a complex conjugate pair, implying damped oscillations with a period centred around 9.93 years; see formula (6.4.5). Similar oscillations may be expected in (5.7). The best way of examining such stochastic properties is by computing the spectral density matrix. Chan and Wallis report that the spectra of the two series exhibit considerable power at frequencies corresponding to the ten-year cycle, and that the phase diagram indicates that muskrat leads mink by 2–4 years in this frequency range.

For the vector $AR(1)$ model in (5.7), predictions can be computed from the recursion

$$\tilde{\mathbf{y}}_{T+l|T} = \begin{bmatrix} 0.79 & -0.68 \\ 0.29 & 0.51 \end{bmatrix} \tilde{\mathbf{y}}_{T+l-1|T}, \qquad l = 1, 2, \ldots$$

with $\tilde{\mathbf{y}}_{T|T} = \mathbf{y}_T$. Since the process is stationary, $\mathbf{\Phi}^l \to 0$ as $T \to \infty$. The predictions emerge as damped oscillations. Taking $y_{1T} = y_{2T} = 1$,

$$\tilde{\mathbf{y}}_{T+1|T} = \begin{bmatrix} 0.79 - 0.68 \\ 0.29 + 0.51 \end{bmatrix} = \begin{bmatrix} 0.11 \\ 0.80 \end{bmatrix}$$

$$\tilde{\mathbf{y}}_{T+2|T} = \begin{bmatrix} 0.79 \times 0.11 - 0.68 \times 0.80 \\ 0.29 \times 0.11 + 0.51 \times 0.80 \end{bmatrix} = \begin{bmatrix} -0.46 \\ 0.44 \end{bmatrix}$$

and so on.

Exactly the same predictions would be obtained by working with the final equations obtained by solving (5.7). Since this is a vector $ARMA(2, 1)$ process, the predictions for each series are governed by the same difference equations, based on (5.9). This makes it clear exactly why the period of the oscillations in the predictions of the two series is identical.

7.6 Structural Time Series Models

Structural time series generalise to multivariate series in a number of ways. Here attention is focused on two classes of models. In both cases only the generalisation of the random walk plus noise model is considered, since although this model is the simplest, it clearly demonstrates the main issues involved.

Seemingly Unrelated Time Series Equations

Suppose the $N \times 1$ vector $\mathbf{y}_t$ is a set of observations on a cross-section of firms, countries or individuals. The series do not interact with each other in any causal sense, but are subject to the same environment, so their movements are likely to be correlated. These considerations lead to the following multivariate local level model.

$$\mathbf{y}_t = \boldsymbol{\mu}_t + \boldsymbol{\varepsilon}_t \qquad \text{Var}(\boldsymbol{\varepsilon}_t) = \boldsymbol{\Sigma}_\varepsilon \tag{6.1a}$$

$$\boldsymbol{\mu}_t = \boldsymbol{\mu}_{t-1} + \boldsymbol{\eta}_t, \qquad \text{Var}(\boldsymbol{\eta}_t) = \boldsymbol{\Sigma}_\eta \tag{6.1b}$$

where $\boldsymbol{\mu}_t$ is an $N \times 1$ vector of level components, and $\boldsymbol{\varepsilon}_t$ and $\boldsymbol{\eta}_t$ are $N \times 1$ vectors of multivariate white noise disturbances which are uncorrelated with each other in all time periods. The permanent movements in the series are linked by the off-diagonal elements in the covariance matrix Σ_η, while the correlation between short-term movements depends on the off-diagonal elements in Σ_ε. If these matrices are both diagonal, the model reduces to N univariate local level models.

The model in (6.1) may be regarded as analogous to the seemingly unrelated regression equation (SURE) model proposed by Zellner (1963). Hence it is appropriate to refer to it as a system of *seemingly unrelated time series equations* – a SUTSE model.

The time domain properties of (6.1) are obtained by differencing to give the stationary process

$$\Delta \mathbf{y}_t = \boldsymbol{\eta}_t + \boldsymbol{\varepsilon}_t - \boldsymbol{\varepsilon}_{t-1} \tag{6.2}$$

The autocovariance matrices are then:

$$\boldsymbol{\Gamma}(0) = \boldsymbol{\Sigma}_\eta + 2\boldsymbol{\Sigma}_\varepsilon$$

$$\boldsymbol{\Gamma}(1) = \boldsymbol{\Gamma}'(-1) = -\boldsymbol{\Sigma}_\varepsilon \tag{6.3}$$

$$\boldsymbol{\Gamma}(\tau) = \mathbf{0}, \qquad \tau \geqslant 2$$

The symmetry of the autocovariance matrices arises because the covariance matrix Σ_ε is symmetric.

The form of the ACF in (6.3) suggests that the reduced form of the model is a vector $\mathrm{ARIMA}(0, 1, 1)$ process

$$\Delta \mathbf{y}_t = \boldsymbol{\xi}_t + \boldsymbol{\Theta}\boldsymbol{\xi}_{t-1} \tag{6.4}$$

For a univariate model, it was shown in (5.3.15) that only negative values of the MA parameter are admissible in the reduced form. In the multivariate case, the structural form in (6.1) not only restricts the parameter space of $\boldsymbol{\Theta}$, it also reduces the number of free parameters. Each of the matrices, $\boldsymbol{\Sigma}_\eta$ and $\boldsymbol{\Sigma}_\varepsilon$, contains $N(N+1)/2$ parameters, making a total of $N(N+1)$, as against a total of $N^2 + N(N+1)/2$ in the unrestricted form of (6.4).

Estimation

ML estimation of (6.1) can be carried out straightforwardly in the time domain by means of the Kalman filter. The model goes into state space form in the same way as its univariate counterpart, initial values are formed from $\mathbf{y}_1$, and the likelihood is formed from the prediction error decomposition (4.3.8). Numerical optimisation can be carried out with respect to the lower triangular matrices $\boldsymbol{\Sigma}_\eta^*$ and $\boldsymbol{\Sigma}_\varepsilon^*$ defined such that $\boldsymbol{\Sigma}_\eta^{*\prime}\boldsymbol{\Sigma}_\eta^* = \boldsymbol{\Sigma}_\eta$ and $\boldsymbol{\Sigma}_\varepsilon^{*\prime}\boldsymbol{\Sigma}_\varepsilon^* = \boldsymbol{\Sigma}_\varepsilon$. This ensures that the estimates of $\boldsymbol{\Sigma}_\eta$ and $\boldsymbol{\Sigma}_\varepsilon$ are positive semi-definite.

When $\boldsymbol{\Sigma}_\eta$ and $\boldsymbol{\Sigma}_\varepsilon$ are proportional so that $\boldsymbol{\Sigma}_\eta = q\boldsymbol{\Sigma}_\varepsilon$, where q is a non-negative scalar, the model is said to be *homogeneous*. In this case all the series have the same signal–noise ratio, q, and hence the same ACF for the first differences. Estimation is simplified considerably, since the likelihood function can be constructed by applying the same univariate filter to each individual series. Furthermore Σ_ε can be concentrated out of the likelihood function, so numerical optimisation is carried out only with respect to the single parameter, q.

As regards estimation in the frequency domain, the log–likelihood function for a circular stationary multivariate process is given by the generalisation of (6.8.1)

$$\log L = -\frac{NT}{2} \log 2\pi - \frac{1}{2} \sum_{j=0}^{T-1} \log|\mathbf{G}_j| - \pi \operatorname{tr} \sum_{j=0}^{T-1} \mathbf{G}_j^{-1} \mathbf{I}(\lambda_j) \quad (6.5)$$

where $\operatorname{tr}(\cdot)$ denotes the *trace* of a matrix, $\mathbf{G}(\lambda)$ is the multivariate spectral generating function (SGF) such that $\mathbf{G}(\lambda) = 2\pi\mathbf{F}(\lambda)$, and $\mathbf{I}(\lambda_j)$ is the multivariate sample spectrum,

$$\mathbf{I}(\lambda_j) = \frac{1}{2\pi} \sum_{-(T-1)}^{T-1} \mathbf{C}(\tau)\, e^{-i\lambda\tau} \quad (6.6)$$

The symmetry of the autocovariance function means that $\mathbf{G}(\lambda)$ is real and symmetric around $\lambda = 0$, being given by

$$\mathbf{G}(\lambda) = \Sigma_\eta + 2(1 - \cos \lambda)\Sigma_\varepsilon$$

Thus only the real part of $\mathbf{I}(\lambda_j)$ need be computed.

For a homogeneous model

$$\mathbf{G}(\lambda) = [q + 2(1 - \cos \lambda)]\Sigma_\varepsilon$$

As in the time domain, ML estimation is simplified considerably with Σ_ε being concentrated out of the likelihood function. Furthermore, a Lagrange multiplier test of the null hypothesis of homogeneity can be constructed quite easily; see Fernandez (1990) and FSK, sections 8.2 and 8.3.

Dynamic Factor Models

The principal feature of a structural time series model is that it is formulated in terms of components which have distinctive dynamic properties. A natural generalisation of the SUTSE class of models is therefore to allow them to have certain of their components in common. Just as prior considerations may help in formulating a model in terms of components, so they may help in deciding which components may be candidates for common factors. The fact that some of these components may be non-stationary does not pose any difficulties. In fact it is an asset. The more different are the properties of components, the more easy they are to distinguish.

Consider the random walk plus noise SUTSE model, (6.1). Common factors may be introduced by the modification

$$\mathbf{y}_t = \mathbf{\Theta}\boldsymbol{\mu}_t + \boldsymbol{\mu}^* + \boldsymbol{\varepsilon}_t, \qquad \text{Var}(\boldsymbol{\varepsilon}_t) = \boldsymbol{\Sigma}_\varepsilon \qquad (6.7a)$$

$$\boldsymbol{\mu}_t = \boldsymbol{\mu}_{t-1} + \boldsymbol{\eta}_t, \qquad \text{Var}(\boldsymbol{\eta}_t) = \boldsymbol{\Sigma}_\eta \qquad (6.7b)$$

where $\boldsymbol{\mu}_t$ is a $K \times 1$ vector of *common trends*, $\mathbf{\Theta}$ is an $N \times K$ matrix of factor loadings and $0 \leqslant K \leqslant N$. The covariance matrices $\boldsymbol{\Sigma}_\varepsilon$ and $\boldsymbol{\Sigma}_\eta$ are $N \times N$ and $K \times K$ respectively and are PD, while $\boldsymbol{\mu}^*$ is an $N \times 1$ vector which has zeros for its first K elements while its last $N - K$ elements consist of an unconstrained vector $\bar{\boldsymbol{\mu}}$.

As it stands, (6.7) is not identifiable. For any non-singular $K \times K$ matrix $\mathbf{H}$, the matrix of factor loadings and the trend component could be redefined as $\mathbf{\Theta}^\dagger = \mathbf{\Theta}\mathbf{H}^{-1}$ and $\boldsymbol{\mu}_t^\dagger = \mathbf{H}\boldsymbol{\mu}_t$ respectively, and so

$$\mathbf{y}_t = \mathbf{\Theta}^\dagger \boldsymbol{\mu}_t^\dagger + \boldsymbol{\mu}^* + \boldsymbol{\varepsilon}_t \qquad (6.8a)$$

$$\boldsymbol{\mu}_t^\dagger = \boldsymbol{\mu}_{t-1}^\dagger + \boldsymbol{\eta}_t^\dagger \qquad (6.8b)$$

where $\boldsymbol{\eta}_t^\dagger = \mathbf{H}\boldsymbol{\eta}_t$ and $\text{Var}(\boldsymbol{\eta}_t^\dagger) = \mathbf{H}\boldsymbol{\Sigma}_\eta\mathbf{H}'$. This model is indistinguishable from (6.7). There are an infinite number of parameter sets which give the same joint density function for the observations; see the discussion on identifiability in EATS, chapter 3.

In order for the model to be identifiable, restrictions must be placed on $\boldsymbol{\Sigma}_\eta$ and $\mathbf{\Theta}$. In classical factor analysis, the covariance matrix of the common factors is taken to be an identity matrix. However, this is not sufficient to make the model identifiable since if $\mathbf{H}$ is an orthogonal matrix, (6.8) still satisfies all the restrictions of the original model because $\text{Var}(\boldsymbol{\eta}_t^\dagger) = \mathbf{H}\mathbf{H}' = \mathbf{I}$. Some restrictions are needed on $\mathbf{\Theta}$, and one way of imposing them is to require that the ijth element of $\mathbf{\Theta}$, θ_{ij}, be zero for $j > i$, $i = 1, \ldots, K - 1$. Alternatively, $\boldsymbol{\Sigma}_\eta$ can be set equal to a diagonal matrix while $\theta_{ij} = 0$ for $j > i$ and $\theta_{ii} = 1$ for $i = 1, \ldots, K$. Note that when $K = N$, the model reverts to (6.1) since $\mathbf{\Theta}\boldsymbol{\mu}_t$ is then the PSD matrix $\mathbf{\Theta}\boldsymbol{\Sigma}_\eta\mathbf{\Theta}'$.

Example 1   Suppose that $N = 2$ and $K = 1$. The model may be written as

$$\begin{bmatrix} y_{1t} \\ y_{2t} \end{bmatrix} = \begin{bmatrix} 1 \\ \theta \end{bmatrix} \mu_t + \begin{bmatrix} 0 \\ \bar{\mu} \end{bmatrix} + \begin{bmatrix} \varepsilon_{1t} \\ \varepsilon_{2t} \end{bmatrix} \qquad (6.9a)$$

$$\mu_t = \mu_{t-1} + \eta_t \qquad (6.9b)$$

with $\text{Var}(\eta_t) = \sigma_\eta^2$. Imposing identifiability in this case simply amounts to normalising the 2×1 vector $\boldsymbol{\theta}$ so that its first element is unity. The parameter θ is just a scaling factor for the trend in the second series, while $\bar{\mu}$ determines its intercept.

The identifiability restrictions mean that the common trends are uncorrelated with each other. This is quite an attractive property. The restrictions on the $\boldsymbol{\Theta}$ matrix are less appealing, since they imply that y_{1t} depends only on the first common trend, and not the others. Similarly y_{2t} depends only on the first two common trends and so on until we reach y_{Kt}. This depends on all the common trends, as do $y_{K+1,t}, \ldots, y_{N,t}$. Clearly this is arbitrary, and defining the common trends in this way may not lead to a particularly useful interpretation. However, once the model has been estimated, an orthogonal $\mathbf{H}$ matrix can be used to give a *factor rotation*. The new common trends are then the elements of $\boldsymbol{\mu}_t^\dagger$ in (6.8). A number of methods for carrying out factor rotation have been developed in the classical factor analysis literature. There is no reason why these should not be employed in the present context. Often one of the aims in factor rotation is to give factor positive loadings for some variables while the other variables get a loading near zero. Thus the movements in a variable may be identified with only a subset of the factors. This may enable the factors to have a useful interpretation. An example can be found in Harvey *et al.* (1992).

7.7 Co-integration

In a non-stationary multivariate ARIMA model, there is nothing to keep the individual series moving together in the long run. This may be a shortcoming for a time series model to have, particularly in economics where notions of equilibrium suggest that series cannot go on drifting further and further apart. The idea that non-stationary series may keep together in the long run is captured by the concept of co-integration; see Engle and Granger (1987).

It will be recalled that if a series with no deterministic component has a stationary, invertible ARMA representation after differencing d times, it is said to be integrated of order d. This is expressed by writing $y_t \sim \mathrm{I}(d)$. If two series, y_{1t} and y_{2t}, are both $\mathrm{I}(d)$, it will normally be the case that any linear combination is also $\mathrm{I}(d)$. However, it is possible that there is a linear combination of the two series for which the order of integration is smaller than d. In this case the series are said to be co-integrated. More generally we have the following definition. The components of the vector $\mathbf{y}_t$ are said to be *co-integrated of order d, b* if

(a) all components of $\mathbf{y}_t$ are $\mathrm{I}(d)$; and
(b) there exists a non-null vector, $\boldsymbol{\alpha}$, such that $\boldsymbol{\alpha}'\mathbf{y}_t$ is $\mathrm{I}(d-b)$ with $b > 0$.

This may be expressed as $\mathbf{y}_t \sim \mathrm{CI}(d, b)$. The vector $\boldsymbol{\alpha}$ is called the *co-integrating vector*.

The presence of co-integration implies the need to impose certain constraints on a multivariate time series model. Before examining the nature of these constraints in ARIMA and AR models, we first look at how co-integrating restrictions are imposed explicitly in a structural model by common trends.

Common Trends

The common trends model (6.7) explicitly sets up a co-integrated system because of the restriction on the number of non-stationary components. The formal definition of co-integration given above is satisfied because $\mathbf{y}_t$ is $I(1)$ while $N - K$ linear combinations of $\mathbf{y}_t$ are stationary. The model is therefore co-integrated of order $(1, 1)$. The co-integrating vectors are the $N - K$ rows of an $(N - K) \times N$ matrix $\mathbf{A}$ which has the property that $\mathbf{A}'\boldsymbol{\Theta} = \mathbf{0}$. Hence

$$\mathbf{A}\mathbf{y}_t = \mathbf{A}\boldsymbol{\mu}^* + \mathbf{A}\boldsymbol{\varepsilon}_t \tag{7.1}$$

and $\mathbf{A}\mathbf{y}_t$ is an $(N - K) \times 1$ stationary process. In fact in this case it is simply multivariate white noise with mean $\mathbf{A}\boldsymbol{\mu}^*$ and covariance matrix $\mathbf{A}\Sigma_\varepsilon\mathbf{A}'$.

Example 1 In the special case considered in (6.9), the matrix $\mathbf{A}$ denotes the single co-integrating vector. This may be normalised as $\mathbf{A} = (1 \; \alpha)$. Since it must be the case that

$$1 + \alpha\theta = 0$$

it follows that

$$\alpha = -1/\theta \tag{7.2}$$

Multiplying (6.9a) through by $\mathbf{A}$ gives

$$y_{1t} = (1/\theta)y_{2t} + (-1/\theta)\bar{\mu} + \varepsilon_t \tag{7.3}$$

where $\varepsilon_t = \varepsilon_{1t} - \varepsilon_{2t}/\theta$. Thus there is a levels relationship between y_{1t} and y_{2t}.

A model of a similar form to (6.9), but slightly more general in that the common trend component contained a drift term while ε_t was VAR(2), was estimated by Harvey and Stock (1988) for US GNP and consumption. The variables were in logarithms and it was found that θ could be set to unity, implying a long-run elasticity of unity between the permanent components of income and consumption. Taking antilogs in (7.3) shows that $\exp(-\bar{\mu})$ can be interpreted as the average propensity to consume.

A final point which is clearly seen in the common trends formulation is the way in which a co-integrated model preserves the long-run levels relationships between the variables when forecasts are made.

Granger Representation Theorem

The implications of co-integration for multivariate time series models were considered by Engle and Granger (1987). For simplicity, we restrict attention to the CI(1, 1) case.

If $\mathbf{y}_t$ is an $N \times 1$ vector of $I(1)$ variables, the Wold representation is

$$\Delta\mathbf{y}_t = \mathbf{\Psi}(L)\boldsymbol{\xi}_t, \qquad \boldsymbol{\xi}_t \sim \text{WN}(\mathbf{0}, \boldsymbol{\Sigma}) \tag{7.4}$$

where the infinite moving average polynomial,

$$\mathbf{\Psi}(L) = \sum_{j=0}^{\infty} \mathbf{\Psi}_j L^j$$

has roots outside or on the unit circle and $\mathbf{\Psi}_0 = \mathbf{I}$. This polynomial can be written as

$$\mathbf{\Psi}(L) = \mathbf{\Psi}(1) + \Delta\mathbf{\Psi}^\dagger(L) \tag{7.5}$$

where $\mathbf{\Psi}(1)$ denotes the sum of the coefficient matrices, that is

$$\mathbf{\Psi}(1) = \sum_{j=0}^{\infty} \mathbf{\Psi}_j \tag{7.6a}$$

and

$$\mathbf{\Psi}_i^\dagger = -\sum_{j=i+1}^{\infty} \mathbf{\Psi}_j, \qquad i = 0, 1, \ldots \tag{7.6b}$$

The identity in (7.5) was also employed in the section on unit root tests in (5.4.7), except that there it was used on a finite univariate AR polynomial.

If $\mathbf{\Psi}(1)$ is a matrix of zeros in (7.5), the difference operators cancel, and the process is stationary, with MA coefficients given by the $\mathbf{\Psi}_i^\dagger$s. In a co-integrated system, $\mathbf{\Psi}(1)$ is non-zero, but is less than full rank. Thus $\Delta\mathbf{y}_t$ is strictly non-invertible since $L = 1$ is a solution to the determinantal equation, $|\mathbf{\Psi}(L)| = 0$; see section 7.3. One consequence of this strict non-invertibility is that $\Delta\mathbf{y}_t$ cannot be modelled as a vector autoregression.

The number of co-integrating vectors depends on the rank of $\mathbf{\Psi}(1)$. Specifically if the rank of $\mathbf{\Psi}(1)$ is K, where $0 < K < N$, the number of co-integrating vectors is $N - K$. The *Granger Representation theorem* proves this result and gives the restrictions on the Wold representation (7.4) in terms of $\mathbf{\Psi}(1)$ and the matrix, $\mathbf{A}$, of co-integrating vectors. Specifically, it states that *the existence of an $(N - K) \times N$ matrix $\mathbf{A}$ of rank $N - K$ such that $\mathbf{A}\mathbf{y}_t$ is $I(0)$ implies, and is implied by,*

$$\text{rank}[\mathbf{\Psi}(1)] = K \tag{7.7}$$

and

$$\mathbf{A}\mathbf{\Psi}(1) = \mathbf{0} \tag{7.8}$$

In addition, *there is an $N \times (N - K)$ matrix $\mathbf{\Gamma}$ such that*

$$\mathbf{\Psi}(1)\mathbf{\Gamma} = \mathbf{0} \tag{7.9}$$

The restrictions on the Wold representation translate into a multivariate ARMA model as follows:

$$\mathbf{\Phi}(L)\mathbf{y}_t = \theta(L)\boldsymbol{\xi}_t \tag{7.10}$$

where $\theta(L)$ is a scalar polynomial, the roots of the pth-order matrix polynomial $\Phi(L)$ lie on or outside the unit circle and

$$\text{rank}[\Phi(1)] = N - K = r \quad \text{and} \quad \Phi(1) = \Gamma A \quad (7.11)$$

If $\text{rank}[\Phi(1)] = N$, then $\Psi(1) = 0$ and y_t is stationary. On the other hand, if $\Phi(1) = 0$, then $\text{rank}[\Psi(1)] = N$ and $y_t \sim I(1)$ and there is no co-integration. There is a connection with the unit root tests described in section 5.4. In that case, we saw that a unit root is present in the AR polynomial, and hence the process is non-stationary, if $\phi(1) = 0$. Here, unit roots are present if $|\Phi(1)| = 0$, implying that $L = 1$ is a solution to the determinantal equation $|\Phi(L)| = 0$. It was convenient to reformulate the univariate AR model in terms of differences and a single levels variable, as in (5.4.7), since the coefficient of the levels variable is then $\phi(1)$. The same idea may be applied to (7.10) to yield the *error correction model* (ECM) representation

$$\Phi^\dagger(L)\Delta y_t = -\Gamma z_{t-1} + \theta(L)\xi_t = -\Phi(1)y_{t-1} + \theta(L)\xi_t \quad (7.12)$$

where $z_t = A y_t$ and $\Phi^\dagger(L) = I - \Phi_1^\dagger L - \cdots - \Phi_{p-1}^\dagger L^{p-1}$ is the multivariate generalisation of (5.4.7), that is

$$\Phi_j^\dagger = \sum_{k=j+1}^{p} \Phi_k, \quad j = 0, 1, \ldots, p-1 \quad (7.13)$$

Single equation ECM's are of considerable practical importance in econometric modelling, since they are able to incorporate long-run relationships between variables; see EATS, chapter 8, section 5.

Example 2 A simple illustration of the above results is provided by the model

$$y_{1t} = \beta y_{2t} + \varepsilon_t \quad (7.14a)$$

$$y_{2t} = y_{2,t-1} + \eta_t \quad (7.14b)$$

where ε_t and η_t are uncorrelated white noise disturbances. It can be seen immediately that this model is CI(1, 1), with the co-integrating relationship given directly by (7.14a). The Wold representation (7.4) is obtained by differencing (7.14a) and substituting for Δy_{2t}, to give

$$\Delta y_{1t} = \beta \Delta y_{2t} + \Delta \varepsilon_t = \beta \eta_t + \varepsilon_t - \varepsilon_{t-1} \quad (7.15a)$$

$$\Delta y_{2t} = \eta_t \quad (7.15b)$$

and then setting $\xi_t = (\varepsilon_t + \beta\eta_t, \eta_t)'$ so that

$$\Psi(1) = \Psi_0 + \Psi_1 = \begin{bmatrix} 1 & 0 \\ 0 & 1 \end{bmatrix} + \begin{bmatrix} -1 & \beta \\ 0 & 0 \end{bmatrix} = \begin{bmatrix} 0 & \beta \\ 0 & 1 \end{bmatrix}$$

The rank of $\mathbf{\Psi}(1)$ is obviously one. Furthermore it can be seen directly from (7.14a) that the co-integrating vector, and hence the matrix $\mathbf{A}$, is $(1, -\beta)$, and so (7.8) is satisfied, that is $\mathbf{A}\mathbf{\Psi}(1) = \mathbf{0}$.

A different re-arrangement of (7.14) gives the ECM representation

$$\Delta y_{1t} = -y_{1,t-1} + \beta y_{2,t-1} + \xi_{1t} \qquad (7.16a)$$

$$\Delta y_{2t} = \qquad\qquad \xi_{2t} \qquad (7.16b)$$

In terms of (7.12), $\theta(L) = 1$ and

$$\mathbf{\Phi}(1) = \begin{bmatrix} 1 & -\beta \\ 0 & 0 \end{bmatrix} = \mathbf{\Gamma}\mathbf{A} = \begin{bmatrix} 1 \\ 0 \end{bmatrix}(1-\beta)$$

Vector Autoregressions

Multivariate ARMA models of the form (7.10) or (7.12) are rarely estimated in practice. Instead it is assumed that $\mathbf{\Phi}(L)$ is of finite order and $\theta(L) = 1$, so that a VAR model can be fitted. The co-integration constraints of (7.11) can be imposed by working with the ECM as in (7.12) or with a re-arranged version

$$\mathbf{\Phi}^*(L)\,\Delta y_t = -\mathbf{\Phi}(1)\mathbf{y}_{t-p} + \xi_t \qquad (7.17)$$

where $\mathbf{\Phi}_0^* = \mathbf{I}$, and

$$\mathbf{\Phi}_j^* = \sum_{i=1}^{j} \mathbf{\Phi}_i - \mathbf{I}, \qquad j = 1, \ldots, p-1 \qquad (7.18)$$

This is the form preferred by Johansen (1988); see also Ahn and Reinsel (1990). Having decided on the *co-integration rank*, $r = N - K$, the constrained Gaussian model is estimated by ML as follows.

If p were unity, the matrix $\mathbf{\Phi}(1)$, and the parameter matrices $\mathbf{A}$ and $\mathbf{\Gamma}$, could be estimated by a multivariate *reduced rank regression* of Δy_t on $\mathbf{y}_{t-1}$. However, with p greater than zero, it is necessary first to remove the influence of the lagged differences, $\Delta \mathbf{y}_{t-1}, \ldots, \Delta \mathbf{y}_{t-p+1}$. This is done by regressing $\Delta \mathbf{y}_t$ and $\mathbf{y}_{t-p}$ on the lagged differences to give $N \times 1$ vectors of residuals, $\mathbf{e}_{0t}$ and $\mathbf{e}_{pt}$ respectively. The reduced rank regression is then carried out with these residuals; this is rather like detrending before running a regression.

Define the cross-product matrices

$$\mathbf{S}_{00} = T^{-1} \sum \mathbf{e}_{0t}\mathbf{e}_{0t}', \qquad \mathbf{S}_{pp} = T^{-1} \sum \mathbf{e}_{pt}\mathbf{e}_{pt}' \qquad \text{and} \qquad \mathbf{S}_{0p} = T^{-1} \sum \mathbf{e}_{0t}\mathbf{e}_{pt}'$$

and let $\mathbf{G}$ be a lower triangular matrix with positive diagonal elements satisfying $\mathbf{G}\mathbf{S}_{pp}\mathbf{G}' = \mathbf{I}$, that is the Cholesky decomposition. Noting that $\mathbf{S}_{p0} = \mathbf{S}_{0p}'$, first compute the eigenvalues of $\mathbf{G}\mathbf{S}_{p0}\mathbf{S}_{00}^{-1}\mathbf{S}_{0p}'\mathbf{G}'$. Denote the eigenvalues by

$$\lambda_1 \geqslant \lambda_2 \geqslant \cdots \geqslant \lambda_N$$

and the corresponding eigenvectors by $v_1, \ldots, v_N$. If r is less than N, the $N - r$ smallest eigenvalues are taken to be zero, and the ML estimators of $\mathbf{A}$ and $\boldsymbol{\Gamma}$ are:

$$\tilde{\mathbf{A}} = [v_1, \ldots, v_r]'\mathbf{G} \tag{7.19a}$$

$$\tilde{\boldsymbol{\Gamma}} = -\mathbf{S}_{0p}\tilde{\mathbf{A}}'(\tilde{\mathbf{A}}\mathbf{S}_{0p}\tilde{\mathbf{A}}')^{-1} \tag{7.19b}$$

and the ML estimators of $\boldsymbol{\Phi}_1^*, \ldots, \boldsymbol{\Phi}_{p-1}^*$ are obtained by a multivariate regression of $\Delta\mathbf{y}_t - \tilde{\boldsymbol{\Gamma}}\tilde{\mathbf{A}}\mathbf{y}_{t-1}$ on $\Delta\mathbf{y}_{t-1}, \ldots, \Delta\mathbf{y}_{t-p+1}$. The maximised likelihood function is

$$\log L = -\frac{T}{2}\left[N + N\log 2\pi + \log|\mathbf{S}_{00}| + \sum_{i=0}^{r}\log(1 - \lambda_i)\right] \tag{7.20}$$

The asymptotic properties of the estimators reflect the fact that we are dealing with a generalisation of the univariate AR model in section 5.4. Thus the estimators of the $\boldsymbol{\Phi}_j^*$ matrices converge to multivariate normal distributions when multiplied by $T^{1/2}$, while the estimator of $\boldsymbol{\Phi}(1)$ is superconsistent, converging to a non-normal limiting distribution when multiplied by T. Unfortunately, we cannot claim that the estimators of $\mathbf{A}$ and $\boldsymbol{\Gamma}$ are consistent since without further restrictions they are not identifiable. Note that the asymptotic properties change if there is a constant in the error correction term, or in all the equations; see Lütkepohl (1991, section 11.2).

Sims *et al.* (1990) derive the asymptotic properties of the unconstrained multivariate least squares estimator in a co-integrated VAR model. Again the estimator of $\boldsymbol{\Phi}(1)$ is superconsistent, and because of this, estimators of linear combinations of the parameters in the $\boldsymbol{\Phi}_j^*$ matrices of (7.18) will have the same asymptotic distribution as corresponding estimators obtained from constrained estimation. Thus standard errors and t-statistics associated with such estimators may be used in the same way as in a stationary VAR. However, one should bear in mind that there may be substantial differences between large and small sample properties.

Testing for the Order of Co-integration

The constrained estimation procedure described in the previous sub-section depends on knowing the co-integration rank, r. In large samples, this is easy. We simply carry out unconstrained least squares estimation of the VAR and then compute the eigenvalues of the resulting estimator of $\boldsymbol{\Phi}(1)$ in order to assess its rank. However, although the estimator of $\boldsymbol{\Phi}(1)$ is superconsistent, it may be subject to considerable bias in small samples, as is the estimator of ϕ in the univariate AR model, (5.4.7). Thus the estimator of $\mathbf{\Phi}(1)$ may not give a good indication of r in practice, just as an examination of the value of a univariate estimate of ϕ does not give a reliable indication of whether its true value is unity.

Within the framework of constrained estimation, an LR test of a specific co-integration rank, r_0, against a higher rank, $r_1 \leqslant N$, may be carried out. It is easily seen from (7.20) that the LR statistic is just

$$\lambda(r_0, r_1) = -T \sum_{i=r_0+1}^{r_1} \log(1 - \lambda_i) \tag{7.21}$$

This statistic depends only on the eigenvalues obtained from the cross-product matrices of the residual vectors and so computing the ML estimators of the model parameters for specific values of r is unnecessary. As might be expected, the asymptotic distribution of $\lambda(r_0, r_1)$ under the null hypothesis is not χ^2. Fortunately it just depends on $K = N - r_0$ and r_1, so significance points can be tabulated; see Johansen and Juselius (1990). These points differ when constant terms are included.

Other tests have been proposed; see, for example, Stock and Watson (1988) and Phillips and Ouliaris (1990). How effective these tests are for determining co-integration rank in practice has yet to be determined.

Exercises

1. Suppose that

$$y_t = \beta x_{t-2} + \varepsilon_t$$

   where x_t is the MA(1) process

$$x_t = \eta_t + \theta \eta_{t-1}$$

   and ε_t and η_t are mutually uncorrelated white noise processes. Derive the cross-correlation function $\rho_{yx}(\tau)$.

2. Evaluate the autocorrelation matrices at all finite lags in the vector MA(1) process

$$\begin{bmatrix} y_{1t} \\ y_{2t} \end{bmatrix} = \begin{bmatrix} \varepsilon_{1t} \\ \varepsilon_{2t} \end{bmatrix} + \begin{bmatrix} 0.5 & -0.3 \\ 0.7 & 0.6 \end{bmatrix} \begin{bmatrix} \varepsilon_{1,t-1} \\ \varepsilon_{2,t-1} \end{bmatrix}$$

   Is the process invertible?

3. Consider the non-stationary processes

$$y_{1t} = y_{1,t-1} + \varepsilon_{1,t} + \theta\varepsilon_{1,t-1}, \qquad |\theta| < 1$$
$$y_{2t} = \phi y_{1t} + \varepsilon_{2,t}, \qquad\qquad |\phi| < 1$$

   Show that the vector of first differences, $(\Delta y_{1t}, \Delta y_{2t})'$, is a strictly non-invertible vector MA(1) process.

4. Is the following VAR stationary?

$$\begin{bmatrix} y_{1t} \\ y_{2t} \end{bmatrix} = \begin{bmatrix} 1 & 1 \\ -1.62 & -0.80 \end{bmatrix} \begin{bmatrix} \varepsilon_{1t} \\ \varepsilon_{2t} \end{bmatrix}$$

What are the univariate models for the two series? Would you expect pseudo-cyclical behaviour?

5. Consider the stochastic cycle model, (6.5.6).

   (a) By treating the model as a VAR(1), show that the ACF of ψ_t is as given by (6.5.11).

   (b) Show that ψ_t is a special case of an ARMA(2, 1) process. Express the roots of the autoregressive polynomial of this process in terms of ρ and λ_c. Derive a formula expressing the moving average parameter in terms of ρ and λ_c. What restrictions are effectively placed on the parameters of the reduced form ARMA process?

   (c) What is meant by a common factor in the context of an ARMA(2, 1) model? If such a model is subject to the restrictions imposed by a cyclical structural form can it have a common factor?

6. The following statistic has been proposed for testing the hypothesis that $\boldsymbol{\Phi} = \boldsymbol{\Phi}_0$ in the vector AR(1) model

$$\mathrm{tr}(\tilde{\boldsymbol{\Phi}} - \boldsymbol{\Phi}_0) \left[\sum_{t=2}^{T} \mathbf{y}_t \mathbf{y}_t' \right] (\tilde{\boldsymbol{\Phi}} - \boldsymbol{\Phi}_0) \tilde{\boldsymbol{\Omega}}^{-1}$$

This is tested as a χ^2 variate with N^2 degrees of freedom. Is this test related to any of those discussed in the text?

7. Determine the autocovariance matrices of the first differenced observations in the common trends model (6.9).

8. Consider two series generated by the following process:

$$y_{1t} = \phi y_{1,t-1} + \beta y_{2,t-1} + \varepsilon_t$$

$$y_{2t} = \qquad\qquad y_{2,t-1} + \eta_t$$

where ε_t and η_t are mutually uncorrelated white noise processes, and ϕ and β are parameters.

   (a) Write down a model for the differenced series, $\Delta \mathbf{y}_t = (\Delta y_{1t}, \Delta y_{2t})'$. If $\boldsymbol{\Psi}(L)$ denotes the matrix polynomial in the lag operator for the moving average representation of $\Delta \mathbf{y}_t$, find an expression for $\boldsymbol{\Psi}_i$, the matrix associated with L^i, in terms of ϕ and β. Evaluate $\boldsymbol{\Psi}(1)$, and comment on it.

   (b) Find an expression for $\mathbf{F}(\lambda)$, the power spectrum of $\Delta \mathbf{y}_t$, at $\lambda = 0$. What is its rank?

   (c) Find the cross-covariance function between the differenced series. Does this indicate the form of the relationship between the two series?

   (d) Write down the multivariate error correction representation of $\mathbf{y}_t$. What is the co-integrating vector in this case?

8

Non-Linear Models

8.1 Introduction

Relaxing the requirement that time series models be linear opens up a vast range of possibilities. This chapter provides an introduction to non-linear modelling, by pointing out some of the implications of non-linearity and looking at some of the basic models. It is shown how models formulated in terms of one-step ahead conditional distributions, or more specifically conditional Gaussian distributions, can be handled. Some attention is paid to the question of modelling stochastic movements in variance and this leads to a consideration of a class of models exhibiting a property known as ARCH and to a class of stochastic volatility models. Both these classes of models have proved to be extremely useful in modelling movements in financial time series.

Since the aim is to introduce the main concepts, attention is restricted to univariate models. Many of the ideas extend quite naturally to multivariate models and models with explanatory variables. Further discussion on the subject as a whole can be found in the book by Tong (1990).

Linear Models

Before examining non-linear models, it is necessary to define what is meant by a linear model. Unfortunately there seems to be no generally agreed definition in the literature. A necessary requirement is that the MMSEs of future observations should be linear combinations of sample observations. However, linearity in predictions of the mean is not sufficient to rule out many models which clearly exhibit non-linear effects.

It is important to make a distinction between uncorrelated and independent random variables. The linear process defined in (2.1.23) does not satisfy the requirements of a linear *model* for the simple reason that uncorrelated disturbances do not rule out the possibility that the MMSE of a future observation may be non-linear; see the next sub-section. The same is true of a linear state space form, which is a system defined as in (4.1) with non-stochastic, but possibly time-varying, system matrices and uncorrelated disturbances. The complete specification of the time series models employed in previous chapters included the assumption of Gaussianity. *Any model which has a linear state space form and Gaussian disturbances is certainly linear.* Not only are the MMSE's of future observations linear in the observations, but also their predictive distributions are completely specified since they are known to be Gaussian.

It is generally felt that defining a linear model as a linear Gaussian state space model is too strong. Assuming a univariate framework for simplicity, a weaker definition of linearity is the requirement that the model can be written in the form

$$y_t = \sum_{j=0}^{t-1} \psi_{jt}\varepsilon_{t-j} + \lambda_{0t}, \qquad t = 1, 2, \ldots, T \qquad (1.1)$$

where the ψ_{jt}'s are non-stochastic weights, λ_{0t} denotes observable initial conditions, which may be fixed or random, and ε_t is a sequence of *independent* random variables with mean zero. The importance of the independence assumption was noted in the discussion on the prediction of ARMA processes in section 2.6. The expression in (1.1) is reasonably general in that it takes account of time variation, non-stationarity and finite samples; compare Priestley (1981, p. 867). The MMSE of a future observation can be expressed as a linear combination of current and past observations, while the corresponding prediction error can be written as a linear combination of future values of the ε_t's just as in (2.6.8). Moments of the predictive distribution can be computed, assuming that the corresponding moments of the disturbances exist. However, without the assumption that the disturbances are Gaussian, it will not, in general, be possible to write down a formula for the distribution itself.

Law of Iterated Expectations

An important result for analysing non-linear models is the *law of iterated expectations*, the statistical basis of which is set out in the appendix. In the present context it means that the expectation of the current observation, or a function of it, $g(y_t)$, with respect to information available at time $t - J$ can be found by first taking the expectation conditional on the information in the previous time period, $t - 1$, and then taking the expectation conditional on information in the period before that and so on, back to $t - J$. Thus, if the time subscript below the expectation operator indicates that we are taking expectations with respect to information available at that time, the expectation of $g(y_t)$ at time $t - J$ can be written as

$$\underset{t-J}{E}\,[g(y_t)] = \underset{t-J}{E}\,\cdots\,\underset{t-1}{E}\,[g(y_t)] \qquad (1.2)$$

The unconditional expectation is found by letting J go to infinity, in which case the time index will be dropped. If the process is regarded as starting at time $t = 0$, the expectation given the initial conditions is given by setting $J = t$.

When used in connection with the prediction of some function of a future observation at time $T + l$, (1.2) applies with t set to $T + l$ and J set to l.

When is White Noise not White Noise?

White noise (WN) is defined as a sequence of uncorrelated random variables with constant mean and variance. Contrary to what one might expect, it is sometimes possible to make non-trivial predictions from series which have the white noise property. Only if the variables are independent is it impossible to make use of current and past values to predict any feature of future values. We must therefore differentiate between white noise and *strict* white noise, the latter being a sequence of independent and identically distributed (IID) random variables. Note that if a WN sequence is assumed to be Gaussian, then it must also be strict WN.

The relevance of the distinction between WN and strict WN is that observations generated by a non-linear model may have the WN property. This introduces an interesting possibility if an analysis of the correlogram of a series of observations, such as stock returns, indicates white noise. Although we might conclude, quite correctly, that there is no point in trying to fit a linear model, there may be a non-linear model which is of some value in prediction.

Example 1   Consider the model

$$y_t = \varepsilon_t + \beta\varepsilon_{t-1}\varepsilon_{t-2}, \qquad \varepsilon_t \sim \text{IID}(0, \sigma^2), \qquad t = 1, \dots, T \qquad (1.3)$$

where β is a fixed parameter and $\varepsilon_0 = \varepsilon_{-1} = 0$. The expected value of y_t is zero, while its variance is

$$\begin{aligned}
\text{Var}(y_t) = E(y_t^2) &= E(\varepsilon_t^2) + 2\beta E(\varepsilon_t\varepsilon_{t-1}\varepsilon_{t-2}) + \beta^2 E(\varepsilon_{t-1}^2\varepsilon_{t-2}^2) \\
&= \sigma^2 + \beta^2 E(\varepsilon_{t-1}^2)E(\varepsilon_{t-2}^2) = \sigma^2 + \beta^2\sigma^4 \\
&= (1 + \sigma^2\beta^2)\sigma^2 \qquad (1.4)
\end{aligned}$$

The autocovariances

$$\begin{aligned}
\gamma(\tau) = E(y_t y_{t-\tau}) &= E(\varepsilon_t\varepsilon_{t-\tau}) + \beta E(\varepsilon_{t-1}\varepsilon_{t-2}\varepsilon_{t-\tau}) \\
&\quad + \beta E(\varepsilon_t\varepsilon_{t-\tau-1}\varepsilon_{t-\tau-2}) + \beta^2 E(\varepsilon_{t-1}\varepsilon_{t-2}\varepsilon_{t-\tau-1}\varepsilon_{t-\tau-2})
\end{aligned}$$

are all zero at non-zero lags since in each term there is always at least one disturbance whose time subscript is different to the others. Hence the y_t series is white noise, although unlike the ε_t series it is not independent. The significance of this particular pattern of dependence emerges when predictions are made. The values of current and past ε_ts may be computed from the recursion

$$\varepsilon_t = y_t - \beta \varepsilon_{t-1} \varepsilon_{t-2}, \qquad t = 1, \ldots, T \tag{1.5}$$

and so it is possible to construct the MMSE of y_{T+1} as

$$\tilde{y}_{T+1|T} = \beta \varepsilon_T \varepsilon_{T-1} \tag{1.6}$$

The MSE is just the variance of the future unpredictable variable ε_{T+1}, that is σ^2. On the other hand, the MMSLE gives the trivial prediction of zero, with an MSE of (1.4).

Another concept which has relevance in the characterisation of random series is that of *martingale difference* (MD). Assuming that $E|y_t| < \infty$, an MD has the property that its expectation, conditional on past information, is zero. That is,

$$\underset{t-1}{E}\ (y_t) = E(y_t|Y_{t-1}) = 0 \tag{1.7}$$

where Y_{t-1} denotes all the information up to and including the observation at time $t-1$. It follows immediately from the law of iterated expectations that the unconditional expectation of y_t is zero, that is

$$E(y_t) = E[E(y_t|Y_{t-1})] = 0$$

Furthermore y_t is uncorrelated with any function of the past observations, $f(Y_{t-1})$. This follows because

$$E[y_t f(Y_{t-1})|Y_{t-1}] = f(Y_{t-1})E(y_t|Y_{t-1}) = 0$$

and so the unconditional expectation of $y_t f(Y_{t-1})$ is also zero.

The relationship between an MD sequence and the various concepts of WN is therefore as follows:

(a) All MD's are serially uncorrelated, but, as can be seen from (1.6), the converse is not true. If the variance of an MD is constant, it is WN.
(b) All zero mean independent sequences are MD's, but not the converse.

The essential point about a series with the MD property is that past observations contain no information which can be used to predict future values of the series. However, it may be possible to construct a non-linear model in which the non-linearity is reflected in higher order moments such as the variance, and this may have implications for assessing the variability of the predictions.

Modelling Volatility

Many time series, especially financial ones such as stock returns and exchange rates, exhibit changes in variance over time. These changes tend to be serially correlated, with groups of highly volatile observations occurring together. This is highly plausible since if a financial market is in a state of uncertainty, perhaps brought about by some international crisis, it will take some time for the price to settle down. An illustration is provided by figure 8.1, which shows first differences of the logged daily exchange rate of the yen against the dollar from 1 October 1981 to 28 June 1985.

There are a number of different ways of modelling changes in variance. The basic set up is to regard the series of interest as being a sequence of independent, identically distributed random variables, ε_t, with unit variance, multiplied by a factor σ_t, the standard deviation, that is

$$y_t = \sigma_t \varepsilon_t, \qquad \varepsilon_t \sim \text{IID}(0, 1) \tag{1.8}$$

One possibility is to adopt a direct approach in which σ_t is modelled by a stochastic process, such as an autoregression. Such models, which are described in section 8.4, are called stochastic variance models. Section 8.3 looks at an alternative approach, known as ARCH, in which the variance is

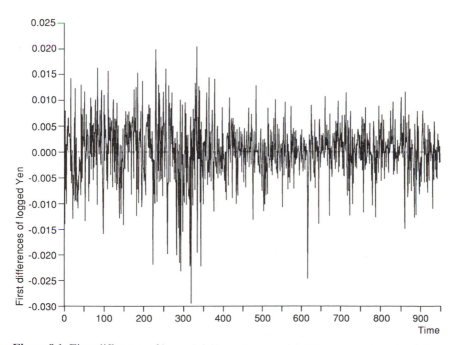

Figure 8.1 First difference of logged daily exchange rate of the yen against the dollar, 1 October 1981 to 28 June 1985.

modelled in terms of past observations. In both cases the observations in (1.8) form an MD sequence although they are not independent.

Detecting Non-Linearity

So far the properties of stationary time series models have been summarised in terms of the ACF or the spectrum. These are based on second-order moments. For a linear model it can be shown that the ACF and the spectrum contain all the relevant information on the dynamic properties of the process. For non-linear models, new information can be obtained from other descriptive statistics.

In the time domain the autocorrelations of powers of the observations may be examined. In particular, for a series, y_t, with mean zero and variance σ_y^2, we may consider the ACF of the squared observations,

$$\rho(\tau; y_t^2) = \frac{E[(y_t^2 - \sigma_y^2)(y_{t-\tau}^2 - \sigma_y^2)]}{E[(y_t^2 - \sigma_y^2)^2]}, \qquad \tau = 0, 1, 2, \ldots \qquad (1.9)$$

If y_t is a linear stationary model with finite fourth moment it can be shown that knowledge of the ACF, $\rho(\tau)$, implies knowledge of the ACF of the squares. Specifically

$$\rho(\tau; y_t^2) = \{\rho(\tau)\}^2 \qquad \text{for all } \tau \qquad (1.10)$$

It follows as a corollary that the absolute value of a particular $\rho(\tau; y_t^2)$ can never exceed the value of the corresponding $\rho(\tau)$.

For IID observations, $\rho(\tau; y_t^2) = 0$ for non-zero lags. This is not necessarily the case for non-linear models which have the WN property. The correlogram of the squared observations may therefore be used as the basis of a test for linearity. If $r(\tau; y_t^2)$ denotes the sample estimator of $\rho(\tau; y_t^2)$, the statistic

$$Q(P) = T(T + 2) \sum_{\tau=1}^{P} (T - \tau)^{-1} \{r(\tau; y_t^2)\}^2 \qquad (1.11)$$

provides a higher order analogue of the portmanteau statistic, and, like the portmanteau statistic, it can be shown to be asymptotically χ_P^2 for Gaussian WN. Thus while the portmanteau test is used to test for randomness, in the sense of uncorrelatedness, (1.11) is testing for a stronger notion of randomness which almost, but not necessarily, amounts to independence. Note that a test for normality is also providing information, albeit indirectly, on possible departures from linearity, since a Gaussian process must be linear.

If we have a stationary series which is not WN, the test based on (1.11) can be applied to the residuals from a fitted model, such as an ARMA process. Again it can be shown that the statistic is asymptotically χ_P^2. Unlike the portmanteau test, no correction is needed for the loss in degrees of freedom; see McLeod and Li (1983).

In the frequency domain, properties of non-linear models may be captured by *polyspectra*, defined as the Fourier transforms of higher order cumulants. The second-order cumulant is the autocovariance, the Fourier transform of which produces the conventional power spectrum, (6.1.4). The third-order cumulant is

$$\gamma(\tau, \upsilon) = E[(y_t - \mu)(y_{t-\tau} - \mu)(y_{t-\upsilon} - \mu)] \tag{1.12}$$

the Fourier transform of which yields the *bispectrum*

$$f(\lambda, \omega) = \left(\frac{1}{2\pi}\right)^2 \sum_{\tau=-\infty}^{\infty} \sum_{\upsilon=-\infty}^{\infty} \gamma(\tau, \upsilon) e^{-i(\lambda\tau - \omega\upsilon)} \tag{1.13}$$

The bispectrum has the property that it is zero everywhere if the process is Gaussian. If it is non-Gaussian, but linear, then the function

$$f^*(\lambda, \omega) = |f(\lambda, \omega)|^2 / \{f(\lambda)f(\omega)f(\lambda + \omega)\} \tag{1.14}$$

is constant for all λ and ω. Subba Rao and Gabr (1981) construct a test for non-linearity based on estimates of the bispectrum and spectrum in (1.14) calculated over a grid of frequencies. A test of normality, based on whether the estimated bispectrum is zero over a grid of frequencies, can also be carried out.

Chaos

Certain *deterministic* non-linear difference equations are able to generate series which have many of the features of stochastic processes. Such models are called *chaotic*. They can, for example, generate white noise series which, given a knowledge of the model and the initial conditions, can be predicted exactly. Hence they provide an extreme illustration of the distinction between uncorrelated and independent processes.

Example 1 The following first-order difference equation is called a *tent map*:

$$y_t = \begin{cases} y_{t-1}/a & \text{if } 0 \leqslant y_{t-1} \leqslant a \\ (1 - y_{t-1})/(1 - a) & \text{if } a \leqslant y_{t-1} \leqslant 1 \end{cases}$$

with $0 < a < 1$. Most realisations of this deterministic equation generate the same ACF as an AR(1) process with parameter $\phi = 2a - 1$. Thus if $a = 0.5$, white noise results.

Chaotic systems have proved to be of some importance in certain of the natural sciences. The extent to which they may be empirically useful in areas like economics has yet to be determined. Certainly detecting a particular chaotic model, and distinguishing it from non-linear stochastic processes, is likely to be very difficult in practice.

Useful references on chaos include Bartlett (1990), Brock and Sayers (1988) and Stewart (1989).

8.2 Conditionally Gaussian Models

A time series model may be specified in terms of a distribution for y_t which depends on information which is available at time $t - 1$. An important feature of models specified in this way is that, given suitable initial conditions, the likelihood function may be computed thereby enabling ML estimation to be carried out. This follows immediately on recalling that the joint density of the observations can be expressed as

$$L = \prod_t p(y_t | Y_{t-1}) \tag{2.1}$$

If the conditional distribution of y_t is normal, the model is said to be *conditionally Gaussian*. Thus we may write

$$y_t | Y_{t-1} \sim N(\mu_t\{Y_{t-1}\}, \sigma_t^2\{Y_{t-1}\}) \tag{2.2}$$

Example 1 If the ε_t's in (1.3) are normally distributed, the observations are conditionally Gaussian with a mean of $\beta\varepsilon_{t-1}\varepsilon_{t-2}$ and a variance σ^2. Maximising the likelihood function is equivalent to minimising the sum of squares function

$$S(\beta) = \sum \varepsilon_t^2 \tag{2.3}$$

where the residuals ε_t are obtained from the recursion in (1.5).

Example 2 The simplest example of a *bilinear* model is

$$y_t = \phi y_{t-1} + \theta\varepsilon_{t-1} + \beta\varepsilon_{t-1}y_{t-1} + \varepsilon_t, \qquad t = 1, \dots, T \tag{2.4}$$

where $\varepsilon_t \sim \text{NID}(0, \sigma^2)$ and ϕ, θ and β are unknown parameters. The model can be regarded as an ARMA$(1, 1)$ generalised by the addition of a cross-product term. If y_0 is a given fixed number and ε_0 is zero, the residuals may be obtained recursively from

$$\varepsilon_t = y_t - \phi y_{t-1} - \theta\varepsilon_{t-1} - \beta\varepsilon_{t-1}y_{t-1}, \qquad t = 1, \dots, T \tag{2.5}$$

and the ML estimators of ϕ, θ and β obtained by minimising a sum of squares function as in (2.3).

The likelihood framework opens up the possibility of constructing LR, Wald and LM tests.

Example 2 (*contd*)   If an ARMA$(1, 1)$ model has been fitted, the LM principle may be used to construct a test for the presence of the bilinear term in (2.4). The derivatives of the residuals in (2.5) are

$$\frac{\partial \varepsilon_t}{\partial \phi} = -y_{t-1} + \theta \frac{\partial \varepsilon_{t-1}}{\partial \phi} + \beta y_{t-1} \frac{\partial \varepsilon_{t-1}}{\partial \phi}$$

$$\frac{\partial \varepsilon_t}{\partial \beta} = -\varepsilon_{t-1} y_{t-1} + \theta \frac{\partial \varepsilon_{t-1}}{\partial \beta}$$

and

$$\frac{\partial \varepsilon_t}{\partial \theta} = -\varepsilon_{t-1} + \beta y_{t-1} \frac{\partial \varepsilon_{t-1}}{\partial \theta}, \qquad t = 1, \ldots, T$$

with the initial derivatives at $t = 0$ being zero. The null hypothesis is that $\beta = 0$, and so the test is carried out by regressing the ARMA residuals on the derivatives evaluated at $\beta = 0$. The resulting TR^2 statistic is tested against a χ_1^2-distribution.

State Space Models

The state space framework may be extended to allow for a very general class of conditionally Gaussian models by allowing the system matrices $\mathbf{T}_t$, $\mathbf{R}_t$, $\mathbf{Z}_t$, $\mathbf{Q}_t$ and $\mathbf{H}_t$ to depend on information available at time $t - 1$. Although models within this class may not be explicitly set up in terms of conditionally Gaussian distributions for the observations, the derivation of the Kalman filter given in section 4.3 remains valid, and so conditional Gaussianity follows as a consequence. The likelihood function emerges as before in terms of the one-step ahead prediction errors.

Example 3   An AR(1) model with a parameter which also follows an AR(1) process may be written as

$$y_t = \phi_t y_{t-1} + \varepsilon_t, \qquad \varepsilon_t \sim \text{NID}(0, \sigma_\varepsilon^2) \tag{2.6a}$$

$$\phi_t = \alpha \phi_{t-1} + \eta_t, \qquad \eta_t \sim \text{NID}(0, \sigma_\eta^2) \tag{2.6b}$$

where α is a fixed parameter. The properties of this model are examined in Weiss (1985), where conditions under which y_t has a finite variance are derived. The model is in state space form with ϕ_t being the state and $\mathbf{Z}_t = y_{t-1}$.

Example 4   A shift in regime can be incorporated into any state space model by letting a parameter, or parameters, take different values according to whether Δy_{t-1} is positive or negative.

Prediction

Although a model may be set up in terms of one-step ahead predictive distributions, obtaining the predictive distribution several steps ahead may not be easy, even for conditionally Gaussian models. The *l*-step ahead predictive distribution is, in principle, given by

$$p(y_{T+l}|Y_t) = \int \cdots \int \prod_{j=1}^{l} p(y_{T+j}|Y_{T+j-1}) \, dy_{T+1} \cdots dy_{T+l-1} \quad (2.7)$$

This expression follows by observing that the joint distribution of the future observations may be written in terms of conditional distributions, that is

$$p(y_{T+l}, y_{T+l-1}, \ldots, y_{T+1}|Y_T) = \prod_{j=1}^{l} p(y_{T+j}|Y_{T+j-1})$$

The predictive distribution of y_{T+l} is then obtained as a marginal distribution by integrating out y_{T+1} to y_{T+l-1}.

The predictive distribution of y_{T+l} will not usually be normal for $l > 1$. Furthermore it is not, in general, straightforward to determine the form of the distribution from (2.7). Evaluating conditional moments tends to be easier, though whether it is a feasible proposition depends on the way in which past observations enter into the system matrices. At the least one would hope to be able to evaluate the conditional expectations of future observations thereby obtaining the MMSEs of these observations.

Evaluation of the conditional moments of the predictive distribution of y_{T+l} is carried out using the law of iterated expectations as in (1.2). Thus the MMSE of y_{T+l} is

$$\underset{T}{E}(y_{T+l}) = \underset{T}{E} \underset{T+1}{E} \cdots \underset{T+l-1}{E}(y_{T+l}) \quad (2.8)$$

The corresponding prediction MSE is obtained by evaluating the conditional expectations of y_{T+l}^2 in the formula

$$\text{MSE}\{\underset{T}{E}(y_{T+l})\} = \text{Var}(y_{T+l}|Y_T) = \underset{T}{E}(y_{T+l}^2) - \{\underset{T}{E}(y_{T+l})\}^2 \quad (2.9)$$

Example 5 For the bilinear model, (2.4), the two-step ahead predictor is constructed by first taking expectations at time $T + 1$ to give

$$\underset{T+1}{E}(y_{T+2}) = \phi y_{T+1} + \theta \varepsilon_{T+1} + \beta \varepsilon_{T+1} y_{T+1}$$

and then taking expectations at time T so that

$$\underset{T}{E}(y_{T+2}) = \phi(\phi y_T + \theta \varepsilon_T + \beta \varepsilon_T y_T) + \beta \sigma^2 = \phi^2 y_T + \phi \theta \varepsilon_T + \phi \beta \varepsilon_T y_T + \beta \sigma^2$$

8.3 Autoregressive Conditional Heteroscedasticity

Engle (1982) suggested that the variance in (1.8) be modelled directly in terms of past observations. The simplest possibility is to let

$$\sigma_t^2 = \gamma + \alpha y_{t-1}^2, \qquad \gamma > 0, \qquad \alpha \geqslant 0 \tag{3.1}$$

the constraints on the parameters γ and α being required to ensure that the variance remains positive. The model therefore specifies a predictive distribution for y_t. If ε_t is Gaussian, so that (1.8) becomes

$$y_t = \sigma_t \varepsilon_t, \qquad \varepsilon_t \sim \text{NID}(0, 1) \tag{3.2}$$

the model itself is conditionally Gaussian, and we could write $y_t | Y_{t-1} \sim N(0, \sigma_t^2)$. Because the variance has an analogous form to the conditional expectation of the mean in a standard AR(1) process, the model is said to exhibit *autoregressive conditional heteroscedasticity*, or ARCH. A wide variety of models based on this idea may be formulated; see the review by Bollerslev *et al.* (1992).

Properties of ARCH

The ARCH model is an MD, and so its unconditional mean is zero and it is serially uncorrelated. The unconditional variance can be found using the law of iterated expectations. Using the notation established earlier, we have

$$\mathop{E}_{t-2} \mathop{E}_{t-1} (y_t^2) = \mathop{E}_{t-2} [\gamma + \alpha y_{t-1}^2] = \gamma + \gamma \alpha + \alpha^2 y_{t-2}^2$$

Repeating this operation until the last expectation is taken at time $t - J$ gives

$$\mathop{E}_{t-J} \cdots \mathop{E}_{t-1} (y_t^2) = \gamma + \gamma \alpha + \gamma \alpha^2 + \cdots + \gamma \alpha^{J-1} + \alpha^J y_{t-J}^2 \tag{3.3}$$

If $\alpha < 1$, letting $J \to \infty$ and summing as an infinite geometric progression gives

$$\text{Var}(y_t) = E(y_t^2) = \gamma/(1 - \alpha) \tag{3.4}$$

The ARCH process is therefore WN, but not strict WN. Furthermore, even though it may be specified to be conditionally Gaussian, as in (3.2), it is not unconditionally Gaussian. Indeed it cannot be unconditionally Gaussian, since if it were, it would be a linear model. The actual unconditional distribution is not of any standard form, but it is easy to see that it is symmetric since all the odd moments are zero. It can also be shown that, if $3\alpha^2 < 1$, the kurtosis is given by $3(1 - \alpha^2)/(1 - 3\alpha^2)$. This is greater than 3 for α positive, and so the ARCH model yields observations with heavier tails than those of a normal distribution. This is an appealing property, because many financial time series are observed to have heavy-tailed distributions.

The dynamics of the ARCH model show up nicely in the ACF of the squared observations. Write

$$y_t^2 = \sigma_t^2 + (y_t^2 - \sigma_t^2)$$

and then use (3.1) and (3.2) to get

$$y_t^2 = \gamma + \alpha y_{t-1}^2 + v_t \tag{3.5}$$

where $v_t = \sigma_t^2(\varepsilon_t^2 - 1)$. The disturbance term, v_t, in (3.5) is an MD since

$$\underset{t-1}{E}\ (v_t) = \sigma_t^2\ \underset{t-1}{E}\ (\varepsilon_t^2 - 1) = 0$$

and, after a little effort, it can be shown to have constant variance. It is therefore WN. Thus (3.5) indicates that the squared observations follow an AR(1) process, the properties of which were established in section 2.2. The ACF is therefore

$$\rho(\tau; y_t^2) = \alpha^\tau, \qquad \tau = 0, 1, 2, \dots \tag{3.6}$$

As regards prediction, the conditional expectation of any future observation is zero, but applying the law of iterated expectations as in (3.3) shows that the prediction MSE, which in this case is just the conditional variance of the future observation, is

$$\text{MSE}(\tilde{y}_{T+l|T}) = \gamma(1 + \alpha + \alpha^2 + \cdots + \alpha^{l-1}) + \alpha^l y_T^2 \tag{3.7}$$

If the series were treated as though it was WN, the prediction would be given by the unconditional variance, (3.4). Expression (3.7) tends to (3.4) as $l \to \infty$, but for a small lead time it could be quite different.

Generalised ARCH

The simple ARCH model based on (3.1) is not entirely satisfactory because the conditional variance depends only on a single observation. A high conditional variance in the previous time period could easily generate an observation close to zero, with the result that the current conditional variance would be relatively small. As a rule, one would expect the variance to change more slowly. This indicates the need to spread the memory of the process over a number of past observations. Thus more lags might be introduced in (3.1) to give

$$\sigma_t^2 = \gamma + \alpha_1 y_{t-1}^2 + \cdots + \alpha_p y_{t-p}^2 \tag{3.8}$$

This is an ARCH(p) process. Obviously in this terminology (3.1) is first-order ARCH or ARCH(1).

The $\text{ARCH}(p)$ model seems to work better in practice if some restrictions are put on the coefficients. Thus, for example, a linear decline might be imposed by setting

$$\alpha_i = \alpha\{(9-i)/36\}, \qquad i = 1, \ldots, 8 \tag{3.9}$$

thereby leaving only two free parameters to be estimated. A better approach is to introduce lagged values of σ_t^2 into the equation to give the *generalised ARCH* model

$$\sigma_t^2 = \gamma + \alpha_1 y_{t-1}^2 + \cdots + \alpha_p y_{t-p}^2 + \beta_1 \sigma_{t-1}^2 + \cdots + \beta_q \sigma_{t-q}^2 \tag{3.10}$$

This model was suggested by Bollerslev (1986) and is termed $\text{GARCH}(p, q)$. The simplest such model is $\text{GARCH}(1, 1)$

$$\sigma_t^2 = \gamma + \alpha y_{t-1}^2 + \beta \sigma_{t-1}^2, \qquad \gamma > 0, \qquad \alpha, \beta \geqslant 0, \qquad \alpha + \beta < 1 \tag{3.11}$$

All GARCH models are MDs. If the sum of the α_i's and β_j's is less than one, the model has constant finite variance and so is WN. This is easy to see in the $\text{GARCH}(1, 1)$ case, where following the derivation for the $\text{ARCH}(1)$ model, we can write

$$\mathop{E}_{t-2} \mathop{E}_{t-1} (y_t^2) = \mathop{E}_{t-2} [\gamma + \alpha y_{t-1}^2 + \beta \sigma_{t-1}^2] = \gamma + (\alpha + \beta)\sigma_{t-1}^2$$

$$= \gamma + (\alpha + \beta)[\gamma + \alpha y_{t-2}^2 + \beta \sigma_{t-2}^2]$$

Repeating this process *ad infinitum*, it can be seen that if $\alpha + \beta < 1$,

$$\text{Var}(y_t) = \gamma/(1 - \alpha - \beta) \tag{3.12}$$

The ACF of the squared observations of a GARCH process is analogous to that of an ARMA process, but the correspondence is not quite as direct as in the pure ARCH case. Following (3.5) write

$$y_t^2 = \gamma + \sum_{i=1}^{p} \alpha_i y_{t-i}^2 + \sum_{j=1}^{q} \beta_j \sigma_{t-j}^2 + v_t$$

where, as before, the disturbance term $v_t = \sigma_t^2(\varepsilon_t^2 - 1)$ can be shown to be WN. Adding and subtracting $\beta_j y_{t-j}^2$ for $j = 1, \ldots, q$, gives

$$y_t^2 = \gamma + \sum_{i=1}^{p} \alpha_i y_{t-i}^2 + \sum_{j=1}^{q} \beta_j y_{t-j}^2 + \sum_{j=1}^{q} \beta_j(\sigma_{t-j}^2 - y_{t-j}^2) + v_t$$

which, on re-arranging and defining $p^* = \max(p, q)$, becomes

$$y_t^2 = \gamma + \sum_{i=1}^{p^*} \phi_i y_{t-i}^2 + v_t + \sum_{j=1}^{p} \theta_j v_{t-j} \tag{3.13}$$

where

$$\phi_i = \alpha_i + \beta_i, \qquad i = 1, \ldots, p^* \qquad \text{and} \qquad \theta_j = -\beta_j, \qquad j = 1, \ldots, q$$

The ACF of y_t^2 is therefore the same as that of the $\mathrm{ARMA}(p^*, q)$ process in (3.13).

In the GARCH(1, 1) model, the ACF is that of an ARMA(1, 1) process as in (2.4.13). Thus if the sum of α and β is close to one, the ACF will decay quite slowly, indicating a relatively slowly changing conditional variance. In introducing GARCH it was argued that this may well happen in practice, and in fact GARCH(1, 1) models with $\alpha + \beta$ close to unity are often found to give a good fit to the data.

Integrated GARCH

If we set $\alpha + \beta = 1$ in the GARCH(1, 1) model, it is no longer weakly stationary since it does not have finite variance. Expression (3.13) becomes

$$y_t^2 = \gamma + y_{t-1}^2 + v_t + \theta v_{t-1} \tag{3.14}$$

where $\theta = -\beta = 1 - \alpha$. Re-arranging as

$$\Delta y_t^2 = \gamma + v_t + \theta v_{t-1} \tag{3.15}$$

indicates an analogy with the ARIMA(0, 1, 1) model from the point of view of defining an ACF of squared observations. Because the squared observations are stationary in first differences, the model is called *integrated GARCH*, or *IGARCH*. However, it does not follow from this that y_t^2 will behave like an integrated process, and, in fact, it turns out, perhaps rather surprisingly, to be strictly stationary. (The existence of moments is not required for strict stationarity.)

The IGARCH model is still an MD, and so forecasts of all future observations are zero. The prediction MSE increases with the lead time, since

$$\mathrm{MSE}(\tilde{y}_{T+l|T}) = \gamma l + \alpha y_T^2 + (1 - \alpha)\sigma_T^2 \tag{3.16}$$

On the other hand, if we set $\gamma = 0$ so as to obtain a constant prediction MSE, the IGARCH process has the rather strange property that, no matter what the starting point, σ_t^2 collapses to zero almost surely, so that the series effectively disappears; see Nelson (1990). Thus it is essential that γ be strictly positive.

Estimation and Testing

The likelihood function for an ARCH or GARCH model can usually be written down directly using (2.1). In the case of a conditionally Gaussian first-order ARCH model, $p(y_t | Y_{t-1})$ is normal with mean zero and variance (3.1) and if y_0 is arbitrarily assumed to be fixed and equal to zero, the log–likelihood function is

$$\log L(\alpha, \gamma) = -\frac{T}{2} \log 2\pi - \frac{1}{2} \sum_{t=1}^{T} \log(\gamma + \alpha y_{t-1}^2) - \frac{1}{2} \sum_{t=1}^{T} \frac{y_t^2}{\gamma + \alpha y_{t-1}^2} \quad (3.17)$$

The method of scoring appears to be a viable procedure for maximising the likelihood function; see Engle (1982) and EATS, pp. 221–3. Bollerslev (1986) considers the estimation of GARCH models when ε_t follows a t-distribution.

A test for ARCH may be carried out using the Q-statistic of (1.11). In fact this may be rationalised as an LM test against an ARCH(P) model; see EATS, section 6.9. Thus there is a direct parallel with the LM interpretation of a portmanteau test of white noise against an AR(P) alternative.

Regression and ARCH-M

A regression model with a first-order ARCH disturbance can be written as

$$y_t = \mathbf{x}_t' \boldsymbol{\beta} + u_t, \qquad t = 1, \dots, T \quad (3.18a)$$

where $u_t = \sigma_t \varepsilon_t$ as in (3.2) and so, conditional on the information at time $t - 1$, u_t is distributed with mean zero and variance

$$\sigma_t^2 = \gamma + \alpha u_{t-1}^2 \quad (3.18b)$$

Since the disturbances in (3.18a) are white noise, it follows from the Gauss–Markov theorem that an OLS regression of y_t on $\mathbf{x}_t$ yields the best linear unbiased estimator (BLUE) of $\boldsymbol{\beta}$. However, although the disturbances are uncorrelated, they are not independent of each other, and so OLS is inefficient. Given a distribution for ε_t, a fully efficient estimator, which takes account of the dependence in variance, can be constructed by maximum likelihood. For a conditionally Gaussian model, the likelihood function is of the form given in (3.17) but with y_t replaced by $y_t - \mathbf{x}_t' \boldsymbol{\beta}$. It can be shown that the information matrix is block diagonal with respect to the regression parameters, $\boldsymbol{\beta}$, and the ARCH parameters, γ and α.

In the ARCH-M model, ARCH effects appear in the mean of the process. Thus (3.18a) becomes

$$y_t = \mathbf{x}_t' \boldsymbol{\beta} + \delta \sigma_t + u_t \quad (3.19)$$

Models of this kind may be appropriate in situations where expected return is partially dependent on risk as reflected in volatility; see Engle *et al.* (1987). ML estimation proceeds as before.

Exponential ARCH

There are a number of drawbacks to GARCH models. Firstly, the conditional variance is unable to respond asymmetrically to rises and falls in y_t, and such effects are believed to be important in the behaviour of stock returns. Secondly, the parameter constraints are often violated by estimated coefficients; furthermore these constraints may unduly restrict the dynamics of the conditional variance process. Thirdly, assessing whether shocks to conditional variance are 'persistent' is difficult because of the somewhat paradoxical behaviour noted earlier for IGARCH.

In order to overcome these problems, Nelson (1991) proposed a class of exponential ARCH, or EGARCH, models. The conditional variance is constrained to be non-negative by assuming that the logarithm of σ_t^2 is a function of past ε_t's. Thus,

$$\log \sigma_t^2 = \gamma + \sum_{i=1}^{\infty} \psi_i g(\varepsilon_{t-i}), \qquad \psi_0 = 1 \tag{3.20}$$

The specification

$$g(\varepsilon_t) = \omega \varepsilon_t + \lambda [|\varepsilon_t| - E|\varepsilon_t|] \tag{3.21}$$

means that $g(\varepsilon_t)$ is a function of both the magnitude and sign of ε_{t-1}, and this enables σ_t^2 to respond asymmetrically to rises and falls in y_t. When ε_t is positive, $g(\varepsilon_t)$ is linear in ε_t with slope $\omega + \lambda$ and when it is negative, $g(\varepsilon_t)$ has slope $\omega - \lambda$.

By construction $g(\varepsilon_t)$ is a zero mean IID process. Thus the stationarity of $\log \sigma_t^2$ depends on whether the sum of squares of the weights, ψ_i, in the infinite sum of (3.20) is finite; compare with (2.1.24). A parsimonious representation of (3.20) can be obtained by modelling the dependence as an ARMA(p, q) process. Thus

$$\log \sigma_t^2 = \gamma + \frac{\theta(L)}{\phi(L)} g(\varepsilon_{t-1}) \tag{3.22}$$

or

$$\log \sigma_t^2 = \gamma(1 - \phi_1 - \cdots - \phi_p) + \phi_1 \log \sigma_{t-1}^2 + \cdots + \phi_p \log \sigma_{t-p}^2$$
$$+ g(\varepsilon_{t-1}) + \theta_1 g(\varepsilon_{t-2}) + \cdots + \theta_q g(\varepsilon_{t-q})$$

The dynamic properties of $\log \sigma_t^2$ are obtained directly from a knowledge of the standard properties of an ARMA(p, q) process. Persistence in conditional variance could be modelled by an ARIMA process in (3.22).

Maximum likelihood estimation of EGARCH models is carried out in essentially the same way as for models in the GARCH class. The lagged values of ε_t which enter into (3.22) are known at time $t - 1$ since σ_{t-1}^2 is known and $\varepsilon_{t-1} = y_{t-1}/\sigma_{t-1}$.

Example 1 Nelson (1991) models the disturbance in (3.19) as an EGARCH process, where the observations are daily returns on a value-weighted stock market index. He finds an ARMA$(2,1)$ model to be appropriate.

8.4 Stochastic Variance Models

An alternative approach is to treat σ_t in (1.8) as an unobserved variable which is assumed to follow a certain stochastic process. Models of this kind are called *stochastic volatility*, or *stochastic variance* (SV), *models*. They fit more naturally into the theoretical framework within which much of modern finance theory, including generalisations of the Black–Scholes result on option pricing, has been developed. Their principal disadvantage is that it is difficult to write down the exact likelihood function. However, they do have other compensating statistical attractions. For example, they are able to overcome the drawbacks to GARCH models noted in the previous sub-section.

A stochastic process is not set up directly for σ_t^2, but is instead formulated for its logarithm thereby ensuring that σ_t^2 is always positive, as in EGARCH. We may therefore write

$$y_t = \sigma_t \varepsilon_t, \qquad \sigma_t^2 = \exp(h_t), \qquad t = 1, \ldots, T \qquad (4.1)$$

and let h_t follow, for example, an AR(1) process

$$h_t = \gamma + \phi h_{t-1} + \eta_t, \qquad \eta_t \sim \text{NID}(0, \sigma_\eta^2) \qquad (4.2)$$

where η_t may, or may not, be independent of ε_t. The key to handling such models is the state space form. Before describing how the method is implemented, the properties of stochastic variance models are derived and compared with those of GARCH processes. To simplify matters, this next sub-section will assume that η_t and ε_t are independent.

Properties

If $|\phi| < 1$ in (4.2), it is known from the standard theory of section 2.2 that h_t is strictly stationary, with mean $\gamma_h = \gamma/(1 - \phi)$ and variance $\sigma_h^2 = \sigma_\eta^2/(1 - \phi^2)$. Since y_t is the product of two strictly stationary processes, it must also be strictly stationary. Thus the restrictions needed to ensure stationarity of y_t are just the standard restrictions needed to ensure stationarity of the process generating h_t.

The fact that y_t is WN follows almost immediately given the independence of ε_t and η_t. The mean is clearly zero, while

$$E(y_t y_{t-\tau}) = E(\varepsilon_t \varepsilon_{t-\tau}) E[\exp(h_t/2) \exp(h_{t-\tau}/2)] = 0$$

because $E(\varepsilon_t \varepsilon_{t-\tau}) = 0$.

The odd moments of y_t are all zero if ε_t is symmetric. If ε_t is Gaussian, the even moments can be obtained by making use of a standard result for the log–normal distribution, which in the present context tells us that since $\exp(h_t)$ is log–normal, its jth moment about the origin is $\exp\{j\gamma_h + \frac{1}{2}j^2\sigma_h^2\}$. Therefore

$$\mathrm{Var}(y_t) = E(\varepsilon_t^2)E\{\exp(h_t)\} = \exp\{\gamma_h + \tfrac{1}{2}\sigma_h^2\} \tag{4.3}$$

The fourth moment is

$$E(y_t^4) = E(\varepsilon_t^4)E\{\exp(2h_t)\} = 3\exp\{2\gamma_h + 2\sigma_h^2\} \tag{4.4}$$

and so the kurtosis is $3\exp\{\sigma_h^2\}$, which is greater than three when σ_h^2 is positive. Thus the model exhibits excess kurtosis compared with a normal distribution.

The dynamic properties of the model appear in $\log y_t^2$ rather than y_t^2. Taking logarithms of the squared observations in (4.1) gives

$$\log y_t^2 = h_t + \log \varepsilon_t^2$$

If ε_t has a standard normal distribution, the mean and variance of $\log \varepsilon_t^2$ are known to be -1.27 and 4.93 respectively, and we may write

$$\log y_t^2 = -1.27 + h_t + \varepsilon_t^* \tag{4.5}$$

where $\varepsilon_t^* = \log \varepsilon_t^2 + 1.27$. It follows that $\log y_t^2$ is the sum of an AR(1) component and white noise and its ACF is

$$\rho(\tau; \log y_t^2) = \phi^\tau/(1 + 4.93/\sigma_h^2), \qquad \tau = 1, 2, \ldots \tag{4.6}$$

Since $\log y_t^2$ is equivalent to an ARMA(1, 1) process, its properties are similar to those of GARCH(1, 1). Indeed, if σ_h^2 is small and/or ϕ is close to one, the correlogram of y_t^2 is very close to that of an ARMA(1, 1) process; see Taylor (1986, pp. 74–5).

The model can be generalised so that h_t follows any stationary ARMA process, in which case y_t is also stationary with variance and fourth moment given by (4.3) and (4.4) respectively. The ACF of $\log y_t^2$ can again be deduced from (4.5) and the dynamic properties of h_t.

As noted earlier, the ARCH model may be generalised by letting ε_t have a Student t-distribution. This is important because the kurtosis in many financial series is greater than the kurtosis which results from incorporating conditional heteroscedasticity into a Gaussian process. A similar generalisation is possible for the SV model. Once again it can be shown that when h_t is stationary, y_t is white noise and it follows immediately from the properties of the t-distribution that the formula for the unconditional variance in (4.3) generalises to $\{v/(v-2)\}\exp(\gamma_h + \frac{1}{2}\sigma_h^2)$, where v is the degrees of freedom. The kurtosis is $3\{(v-2)/(v-4)\}\exp(\sigma_h^2)$.

If ε_t is a t-variable it may be written as

$$\varepsilon_t = \zeta_t/\kappa_t^{1/2} \tag{4.7}$$

where ζ_t is a standard normal variate and $\nu\kappa_t$ is distributed, independently of ζ_t, as a χ^2 with ν degrees of freedom. Thus

$$\log \varepsilon_t^2 = \log \zeta_t^2 - \log \kappa_t \tag{4.8}$$

and it follows from results in Abramowitz and Stegun (1970, p. 260) that the mean and variance of $\log \kappa_t$ are

$$E(\log \kappa_t) = \psi(\nu/2) - \log(\nu/2) \tag{4.9}$$

and

$$\mathrm{Var}(\log \kappa_t) = \psi'(\nu/2) \tag{4.10}$$

where $\psi(\cdot)$ and $\psi'(\cdot)$ are the digamma and trigamma functions respectively. Thus (4.5) becomes

$$\log y_t^2 = -1.27 - \psi(\nu/2) + \log(\nu/2) + h_t + \varepsilon_t^* \tag{4.11}$$

where ε_t^* has a zero mean and a variance equal to $4.93 + \psi'(\nu/2)$. The ACF of $\log y_t^2$ has the same form as before except that $\psi'(\nu/2)$ is added to 4.93 in the expression for $\rho(\tau; \log y_t^2)$ in (4.6).

Estimation

The model fits naturally into state space form with (4.5) being the measurement equation and (4.2) the transition equation. It can be shown that η_t and the disturbance ε_t^* are uncorrelated, even if η_t and ε_t are not; see Harvey *et al.* (1992). The problem is that the disturbance ε_t^* in (4.5) is far from being Gaussian. Thus although the Kalman filter can be applied, it will only yield MMSLEs of the state and future observations rather than MMSEs. Furthermore, since the model is not conditionally Gaussian, an exact likelihood cannot be obtained from the Kalman filter. Nevertheless estimates can be computed by treating the model as though it were Gaussian and maximising the resulting quasi-likelihood function.

An interesting issue is whether or not to use the assumption that ε_t is Gaussian in applying the above procedure. According to the results in Ruiz (1992) there is little gain in efficiency in making such an assumption, even when it is true. Thus it would seem to be much better to estimate the variance of ε_t^* rather than setting it to 4.93. However, leaving the distribution of ε_t unspecified means that γ_h is not identified since the expected value of $\log \varepsilon_t^2$ is unknown. Thus the level of volatility is not determined. If ε_t is assumed to have a t-distribution, the estimated variance of ε_t^* implies a value of ν when set to $4.93 + \psi'(\nu/2)$ and this in turn gives the expectation of $\log \varepsilon_t^2$ from (4.8) and (4.9).¹

An alternative to the quasi-ML method is the generalised method of moments estimation procedure used by Melino and Turnbull (1990).

Non-Stationary Variance

The variance can be allowed to evolve according to a non-stationary process. The simplest option is to let h_t follow a random walk

$$h_t = h_{t-1} + \eta_t, \qquad \eta_t \sim \text{NID}(0, \sigma_\eta^2) \tag{4.12}$$

In this case $\log y_t^2$ is a random walk plus noise. This is one of the simplest structural time series models, and it was shown in section 5.3 that the optimal predictor is an EWMA of past observations. Thus there is a parallel with the IGARCH model where the conditional variance,

$$h_t = \gamma + \alpha y_{t-1}^2 + (1 - \alpha)h_{t-1}$$

is also an EWMA. The crucial difference is that while the IGARCH conditional variance is known exactly, the variance here is an unobserved component, and a better estimate can be obtained by a smoothing algorithm. Although the model based on (4.12) does not yield an exact likelihood, in the way that IGARCH does, it contains one less parameter, and can be estimated quite easily by the quasi-ML procedure outlined above. Like IGARCH it seems to provide a good fit to many data sets, and it generalises easily to multivariate series.

> *Example 1* For daily observations on the pound–dollar exchange rate from 1 October 1981 to 28 June 1985, a sample size of 946, the Box–Ljung Q-statistic for the first differences of logarithms, denoted y_t, is 11.19. The χ^2 5 per cent critical value for ten degrees of freedom is 18.3, and so y_t appears to be a random walk. However, the Q-statistics for y_t^2 and $\log y_t^2$ are 128.25 and 45.47 respectively, and so there is strong evidence of non-linearity.
>
> The stationary AR(1) stochastic volatility model (4.2) was fitted to the differences of the logarithm of the exchange rate, with the mean subtracted. Estimation by quasi-maximum likelihood yielded $\tilde{\phi} = 0.991$. Not surprisingly, the random walk specification (4.12) fits almost as well. The estimate of σ_η^2 is 0.0042 and the Box–Ljung statistic, $Q(10) = 3.52$, gives no indication of residual serial correlation. Figure 8.2, taken from Harvey *et al.* (1992), shows the absolute values, $|y_t|$, for the pound–dollar series, together with the estimated standard deviation, $\exp(\frac{1}{2}\tilde{h}_{t|T})$, where $\tilde{h}_{t|T}$ is the MMSLE of the volatility level, h_t, as given by the smoothing algorithm.
>
> Estimation of the model without the variance of $\log \varepsilon_t^2$ constrained to be 4.93 gives the same result. However, data on the yen–dollar rate over the same period, shown in figure 8.1, gives an unconstrained estimate of 5.30 for the variance of $\log \varepsilon_t^2$. Setting (4.10) to 5.30 minus 4.93 and solving for v suggests that ε_t might be regarded as being from a t-distribution with about six degrees of freedom.

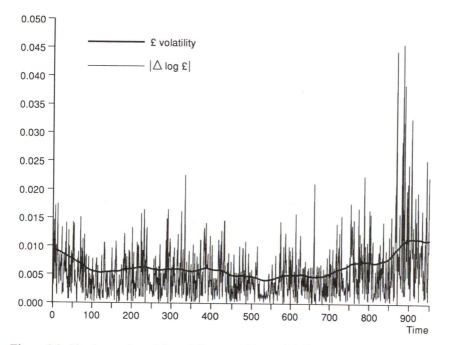

Figure 8.2 Absolute value of first difference of logged daily pound–dollar exchange rate and smoothed estimates of standard deviation, 1 October 1981 to 28 June 1985.

8.5 Qualitative Observations and Markov Chains

Time series sometimes consist of observations on a qualitative variable, which can have two states such as 'Yes/No' or 'True/False'. The variable is therefore binary (dichotomous), taking the values zero or one. Thus $y_t = 0$ or 1 for $t = 1, \ldots, T$. The movement from one state, or *regime*, to another is governed by transition probabilities. In a Markov chain these probabilities depend only on the current state. Thus if $y_{t-1} = 1$, $\Pr(y_t = 1) = \pi_1$ and $\Pr(y_t = 0) = 1 - \pi_1$, while if $y_{t-1} = 0$, $\Pr(y_t = 0) = \pi_0$ and $\Pr(y_t = 1) = 1 - \pi_0$. These transition probabilities may be expressed as in table 8.1.

Table 8.1 State at t

		0	1
State at $t-1$	0	π_0	$1 - \pi_0$
	1	$1 - \pi_1$	π_1

The study of Markov chains is a whole subject in itself. Here we look at the simplest cases and show the connection with classical time series models. In the next section it is shown how Markov chains form the basis for models of *switching regimes*.

Markov Chains and Autoregressions

At first sight the Markov chain defined by the transition probabilities in the table above looks totally different from the kind of stochastic process formulated for a continuous variable. However, it turns out to be an $AR(1)$ process. This follows from first noting that

$$E(y_t|y_{t-1}) = \Pr(y_t = 1|y_{t-1}) = (1 - \pi_0)(1 - y_{t-1}) + \pi_1 y_{t-1}$$
$$= 1 - \pi_0 + (\pi_0 + \pi_1 - 1)y_{t-1}$$

Thus

$$y_t = \theta + \phi y_{t-1} + v_t, \qquad t = 1, \ldots, T \tag{5.1}$$

where

$$\phi = \pi_0 + \pi_1 - 1, \qquad \theta = 1 - \pi_0$$

and the properties of the disturbance term v_t are such that for $y_{t-1} = 1$

$$\Pr(v_t = 1 - \pi_1) = \pi_1$$
$$\Pr(v_t = -\pi_1) = 1 - \pi_1$$

while for $y_{t-1} = 0$

$$\Pr(v_t = \pi_0 - 1) = \pi_0$$
$$\Pr(v_t = \pi_0) = 1 - \pi_0$$

By construction $E(v_t|y_{t-1})$ is zero. Thus it is a martingale difference, its unconditional expectation is zero and it is serially uncorrelated.

If the process is assumed to have started at some point in the remote past, we can substitute repeatedly for lagged values of y_t, as in (2.2.5), to give

$$y_t = \frac{\theta}{1 - \phi} + \sum_{j=0}^{\infty} \phi^j v_{t-j}, \qquad |\phi| < 1 \tag{5.2}$$

It therefore follows that the mean of the process is

$$\mu = E(y_t) = \frac{\theta}{1 - \phi} = \frac{1 - \pi_0}{1 - \pi_0 + 1 - \pi_1} \tag{5.3}$$

This is also the unconditional probability that y_t is one. In the Markov chain literature it is called the steady-state probability.

The unconditional variance of v_t is given by

$$\text{Var}(v_t) = E(v_t^2|y_t = 1)\Pr(y_t = 1) + E(v_t^2|y_t = 0)\Pr(y_t = 0)$$

$$= \pi_0(1 - \pi_0)(1 - \mu) + \pi_1(1 - \pi_1)\mu \tag{5.4}$$

This does not depend on t. Thus (5.1) is an AR(1) model of the form studied in section 2.2 since the disturbance term, v_t, is white noise. Hence its ACF is given by

$$\rho(\tau) = \phi^\tau, \qquad \tau = 0, 1, 2, \ldots \tag{5.5}$$

The process is stationary provided that either π_0 or π_1 lies strictly between zero and one. In the special case $\pi_0 = \pi_1$, the process is said to be *symmetric*. Then $\phi = 2\pi_0 - 1$ and $\text{Var}(v_t) = \pi_0(1 - \pi_0)$. The mean of a symmetric process is always 0.5. In the special case when $\pi_0 + \pi_1 = 1$, y_t is white noise with variance 0.25. In fact, the observations are IID. This is not true, in general, of the v_t's. These are white noise, but, unless $\pi_0 + \pi_1 = 1$, they are not independent since their distribution depends on the state in the previous time period. Thus (5.1) is a non-linear model. The MMSE of y_{t+l} is still the same as the MMSLE, that is

$$\tilde{y}_{T+l|T} = \mu + \phi^l(y_T - \mu) \tag{5.6}$$

because v_t is a martingale difference. However, the MSE is not given by expression (2.6.12), since the distribution of y_{T+l} conditional on Y_T is binomial with a probability that y_{T+l} is one given by $\tilde{y}_{T+l|T}$.

Estimation

Estimation of the Markov chain parameters can be carried out in a fairly obvious way simply by counting the number of changes from one state to another. Let n_{ij}, $i, j = 0, 1$, be the number of times, in a sample of size T, that there is a move from state i to state j. The log–likelihood function is then

$$\log L = n_{00}\log \pi_0 + n_{01}\log(1 - \pi_0) + n_{10}\log(1 - \pi_1) + n_{11}\log \pi_1 \tag{5.7}$$

The ML estimates of π_0 and π_1 are therefore

$$\tilde{\pi}_0 = n_{00}/(n_{00} + n_{01}) \qquad \text{and} \qquad \tilde{\pi}_1 = n_{11}/(n_{10} + n_{11})$$

Example 1 Ignoring the dead heat of 1877, there were 130 boat races between the universities of Oxford and Cambridge up to and including 1985. We can denote a win for Oxford as one, and a win for Cambridge as zero. The runs test clearly indicates serial correlation. Estimating the parameters in a Markov chain model using the 130 observations gives $\tilde{\pi}_0 = 0.662$ and $\tilde{\pi}_1 = 0.623$. Thus the probability of staying in the same state is quite close for the two states; estimating this as a single probability gives 0.643. In a symmetric model, therefore, the probability of last year's winner winning this year is just slightly less than two-thirds.

Extensions and Alternatives

The Markov chain model can be extended so that the probability of staying in the same state depends on both the current state and the states in the preceding $p - 1$ time periods. Such p-dependent Markov chains rapidly become intractable as they contain $2p$ parameters. Imposing symmetry leads to a model with only p parameters. This is analogous to an AR(p) model with known mean. If we wish to allow for the equilibrium probability being different to 0.5, an extra parameter is needed. The most appealing formulation has the logit of π_t depending on the p previous observations and a constant term; see Cox and Snell (1989, pp. 96–105).

Binary observations need not necessarily be modelled by stationary processes. For example, in the boat race example, the fact that Oxford won nearly all the races in the 1980s might lead one to prefer a model in which the probability of an Oxford win was allowed to increase towards the end of the period. This may be done using a variation of the local level structural time series model which explicitly handles dichotomous observations; see FSK, section 6.6.

The above ideas may be extended to situations where there is more than one state. The Markov chain operates as before, with a probability specified for moving from any of the states at time $t - 1$ to any other state at time t. A non-stationary multinomial model is also possible.

8.6 Switching Regimes

The observations in a time series may sometimes be generated by different mechanisms at different points in time. When this happens, we will say that the model is subject to switching *regimes*. If the points at which the regime changes are known in advance, or at least in the previous time period, the Kalman filter provides the basis for a statistical treatment; see section 8.2. However, the concern here is with situations in which the regime is not directly observable but is known to change according to a Markov process. Models of this kind have been proposed by Harrison and Stevens (1976) and Hamilton (1989, 1992). This section follows Hamilton's approach in deriving a filter and a method for ML estimation.

State Space

A state space model may be formulated by specifying a distribution for each observation, y_t, conditional on the state vector, α_t, together with a distribution of α_t conditional on α_{t-1}. In a linear Gaussian state space model, these distributions are expressed in terms of the familiar measurement and transition equations, and the Kalman filter provides the basis for prediction, smoothing and ML estimation. In the general formulation, the observations may be discrete or continuous as may the variables in the state. For continuous state variables the appropriate filter is as given in Kitagawa (1987) and FSK, p. 163. In the present context, our interest lies in a single state variable which is discrete. The filter presented below is the same as the filter for a continuous state, except that integration is replaced by summation.

The state variable takes the values $1, 2, \ldots, m$, and these values represent each of m different regimes. (In the previous section, the term state was used where here we use regime; the use of 'state' for the value of the state variable could be confusing here.) The transition mechanism is a Markov process which specifies $\Pr(\alpha_t = i | \alpha_{t-1} = j)$ for $i, j = 1, \ldots, m$. Given probabilities of being in each of the regimes at time $t - 1$, the corresponding probabilities in the next time period are

$$\Pr(\alpha_t = i | Y_{t-1}) = \sum_{j=1}^{m} \Pr(\alpha_t = i | \alpha_{t-1} = j) \Pr(\alpha_{t-1} = j | Y_{t-1}),$$

$$i = 1, 2, \ldots, m \qquad (6.1)$$

and the conditional PDF of y_t is a mixture of distributions given by

$$p(y_t | Y_{t-1}) = \sum_{j=1}^{m} p(y_t | \alpha_t = j) \Pr(\alpha_t = j | Y_{t-1}) \qquad (6.2)$$

where $p(y_t | \alpha_t = j)$ is the distribution of y_t in regime j. As regards updating

$$\Pr(\alpha_t = i | Y_t) = \frac{p(y_t | \alpha_t = i) \cdot \Pr(\alpha_t = i | Y_{t-1})}{p(y_t | Y_{t-1})},$$

$$i = 1, 2, \ldots, m \qquad (6.3)$$

Given initial conditions for the probability that α_t is equal to each of its m values at time zero, the filter can be run to produce the probability of being in a given regime at the end of the sample. Predictions of future observations can then be made. If $\mathbf{M}$ denotes the transition matrix with ijth element equal to $\Pr(\alpha_t = i | \alpha_{t-1} = j)$ and $\mathbf{p}_{t|t-k}$ is the $m \times 1$ vector with ith element $\Pr(\alpha_t = i | Y_{t-k})$, $k = 0, 1, 2, \ldots$, then

$$\mathbf{p}_{T+l|T} = \mathbf{M}^l \mathbf{p}_{T|T}, \qquad l = 1, 2, \ldots$$

and so

$$p(y_{T+l}|Y_T) = \sum_{j=1}^{m} p(y_{T+l}|\alpha_{T+l} = j)\Pr(\alpha_{T+l} = j|Y_T) \qquad (6.4)$$

An exact smoother may also be derived.

The likelihood function can be constructed from the one-step predictive distributions (6.2) just as in (2.1). The unknown parameters consist of the transition probabilities in the matrix M and the parameters in the measurement equation distributions, $p(y_t|\alpha_t = j)$, $j = 1, \ldots, m$.

Time Series Models with Switching Regimes

The above state space form may be extended by allowing the distribution of y_t to be conditional on past observations as well as on the current state. It may also depend on past regimes, so the current state becomes a vector containing the state variables in previous time periods. This may be expressed by writing the state vector at time t as $\alpha_t = (s_t, s_{t-1}, \ldots, s_{t-p})'$, where s_t is the state variable at time t.

In the model of Hamilton (1989), the observations are generated by an $AR(p)$ process of the form

$$y_t - \mu(s_t) = \phi_1[y_{t-1} - \mu(s_{t-1})] + \cdots + \phi_p[y_{t-p} - \mu(s_{t-p})] + \varepsilon_t \qquad (6.5)$$

where $\varepsilon_t \sim NID(0, \sigma^2)$. Thus the expected value of y_t, denoted $\mu(s_t)$, varies according to the regime, and it is the value appropriate to the corresponding lag on y_t which enters into the equation. Hence the distribution of y_t is conditional on s_t and s_{t-1} to s_{t-p} as well as on y_{t-1} to y_{t-p}.

The filter of the previous sub-section can still be applied although the summation must now be over all values of the $p + 1$ state variables in α_t. The only new problem concerns the initialisation of the filter, which has to be based on the joint density of $y_1, \ldots, y_p, s_1, \ldots, s_p$. For simplicity, let $p = 1$, so that

$$y_t - \mu(s_t) = \phi[y_{t-1} - \mu(s_{t-1})] + \varepsilon_t, \qquad t = 1, \ldots, T \qquad (6.6)$$

and suppose that there are only two regimes. Given an initial assumption about the probability distribution of s_1, denoted $p(s_1)$, the joint probability distribution of s_1 and s_2 is

$$p(s_1, s_2) = p(s_2|s_1)p(s_1)$$

where $p(s_2|s_1)$ depends on the assumed transition probabilities. The four elements of $p(s_2|s_1)$ are $\Pr(s_t = i, s_t = j)$, for $i, j = 1, 2$. Next observe that $p(y_1, y_2|s_1, s_2)$, the joint density of y_1 and y_2 conditional on s_1 and s_2, is multivariate normal with mean vector $[\mu(s_1), \mu(s_2)]'$ and covariance matrix

$$V = \frac{\sigma^2}{1 - \phi^2} \begin{bmatrix} 1 & \phi \\ \phi & 1 \end{bmatrix}$$

Hence, the joint probability density is obtained as

$$p(y_1, y_2, s_1, s_2) = p(y_1, y_2 | s_1, s_2) p(s_1, s_2)$$

The formulae in (6.1) to (6.3) may now be applied by observing that the state vector, α_t, now consists of two variables, s_1 and s_2, each of which has two distinct values. Thus the summations are over four values. The likelihood function is

$$\log L = p(y_2, y_1) \prod_{t=3}^{T} p(y_t | Y_{t-1})$$

where

$$p(y_1, y_2) = \sum_{j=1}^{2} \sum_{i=1}^{2} p(y_1, y_2 | s_1 = i, s_2 = j)$$

Hamilton's model has been applied to modelling cycles in macroeconomic time series and to the term structure of interest rates.

Appendix   Law of Iterated Expectations

It is sometimes easier to evaluate the expectation of a random variable, Y, by first finding its expectation conditional on another variable, X, and then taking the expectation of the resulting expression with respect to the distribution of X. Thus, using obvious notation, the operation we are carrying out is

$$E[E(Y | X = x)] = \int \left[\int y p(y|x) \, dy \right] p(x) \, dx$$

and on re-arranging and substituting the joint density for the product of the conditional and marginal densities, we get

$$\int \int y p(y, x) \, dy \, dx = E(Y)$$

which is the unconditional expectation of Y.

The result generalises to any function of Y, so that

$$E[E\{g(Y) | X = x\}] = E[g(Y)]$$

In the context of this chapter letting Y be the random variable denoting the current observation and X be the variable denoting the previous observation allows us to evaluate the expectation of the current observation, or a function of it, conditional on the information two time periods ago.

Exercises

1. In an AR(1) model, $y_t = \phi y_{t-1} + \varepsilon_t$, the disturbance term, ε_t, is defined such that

$$\varepsilon_t = \begin{cases} v_t, & \text{for } t \text{ even} \\ (v_{t-1}^2 - 1)/\sqrt{2}, & \text{for } t \text{ odd} \end{cases}$$

where $v_t \sim \text{NID}(0, 1)$. Given a sample of ten observations and a value of ϕ, what is the MMSLE of y_{11}? Can you construct a better predictor?

2. Write down the likelihood function for the exponential AR model

$$y_t = \phi_t y_{t-1} + \varepsilon_t, \qquad \phi_t = \phi + \alpha \exp(-\gamma y_{t-1}^2)$$

with $\varepsilon_t \sim \text{NID}(0, \sigma^2)$; see Ozaki (1985).

3. Wecker (1981) proposed the following *asymmetric* time series model

$$y_t = \varepsilon_t + \theta^+ \varepsilon_{t-1}^+ + \theta^- \varepsilon_{t-1}^-, \qquad t = 1, \ldots, T$$

where $\varepsilon_t^+ = \max(\varepsilon_t, 0)$ and $\varepsilon_t^- = \min(\varepsilon_t, 0)$, and $\varepsilon_t \sim \text{NID}(0, \sigma^2)$. Show that, in general, the mean is non-zero. [NB The expected value of $|\varepsilon_t|$ is $(2/\pi)^{1/2}$.] Derive an expression for the first-order autocorrelation, $\rho(1)$. Hence show that the series reduces to white noise if $\theta^+ = \theta^-$. Find the reduction in the one-step ahead forecast MSE in this case if the asymmetric model is used. How would you estimate the parameters in the model?

4. Show that in a Gaussian MA(1) model, the squares of the theoretical autocorrelations are equal to the autocorrelations of the squared observations.

5. Consider a first-order autoregressive model

$$y_t = \phi y_{t-1} + v_t, \qquad t = 2, \ldots, T$$

in which y_1 is fixed and $v_t = h_t^{1/2} \varepsilon_t$, where $\varepsilon_t \sim \text{NID}(0, 1)$ and

$$\sigma_t^2 = \alpha_0 + \alpha_1 v_{t-1}^2, \qquad t = 2, \ldots, T$$

with $v_1 = 0$.

(a) Find an expression for the MMSE of y_{T+2} given the observations up to time T. Derive an expression for its MSE in terms of the parameters ϕ, α_0 and α_1, and any relevant observations.

(b) Explain how you would obtain efficient estimators of the parameters in the model.

(c) Derive the variance and autocorrelation function of y_t. (You may, if you wish, relax the assumption that y_1 is fixed and v_1 is zero.)

6. Consider the stochastic variance model (4.2). How would you test the null hypothesis that ϕ is equal to one, against the alternative that it is less than one, using an augmented Dickey–Fuller test? Would you advise the use of such a test in these circumstances, given that the value of σ_η^2 is typically very small?

7. An observation, y_t, can be drawn randomly from a normal distribution with mean μ and variance σ^2 or it can be equal to the previous observation in the series. If the probability of the first event is π, find the (unconditional) mean and variance of y_t and show that it follows an AR(1) process. Find an expression for the l-step ahead predictor. What is the prediction MSE for $l = 1$? How would you estimate π, ϕ and σ^2?

Answers to Selected Exercises

Chapter 2.– 1. (a) Yes; (b) Yes; see section 6.3; (c) No; (d) No; (e) Yes; roots are $\frac{1}{2} \pm \frac{1}{2}i$; (f) weakly stationary; (g) strictly stationary, but not weakly stationary as moments do not exist.

     2. $0.267, -0.167$.

     5. Yes; there is a common factor of $(1 + 0.8L)$. The model reduces to an $ARMA(1, 1)$ process.

     6. $0.6, 0$.

     7. $1.7, 1.42, 1.19$.

    10. $ARMA(4, 2)$: (a) one common factor.

    11. See Brewer (1973).

Chapter 3.– 1. From Yule–Walker equations, $\tilde{\phi}_1 = 1.11$ and $\tilde{\phi}_2 = -0.39$.

     5. $S(-0.5) = 46.70$.

    12. $\tilde{\phi}(1) = r(1) = 0.7$; $\tilde{\phi}(2) = 0.02$. Suggests $AR(1)$.

    13. $\hat{\theta} = 0.9$ and $\hat{\phi} = -0.5$.

Chapter 5.– 2. $10.8, 11.2, 11.35, \alpha = 10.9, \beta = 0.15$.

     3. (b) Δy_t is $ARMA(1, 1)$ with $\rho(1) = -(1 - \phi)/2 = -0.25$ and $\rho(\tau) = \rho(1)\phi^{\tau - 1}$.

     6. $12.5, 15.0, 17.5$; $\alpha = 10$, $\beta = 2.5$; 20 ± 14.40.

     9. $Tr^2(4)$. Tested as χ_1^2.

    10. See Box and Jenkins (1976, p. 319).

    11. $\tilde{\theta} = -0.39$, $\tilde{\Theta} = -0.48$.

    12. (a) $q = 0.5$, $\sigma_\varepsilon^2 = 2$. (c) Ratio of RMSEs is 0.37; hence government estimator is very inefficient.

    13. Strictly non-invertible. BSM with $\sigma_\zeta^2 = \sigma_\omega^2 = 0$, and $\sigma_\eta^2/\sigma_\varepsilon^2 = 0.5$.

Chapter 6.– 1. Yes; see Anderson (1971, pp. 403–5).

     4. $Ph(\lambda) = \tan^{-1}[-q(\lambda)/c(\lambda)]$.

     8. Moving average filter cuts down high frequencies, but has no phase shift. Difference filter has a phase shift and removes trend, $W(e^{-i\lambda}) = 1 - \exp(-i7\lambda)$.

9. $\rho(1) = -0.5$, $\rho(2) = 0$, $\rho(3) = -0.5\phi$, $\rho(\tau) = \phi\rho(\tau - 4)$ for $\tau \geqslant 4$; $f(\lambda) = 2(1 - \cos\lambda)/(1 + \phi^2 - 2\phi\cos 4\lambda)$.

10. $\hat{y}_t = \dfrac{19}{4} + \dfrac{1}{2}\cos\dfrac{2\pi}{4}t + \dfrac{5}{2}\sin\dfrac{2\pi}{4}t - \dfrac{1}{4}(-1)^t$.

   Standardised coefficients of cosine and sine terms (distributed as $N(0, 1)$) are 0.94 and 4.71 respectively. Standardised coefficient of last term is -0.67.

11. $\text{Avar}(b) = g_0/(T - 1)$; the expression given can be interpreted as a lag window for estimating the spectrum at frequency zero.

Chapter 7.– 1. $\rho_{yx}(\tau) = 0$ for $\tau \leqslant 0$ and $\tau \geqslant 4$.

3. $|\theta(L)| = (1 + \theta L)(1 - L)$.

8. Both $\boldsymbol{\Psi}(1)$ and $\mathbf{F}(0)$ have rank one, indicating co-integration. The cross-covariances are $\gamma_{yx}(\tau) = \beta\phi^{\tau-1}$ for $\tau \geqslant 1$, and $\gamma_{yx}(\tau) = 0$ for $\tau < 1$. The co-integrating vector is $\boldsymbol{\alpha} = (1 - \phi, \beta)'$.

Chapter 8.– 1. The process y_t is WN, but y_{11} can be predicted exactly.

3. $\mu = (\theta^+ - \theta^-)/(2\pi)^{1/2}$; $\gamma(1) = \sigma^2(\theta^+ + \theta^-)/2$.

References

Abraham, B. and J. Ledolter (1983), *Statistical Methods for Forecasting*, John Wiley, New York, NY.

Abramowitz, M. and N. C. Stegun (1970), *Handbook of Mathematical Functions*, Dover Publications Inc., New York, NY.

Ahn, S. K. and G. C. Reinsel (1990), Estimation of partially non-stationary vector autoregressions, *Journal of the American Statistical Association*, **85**, 813–825.

Akaike, H. (1974), A new look at the statistical model identification, *IEEE Transactions on Automatic Control*, **AC-19**, 716–723.

Anderson, B. D. O. and J. B. Moore (1979), *Optimal Filtering*, Prentice Hall, Englewood Cliffs, NJ.

Anderson, T. W. (1971), *The Statistical Analysis of Time Series*, John Wiley, New York, NY.

Ansley, C. F. and R. Kohn (1985), Estimation, filtering and smoothing in state space models with incompletely specified initial conditions, *Annals of Statistics*, **13**, 1286–1316.

Ansley, C. F. and P. Newbold (1980), Finite sample properties of estimators for auto-regressive moving average processes, *Journal of Econometrics*, **13**, 159–184.

Baillie, R. T. (1979), Asymptotic prediction mean squared error for vector autoregressive models, *Biometrika*, **66**, 675–678.

Ball, J. and E. St. Cyr (1966), Short-term employment functions in British manufacturing, *Review of Economic Studies*, **33**, 179–207.

Bartlett, M. S. (1946), On the theoretical specification of sampling properties of autocorrelated time series, *Journal of the Royal Statistical Society, Supplement*, **8**, 27–41.

Bartlett, M. S. (1990), Chance or chaos? (with discussion), *Journal of the Royal Statistical Society*, **153**, 321–347.

Beach, C. M. and J. G. MacKinnon (1978), A maximum likelihood procedure for regression with auto-correlated errors, *Econometrica*, **46**, 51–58.

Beamish, N. and M. B. Priestley (1981), Autoregressive spectral estimation, *Applied Statistics*, **30**, 41–58.

Bollerslev, T. (1986), Generalized autoregressive conditional heteroskedasticity, *Journal of Econometrics*, **31**, 307–327.

Bollerslev, T., Y. Chou and K. F. Kroner (1992), ARCH models in finance: a review of the theory and evidence, *Journal of Econometrics*, **52**, 5–59.

Bowman, K. O. and L. R. Shenton (1975), Omnibus test contours for departures from normality based on $\sqrt{b_1}$ and b_2, *Biometrika*, **62**, 243–250.

Box, G. E. P. and G. M. Jenkins (1976), *Time Series Analysis: Forecasting and Control*, revised edition, Holden-Day, San Francisco, CA.

Box, G. E. P. and D. A. Pierce (1970), Distribution of residual autocorrelations in autoregressive integrated moving average time series models, *Journal of the American Statistical Association*, **65**, 1509–1526.

Box, G. E. P. and G. C. Tiao (1975), Intervention analysis with applications to economic and environmental problems, *Journal of the American Statistical Association*, **70**, 70–79.

Brewer, K. R. W. (1973), Some consequences of temporal aggregation and systematic sampling for ARMA and ARMAX models, *Journal of Econometrics*, **1**, 133–154.

Brock, W. A. and C. L. Sayers (1988), Is the business cycle characterised by deterministic chaos? *Journal of Monetary Economics*, **22**, 71–90.

Brown, R. G. (1963), *Smoothing, Forecasting and Prediction*, Prentice Hall, Englewood Cliffs, NJ.

Chan, W. Y. T. and K. F. Wallis (1978), Multiple time series modelling: another look at mink–muskrat interaction, *Applied Statistics*, **27**, 168–175.

Cheung, Y. W. and F. X. Diebold (1990), On maximum likelihood estimation of the differencing parameter of fractionally integrated noise with unknown mean, Discussion paper 34, Institute for Empirical Macroeconomics, Minneapolis.

Cooley, T. F. and E. C. Prescott (1978), Efficient estimation in the presence of stochastic parameter variation, *Econometrica*, **44**, 167–184.

Cox, D. R. and E. J. Snell (1989), *Analysis of Binary Data*, 2nd edition, Chapman & Hall, London.

Dahlhaus, Z. Z. (1988), Small sample effects in time series analysis: a new asymptotic theory and a new estimate, *Annals of Statistics*, **16**, 808–841.

Davidson, J. E. H. (1981), Problems with the estimation of moving average processes, *Journal of Econometrics*, **16**, 295–310.

Davidson, J. E. H., D. F. Hendry, F. Srba and S. Yeo (1978), Econometric modelling of the aggregate time-series relationship between consumers' expenditure and income in the United Kingdom, *Econometric Journal*, **88**, 661–692.

de Jong, P. (1988), The likelihood for a state space model, *Biometrika*, **75**, 165–169.

de Jong, P. (1991), The diffuse Kalman filter, *Annals of Statistics*, **19**, 1073–1083.

Dent, W. T. and A. S. Min (1978), A Monte Carlo study of autoregressive integrated moving average processes, *Journal of Econometrics*, **7**, 23–55.

Duncan, D. B. and S. D. Horn (1972), Linear dynamic regression from the viewpoint of regression analysis, *Journal of the American Statistical Association*, **67**, 815–821.

Durbin, J. (1969), Tests for serial correlation in regression analysis based on the periodogram of least-square residuals, *Biometrika*, **56**, 1–15.

Engle, R. F. (1974), Band spectrum regression, *International Economic Review*, **15**, 1–11.

Engle, R. F. (1978a), Estimating structural models of seasonality, in A. Zellner (ed.), *Seasonal Analysis of Economic Time Series*, Bureau of the Census, Washington, DC, pp. 281–308.

Engle, R. F. (1978b), Testing price equations for stability across spectral frequency bands, *Econometrica*, **46**, 869–881.

Engle, R. F. (1982), Autoregressive conditional heteroscedasticity with estimates of the variance of UK inflation, *Econometrica*, **50**, 987–1007.

Engle, R. F. and R. Gardner (1976), Some finite sample properties of spectral estimators of a linear regression, *Econometrica*, **44**, 159–166.

Engle, R. F. and C. W. J. Granger (1987), Co-integration and error correction: representation, estimation and testing, *Econometrica*, **55**, 251–276.

Engle, R. F., D. F. Hendry and J. F. Richard (1983), Exogeneity, *Econometrica*, **51**, 277–304.

Engle, R. F., D. M. Lilien and R. P. Robins (1987), Estimating the time varying risk premia in the term structure: the ARCH-M model, *Econometrica*, **55**, 391–407.

Fernandez, F. J. (1990), Estimation and testing of a multivariate exponential smoothing model, *Journal of Time Series Analysis*, **11**, 89–105.

Fishman, G. S. (1969), *Spectral Methods in Econometrics*, Harvard University Press, Cambridge, MA.

Fuller, W. A. (1976), *Introduction to Statistical Time Series*, John Wiley, New York, NY.

Fuller, W. A. and D. P. Hasza (1981), Properties of predictors for autoregressive time series, *Journal of American Statistical Association*, **76**, 155–161.

Galbraith, R. F. and J. F. Galbraith (1974), On the inverse of some patterned matrices arising in the theory of stationary time series, *Journal of Applied Probability*, **11**, 63–71.

Gallant, A. R. and J. J. Goebel (1976), Nonlinear regression with autocorrelated errors, *Journal of the American Statistical Association*, **7**, 961–967.

Garbade, K. (1977), Two methods for examining the stability of regression coefficients, *Journal of the American Statistical Association*, **72**, 54–63.

Gardner, G., A. C. Harvey and G. D. A. Phillips (1980), An algorithm for exact maximum likelihood estimation of autoregressive-moving average models by means of Kalman filtering, *Applied Statistics*, **29**, 311–322.

Geweke, J. and S. Porter-Hudak (1983), The estimation and application of long memory time series models, *Journal of Time Series Analysis*, **4**, 221–238.

Godolphin, E. J. (1976), On the Cramer–Wold factorization, *Biometrika*, **63**, 367–380.

Goldberg, S. (1958), *Difference Equations*, John Wiley, New York, NY.

Granger, C. W. J. and M. Hatanaka (1964), *Spectral Analysis of Economic Time Series*, Princeton University Press, Princeton, NJ.

Granger, C. W. J. and R. Joyeux (1980), An introduction to long memory time series models and fractional differencing, *Journal of Time Series Analysis*, **1**, 15–30.

Granger, C. W. J. and M. J. Morris (1976), Time series modelling and interpretation, *Journal of the Royal Statistical Society*, Series A, **139**, 246–257.

Granger, C. W. J. and P. Newbold (1977), *Forecasting Economic Time Series*, Academic Press, New York, NY.

Griffiths, L. J. and R. Prieto-Diaz (1977), Spectral analysis of natural seismic events using autoregressive techniques, *IEEE Transactions on Geo-Science Electronics*, **GE-15**, 13–25.

Hall, A. (1989), Testing for a unit root in the presence of moving average errors, *Biometrika*, **76**, 49–56.

Hall, R. E. (1978), Stochastic implications of the life cycle–permanent income hypothesis: theory and evidence, *Journal of Political Economy*, **86**, 971–987.

Hamilton, J. D. (1989), A new approach to the economic analysis of nonstationary time series and the business cycle, *Econometrica*, **57**, 357–384.

Hamilton, J. D. (1992), Estimation, inference, and forecasting of time series subject to changes in regime, in C. R. Rao and G. S. Maddala (eds.), *Handbook of Statistics, Vol 11*, North-Holland, Amsterdam.

Hannan, E. J. (1980), The estimation of the order of an ARMA process, *Annals of Statistics*, **8**, 1071–1081.

Hannan, E. J. and M. Deistler (1988), *The Statistical Theory of Linear Systems*, John Wiley, New York, NY.

Harrison, P. J. and C. F. Stevens (1976), Bayesian forecasting, *Journal of the Royal Statistical Society, Series B*, **38**, 205–247.

Hart, B. I. (1942), Significance levels for the ratio of the mean square successive difference to the variance, *Annals of Mathematical Statistics*, **13**, 445–447.

Harvey, A. C. (1984a), A unified view of statistical forecasting procedures (with discussion), *Journal of Forecasting*, **3**, 245–283.

Harvey, A. C. (1984b), Time series forecasting based on the logistic curve, *Journal of the Operational Research Society*, **35**, 641–646.

Harvey, A. C. (1989), *Forecasting, Structural Time Series Models and the Kalman Filter*, Cambridge University Press, Cambridge.

Harvey, A. C. (1990), *The Econometric Analysis of Time Series*, 2nd edition, Philip Allan, Hemel Hempstead and MIT Press, Boston, MA.

Harvey, A. C. and J. Durbin (1986), The effects of seat belt legislation on British road casualties: a case study in structural time series modelling, *Journal of the Royal Statistical Society, Series A*, **149**, 187–227.

Harvey, A. C., B. Henry, S. Peters and S. Wren-Lewis (1986), Stochastic trends in dynamic regression models: an application to the output–employment equation, *Economic Journal*, **96**, 975–985.

Harvey, A. C. and A. Jaeger (1993), Detrending, stylized facts and the business cycle, *Journal of Applied Econometrics*, forthcoming.

Harvey, A. C. and G. D. A. Phillips (1977), A comparison of estimators in the ARMA(1, 1) model, University of Kent, Canterbury (unpublished paper).

Harvey, A. C. and G. D. A. Phillips (1982), The estimation of regression models with time-varying parameters, in *Proceedings of a Symposium in Honour of Oskar Morgenstern*, Vienna, May 1980, Physica-Verlag, Würzburg.

Harvey, A. C., E. Ruiz and N. G. Shephard (1992), *Multivariate Stochastic Variance Models*, London School of Economics Financial Markets Group Discussion Paper, No. 132.

Harvey, A. C. and N. G. Shephard (1992), Structural time series models, in C. R. Rao and G. S. Maddala (eds.), *Handbook of Statistics, Vol 11*, North-Holland, Amsterdam.

Harvey, A. C. and J. H. Stock (1988), Continuous time autoregressive models with common stochastic trends, *Journal of Economic Dynamics and Control*, **12**, 365–384.

Hasza, D. P. (1980), The asymptotic distribution of the sample autocorrelations for an integrated ARMA process, *Journal of the American Statistical Association*, **75**, 349–352.

Hillmer, S. C. and C. C. Tiao (1982), An ARIMA-model-based approach to seasonal adjustment, *Journal of the American Statistical Association*, **77**, 63–70.

Holt, C. C. (1957), Forecasting seasonals and trends by exponentially weighted moving averages, Carnegie Institute of Technology, Pittsburgh, PA, ONR Research Memorandum No. 52.

Hosking, J. R. M. (1980), The multivariate portmanteau statistic, *Journal of the*

American Statistical Association, **75**, 602–607.

Hosking, J. R. M. (1981), Fractional differencing, *Biometrika*, **68**, 165–176.

Jazwinski, A. H. (1970), *Stochastic Processes and Filtering Theory*, Academic Press, New York, NY.

Johansen, S. (1988), Statistical analysis of cointegration vectors, *Journal of Economic Dynamics and Control*, **12**, 131–154.

Johansen, S. and K. Juselius (1990), Maximum likelihood estimation and inference of cointegration – with applications to the demand for money, *Oxford Bulletin of Economics and Statistics*, **52**, 169–210.

Jones, R. H. (1980), Maximum likelihood fitting of ARIMA models to time series with missing observations, *Technometrics*, **22**, 389–395.

Kalman, R. E. (1960), A new approach to linear filtering and prediction problems, *Transactions ASME Journal of Basic Engineering*, **D 82**, 35–45.

Kalman, R. E. and R. S. Bucy (1961), New results in linear filtering and prediction theory, *Transactions ASME Journal of Basic Engineering*, **D 83**, 95–108.

Kang, K. M. (1975), A comparison of estimators for moving average processes, Australian Bureau of Statistics, Canberra (unpublished paper).

Kitagawa, G. (1981), A nonstationary time series model and its fitting by a recursive filter, *Journal of Times Series Analysis*, **2**, 103–116.

Kitagawa, G. (1987), Non-Gaussian state space modeling of nonstationary time series, *Journal of the American Statistical Association*, **82**, 1032–1063.

Kohn, R. and C. F. Ansley (1985), Efficient estimation and prediction in time series regression models, *Biometrika*, **72**, 694–697.

Koopman, S. (1993), Disturbance smoother for state space models, *Biometrika* (forthcoming).

Kunsch, H. (1986), Discrimination between monotonic trends and long-range dependence, *Journal of Applied Probability*, **23**, 1025–1030.

Kuznets, S. S. (1961), *Capital and the American Economy: Its Formation and Financing*, National Bureau of Economic Research, New York, NY.

Levenbach, H. and B. E. Reuter (1976), Forecasting trending time series with relative growth rates, *Technometrics*, **18**, 261–272.

Ljung, G. M. and G. E. P. Box (1978), On a measure of lack of fit in time series models, *Biometrika*, **66**, 67–72.

Lütkepohl, H. (1991), *Introduction to Multiple Time Series Analysis*, Springer-Verlag, Berlin.

McLeod, A. I. and W. K. Li (1983), Diagnostic checking ARMA time series models using squared-residual autocorrelations, *Journal of Time Series Analysis*, **4**, 269–273.

Mann, H. B. and A. Wald (1943), On the statistical treatment of linear stochastic difference equations, *Econometrica*, **11**, 173–220.

Maravall, A. (1985), On structural time series models and the characterization of components, *Journal of Business and Economic Statistics*, **3**, 350–355.

Maravall, A. and A. Mathis (1993), Encompassing univariate models in multivariate time series, *Journal of Econometrics*, forthcoming.

Mélard, G. (1984), A fast algorithm for the exact likelihood of autoregressive-moving average models, *Applied Statistics*, **33**, 104–114.

Melino, A. and S. M. Turnbull (1990), Pricing options with stochastic volatility, *Journal of Econometrics*, **45**, 239–265.

Mittnik, S. (1991), Derivation of the unconditional state covariance matrix for exact maximum likelihood estimation of ARMA models, *Journal of Economic Dynamics and Control*, **15**, 731–740.

Muth, J. F. (1960), Optimal properties of exponentially weighted forecasts, *Journal of the American Statistical Association*, **55**, 299–305.

Nelson, C. R. (1972), The prediction performance of the FRB-MIT-PENN model of the US Economy, *American Economic Review*, **62**, 902–917.

Nelson, C. R. (1974), The first order moving average process, *Journal of Econometrics*, **1**, 121–141.

Nelson, C. R. (1976), Gains in efficiency from joint estimation of systems of autoregressive-moving average processes, *Journal of Econometrics*, **4**, 331–348.

Nelson, C. R. and H. Kang (1984), Pitfalls in the use of time as an explanatory variable, *Journal of Business and Economic Statistics*, **2**, 73–82.

Nelson, C. R. and G. S. O'Shea (1979), Hypothesis testing based on goodness-of-fit in the moving average time series model, *Journal of Econometrics*, **10**, 221–226.

Nelson, D. B. (1990), Stationarity and persistence in the GARCH(1, 1) model, *Econometric Theory*, **6**, 318–344.

Nelson, D. B. (1991), Conditional heteroscedasticity in asset returns: A new approach, *Econometrica*, **59**, 347–370.

Nerlove, M., D. M. Grether and J. L. Carvalho (1979), *Analysis of Economic Time Series*, Academic Press, New York, NY.

Nerlove, M. and S. Wage (1964), On the optimality of adaptive forecasting, *Management Science*, **10**(2), 207–229.

Ozaki, T. (1985), Non-linear time series models and dynamical systems, in E. J. Hannan, P. R. Krishnaiah and M. M. Rao (eds.), *Handbook of Statistics, Vol 5*, North-Holland, Amsterdam, pp. 25–83.

Pantula, S. (1991), Asymptotic distributions of unit-root tests when the process is nearly stationary, *Journal of Business and Economic Statistics*, **9**, 63–71.

Parzen, E. (1969), Multiple time series modelling, in P. R. Krishnaiah (ed.), *Multivariate Analysis*, Vol II, Academic Press, New York, NY, pp. 389–409.

Phillips, P. C. B. (1987), Time series regression with a unit root, *Econometrica*, **55**, 277–302.

Phillips, P. C. B. and S. Ouliaris (1990), Asymptotic properties of residual based tests for cointegration, *Econometrica*, **58**, 165–193.

Phillips, P. C. B. and P. Perron (1988), Testing for a unit root in time series regression, *Biometrika*, **75**, 335–346.

Poskitt, D. S. and A. R. Tremayne (1980), Testing the specification of a fitted autoregressive-moving average model, *Biometrika*, **67**, 359–363.

Prest, A. R. (1949), Some experiments in demand analysis, *Review of Economics and Statistics*, **31**, 33–49.

Priestley, M. B. (1981), *Spectral Analysis and Time Series*, Academic Press, London.

Reed, D. (1978), Whistlestop: a community alternative for crime prevention. Unpublished Ph.D. thesis, Department of Sociology, Northwestern University, Chicago.

Rosenberg, B. (1973), Random coefficient models: the analysis of a cross section of time series by stochastically convergent parameter regression, *Annals of Economic and Social Measurement*, **2**, 399–428.

Ruiz, E. (1992), Quasi-maximum likelihood estimation of stochastic variance models,

LSE Econometrics discussion paper, London School of Economics.

Said, S. E. and D. A. Dickey (1984), Testing for unit roots in autoregressive moving average models of unknown order, *Biometrika*, **71**, 599–607.

Sargan, J. D. and A. Bhargava (1983), Maximum likelihood estimation of regression models with first order moving average errors when the root lies on the unit circle, *Econometrica*, **51**, 799–820.

Schaefer, S., R. Brealey, S. Hodges and H. Thomas (1975), Alternative models of systematic risk, in E. Elton and M. Gruber (eds.), *International Capital Markets: An Inter and Intra Country Analysis*, North-Holland, Amsterdam, pp. 150–161.

Schwert, G. W. (1989), Tests for unit roots: A Monte Carlo investigation, *Journal of Business and Economic Statistics*, **7**, 147–160.

Shenton, L. R. and W. L. Johnson (1965), Moments of a serial correlation coefficient, *Journal of the Royal Statistical Society, Series B*, **27**, 308–320.

Shephard, N. G. (1993), Maximum Likelihood Estimation of Regression Models with Stochastic Trend Components, *Journal of the American Statistical Association*, forthcoming.

Shephard, N. G. and A. C. Harvey (1990), On the probability of estimating a deterministic component in time series models, *Journal of Time Series Analysis*, **11**, 339–347.

Silvey, S. D. (1970), *Statistical Inference*, Chapman & Hall, London.

Sims, C. A., J. H. Stock and M. W. Watson (1990), Inference in linear time series models with some unit roots, *Econometrica*, **58**, 113–144.

Sneek, J. M. (1984), *Modelling procedures for economic time series*, Free University Press, Amsterdam.

Stewart, I. (1989), *Does God Play Dice? The Mathematics of Chaos*, Basil Blackwell, Oxford.

Stock, J. H. and M. Watson (1988), Testing for common trends, *Journal of the American Statistical Association*, **83**, 1097–1107.

Subba Rao, T. and M. M. Gabr (1981), A test for linearity of stationary time series, *Journal of Time Series Analysis*, **2**, 155–171.

Taylor, S. J. (1986), *Modelling Financial Time Series*, John Wiley, Chichester.

Tong, H. (1990), *Non-Linear Time Series: A Dynamic System Approach*, Clarendon Press, Oxford.

Tunnicliffe-Wilson, G. (1973), The estimation of parameters in multivariate time series models, *Journal of the Royal Statistical Society, Series B*, **35**, 76–85.

Walker, A. M. (1964), Asymptotic properties of least squares estimates of the spectrum of a stationary non-deterministic time series, *Journal of the Australian Mathematical Society*, **4**, 363–384.

Wallis, K. F. (1974), Seasonal adjustment and relations between variables, *Journal of the American Statistical Association*, **69**, 18–31.

Wecker, W. E. (1981), Asymmetric time series, *Journal of the American Statistical Association*, **76**, 16–21.

Weiss, A. A. (1985), The stability of the AR(1) process with an AR(1) coefficient, *Journal of Time Series Analysis*, **6**, 181–186.

West, M. and P. J. Harrison (1989), *Bayesian Forecasting and Dynamic Models*, Springer-Verlag, New York, NY.

Winters, P. R. (1960), Forecasting sales by exponentially weighted moving averages, *Management Science*, **6**, 324–342.

Yamamoto, T. (1976), A note on the asymptotic mean square error of predicting more than one step ahead using the regression method, *Applied Statistics*, **25**, 123–127.

Zellner, A. (1963), Estimation for seemingly unrelated regression equations: some exact finite sample results, *Journal of the American Statistical Association*, **68**, 977–992.

Subject Index

Author Index